Therapeutic
Experiencing

The Process of Change

BOOKS BY ALVIN R. MAHRER

Psychotherapeutic Change: An Alternative Approach to Meaning and Measurement (1985)

Experiential Psychotherapy: Basic Practices (1983)

Experiencing: A Humanistic Theory of Psychology and Psychiatry (1978)

(Editor with L. Pearson) Creative Developments in Psychotherapy (1971)

(Editor) New Approaches to Personality Classification (1970)

(Editor) The Goals of Psychotherapy (1967)

A NORTON PROFESSIONAL BOOK

Therapeutic Experiencing

The Process of Change

ALVIN R. MAHRER, Ph.D.

Professor of Psychology
University of Ottawa

W · W · NORTON & COMPANY · NEW YORK · LONDON

Published simultaneously in Canada by Penguin Books Canada Ltd,
2801 John Street, Markham, Ontario L3R 1B4

Printed in the United States of America.

First Edition

Library of Congress Cataloging in Publication Data

Mahrer, Alvin R.
  Therapeutic experiencing.

  "A Norton professional book"—P.
  1. Experiential psychotherapy.   2. Personality
change.   I. Title.
RC489.E96M35   1986   616.89′14   85-15326

ISBN   0-393-70008-9

W. W. Norton & Company, Inc., 500 Fifth Avenue, New York, N.Y. 10110

W. W. Norton & Company Ltd., 37 Great Russell Street, London WC1B 3NU

1 2 3 4 5 6 7 8 9 0

FOREWORD

WHEN KARL MENNINGER was recently visiting in our home, I asked him what he, from his long perspective of being identified with the mental health movement in this country for the last 50 years, would answer to the question: What is therapy? His reply was, "People have been talking to each other as long as they have existed on this planet. The question is: How did it become worth $60.00 an hour?"

So the question remains: What is the special kind of communication of one person to another we call psychotherapy? This is the question Alvin Mahrer addresses in this important book.

Our age could well be called the Age of Therapy. The tremendous number of people going into this profession, and the equally tremendous number of people who come to therapists for help, are an amazing development to say the least. It will help us to get a historical perspective on the development of psychotherapy.

We need to keep in mind that therapy burgeons at a particular time in the historical development of a society. Therapy arises at the time when the society fails to provide its members with the myths, values, and techniques for meeting severe anxiety, guilt feelings and other disruptive emotions. Therapy is not present, at least in the same degree, in the times when society does give its members the means of allaying severe anxiety and consoling people for their guilt.

This means that therapy appears in a culture at the time when that culture is in radical transition. Take the Greek society for example. In the sixth and fifth centuries B.C., when Greek society was at its height in the so-called "golden age" of Greece, the time of Plato and Aeschylus and Sophocles and Pericles and Socrates, it is impossible even to find the words "anxiety" or "guilt" in their writings. Pericles, for example, delivered his oration to the widows and orphans of the soldiers killed in the Peloponnesian War, but he never mentions anxiety; he emphasizes only that these men were proud to die for Athens.

But during the second and first century B.C., when Hellenistic Greek society was in radical transition, and no one believed in the myths or had values which allayed anxiety and gave consolation to the people, anxiety was rampant. Lucretius for example, in his long poem, *On the Nature of the Universe*, writes, describing his teacher,

Epicurus saw that, practically speaking, all that was wanted to meet men's vital needs was already at their disposal, and . . . their livelihood was assured. He saw some men in full enjoyment of riches and reputation, dignity and authority, and happy in the fair fame of their children. Yet, for all that, he found aching hearts in every home, racked incessantly by pangs the mind was powerless to assuage and forced to vent themselves in recalcitrant repining.

This sounds exactly like anxiety in our contemporary times.

For the same is true in our own 20th century. When the modern age was born in the Renaissance, there were present the beliefs, myths and values which served to allay severe anxiety and console grief. The belief of Descartes is a good example, "I think, therefore I am." This served to give birth to the myths and values associated with the rationalism and the individualism of the modern period. These beliefs were fundamental to the birth of Protestantism, the vast explorations of the known world, the progress of science, the age of Capitalism and the Industrial Age. The problems which arise in our 20th century were not present; people could believe in themselves, in their science, in human greatness and so on.

In fact, it was predicted in the first decade of the 20th century that this would be a time of reason and peace. But just the opposite turned out to be the case. The Titanic, built in the first decade of this century was a vivid symbol: It was arrogantly called the "unsinkable ship." When this ship hit an iceberg and sank in 1913 on its first voyage, we saw a symbol of the vast upheavals which were to occur.

So in our contemporaneous decades we see radical upsets like those which occurred in the Hellenistic and other catastrophically transitional ages. Instead of reason and peace in the 20th century, we have had the two World Wars, which were the most cruel in history, the Great Depression, radical changes in sexual mores, upheavals in marriage and family life, the destruction of Hiroshima and Nagasaki, and so on and on.

As a result people experience in our century the widespread feelings of anxiety, loneliness, feelings of the loss of self and all the other symptoms which we choose to call neurosis and psychosis. I am told that the '80s are the age of bulimia and anorexia, which are physical expressions of the psychological experience of having "nothing inside," the feeling of loss of self. We have seen about us the development of cults of all sorts, radical changes in religious practices. People are crying for myths, for new ways of life, new heroes to fill the emptiness given them by a society which has lost its means of allaying anxiety, assuaging their loneliness and relieving their excessive guilt.

Hence the vast development of psychotherapy in our century. Our therapy is called forth by the great needs about us. One index is that in 1918 there were in the American Psychological Association 318 members, and now there are over 60,000. Roughly the same growth has occurred in psychiatry. Freud, Jung, Adler and their hundreds of followers of various names were called forth as an answer to this great need.

As I have said, we live in the age of therapy. The helping professions have indeed burgeoned, including not only psychiatry and psychology but social work, religious healing, and educational counseling. We are told that, as of this moment, there are over 300 identifiable kinds of therapy in this country.

Alvin Mahrer's book is a sensitive and penetrating work on this important topic and helps us to get our bearings in a confusing field. It is written from the existential-humanistic viewpoint, thus expressing developments in our whole culture which give profundity and solidity to the ideas. Speaking of the groups he is addressing, Alvin Mahrer writes that one group . . .

> is extremely large. It is comprised of those who do any kind of psychotherapy—whether they like to refer to this as case work, counseling, "analysis," or whatever—and who are intrigued with the guts of our practice. These are the people who worry about how to be better therapists, who ruminate about therapeutic issues, who can be surprised by something new in therapy, who are intrigued with the phenomena of psychotherapeutic practice.

Mahrer is sensitive to the larger issues in therapy, such as the relationship of the two people in therapy, transference and so on, but he never loses sight of the "simple" aspects of the profession as well,

> Even before the therapist says or does something, the way the therapist listens and what the therapist listens for will either further the patient's attention or deflect it away. It is remarkable how much of what therapists do tends to deflect patients' attention away from focused centering and the carrying forward of experiencing.

This book is important not only for the persons engaged in training for the profession of therapy but also for all those interested in the psychological workings of themselves and their loved ones. Whether we disagree with Mahrer in a few details is not important; the book stimulates us to "worry about how to be better therapists," as he put it. I do not see how anyone can seriously read this book without finding that he or she has had a rich learning experience.

Rollo May

CONTENTS

INTRODUCTION

Purpose

THERE ARE DIFFERENT kinds of psychotherapy. For example, there are rational-emotive therapy, Sullivanian psychoanalysis, cognitive behavior therapy, Freudian psychoanalysis, Ericksonian hypnotherapy, Gestalt therapy, and many more. There is also experiential psychotherapy. The purpose of this book is to show how to do experiential psychotherapy.

What is experiential psychotherapy? One way of answering goes like this. The various psychotherapies can be organized into a number of categories. I like a four-fold division into the behavior therapies, the psychoanalytic-psychodynamic therapies, the experiential psychotherapies, and "others." So "experiential" is a big family. It includes Daseinsanalysis, Gestalt therapy, encounter therapy, logotherapy, existential therapy, feeling-expressive therapy, provocative therapy, intense feeling therapy, and many more members of the large family (e.g., Brown, 1973; Nichols & Zax, 1977; Olsen, 1976; Rowen, 1983). A second way of answering is that it is a psychotherapy which is conceptually linked with an existential-humanistic body of thought. A third way of answering is that it brings about change through something it refers to as "experiencing" rather than by counting upon such other mechanisms of change as trying to build the right kind of therapist-patient relationship, trying to effect insight or understanding, or trying to alter whatever the patient's behavior is supposed to be contingent upon.

What is distinctive about this book? There already are books on the various therapies which fall in the experiential family. What does this book offer over and above what these others do? The purpose of this book is to build upon the various members of the experiential family and to propose a single theory of experiential psychotherapy complete with its own methods of bringing about therapeutic change. It takes its theory of practice from many of the family members and organizes it into something new, something different. It also borrows from the methods used by the various family members and organizes them into something new, something different. One contribution that is distinctive is the proposed organized theory and methods of experiential psychotherapy.

Another distinctive contribution is that the reader is shown how to undertake therapeutic change by means of "therapeutic experiencing." This is proposed as an efficient and effective means of undergoing the process of profound therapeutic change. The challenge is that the theory and methods of experiential psychotherapy are the most effective means of opening up the kinds of changes set forth by existential-humanistic conceptualizations of what human beings are like and what human beings can become.

The purpose of a previous book (Mahrer, 1983a) was to describe the basic practices which prepare the way for the processes of change in experiential psychotherapy. That book aimed at showing how to begin each session by reaching the proper experiential state. The distinctiveness of the present book is that it takes up from there. Compared with the earlier book, which showed how to get ready, the present book tells what to do from then on throughout each session.

How complete is this book? Is it designed to show how to do experiential psychotherapy? It is just about complete, yes. And it is designed to show how to do experiential psychotherapy. If the reader digests the theory of practice, and if the reader uses the methods described, then the reader should be able to do this therapy. That is the purpose.

There are three conditions, however. One is that the reader has some understanding of existential-humanistic thought. The reader's explicit or implicit sense of what human beings are like, how and why they feel good and bad, how human beings build their worlds and live with one another, what they can become, and how changes come about—the reader's answers must at least be cordial to existential-humanistic theory (e.g., Binswanger, 1967; Heidegger, 1949; Jaspers, 1957; Mahrer, 1978a; May, Angel, & Ellenberger, 1958). For readers who share this theory of human beings, the book is relatively complete and designed to show how to do experiential psychotherapy.

The second condition is that the reader understand how to start each session of experiential psychotherapy. Essentially, each session begins with the patient reclining in a comfortable chair, feet on a hassock, eyes closed. The therapist has the same posture and position. Then the therapist shows the patient how to move into an experiential state in which most of the patient's attention is on a meaningful center, not on the therapist. That means there are at least moderate sensations in the patient's body. This is the place where experiential work begins.

It is the first step in each session (Figure 1). A detailed description of how and why to start this way is given elsewhere (Mahrer, 1983a).

The third condition is that the therapist know how to listen "experientially" to what the patient says and does. This means that the therapist takes steps to resonate with the patient, to get into the phenomenological world of the patient. The therapist resonates with the patient's bodily sensations, inner thoughts and feelings. The therapist moves close enough to the patient to see the world in which the patient is existing this moment. The therapist moves into the space occupied by the patient's own thoughts and feelings, body sensations and behaviors, inner sensings and ways of seeing the world. In short, the therapist shares the phenomenological world of the patient. Everything is as if it were flowing out of both patient and therapist: the pauses, voice intonation, the words, the bodily posture, the timbre and amplitude of the voice, the nervous little laugh, the flow of inner bodily sensations, the meaningful pauses, the attitude toward the other one, the content and significance of everything which is behaved, acted, implied, meant, spoken. The net result is that the therapist now immediately and momentarily exists in a world, a scene, a situation, and there is experiencing occurring in the therapist. These are the fruits of experiential listening. Again, a detailed description of how to enter into the phenomenological world of the patient and how to listen "experientially" is given elsewhere (Mahrer, 1983a).

Given these three conditions, the therapist is ready to carry out therapeutic experiencing as described in this book.

What is covered in the book? Every session goes through five steps in a relatively natural sequence (Figure 1) (cf. Cashdan, 1973; Gottman & Leiblum, 1974; Hackney, Ivey, & Oetting, 1970; Mahrer, 1978b; Mahrer, Nifakis, Abhukara & Sterner, 1984; Paul, 1978). It applies to the initial session, to the middle sessions, and to the final session. The opening step is one in which the patient's attention is largely on whatever is meaningful for the patient right now, with at least moderate sensations in the body. In Figure 1, this is referred to as attention-centered bodily experiencing. Now we are ready to begin therapeutic experiencing.

At this point, with some patients, there is a carrying forward of whatever experiencing is occurring in the patient right now. This is indicated in Figure 1 as the carrying forward of potentials for experiencing. Chapter 1 provides the theory for this step, some of the conceptual considerations, and some of the relevant clinical issues involved. Chapter 2 concentrates on the actual methods given in Figure 1.

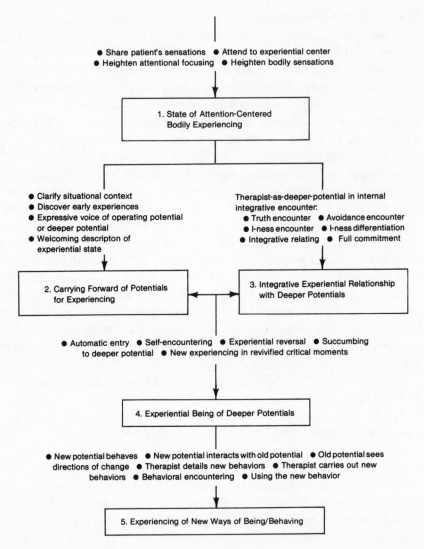

● Share patient's sensations   ● Attend to experiential center
● Heighten attentional focusing   ● Heighten bodily sensations

1. State of Attention-Centered Bodily Experiencing

● Clarify situational context
● Discover early experiences
● Expressive voice of operating potential or deeper potential
● Welcoming descripton of experiential state

Therapist-as-deeper-potential in internal integrative encounter:
  ● Truth encounter   ● Avoidance encounter
  ● I-ness encounter   ● I-ness differentiation
  ● Integrative relating   ● Full commitment

2. Carrying Forward of Potentials for Experiencing

3. Integrative Experiential Relationship with Deeper Potentials

● Automatic entry   ● Self-encountering   ● Experiential reversal   ● Succumbing to deeper potential   ● New experiencing in revivified critical moments

4. Experiential Being of Deeper Potentials

● New potential behaves   ● New potential interacts with old potential   ● Old potential sees directions of change   ● Therapist details new behaviors   ● Therapist carries out new behaviors   ● Behavioral encountering   ● Using the new behavior

5. Experiencing of New Ways of Being/Behaving

Figure 1. Operations and Steps in a Session of Experiential Psychotherapy

Alternatively, therapeutic change begins with the relationships between the patient and deeper personality processes or "potentials." In this step, there is experiencing of these inner relationships. In Figure 1, this is indicated as the integrative experiential relationship with deeper potentials. The theory behind this step is given in chapter 3, and the methods in chapter 4.

The next step in the process of therapeutic change is for the patient to leave behind or disengage from the ordinary, continuing personality in which he or she typically exists, and to get into or "be" the deeper insides. In effect, the patient undergoes a significant, qualitative shift in the person whom the patient is. In Figure 1 this is indicated as the experiential being of the deeper potentials. Chapter 5 deals with the theory underlying this step, and chapter 6 discusses the operations or methods (Figure 1) for accomplishing this step.

Finally, each session culminates with the patient tasting or sampling what it is like to be this changing new person within the context of the real world outside the therapy room. This final step is the experiential consideration of change in the person's ways of being and behaving in real life. In Figure 1, this is indicated as being/behavior change. The theory behind this final step is given in chapter 7, and the methods or operations in chapter 8.

This book begins with the patient in a state of attention-centered bodily experiencing, and presents the theory and the operations or methods for moving through the subsequent four kinds of therapeutic experiencing which constitute the process of change in each session of experiential psychotherapy. In effect, Figure 1 is a resumé of the operations and methods of the experiential psychotherapist. It is a procedural guide for all the methods and operations of experiential psychotherapy.

The readers for whom this book is written. The immediate group I had in mind includes psychotherapists who look out upon the world and themselves from an existential-humanistic conceptualization, and who are included in the large family of experiential psychotherapies, i.e., who count upon some kind of therapeutic experiencing as the process of therapeutic change. This group goes all the way from students, for whom psychotherapy is something they might want to do, to accomplished therapists. What is more, this group cuts across psychologists, social workers, psychiatrists, psychoanalysts, and the whole spectrum of those who use any kind of therapeutic experiencing in their work.

The second group I had in mind is extremely large. It is comprised of those who do any kind of psychotherapy — whether they like to refer to this as case work, counseling, "analysis," or whatever — and who are intrigued with the guts of our practice. These are the people who worry about how to be better therapists, who ruminate about therapeutic issues, who can be surprised by something new in therapy, who are intrigued with the phenomena of psychotherapeutic practice.

Another group of readers includes those who are especially taken with individual work with adults. I know very little about experiential therapy with couples, families (cf. Kempler, 1968, 1974, 1981; Yalom, 1980), small groups, or children (cf. Mahrer, 1976a; Moustakas, 1966; Rogers, 1967). This book is for those interested in individual work with women and men, psychologically sophisticated and not so, adolescents and really old people, people who come for one session or a fair number or for years, people who get along well in their lives and people who don't seem to, people seen in clinics and institutions as well as private practice, and so on. There is no emphasis on a particular population or "problem" or category, diagnostic or otherwise.

It is also for persons who are or who might be patients. I believe these persons have a right to know both the methods and the theory of practice of experiential psychotherapy to help them decide whether this work seems appropriate for them.

On the other hand, there are many psychotherapists whose theory of practice is not only in place, but is distinctly not experiential, and whose conceptualization of human beings is solidly entrenched, and is distinctly not existential-humanistic. While these readers may find the book interesting and challenging, they were not among the target groups I had in mind.

Some Persons to Whom Acknowledgment Is Extended

There are some persons who go deeply into psychotherapy. They are masters of the craft, and they have many years of experience. But there is also something quite distinctive about this group. They all think about psychotherapy. They formulate the right questions. They try to put into words their thinkings about psychotherapy. Because of their excellence as therapists, they are compelled by phenomena which are important, and because they think well they provide readers with new ideas, new thoughts, new problems and questions. These are the clinical theorists. They worry about the guts of what happens in psychotherapy, and they discover things in and about psychotherapy. Their writings (and, for some, their correspondence) are an inspiration to me. I respect and cherish this breed of clinical theorists.

Here are some of these special people who wrote about the inner workings of psychotherapy in ways which bring forth my heartfelt respect and acknowledgments: Medard Boss, James Bugental, Henri Ellenberger, Sigmund Freud, Eugene Gendlin, Ludwig Binswanger, Rollo May, Otto Fenichel, Ronald Laing, Leston Havens, Claudio

Naranjo, Carl Whitaker, Andras Angyal, Sandor Rado, Carl Jung, Sandor Ferenczi, Karl Abraham.

And here are two special people to whom heartfelt acknowledgment
and thanks are extended: Susan E. Barrows, director of Norton Professional Books, and Patricia A. Gervaize, Ph.D., colleague and partner.

A Note About "Verbatim" Excerpts

None of the excerpts in this book are verbatim. The reason is that
I wish to preserve the anonymity and confidentiality of both the therapists and the patients. All of the words in all of the excerpts are for
purposes of illustration. Accordingly, I started with verbatim excerpts
and then altered sexes, names, places, distinctive and singular phrases,
dates and times. I altered the situational contexts and the nature of
the incidents. Changes were made to preserve the illustrative value of
the excerpts while significantly modifying everything that belongs to
the person who is the therapist and the person who is the patient.

Therapeutic Experiencing

The Process of Change

CHAPTER 1

Carrying Forward the Potentials for Experiencing: Introduction

IN THE BEGINNING of the session, the patient enters into the experiential process by letting attention go to a meaningful center, one which is accompanied with at least moderate bodily sensations. Then therapeutic experiencing takes place. The purpose of chapter 1 is to provide an introduction to one kind of therapeutic experiencing, the carrying forward of the potentials for experiencing. The theory, background, and rationale are given in this chapter, and the methods are presented in chapter 2.

The General Principle

Therapeutic change occurs when there is a carrying forward (deepening, enhancing) of the experiencing occurring right now in the patient. The experiencing may be at the surface, operating level, or it may be deeper within the patient. The process is one of letting it happen more, more fully, more deeply, with greater depth and breadth and saturation (e.g., Bugental, 1976; Farrelly & Brandsma, 1974; Pierce, Nichols, & DuBrin, 1983; Rogers, 1959). "The therapist's task is to help the patient make as alive and vivid as possible whatever he is experiencing at any particular point in time . . . " (Shaffer, 1978, p. 87). This " . . . consists in letting the patient experience what he or she is doing until the experience really grasps him" (May, 1958, p. 83).

The nature of experiencing which is carried forward. In general, the aim is to enable experiencing to become fuller and deeper, to carry forward. But this has a rather explicit meaning. There are at least three aspects to the nature of experiencing which is carried forward. One is that it is the *experiencing* which is carried forward, as contrasted with the feelings which are associated with the experiencing (Greenwald, 1974; Jackins, 1965; Mahrer & Gervaize, 1984; Perls, 1969a; Watts, 1961). It is not a matter of feeling even more pain, suffering, anguish or turmoil. Experiencings may be accompanied with feelings which are delightful and pleasurable, or feelings which are awful and painful. We speak of the experiencing of dominating, overcoming, being superior, or an experiencing of provoking, antagonizing, getting the other all worked up. Whatever the nature of the experiencing, that is what is to carry forward. As the patient is experiencing a sense of withdrawing, pulling away, there may be strong feelings of hurt and anguish, but it is the experiencing of the pulling away and withdrawing which are to deepen. We distinguish between the nature of the experiencing and the good or bad feelings which may accompany the experiencing. In Figure 2, the potentials for experiencing are indicated as circles, with OP1 signifying an operating potential and DP2 signifying a deeper potential.

Second, when experiencing is carried forward, there is a change in how the patient is being/behaving, and the external world in which this takes place. If the "carried-forward" experiencing is the sense of

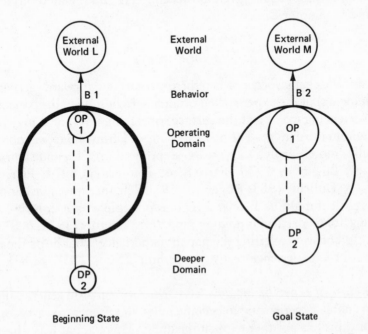

Figure 2. The In-therapy Change: Carrying Forward of Potentials for Experiencing

dominating, overcoming, being superior, the patient is being a substantially new person, being and behaving in a new dominating, overcoming, superior way, and the patient is existing in a substantially new world in which this heightened dominating, overcoming superiority is occurring. Here is a significant change in how the patient is being/behaving, and the world in which the patient exists. In Figure 2, the change in behavior is indicated by the change from B1 on the left to B2 on the right, and the change in the external world is indicated by the change from External World L on the left to External World M on the right.

Third, when experiencing is carried forward, bodily sensations are stronger and occur throughout more of the body. It is the difference between orgasmic bodily sensations confined to the genitals as compared with orgasmic bodily sensations filling the entire body. It is the difference between moderate butterflies in the stomach as compared with powerful butterflies throughout the whole body. It is that all-over lightness and buoyancy as compared with a slight dizziness in the head. It is the state of whole-body trembling versus a quivering in the right hand. Bodily sensations are stronger and occupy more of the body, whether they are good-feelinged or bad-feelinged bodily sensations.

All of this occurs at least momentarily. All the patient has to do is to attain this state. The patient may attain this state for a single second, or it may last for a few seconds, for a minute or so, or even longer. The key is that it be reached even for a brief moment. Fenichel (1953a) puts it this way:

> Now there came a sensation which lasted only a moment and did not recur, but shook the patient deeply: a sort of pressure on the head — as if a ring should press very hard against the back of her head, giving her an indescribable feeling. The whole thing lasted but an instant, and with it the anxiety was gone for good (p. 31).

This is the nature of experiencing which is carried forward. According to our general principle, this is one kind of therapeutic experiencing. But what is "therapeutic" about experiencing which is carried forward?

The therapeutic significance of carrying forward experiencing. Suppose that experiencing is carried forward in good measure for a few seconds or a few minutes or so. What is the therapeutic significance of accomplishing this? There are at least six ways in which this is therapeutically significant, and these apply whether the experiencing is at the operating or the deeper level.

• Not only is the potential experienced more, but there is a qualitative change toward its "good form." Whatever the nature or content of the potential, regardless whether we are referring to an operating or a deeper potential, carrying forward means that is takes on some added qualities, new fibers, altered colors or shapes. It evolves just a bit toward a better form. The experiencing of bawling someone out, of being righteously tough, may take on an added new quality of a kind of exciting playfulness or a kind of friendly sparring or a sort of parental chiding. Whatever the added quality, it is more than a matter of just more intense experiencing of the same content. The potential carries forward toward a better form. So there is an evolving transformation of the very nature of the experiencing.

• As experiencing carries forward, there are new behaviors. Heightened experiencing opens new behaviors, and new behaviors open heightened experiencing. The heightened experiencing of bawling out the other person is accompanied by new ways of doing this. It may consist of new voice quality, new bodily postures and gestures, new words, new ways of thinking, new interrelatings, new ways of reacting to the other, new ways of taking control. The person is behaving in new ways. In Figure 2, this is indicated as the change from B1 to B2.

• There is a new external world. The world in which the carried-forward experiencing occurs undergoes change (External World L and M in Figure 2). It changes because of and in relation to the heightened experiencing. As the person undergoes the carrying forward of the experiencing of bawling out the other figure, the situational context including and encompassing that other figure changes. The figure softens, or now there is a mutual exchange; there is a new world of charged confrontation; the other figure is allowed to be vulnerable or more monstrous or is freed to be violent or reachable or childish or apologetic. In any case, the person is existing in a significantly changed external world.

• Whether the carrying forward refers to the operating or deeper potential, there is a rising upward of the deeper potential. Even when the experiencing refers to the operating potential, it is as if the sheer experiencing at the operating level potentiates or lifts up or activates the deeper potential. The patient begins to feel the deeper potential, to sense its imminence. The sheer experiencing of an operating potential of bawling out the other one has the consequence of lifting up whatever is the nature of a deeper potential, e.g., the experiencing of closeness and intimacy or the experiencing of frenetic rage or the experiencing of chaotic splintering or whatever.

This change is indicated in two ways in Figure 2. One is that the deeper potential (DP2) is now closer into the operating domain. In addition, the boundary of the operating domain moves from thicker to thinner. What this signifies is that the person senses and feels the deeper potential more, is more vulnerable or receptive to what is deeper, is more attuned to it. For better or for worse, the person is less insulated and sealed off from deeper experiencings. And this bringing together of operating domain and deeper experiencing occurs whether what is carried forward is the operating potential or the deeper potential.

• Carrying forward experiencing paves the way for the next step in the session. As indicated in Figure 1, when there has occurred a genuine carrying forward of the potentials for experiencing (step 2), this opens the way for the patient to move out of the operating domain and into the actual being of the deeper domain (step 4). In other words, as the deeper potential lifts up and into the person or operating domain, as the distance is reduced, as the deeper potential is activated and felt, as the boundary around the operating domain is more permeable, the stage is set for the very heart of the person to disengage from the operating domain and enter into the deeper potential. So the carrying forward of experiencing is instrumental for the next therapeutic step in the session.

• Finally, at a higher level, those precious moments in which experiencing reaches the higher plateau are tantamount to a taste of what in existential-humanistic thinking is called "actualization" (e.g., Berne, 1972; Chang, 1959; McGill, 1967). That is, the person is sampling a little of what it could be like to fully experience in a good form what the person has available.

Here, then, are six ways of answering the question: What is the therapeutic significance of carrying forward experiencing?

How the Therapist Fits Into the Process of
Therapeutic Change

One kind of therapeutic change consists of the carrying forward of experiencing. How does the therapist fit into this process of therapeutic change?

What makes therapeutic change possible? Our answer is that the wellsprings of change lie in the patient's capacity for heightened experiencing. When we understand the human being from the perspective of an existential-humanistic theory, the person is comprised of potentials for experiencing, and these potentials are capable of undergoing further and deeper experiencing. In other words, we hold that experiencing can carry forward, that there is a readiness for further and deeper experiencing. With the right methods (chapter 2), the therapist can enable that experiencing to carry forward. Without the capacity for further and deeper experiencing, the methods could not work. Likewise, without proper methods for carrying forward the experiencing, there will be little or no therapeutic change.

Our answer differs from Freud's. Where we count upon the capability of potentials to undergo further experiencing, Freud counted upon the patient's suffering and wish to be cured. "The primary motive-power used in therapy is the patient's suffering and the wish to be cured which arises from it" (Freud , 1959, p. 364). This is quite different from each person's characteristic capability for carrying forward experiencings.

We start with the patient's inner experiencings that are ready to be carried forward. Psychoanalytic therapies and their derivatives start with the patient's suffering and the wish to be cured (Allport, 1937; Berne, 1966; Freud, 1976f; Hartmann, 1958; Maddi, 1972; Saul, 1958). Both need something in the patient to start with. In contrast, in behavior therapies, the wellsprings of the therapeutic process start with largely external cues and events upon which behavior is presumed to be contingent. The change process is set into motion by behavioral methods which set about altering these largely external contingencies (e.g., Kanfer & Phillips, 1970; Lazarus, 1971; Mischel, 1968; Sherman, 1973).

How the therapist fits into the therapeutic process differs depending on the theory's position on what makes change possible in the first place.

When the patient is doing something, what is the locus (stance, posture) of the therapist? This refers to when the patient is talking, responding, being, doing something. The condition is not when the patient is being given instructions by the therapist, but rather when the patient is carrying the ball, is attending to whatever the patient is attending to, and is doing whatever the patient is doing. Under this condition, it is as if the therapist moves alongside the patient, melds into the patient, resonates with the patient.

It is as if the therapist says the words the patient is saying in the same way as the patient. There is the same feeling, the same tone of voice, the same pitch and cadence, the same loudness, the same pauses. It is as if the patient's way of being is coming from the therapist. The therapist is right alongside the patient, letting what the patient is doing come also from the therapist.

This means that the therapist is ready, passively, to experience whatever starts to happen as the patient behaves, feels, says whatever the patient is saying. As the patient says, "My problem is that no one really understands me," those words come as if from the therapist, and the therapist is passively ready to experience whatever percolates as these words come out. This means also that the therapist is ready, passively, to exist and to be in whatever scene or situational context appears. It is as if the therapist is someplace, somewhere, with some context around him. As the patient says, "My problem is that no one really understands me," the therapist may be in a scene including some other person, a therapist-person, and there is some charged distance between the person who is saying these words in this way, and the therapist-person who is at some charged distance away.

This locus or posture of the therapist is called "experiential listening." It is listening by aligning with what the patient is doing as if all of that is coming in and through the therapist. It has been described in detail elsewhere (Mahrer, 1983a). But in terms of the process of therapeutic change, this locus, this way of listening, means that the therapist is a part of the process (Bugental, 1965; Fromm, Suzuki & de Martino, 1960; Havens, 1973; Minuchin, 1974; Polster & Polster, 1974). The therapist undergoes the process. The therapist has the experiencing, shares in it. The therapist also lives and exists in the particular scene or situational context which is linked to the experiencing. If the process of change means the carrying forward of the immediate experiencing of an inner defiant challenging, and if this takes place in a scene involving some therapist-like external figure, then the therapist is already a part of this experiencing and this meaningful situational context.

The patient is the one who determines what the therapist does, and the therapist is postured, ready, and skilled to do it. The therapist must be aligned with the patient, sharing the patient's inner and outer world. This is the correct posture. But, in order to fit into the therapeutic process, the therapist is also ready to receive whatever experiencing starts up when the patient says and does something. The therapist has a welcoming readiness to receive as broad a range of experiencings as possible. One of the greatest handicaps to therapeutic movement is the therapist's own screening, blocking, and deft avoidance of the experiencing that is activated in and by the patient. More bluntly, the problem in therapeutic movement is mainly the therapist — not the patient. Patients are generally ready to carry forward experiencing; it is the therapist who typically blocks and avoids this process.

As stated by Whitaker, Warkentin, and Malone (1959, p. 256), the depth of experiential psychotherapy is determined by the depth of the therapist. When the patient says and does something, what gets started in the therapist is an experiencing at either the operating or the deeper levels. In order to fit into the therapeutic process, the therapist must be receptive to what the patient is stirring up at this deeper level. In experiential psychotherapy, the therapist is not outside, trying to make some sense of " . . . the scattered information received from the patient in order to respond to it in therapeutically useful ways" (Angyal, 1965, p. 204; see also Bucklew, 1960, 1968; Freud, 1976b; Locke, 1971; Wolberg, 1954). Instead, the therapist is aligned into the patient, resonatingly receptive to the experiencings occurring on the surface, at the operating level, and also deeper within, at the deeper level. The effective therapist can receive and have these experiencings; the ineffective therapist will screen these away.

The therapist must also be ready to allow these experiencings to carry forward in her. That is, whatever the nature of the immediate experiencings that are invoked when the patient says or does something, the therapist must not only be able to receive them, but also to let them come forth, heighten, carry forward. This is the experiential meaning of the therapist as a welcoming, accepting, congruent person (Mahrer, 1976b; Overstreet, 1949; Prescott, 1957). Not only will the therapist sense, and resonate, and have the operating and deeper experiencings occurring in the patient, but the therapist will be welcoming to them, let them occur more fully and deeply within the therapist.

Finally, the therapist must be skilled. This means the therapist must have the technical competencies (described in chapter 2) to carry forward these experiencings. Merely sharing the patient's experiencings is necessary, but not sufficient. Indeed, the therapist must be technically skilled enough to carry forward the experiencing gracefully and easily, without thinking about what to do and how to do it. This is the difference between the beginner and the effectively competent therapist who is sufficiently competent in these skills to use them "naturally" and "automatically" (cf. Arbuckle, 1975, p. 178; see also Greenson, 1967; Ritvo, 1971; Thorne, 1973).

The therapist is postured, ready, and technically skilled to carry forward the experiencing. Everything else is up to the patient. The patient is the one who determines what the therapist does. The patient sets the therapist into therapeutic motion, and the patient does so in one of three explicit ways:

First of all, the words and behavior of the patient right this moment illuminate or bring forth some attentional center. It is highlighted, lifted forward, brought into attention, activated. All the therapist does is to be in the proper experiential posture, ready. What the therapist does is partially determined by that image of the look on mother's face, or the image of the cancer eating away at the tissue, or the son lying in the hospital bed before the operation.

Second, the patient's immediate words and behavior may illuminate the operating potential, the experiencing that is occurring more or less on the surface. For example, while the image may be that of the look on mother's face, the highlight may be on the operating experiencing of loving concern, the sense of gentleness toward mother. The immediate words and behavior of the patient have the determining power of activating either the look on mother's face or the operating experiencing of gentle loving concern toward her.

Third, the patient's immediate words and behavior have the power of illuminating a deeper potential, a deeper experiencing. While the image may be that of the look on mother's face, the inner deeper experiencing may consist of the wholesale protection of her, a nurturing ownership of her. It is this inner deeper experiencing that is activated and that is the "center of gravity" as the patient is saying and doing something right now.

The graceful naturalness in this therapy lies in working with whichever of these three domains of data the patient's own immediate words and behavior bring forth. In this sense, the patient is the one who determines what the therapist does, and the therapist does little or no "think-

ing." The therapist does no selecting out, no informational processing, no private inner inference-building. It is the patient who illuminates
some image (scene, situation, attentional center), some experiencing
at the operating level, or some inner, deeper experiencing. And the
therapist floats, attentive, postured, ready, and technically competent
to carry forward the experiencing.

The continuous freshness and immediacy of the data. Because the
patient is the one who determines what the therapist does, there is a
continuous freshness and immediacy to the data. When the patient says
and does something, the therapist resonates to the data that occur in
the form of some image (scene, situational context) and in the form
of some experiencing. On the basis of this imagery and this experiencing, the therapist does something to carry forward the experiencing;
the instant the therapist finishes, everything starts again from the beginning. In other words, each time the patient has his turn to say and do
something, the therapist is ready to receive data which are fresh and
immediately new.

This happens more or less naturally because the therapist is always
in the posture of experiential listening whenever the patient says or does
something. This means there is a kind of easy rhythm in this therapy.
First the patient says and does something as the therapist is listening
experientially. Then the therapist is activated to one or another method
of carrying forward the experiencing. Then it all starts up again as the
therapist returns to experiential listening posture to receive what the
patient next says and does. Accordingly, each time the patient says or
does something, the experientially listening therapist is ready to have
fresh imagery and experiencing.

Carrying Forward of Experiencing Versus
Therapist's Assessment of Patient's
"Readiness"

Who determines whether or not the patient is ready to deal with
whatever the therapist may say or do? Is it part of the therapist's job
to assess whether or not the patient is ready to hear what the therapist
says right now? On what basis is it determined that the patient is not
"ready," but that in a subsequent phase of therapy—perhaps in three
to six months or so—the patient might be "ready"?

There is only one way in which the therapist determines whether or not the patient is ready to carry forward experiencing. The method of experiential psychotherapy says that carrying forward of the potentials for experiencing comes after the patient is ready to begin therapeutic work, i.e., with eyes closed, most of the attention on something meaningful, and at least moderate sensations in the body. As long as the patient is in that state, the patient is ready for the therapist to carry forward experiencing.

The patient's behavior and words will in effect say, "Here is the kind of experiencing that is occurring right now." This is followed by the behavior and words of the therapist, which in effect say, "And I am now carrying forward that experiencing." That is all. Because the therapist is in a posture of experiential listening, because the therapist is sharing the patient's experiencing and the patient's attentional world, the therapist is not in the same locus as the external therapist who can engage in private assessments about whether or not the patient is ready to receive what the external therapist might say.

Now the issue of readiness becomes a matter of what the patient does when the therapist carries forward what the patient got started. It is the patient's turn to move forward with that experiencing, or not to. In experiential psychotherapy, that choice is the right and the responsibility of the patient. Whatever the patient does next starts the whole process over again. Each time the patient behaves or talks, the patient is choosing whether or not to go along with the carrying forth of the experiencing.

An alternative approach, one followed by many psychotherapies, is for the therapist to be external to the patient, and for the therapist to make determinations of whether the patient is "ready" for something the therapist might do or say. It is from this standpoint that, for example, the therapist will weigh the nature of the patient's defenses, the supportive strength of the patient's relationship with the therapist, and the judged severity of the patient's psychopathology (e.g., Bibring, 1954; Boverman, 1953; Guntrip, 1969; Loevinger, 1976; Reich, 1945; Wolberg, 1954).

In experiential psychotherapy, the therapist carries forward whatever experiencing is brought forth by the patient. The choice and responsibility for what the patient does immediately thereafter are within the domain of the patient, and what the patient is ready to do next will show in exactly what the patient does next. The therapist does not get into an external location, judge the patient's readiness, and either go ahead and do it or withhold doing it until later when the therapist judges the patient to be "ready."

When the experiential process stops, the therapist starts from the beginning, and gives instructions. There is one condition under which the therapist does not simply carry forward experiencing. It is when the experiencing process stops. The patient is no longer "ready" when experiencing shuts down in the therapist. When this occurs, the therapist is almost automatically placed outside the patient, external to the patient, attending mainly to the patient. When this happens, the therapist is the instruction-giver who tells the patient what may be done next, and how to do it.

When the patient's experiential process stops, there are two main indicators. One is that the therapist is no longer living and being in the patient's phenomenological world. That is, there is no image, no situational context, no scene. Instead, the therapist is attending to the patient, is aware of and being with the patient. The second indicator is that the therapist's experiencing and bodily sensations have sunk to a neutral level. Along with this change, the therapist now has thoughts about the patient: "I wonder why he stopped what he was doing. . . . For a while I was with him, but now he seems so pulled back. . . . Well, this has been a pretty good session so far. . . . " The therapist is outside the patient, external to the patient, with thoughts directed toward the patient, and with rather inert experiencing and bodily sensations. This is the second indicator that the experiential process has stopped.

When the therapist is outside the patient, external to the patient, attending to the patient, having thoughts about the patient, the experiential process has shut down. What does the therapist do? The therapist starts the whole process from the very beginning. The therapist gives the patient the initial instructions. In effect, the therapist invites the patient to deploy most of the attention on whatever is significant, to return to the experiential state, and to allow at least moderate bodily sensations to occur. These instructions allow free choice on the part of the patient. They include such phrases as, " . . . if you are ready . . . if you want to do this . . . we can do this now if you wish. . . . " Within the vocabulary of Ericksonian psychotherapy, the wording is that of "implied directives" rather than direct commands (Erickson, Rossi & Rossi, 1976; Lankton, Lankton & Brown, 1981). We may go back to where the patient and therapist were before experiencing shut down and the therapist was moved out into being the instruction-giver. We may start somewhere else. But the therapist gives the patient instructions for again entering into the experiential state.

When the experiential process shuts down, the therapist gracefully and automatically becomes the external provider of instructions. This answers the question of what the therapist does when experiencing shuts down. The experiential therapist does not interpret the patient's shutting off of therapeutic work (cf. Fromm-Reichmann, 1958), nor does the therapist try to force the patient back to where the shutdown occurred, nor does the therapist somehow use the private inner thoughts which signal the shutting down. The therapist merely gives instructions for allowing the patient to start the experiential process going again, the same instructions as are used to begin each session (Mahrer, 1983a).

The immediate carrying forward of the patient's experiencings toward therapy and the therapist. Consider those patients who, in the initial sessions, have experiencings centered upon therapy and upon the therapist. These are the patients who experience a sense of never being cherished and treasured, and who are ready to prove that the therapist will eventually fail the test. These are the patients who are ready to make the therapist the sole center of their lives. These are the patients who are ready to resist the therapist's swallowing them up, to wholly entrust themselves to the therapist, to be with the ideal parent, win out over the therapist's best efforts, have an endless sparring contest, worship the therapist, be a nasty little kid to the scolding therapist, enter into a long-term career as patient, prove that therapy will fail, seduce or be seduced by the therapist, use therapy to justify their failures or their unwelcome acts or their intrinsic worth or their utter worthlessness or their inability to succeed.

Do we carry forward these experiencings when they surface, in the first few sessions for example, or do we consider some sort of "readiness" and wait until the right conditions appear? Our answer is that these experiencings are carried forward right now. There is no consideration of patient "readiness"; rather, the presence of these experiencings is tantamount to readiness.

Suppose that the experiencing is that of challenging and jousting. This may be an operating potential, right here on the surface, or it may be a deeper potential. In either case, suppose that the target is the therapist. Because the therapist is aligned with the patient, sharing the patient's experiencing and situational context, the therapist will tend to share the inner experiencing, the sense of challenging and jousting, and the therapist will be sharing the situational context. Accordingly, it is gracefully natural that the therapist will carry forward the experiencing of jousting and challenging, and do so within the appropriate situational context (such as the therapy situation), and directed toward the appropriate figure (probably that of the therapist).

Regardless of the nature of the experiencing, as long as it is present and involves the therapist or therapy, these experiencings are carried forward by the therapist. It is carried forward by the therapist who shares the patient's immediately ongoing experiencing, and who shares the situational context including therapy itself or the therapist-figure.

This process replaces the common opening game-play in which therapist and patient try each other on for size. Typically, with external-therapists who work out of some sort of relationship with the patient, the patient and therapist court each other for a few sessions, find out that there is little goodness-of-fit, and part company. Instead, the patient's opening overtures are used as grist for the therapeutic mill, even in initial sessions.

This process mobilizes those role-relationship feelings which turn therapy into a predetermined career. Consider the patient whose initial experiencing has to do with the anguish of being disappointed by the special one who promises so much. With the experiential therapist, this experiencing is carried forward right from the very beginning. In contrast, a typical alternative career is the slow building of a therapist-patient relationship which heads, often after months of mutual construction, into the final fruition in which the patient is indeed disappointed by the special therapist who had promised so very much, and the relationship ends in the anguished unhappiness which was present in the very beginning.

Finally, this process can accommodate an extremely broad range of patient experiencings relating to therapy and to the therapist. Because this process does not require the presence and involvement of the external therapist, and because this process is not a conjoint enterprise of external patient and external therapist, virtually any kind of experiencing can be carried forward. The patient whose initial experiencing is of a wrenching surrender to the mammoth and all-powerful whirlpool of therapy can be carried forward even if the external therapist is completely free from representing such a meaning for therapy. The patient whose initial experiencing is of the mystical sanctuary of the therapy union can be accommodated even when the external therapist does little or nothing to fulfill this meaning of therapy. Virtually all kinds of therapist-related and therapy-related experiences can be accommodated and carried forward by means of this paradigm, even or especially in the first few sessions.

All in all, the carrying forward of experiencing just moves ahead.

The therapist is not outside, interacting with the patient, making determinations of whether or not the patient is ready for what the therapist elects to do or say.

Carrying Forward of Experiencings Versus Preselected Screening

Experiencing is carried forward when the therapist is sharing the patient's experiencing and sharing the patient's attentional center (or situational context or phenomenological world). That means the therapist who is sharing the patient's experiencing and world cannot stand off and screen in some things, screen out other things, select this as something to push, select that as something to file away for later use. The process enjoins the therapist " . . . to feel one's way, to transpose oneself into the object, instead of picking out and enumerating individual properties and characteristics" (Wyss, 1973, p. 390). Carrying forward means processing whatever comes along.

There is a glaring exception, however. If the experiential therapist is unwilling or unable to share a particular kind of experiencing, that one will not be carried forward. The gatekeeper is the therapist. In experiential therapy, the gate is to be wide open. If the therapist cannot be touched by the experiencing, whatever its nature, experiencing is not carried forward, and that is unfortunate.

The process is naively unselective. No matter what the nature or the content of the experiencing, the therapist carries it forward in the naively unbiased simplicity of the phenomonological approach (Ellenberger, 1958, p. 96).

The patient may be experiencing an avoiding, a withdrawing back from. The patient may be experiencing a sense of defensiveness as he is rushing into all sorts of intellectual deflections (Guntrip, 1969, p. 297). The patient may be undergoing a sense of defying against, resisting, rebelling. It does not matter. The process is one of carrying it forward in the spirit of what Erickson calls a utilization technique (Haley, 1963, p. 52) or what is called exaggeration in Gestalt therapy (Enright, 1970; Shaffer, 1978, pp. 87–88).

It does not matter how the external therapist would describe what the patient seems to be doing. Where the external therapist might want to dissuade the patient from concentrating upon external material (cf. Angyal, 1965, p. 279), the experiential therapist just carries forward the experiencing. When the patient seems to be communicating in an autistic manner (e.g., Gendlin, 1972, p. 366), the therapist just carries forward whatever experiencing is going on. If the external therapist describes the patient as having hallucinations or delusions, the experiential therapist just carries forward whatever experiencing is going on (Needleman, 1967, p. 30). If the patient is commenting on what just occurred ("It's amazing! My headache just went away! It just seemed to ease up and go away. What a great thing!"), the therapist merely carries forward whatever is the ongoing experiencing.

The naively unselective nature of the process contrasts with one in which the therapist actively searches for the kind of data his or her therapy is designed to handle. For example, if the therapy is designed to provide insight on underlying "Oedipus conflicts," then the therapist will guide and mould the patient to produce Oedipus conflict material. If a therapy is designed to mobilize a woman's anger into productive political activity, the therapist will twist and turn until the woman's anger is discovered. Because Wolpe's therapy is geared toward the patient's anxiety, the therapist will sort through material until the anxiety is found:

> The anxiety is often immediately manifest in neurosis. . . . But there
> are neuroses in which the anxiety is not at all obvious. Take, for example, impotence and frigidity, sexual deviations like homosexuality
> and transvesticism, psychosomatic states like asthma or neurodermatitis,
> or reactive depression. Anxiety may not be evident when the patient
> comes to you, and yet if you do a behavioral analysis you will almost
> always find it (Wolpe, 1976, p. 58).

The carrying forward of whatever experiencing is present is naively unselective in that it accepts whatever experiencings are there. This contrasts with an approach in which only certain kinds of experiencings are carried forward, or with an approach whose therapeutic work requires the active searching and locating of material that is not present here and now.

It is setting into motion a process of change rather than applying a program of treatment. Freud (1976e) and Jung (1929, 1934) distinguished between psychotherapy as a process of personality change and development and focused treatment of some defined problem. Both of them favored the former. Freud referred to this as character analysis; Jung referred to this as self-realization, as personality individuation, as transformation. So too is the carrying forward of any and all ongoing experiencings a mere setting into motion of a process of change. Freud puts it in these words:

> The analyst is certainly able to do a great deal, but he cannot determine beforehand exactly what results he will effect. He sets in operation a certain process, the "loosening" of the existing repressions: he can watch over it, further it, remove difficulties in the way of it, and certainly do much also to vitiate it; but on the whole, once begun, the process goes its own way and does not admit of prescribed direction, either in the course it pursues or in the order in which the various stages to be gone through are taken (Freud, 1959, p. 350).

For Rogers, this is the therapeutic creation of a climate in which the patient grows (1963), a granting of a freedom to be (Rogers, 1958) without any preconceived direction or preestablished outcome. While there may be a kind of hierarchical ordering to the material which comes forth (Gendlin, 1964, p. 131), the whole process is merely an opening up of whatever is there for this particular patient right now.

The carrying forward of whatever experiencings are present may be contrasted with a traditional strategy of figuring out a treatment program to cure the problem and applying this strategy to the patient (Chrzanowski, 1977, 1978, 1980; Fromm, 1981; Michels, 1977; Rosen, 1955; Saretsky, 1981; West, 1978). The therapist cannot follow both strategies, i.e., carry forward whatever experiencing is going on and, at the same time, define this patient as an alcoholic whom the therapist wants to feel nauseous whenever he raises a glass of booze to his lips. The carrying forward of whatever experiencing is here contrasts with the therapist's active efforts to get this person to be more normal, to adopt healthy behaviors, to be more socially acceptable, to move " . . . toward the therapist's conception of what constitutes value in life" (Whitehorn, 1959, p. 5). A preselection that this patient has a drinking problem, is obese, is sexually promiscuous, has dependency problems means that the therapist cannot receive and carry forward whatever experiencing comes along. A preselection that this drinking problem is to drink less, this obese person is to lose weight, this dependent individual is to be less dependent—this virtually insures that the therapist will be unable merely to carry forward whatever experiencing is here.

Indeed, even when the patient is the one to define the problem, the two strategies use altogether different data for altogether different purposes. From one perspective, a patient may be understood as talking about his problem, e.g., the cancer or the temper outbursts or the drinking. On the basis of this mode of listening, the therapist will do something in accord with a preselected treatment program. For example, the therapist will seek out certain kinds of background information about the problem, or interpret something about the meaning of the problem. If, however, the therapist merely carries forth whatever experiencing is present, the patient's identifying of a problem becomes part of the experiential process. It is the ongoing experiencing which is paramount, not the referred-to problem. Treatment programs aimed at the referred-to problem pass right by the experiencing.

When a patient speaks about "my problem" and fills in the nature of the problem, its nuances and refinements, its history and development, experiential listening will highlight the constructed imagery and the nature of the experiencing. For example, the experiencing may be a pressured urgency to love and protect the problem, to nurture and succor the problem, to regard it as precious and special. Experiential therapists learn a great deal about the incredible bond between the patient and "my problem" by sensing the experiencing which occurs as the patient describes the problem. It would be an error for the experiential therapist to apply desensitization, relaxation, or other programs designed to "do something" to the precious problem.

All in all, the simple carrying forward of any experiencing which is present is the setting into motion of a process of personality change and development. It contrasts sharply with a strategy of applying some sort of a treatment program. The therapist may do one or another, but not both.

Ongoing experiencing versus referred-to, denoted content. The experiential therapist just carries forward whatever experiencing is going on. This contrasts with tying a treatment program to the referred-to or denoted content. Suppose that the patient talks about (refers to) masturbation: "I am really worried. It's starting again. I started masturbating. It's just as bad as ever!" If the experiencing is a sense of having no right to do bad things, of having to be a good boy, of being a hateful object, then that experiencing is carried forward. On the other hand, if the therapist chooses to select out the referred-to content, then what the therapist does is at least in part a function of, for example, whether the therapist regards that masturbating in that patient as normal or pathological (cf. Fenichel, 1954d).

The patient may refer to anxiety, forgetting things, not sleeping well, getting headaches, work, or writer's cramp. The experiential therapist will carry forward whatever experiencing is here as the patient refers to any of these. The patient may say, simply, "I've had writer's cramp ever since I was in elementary school. I've been to doctors all my life. No one's been able to help me! I just write a few words and it happens. I doubt if anyone can do anything about it." For the experiential therapist, these words, spoken in the right manner, may invoke an experiencing of stubborn challenge within the context of the therapist and others who dared to "do something" about my "problem." What is carried forward is this experiencing. In contrast, external therapists may well be drawn to the referred-to, denoted content, i.e., to the writer's cramp. They then make some sense of the writer's cramp, for example, from the Freudian psychoanalytic perspective as an excessive eroticization of the pen and the act of writing, or from the Daseinsanalytic perspective as tension and unfreedom (Condrau & Boss, 1971, pp. 509–510), from a behavioral position as a skill-learning deficiency, and so on. Then the therapist goes to work on the writer's cramp by interpreting it, showing the patient how to relax, getting at the underlying psychodynamics, teaching the subject the proper handwriting skills, and so on. The difference is that the patient is not right now having a writer's cramp, or anxiety, or forgetting things, having a headache, staying up nights, being annoyed; the patient is merely talking about them, referring to them, denoting them. The experiential therapist is carrying forward the immediate ongoing experiencing as the patient is talking about and referring to all those things to which the external therapist may be applying a treatment program.

In general, once the therapist shares the patient's experiential world, all the therapist does is carry forward whatever experiencings are present. It is naively unselective in that it carries forward whatever experiencings are here, and it works with the experiencing that is present rather than with the denoted or referred-to data. It is a setting into motion of a process of personality change rather than an application of a program designed to treat an identified (and generally referred-to) problem.

Carrying Forward of Experiencing Versus Blocking and Containing

When an experiencing is here, does the therapist carry it forward, or are there certain kinds of experiencings which are blocked off and contained? The answer is that every experiencing is carried forward; none is blocked off and contained. One of the reasons is that the therapist is aligned with the patient, sharing the patient's world and the patient's experiencing. In this posture, the therapist is less open to the private thoughts available to the external therapist: "Here comes some dangerous material, I better push that down. . . . That is wild stuff, it needs to be sealed off." A second reason is that the experiential therapist is generally on integrative terms with the experiencing. While the patient may draw back in dread from her disintegrative relationship with the bad form of the experiencing, the therapist is free to carry forward the good form of the experiencing. It is the difference between suppressing the awful "infantile tendencies" and being able " . . . to allow himself, for once, to be cared for like a child" (Boss, 1963, p. 201). Indeed, the internal therapist who merely carries forward the experiencing is typically unaware of the external therapist's perception of that material as calling for blockading and containment. Our work is that of carrying forward, not blocking and sealing off (Denes-Radomisli, 1977; Gendlin, 1972).

The external therapist will tend to push down, defend against, block, and contain material which his theory labels as delusional, hallucinatory, an unbearable surplus of repressed impulses, psychotic, dangerous acting-out, primitive, homicidal, suicidal, wild, crazy, schizophrenic (e.g., Fromm-Reichmann, 1958; Levine, 1976; Noyes & Kolb, 1967; Weiss, 1969). The ego will be shattered. The patient is too sick, disturbed, to tolerate the breaking through of such impulses. Acting-out impulses must be countered and blocked. The patient must be supported against such wild and dangerous material. Open the gate a little and primitive impulses will come bursting forth. Watch out for symptoms of pathology, illness, psychosis.

Our theory sees the experiencing which is present, and our theory of practice calls for the carrying forward of that experiencing; " . . . we should not turn away from someone who is 'latently psychotic' because we fear (as the contents-in-people theory implies) that the psychosis in people will 'erupt'" (Gendlin, 1966, p. 242). What many external therapists would block off and contain as psychotic and dangerous is qualitatively different from the experiencings which the therapist carries forward. This is more than merely different perspectives on "it." We work with the experiencings, and there is no place in our theory for psychotic impulses, schizophrenic material, or shattered egos.

We carry forward the experiencing whether or not anxiety, for example, is attached to it (cf. Angyal, 1965). In contrast, some other approaches target upon the anxiety, and employ methods designed expressly to reduce or block out the anxiety (e.g., Hobbs, 1962; Salter,

1949; Wolpe, 1964). The strategy of blocking and containing that about which the patient is anxious not only is counter to the carrying forward of experiencing, but also acts further to push down and seal off whatever experiencing is responsible. In the same vein, what happens if the experiencing has to do with resisting, defying, rebelling, being negative and abrasive, and fighting? The experiential therapist carries this forward (Levitsky & Perls, 1970; Mahrer, 1983b, 1984a). In some other therapies, such experiencings are discouraged, blocked, avoided, or interpreted away. It is bad and should not be tolerated: "Negativism is an attempt to get attention, used by people whose insecurity hinders them in relating themselves significantly to their fellowmen in more pleasantly effective ways" (Fromm-Reichmann, 1958, p. 116).

We carry forward the experiencing of snarling, combatting, resisting, even when the target is the therapist. In contrast, some approaches isolate this as bad, as requiring blocking and control. If the patient is inclined to take over the therapist, the therapist is to block and contain that tendency. Label it as paranoid and keep distance from it: "Give them (so psychoanalysts feel about their paranoid patients as their paranoid patients feel about them) an inch, and they will take a mile. Give them your little finger, and they will devour you whole. The generality of psychoanalysts believe that it is wise to keep an especially safe distance from those people they feel that way about" (Laing, 1982, p. 49). If they are not hurting enough or worshipful enough, or engaging in whatever the therapist regards as the good relationship, they are bad. All attempts by the patient to attack the therapist, to threaten the therapist, or to fight against the role the therapist wishes them to fulfill—these are to be dissuaded, discouraged, blocked and contained.

What is more, by forcing the patient to be good, to be in whatever role relationship the therapist forces upon the patient, the net result is that the deeper experiencing is even further blocked and contained. Forcing the patient to be hurting blocks and contains experiencing of being pleased, outrageous, or even happy. Forcing the patient into being a dependent child blocks and contains experiencing of being an aggressive child or a mature adult. Every role the therapist forces onto the patient blocks and contains experiencings that do not fit that role.

The net result is that the experiential therapist merely carries forward whatever experiencing is here, either at the operating or deeper levels. There is no pushing down or blocking or suppressing or containing of certain experiencings. In contrast, some approaches have all sorts of material which they regard as mad, bad, dangerous, and as requiring blockading and containment for all sorts of justifying reasons.

Carrying Forward Experiencing Versus
Intensifying Emotion or Unbridling
Wild Behavior

Carrying forward of experiencing is not the same as intensifying an emotion, or having some painful bodily sensation more intensely, or throwing open the floodgates of unbridled wild behavior. "We should not confuse intensity of emotion with experiencing" (Gendlin, 1966, p. 241), nor should we confuse intensity of bodily sensations with experiencing, or sheer behavioral expression with experiencing (cf. Janov, 1971; Janov & Holden, 1975; Mahrer, 1980a; Nichols & Zax, 1977).

An experiencing of defying, of absolutely resisting, may be accompanied with a moderate headache. Carrying forward means the furthering of the experiencing of defying, of absolutely resisting, rather than an intensifying of the headache. A dizzy sensation in the head is not to be whipped into a swirling passing out. Bodily nauseousness is not to become vomiting. A sensation of tension is not to become-locked, cramped muscles. It is the nature of the experiencing which is carried forward, not bodily sensations. The patient may be experiencing the trusting safety of being a little boy, curled up in grampa's lap, and there are tears. Carrying forward experiencing means heightened experiencing of trusting safety, not churning up the quiet tears into agonizing bawling. The goal is not to twist painful emotions into utter anguish, but rather to carry forward the experiencing.

The carrying forward of whatever experiencing is here is quite different from churning up raw emotions by having a group scream insults at the patient, forcing the patient to undress, wrestling with the patient, or having a group throw the patient in the air. The carrying forward of experiencing is quite different from intensifying bodily sensations by digging hard at the muscles, having the patient scream louder and louder, instructing the patient to slam the mat with increasing intensity, or leaning back as far as you are able and holding that position for 12 minutes.

The carrying forward of experiencing is not to be confused with unbridling behavior which is wild and crazy, behavior which wreaks havoc on others and oneself. The process emphasizes the experiencing rather than stealing around in the dead of night and slashing old people, sitting in towers and machine-gunning passers-by, blowing up city hall, erupting into frenzies of screaming hatred at innocent waiters or bus drivers, ripping off the clothes of priests and nuns, holding group orgies on the front lawn. What is carried forward is the inner experiencing, not behaviors.

Carrying forward of experiencing is not the equivalent of letting it all hang out, releasing libido, acting out sexual and aggressive impulses, catharsis or abreaction. All too often, these phrases refer to the therapist's attempts to get the patient to bawl and yowl, scream and yell, kick and strike, bite and scratch, beat and pound. The carrying forward of experiencing refers to experiencing and not to behaving, and, while some behaviors may be a means of promoting the carrying forward of experiencing, these behaviors do not correspond to those ordinarily included under catharsis and abreaction, or releasing libido or impulses.

Methods of Carrying Forward Experiencing:
Some Soft Hintings

Chapter 2 deals with the actual methods of carrying forward experiencing. These are taken from other methods used in approaches both in and out of the larger experiential family. The purpose of this section is to give some of the background of some of the methods presented in chapter 2.

Experiential use of the meaningful situational context. The idea is simple, and the method is found in many different therapies. If the patient actually lives and exists in the right situational context, the consequence is that experiencing moves ahead. This calls for the right situational context, the meaningful scene. Not just any one will do. This also calls for actually living and existing in that situation, in that scene. The patient is really back in the drugstore when the peculiar incident happened yesterday, or the patient is truly being a five-year-old boy riding on the motorcycle behind his older brother. As in implosive therapy (Stampfl, 1977), the patient is placed in a meaningful scene, one reproduced in detail, and it becomes reality. Then the experiencing carries forward. One feels more in the right situational context, especially as one exists and interacts in that situation (Gendlin, 1968).

It means actually being and existing in the situation, thinking and feeling in that situation (Enright, 1970). Being outside the scene and talking about it will not work; then it is the therapist's job to get the patient fully in that actual situation (Bandler & Grinder, 1982). Talking about oneself in that situation, or even having an image of oneself in the situation, is insufficient. Those who use this method emphasize how important it is actually to be in it, seeing what is here, living and breathing and being in this immediate scene.

Almost always there is another figure, a person with whom you are in direct and immediate interaction. The situation is made more real, and genuine experiencing is carried forward, by making that interaction live and real. Not only does the person talk to that other one (Enright, 1970; Levitsky & Perls, 1970; Perls, 1969a), but the other one is so live and real that there is a meaningful response, a genuine being-here-with and interaction (Gendlin, 1972). As you see your Daddy, and as the situation is real, and as you talk to and interact with him, so too he will stiffen up or smile or reach out or respond in some real way. This promotes the carrying forward of experiencing.

All of this requires that the words of the therapist be concrete, explicit, detailing, defining the specifics of the situation, the responses, the inner thoughts and feelings, pictorializing the explicit inner and outer minutiae of what is occurring. "The language one uses is an important factor; it should be pictorial, the more concrete the better. . . . One must give pictures, because the unconscious speaks in pictures . . . " (Angyal, 1965, p. 246). Even the use of client-centered reflections carries forward experiencing by detailing the exact nature of the feeling and the situational context. The therapist does not say, "You love your father," but "You just can't quite express all the love there is in you right now for your father, now that he is lying helpless in the hospital bed, sick and scared and vulnerable." "Rogers found that, while interpretations, deductions, and conceptual explanations were useless and usually resisted, the *exact* referring to the client's own momentarily felt meaning was almost always *welcome* to the client and seemed to release him into deeper and further self-expression and awareness" (Gendlin, 1964, p. 108). In Ericksonian hypnotherapy, there is incredible detailing of the exact childhood situation, the child's deeply personal thoughts and ideas, feelings and bodily sensations in the precise scene (Lankton & Lankton, 1983; Zeig, 1980). Throughout many approaches, experiencing is carried forward by emphasis upon the exact and concrete detailing of the inner and outer parts of the precise situation.

However, in none of these considerations is the scene or meaningful situational context that of the patient-therapist relation or the therapeutic situation itself. Whatever importance or therapeutic significance may occur in the patient-therapist relation or the therapeutic situation (cf.

Perls, 1969b) is given far more experiential punch by placing it within the more meaningful scenes and situational contexts within the patient's own personal world. In addition, the problems inherent in patient-therapist relationships (Mahrer, 1983a) are minimized by using situational contexts from the patient's own meaningful world. Even the experiencings involving actual physical cuddlings, strugglings, holdings, poundings are more effectively carried forward within actual situational contexts from within the patient's own world as compared with the therapeutic situation (cf. Whitaker, Warkentin, & Malone, 1959).

Phenomenological description and the opening of experiencing. If you pick the right attentional center, and if you describe it in the right way, then the consequence is that experiencing is opened up. Picking the right attentional center is something the experiential psychotherapist knows a lot about, for it is whatever the patient puts most of her attention into so that at least moderate sensations occur in the body. We already know about that. It is here that we learn from phenomenology. If we go into that attentional center with proper and careful description, the consequence is the carrying forward of experiencing. That is the lesson.

Phenomenologists emphasize the importance of simple, mere, unbiased, naive, non-explanatory description of events (Edie, 1976; Farber, 1966; Gurwitsch, 1974; Roche, 1973; Wyss, 1973). Ellenberger (1958) is one of the pioneers who showed how this method can be used in psychotherapy. Where Freud's method of free association may bring the patient into the vicinity of experientially meaningful material, the very nature of the method itself takes the person away rather than going down further into whatever material may be found. In contrast, Ellenberger shows how Husserl's phenomenological method of epoche or phenomenological reduction enters more deeply into the event:

> In the presence of a phenomenon (whether it be an external object or a state of mind), the phenomenologist uses an absolutely unbiased approach; he observes phenomena as they manifest themselves and only as they manifest themselves. . . . Husserl's principle is the unbiased contemplation of phenomena, putting aside any intellectual consideration (Ellenberger, 1958, p. 96).

There is no figuring out, no understanding, no explanation. Instead, by a process of step-by-step further description, the phenomenon is illuminated, opened up, lifted out, revealed, unfolded:

. . . Daseinsanalysis is phenomenologically oriented; it is not concerned with 'explaining', with a deduction of Something from something Else, but with laying clear, revealing. Daseinsanalysis does not seek to prove anything at all, but "merely" tries to show and understand the immediately perceptible phenomenon in its full meaning content (Condrau & Boss, 1971, pp. 505–506).

In phenomenological experience, the discursive taking apart of natural objects into characteristics or qualities and their inductive elaboration into types, concepts, judgements, conclusions and theories is replaced by giving expression to the content of what is purely phenomenally given and therefore is not part of "nature as such" in any way. But the phenomenal content . . . can unfold itself only if we approach and question it by the phenomenological method (Binswanger, 1958a, p. 192).

Stay with the phenomenon. Go further into it. Use words to describe it. The consequence is the opening up of the meaning of it (Wyss, 1973). For the psychotherapist, the actual methods include, for example, the Gestalt method of staying with a given feeling, and the key is staying with it, describing the feeling, going deeper into it — and not rushing away from the feeling in an effort to understand:

Let us say he has arrived at a point where he feels empty or confused or frustrated and discouraged. The therapist says, "Can you stay with this feeling?" . . . The therapist . . . asks him deliberately to remain with whatever psychic pain he has at the moment. The patient will be asked to elaborate the *what* and *how* of his feelings. "What are your sensations?" "What are your perceptions, fantasies, expectancies?" (Levitsky & Perls, 1970, pp. 148–149).

In Ericksonian hypnotherapy, the meaning of a headache is disclosed by a progressively deeper description of the headache itself (e.g., Lankton & Lankton, 1983, p. 206). Gendlin's sensitive work shows how the experiential process carries forward by a progressive going further into the felt meaning of it, whatever "it" is (1964, 1969, 1978). The commonality here is that the further and deeper meaning of a phenomenon emerges by careful and sensitive phenomenological description of the phenomenon itself, and not from traditional methods of rushing into its causes or its symbolic meaning or its origins or anything else which takes the person away from it. For experiential psychotherapists this means that one of the consequences of phenomenological description is the carrying forward of experiencing.

Amplifying bodily sensations. There are many methods which aim at amplifying bodily sensations, at heightening the bodily-felt aspect of feelings. Methods of emotional flooding (e.g., Rose, 1976) and psycho-imagination therapy (Shorr, 1972, 1974) amplify and intensify bodily sensations. Perls (1969a) uses methods of exaggerating, amplifying, celebrating all kinds of bodily sensations, all in an effort to take whatever is happening in the body and carry it forward. Of the wealth of methods to amplify bodily sensations, perhaps Gestalt therapy is foremost in organizing them into a set of explicit rules and procedures such as sheer repetition. While other theories (e.g., Bandura, 1961; Dunlap, 1932) may provide explanations of how repetition works, Gestalt is notable in refining this into a simple therapeutic method in which " . . . a patient may make a statement of importance but has perhaps glossed over it or in some way indicated that he has not fully absorbed its impact. He will be asked to say it again—if necessary a great number of times—and, where necessary, louder and louder" (Levitsky & Perls, 1970, pp. 147–148). Similarly, there are methods of phrasing statements so as to amplify bodily sensations. For example, instead of "my hand is shaking," the patient says, "I am shaking"; instead of "I can't go with you," the patient says, "I won't go with you"; instead of "I feel guilty about this," the patient says, "I resent this," and so on (e.g. Levitsky & Perls, 1970; Perls, 1969a; Shaffer, 1978). Gestalt methods are by no means unique in amplifying bodily sensations. Many approaches offer all sorts of methods designed to amplify the bodily aspect of experiencing (Keleman, 1973), methods of carrying forward experiencing through the medium of bodily feelings and sensations.

Beyond empathy: sharing the patient's world, and using the therapist's own inner experiencings. Client-centered therapy is the owner of the word "empathy," and much of the practice of empathic responding, research on empathy in theory, and theoretical grasp of the meaning of empathy must be credited to the client-centered family. The point of this section is that there are interesting explorations in the theory and practice of methods that hold promise of going well beyond our current meanings and methods of empathy.

The history of psychotherapy contains many attempts to get inside and to share the patient's inner experiencings. For example, Ellenberger (1958) describes some of the pioneering attempts in the early 1900s to solve the problem of understanding the world of "psychotic" individuals by actually entering into their subjective experience, literally to share their inner experiencings of vague threat, depersonalization, numbness, acute withdrawal. The key was the actual sharing of their world of experiencings. But what methods are effective to enable the therapist to be one with the patient, undergoing at least some of what the patient is undergoing. There are some methods which are effective in doing this, in putting the therapist inside the patient's world of experiencings.

Fromm-Reichmann (1958) and Whitaker, Warkentin, and Malone (1959) are representative of those who describe how the therapist duplicates, imitates the immediate physical posture of the patient and the nature of the immediate bodily sensations which are prominent in the patient's chest, arms, legs, back and so on. The method is designed to enable the therapist to get inside the patient's world by literally sharing the patient's immediate bodily-physical state.

Many therapists describe what it is like to leave go of their own conscious controls and cognitive processes, and to dip down into their own deeper personality processes, unconscious thoughts, associations, imagery, impulses. There is a curiously intriguing limbo state in which the therapist is perhaps no longer external to the patient, reacting to and affected by the impact of the patient, but in a somewhat different state which comes quite close to sharing what is occurring in the experiential world of the patient (cf. Bachrach, 1968; Greenson, 1960; Reik, 1948; Schaffer, 1958). In this limbo state, for example, apparently spontaneous thoughts of the therapist ("That is delusional . . . I am getting scared . . . I can't quite remember what just happened") simultaneously occur in the therapist and are verbalized by the patient. This is the kind of material Carkhuff and Berenson (1967, p. 27) refer to when they speak about higher levels of empathy: "The therapist's ability to communicate at high levels of empathic understanding appears to involve the therapist's ability to allow himself to experience or to merge in the experience of the client. . . . " It almost seems that the higher levels of empathy include access to the therapist's own inner experiencings, which take on a new meaning in terms of a kind of merging of the therapist into the world of the patient.

In this connection, many reflective and interpretive statements seem to require that the therapist know what to reflect or to interpret by first getting inside the patient's world. In reflections especially, in order for the therapist to know the feeling, to sense and touch what the feeling is like, the therapist shares the patient's feeling world; then the therapist can reflect the nature of the feeling. Similarly, with many interpretations, the therapist can know what to interpret and when to say it after the therapist has dipped into the patient's world for a moment or so (Fenichel, 1945, p. 25).

Interpretations and reflections are the backbone of many psychotherapies. If we ask where the therapist gets the data to reflect or to interpret, one answer is that the data come from the external therapist who relates with and observes the patient. But that is only one answer. Some interpretations and reflections come from the therapist's momentarily inserting herself into the patient's world of feelings, of personality processes, or whatever is to emerge as a reflective or interpretive statement. There seems to be a state which may be described as the higher levels of empathy or perhaps even beyond empathy. It involves sharing of the patient's immediate experiential world, and the methods of going beyond empathy are quite useful for the carrying forward of the patient's experiencing.

This means that the important data, the data which are trusted and used by the therapist, are those which occur in the sharing, merging, aligned with, highly empathic therapist—rather than the external therapist's observations of or reactions to the separated, external patient. Now the criterion shifts from the accuracy of the therapist's observation or interpretation to the degree to which the therapist is sharing, merging, aligned with, in a state of higher empathy with the patient (Mahrer, 1982, 1983a; Whitaker, Warkentin, & Malone, 1959).

The significant data now include the therapist's own inner momentary fantasies and fleeting dreams (Whitaker, Warkentin, & Malone, 1959), the therapist's inner images and feelings and experiencings (Guntrip, 1969), the naively non-"interpreted" and non-"symbolic" pictures occurring to the therapist (cf. Frankl, 1949, 1965), the therapist's own bodily-physical sensations (Whitaker, Warkentin, & Malone, 1959, p. 247). All of this and more are welcomed, expressed, described, and shown by the therapist who has achieved the state of going beyond empathy. And the therapeutic consequence is the carrying forward of the patient's experiencings.

These are some of the sources of the methods for carrying forward experiencing. We borrow methods from therapists who show how to use meaningful situational contexts and how to use what is occurring in the body. We borrow methods from clinical phenomenologists and from those who have taken the idea of empathy a step beyond. Experiential methods have roots into many ways of carrying forward experiencing, roots which go beyond the experiential family.

The Therapeutic Significance and
Use of Early Life Events

What kinds of early life events are therapeutically significant? How are early life events used to help the therapeutic process? What does the therapist do with early life events? The purpose of this section is to provide a general overview of the therapeutic significance and use of early life events, and to show which kinds of early life events are useful and significant for experiential psychotherapy. While some approaches put little therapeutic value on these events, each school may have its own way of identifying the kinds of early events which it regards as significant, and each may have its own way of using the early life events it selects as significant.

To gain insight and understanding. One of the most common uses of early life events is to facilitate the patient's insight and understanding of genetic themes and connections. "This means understanding what these warping influences are and the effects that they produce — what childhood emotional patterns persist unconsciously, how they operate and what is needed to correct them therapeutically" (Saul, 1958, p. 4).

If the therapist can study early events and see what emotional patterns arose and are still continuing in the present, insight and understanding can be furthered. A variation on this use is to identify connec tions between present and past ways of being, i.e., to see how present patterns are similar to early ones, or to see how early ones persist into the present. Another variant is to identify etiological roots of present ways of being in early life events. This may go all the way from isolated traumas to patterns of development over the early years. "In the early days of psychoanalysis, great emphasis was placed on the early origins of neurotic disturbances. Analysis was assumed to be deeper, the more complete and effective, the further back the symptoms could be traced into the pre-Oedipal phases" (Angyal, 1965, p. 264).

For purposes of gaining insight and understanding, certain kinds of early experiences are especially illuminated. If the therapist searches for psychoanalytic warping influences in childhood, he will be on the active lookout for certain predefined kinds of early events. Depending on the kinds of early events which are held as significant, the therapist may look for early determinants of problematic life scripts (Karpman, 1968; James & Jongeward, 1971; Steiner, 1974) or any number of early events including effectance learnings, cognitive development, schizophrenogenic influences, separation-individuation, psychoanalytic traumas, birth experiences, breast-feeding, cultural influences, family interaction patterns, and hundreds of other kinds of categories of whatever a particular approach identifies as significant early life events for insight and understanding.

Experiential psychotherapy does not use early life events for purposes of insight and understanding. Therefore, this psychotherapy does not search for the same early life events as approaches which count upon insight and understanding. For purposes of carrying forward of experiencing, particular kinds of early events are useful, but generally the kinds of early life events that are useful for insight and understanding are not necessarily those which contribute to the carrying forward of experiencing (see chapter 2). Nevertheless, some early events are regarded as significant in terms of their use in fostering insight and understanding, but not within experiential psychotherapy.

To correct the effects of early parental relationships. In some approaches significant early life events are those involving important relationships with parental figures. Once the therapist knows what these relationships were like, especially those which caused problems, then the therapist can provide the kind of relationship which corrects or counteracts the effects of those problematic early relationships.

There are at least two ways of accomplishing this. In one, the therapist finds out what the faulty early relationships were like, and then the therapist provides a relationship which is corrective. If the early relationships were with a severely punitive father, then the therapist can behave in a "calculatedly permissive manner" in order to provide the "corrective emotional experience" (Alexander, 1963; Alexander & French, 1948). This method " . . . emphasized the therapeutic significance of the difference between the old family conflicts and the actual doctor-patient relationship. This difference is what allows a 'corrective emotional experience' to occur, which I consider as the central therapeutic factor both in psychoanalysis proper and also in analytically oriented psychotherapy" (Alexander, 1963, p. 441).

In a second method, the therapist expressly sets out to duplicate the early problematical (pathological) parental relationship, and then the therapist applies a corrective resolution by means of a more wholesome or salutary therapist-patient relationship. The strategy depends upon " . . . the acting-through of the relationship with the patient which was similar to the relationships which the patient had earlier in life and which gave rise to the patient's problems in the first instance. . . . Such reactivation of early traumatic experiences is of no value unless there is some different resolution to the experience than that which the patient had experienced in early life" (Whitaker, Warkentin, & Malone, 1959, p. 226; see also Whitaker & Malone, 1953). The development of a psychoanalytic transference can work here provided that instead of interpreting the transference the therapist supplies the corrective therapist (i.e., parental) relationship.

In all of this, the significant early life events consist of problematic parental relationships. For experiential psychotherapy, however, this method does not serve to carry forward the patient's experiencings. Indeed, the attempt to correct the effects of early parental relationships is contrary to the carrying forward of experiencing. Whatever experiencings were involved in the early parental relationships would not only fail to be carried forward, but also be further barricaded and sealed off through such a strategy. Accordingly, experiential therapists would not look for problematic early parental relationships, nor would experiential therapists seek to correct the effects of these early parental relationships, for none of this contributes to the carrying forward of the patient's experiencings.

To live out the early event. Another use of early life events is to finish them out, complete the unfinished business, live out whatever was begun, stopped, curtailed, prevented from occurring, opened up but not carried out to its finality, begun but not completed. This procedure generally calls for the patient's returning into the vivid reality of the early event, thereby providing the living out process with what Levitsky and Perls (1970) refer to as "the impact of immediacy." The aim is to exist as fully as possible in the early context, and to live out or carry forth what was there to be lived out and carried forth:

> We found, at first to our greatest surprise, that the individual hysterical symptoms immediately disappeared without returning if we succeeded in thoroughly awakening the memories of the causal process with its accompanying affect, and if the patient circumstantially discussed the process in the most detailed manner and gave expression to the affect (Breuer & Freud, 1936, pp. 3–4).

Whereas many psychoanalytic therapists prefer having the patient live out the early events within the context of the current therapist-patient relationship (e.g., Wolberg, 1954), other therapists value the context of the early event itself (Stampfl & Levis, 1973). It is a matter of going back into these scenes themselves and living them out; " . . . he relives some of the crises of his early life, allowing himself to feel the emotions he felt forced to cut off as a child. In essence he is finishing off old, uncompleted scenes . . . " (Rose, 1976, p. 86). The patient lets the feelings be expressed and completed (Bergman, 1949; Kempler, 1968) in a reliving and further living, all within the explicit context of the early scene (Angyal, 1965).

For these purposes, which early events are the significant ones? They are the ones which provide the most useful context for affect, feelings, experiencings which are and were strong, and which are to be lived out (Mahrer, 1978a, 1984b). They include moments of great pain or great joy. There may have been explosively active behavings or none at all. Feeling and affect and experiencing may have been quite intense or sharply curtailed. The scene may be vividly etched in the patient's memory, vaguely obscure or essentially unremembered. It may have been the quiet beginning of a new way of being and behaving, or it may have been the peak moment of experiencing. What is common to all of these is that the early event constitutes the best context for the further living out and carrying forward of the personality process, whether that is referred to as experiencing, conditioned learning, symptom formation, affect, feeling, or whatever.

For purposes of carrying foward experiencing, these kinds of early life events are quite useful. "Living out" and "carrying forward of experiencing" are not exactly the same, but the former is close enough to be a soft hint for the latter.

To discover new possibilities. Early life events are a rich and untapped resource of new possibilities. They can be used to discover new personality processes, new feelings, new ways of being and behaving.

Some of these new possibilities are simply there for the finding. They contain wonderful possibilities that were there then but are not part of what the patient is now. In the vocabulary of existentialism, this is the "having-been" that constitutes the person's immediate "being-able-to-be." "In this 'having-been' are founded the capabilities by virtue of which the existence exists. Indeed, existence does not mean being-on-hand, but being-able-to-be . . . " (Binswanger, 1958c, p. 303). Condider the person who rarely has the sense of soft intimacy, yet there were precious moments in early childhood when this is precisely the feeling when he cupped the pet pigeon in his hands and brought his cheek against the body of the pigeon, aware of the soft cooing, the touch of the body, and the beating of the blood in his closest friend.

There are all sorts of early childhood learnings which can be discovered and used today. "In psychotherapy you teach a patient to use a great many of the things that they learned, and learned a long time ago, and don't remember learning" (Zeig, 1980, p. 38).

Looking for these early possibilities opens up whole new worlds of early life experiences which are seldom if ever disclosed in many therapies. Leaving aside the problems and the pains, there are early events in which the child had precious feelings and ways of being and experiencings that are not used today. The work of Milton Erickson (Erickson, 1980; Erickson & Rossi, 1981; Erickson, Rossi, & Rossi, 1976) contains hundreds of examples. Do you remember what it was like to be a very young child, and to notice how the other person's face changes when the person smiles, to study your fingers and know they are your fingers, rolling snow to make a snowball, jumping into a large pile of leaves, playing a game with a friend, watching your mother brush her hair, learning how to tie a shoe, slapping the water in the tub, looking through your legs and seeing things upside down, getting all the way through the recitation of the alphabet, making faces in the mirror, watching ants go down the tiny hole, climbing a tree and looking down, touching a spider's web?

There are precious new possibilities lying exposed on the surface of the early life events. Once you find the early event in which you were about three years old, standing in the driveway, with your head between your legs, seeing everything upside down, the possibilities leap forth—the whimsical silliness, how easy it is to turn the sky upside down, the exhilaration of turning everything topsy-turvy. On the other hand, there are also early life events where therapist and patient must do a little therapeutic work to open up the good possibilities. Angyal (1965) shows how, with a little therapeutic digging and opening up, long-standing feelings of guilt may yield underlying potentials for belongingness or tough survival or willingness to risk. Nightmarish memories of being in a pitch-black room, not being able to find the door, not knowing where Mommy and Daddy are or even whose house this is—with proper therapeutic work what is disclosed is a newfound deeper physical flailing, open expressiveness, wild yelling and howling.

All sorts of early events may be recollected quite painfully, wrapped in anguish or hurt or terror. With careful work, each of these can be opened up, lifted out, moved ahead, gone into, carried further along, allowed to disclose further, illuminated, helped to dilate, given fuller play. All of these phrases contain the idea that some kind of opening up or carrying forward yields a new potential. Rose expresses this idea in one particular way: "It is like a dream or a play in which the patient is the author, producer, actors, director, even scenery . . . he can allow the emergence of hitherto suppressed and repressed emotions. . . . He can behave and feel in entirely new ways" (1976, p. 92).

Experiential psychotherapy accepts these significant and useful classes of early life events to discover new possibilities.

To get at universally basic early events. Many approaches presume that if you want to get at the most basic material, the real foundations of what makes this person the way she is, you must get at certain kinds of very early life events. Furthermore, this presumption includes the idea that these life events are universal and that these kinds of early life events have a universal meaning and significance.

In primal therapy (Janov, 1970, 1971; Janov & Holden, 1975; Rose, 1976), the truly basic early life events, for all patients, involve the baby's deepest possible frustrations in interactive contact with the mother. In many schools of psychoanalytic therapy, the deepest and most basic personality processes consist of the Oedipal complexes. Early Oedipal material is the very foundation of every person's problems; early life events which are truly basic must revolve around such Oedipal material:

> Since the Oedipus complex is considered by Freud to be the nucleus of every neurosis, its analysis and resolution . . . constitutes a primary focus. Where the Oedipus complex is not revealed, where its pathologic manifestations are not thoroughly analyzed and worked through, and where forgotten memories of early childhood are not restored, treatment is considered incomplete (Wolberg, 1954, p. 61).

Object relations psychoanalysts (Fairbairn, 1952; Horner, 1979; Kernberg, 1975, 1976; Kohut, 1971, 1977) replace the universally significant Oedipal events with universally significant experiences around a scared infant ego. Guntrip (1969) sees " . . . the terrified infant in retreat from life and hiding in his inner citadel. . . . Psychotherapy . . . cannot be radical unless it reaches and releases this lost heart of the total self, which is not only repressed but in too great fear to re-emerge" (pp. 282–283). Again, this is the basic core of personality, and it is universally significant for all persons.

Many approaches share the two guiding propositions. One is that every person has some shared, common, universal kind of basic personality process. This may consist of sexual and aggressive instincts, or common cultural archetypes, or spiritual problems, or separation-individuation, or original sin, or social interest, or whatever that approach regards as the basic problems for all persons. A second is that truly significant life experiences are those which involve those particular basic universal problems. Accordingly, the most basic and significant and useful early life events have to do with birth trauma, or being seduced, or separation-individuation, or breast-feeding, or screaming at mother, or developing social interest, or finding one's place in the family, or whatever.

Experiential psychotherapy declines the special significance of such designated kinds of early events. The existential-humanistic theory of human beings tells a story in which each person may have a singular set of basic potentials. There are no common basic instincts or impulses or needs or whatever. Because we decline the proposition of common, shared, universal basic personality processes, we also decline the presumption of certain kinds of early life events as supremely significant. Even the basic potentials for experiencing may be carried forward without ever dealing with each patient's Oedipal life events, or being a scared little infant, or the trauma of being born, or nursing experiences.

In experiential psychotherapy, then, early life events are of invaluable significance and use in the carrying forward of experiencing. In this section I suggested that there are at least five ways that psychotherapists in general value early life events. Of these, experiential psychotherapy accepts two, namely, to live out the early event, and to discover new possibilities. Because we value the carrying forward of experiencing, we do not attach special value to using early life events to gain insight or understanding, to correct the effects of early parental relationships, or to get at supposedly universal basic early events.

Methods of Carrying Forward Experiencing: Some Learnings About What Does Not Work

When therapists look for effective methods of carrying forward experiencing, there are some methods which look as if they work, but a fair measure of clinical experience with those methods seems to indicate they are not very effective. In addition, there are some methods which are commonly used in therapy, and it would seem reasonable to use these in carrying forward experiencing. But again, clinical experience suggests these methods are not effective. The purpose of this section is to discuss some methods which do not work in carrying forward experiencing, methods which many therapists would easily think ought to be reasonably effective.

Insight and understanding, interpretation and explanation. Experiencing is our central axis of therapeutic change, the heart of our therapeutic process. In several other approaches, the central axis of therapeutic change is insight or understanding. Interpretation and explanation are major methods of bringing about insight and understanding. Although it is possible to mix and match, my conviction is that experiencing is not carried forward through insight and understanding, nor through the methods of interpretation and explanation. I am not aware of any research on this question (Mahrer, Durak, Lawson, & Nifakis, in press), and therefore we may turn to clinical theory and experience to see whether interpretation, explanation, and similar methods of furthering insight and understanding are useful for carrying forward experiencing.

My answer is no. Interpretations of all kinds and types are not able to carry forward experiencing. Explanations of the patient's personality patterns or relationships with the therapist and any other figures do not carry forward experiencing. Methods of promoting insight and understanding are not effective in carrying forward experiencing (Perls, 1969b). Causal or genetic explanations are not useful for our purpose (Binswanger, 1958a; Gendlin, 1968):

> Whether the explanatory concepts are simple and foolish, or sophisticated and quite correct, they are useless unless one employs them as pointers to momentarily name and hold onto a directly felt meaning. Without that, one cogitates in a vacuum and gets "no further." The explanatory "runaround" races the mental engine, disengaged from the wheels (Gendlin, 1964, p. 125).

There are lots of methods to name (label, identify) something which is hidden or deeper in the patient, but even doing this accurately and sensitively does not carry forward the patient's hidden or deeper experiencing; " . . . the hidden is only named—i.e. determined as here and now existent in the organism—but by no means is it revealed in its being or essence" (Binswanger, 1958b, p. 230).

Interpretive methods often use as data what is occurring in the patient-therapist relationship. The way the patient is with the therapist is seen as representative of the way the patient is with most people or with key figures. Or, much of what the patient talks about is stimulated by and reflective of the ongoing relationship with the therapist (cf. Langs, 1978, 1982). Or, the here-and-now therapeutic situation amplifies deeper material within the patient. Distorted reactions to and perceptions of the therapist are to be corrected, and there are all sorts of methods to maximize the patient's distorting and misperceiving the therapist so that the therapist can use this rich material to foster insight and understanding. However, these methods are only haphazardly useful in the carrying forward of the patient's inner experiencings, regardless of their usefulness in fostering insight and understanding of the patient's interpersonal relationships.

Indeed, efforts to provide insight and understanding are counterproductive to the carrying forward of experiencing. To the extent that a patient is experiencing, methods of gaining insight or understanding serve to dilute or deaden that experiencing rather than carry it forward. If a patient is experiencing strong sexual feelings, they tend to become neutralized as methods are used to help the patient gain insight and understanding of the genetic roots of the sexual experiencing, the relationship between the sexual experiencing and aggressive experiencing, or the thematic connection between sexual experiencing and the recent outbreak of symptomatic rashes on the forehead. Interpretations and explanations are instrumental for providing insight and understanding, but relatively inert or counterproductive to the carrying forward of experiencing.

Many patients (and therapists) move from one grand and exciting insight-explanation to another and another as the last one fades and becomes stale. The process is fun and intellectually stimulating, but it is quite different from experiencing. Freud spent years ruminating about children having sexual attraction toward one parent and fearful jealousy toward the other parent until he actually experienced these feelings toward his own mother and father. There is a gripping experiential meaningfulness which makes it real, and only then was he convinced of what he labeled Oedipal feelings (Freud, 1976c). Patients who have spent years coming to understand their sexual feelings toward one parent, who exhibit a kind of mature glibness in referring to these "Oedipal" feelings, enter a dramatically different state when they experience coitus with that parent.

All in all, interpretive and explanatory methods of promoting insight and understanding are not effective in carrying forward experiencing, and generally are countereffective for our purposes.

"Talking about" versus experiencing. When therapist and patient "talk about" something, experiencing is not carried forward. Instead,

experiencing tends to be quite low. It does not matter whether they are talking about feelings or affect-laden material or anything else; "talking about" suffocates experiencing.

Talking about one's sexual wishes toward mother not only is a far cry from experiencing sex with her, but also tends to truncate the experiencing. Talking about intimacy is not the same as experiencing intimacy and even serves to put a lid on experiencing (Shephard, 1979; Suttie, 1935; Wheelis, 1958). In many therapies, a fair proportion of time is spent with both therapist and patient talking about feelings. The therapist asks about the feeling, ventures statements about the feeling, invites the patient to describe more about the feeling. Yet with all this talking about, the patient is not having the feeling.

The patient may be saying, "I am feeling a lot of hurt right now, a deep hurt." Most therapies make what we would consider an error by presuming that the patient is indeed feeling hurt. But talking about deep hurt is not experiencing deep hurt. What is more, the act of talking about it truncates any experiencing, whether of that about which they are talking or of that which is occurring as they are talking about it. In this sense, much of what is common in many therapies — talking about something — is held as experientially inert, ineffective, or even truncating.

Reflective statements are the backbone of client-centered therapy, and they are rather common in many therapeutic approaches. Reflections often refer to a feeling, and the therapist statements talk about some referred-to feeling. For our purposes, however, reflective statements do not carry forward experiencing. The patient is practically never feeling whatever the reflective statement talks about. Instead, the patient is typically talking about some feeling, and the therapist reflects by likewise talking about some referred-to feeling. But neither is experiencing that feeling. Even the formal structure of the therapist's reflective statement insures that neither therapist nor patient feels it; they talk about it. At best, reflective statements may perhaps succeed in raising the level of experiencing from neutral to somewhat moderate. But reflective statements are ineffective in carrying forward experiencing to high levels.

On balance, "talking about" is not only ineffective in carrying forward experiencing but also tends instead to act as a blanket upon sheer experiencing.

Developing and using therapist-patient relationships. In terms of carrying forward the patient's experiencings, use of the therapist-patient relationship is rather ineffective and perhaps counterproductive. I am referring to the building of whatever the therapist regards as a good therapeutic relationship, including everything from a warm and friendly rapport to a client-centered facilitating relationship to a psychoanalytic transference relationship. I am also referring to interactions in which the therapist fulfills any kind of role in relation to the patient, usually with some sort of explicit therapeutic justification.

A great deal depends upon the issue of whether the patient's own experiencing is carried forward most effectively within a context of the patient's own life or within a context of the therapeutic relationship. If the experiencing is that of being a truly unwanted person, disdained and ridiculed, abandoned and rejected, our theory (Mahrer, 1983a) holds that this experiencing occurs most effectively within the context of carefully selected life situations from within the patient's own world, e.g., a context involving his wife's leaving him, or a context in which his parents were utterly disgusted at him and never again treated him as a member of the family. Our theory holds that therapist-patient relationships and interactions are much less effective in providing the appropriate context for these experiencings, no matter whether the therapist tries to be a blank screen, offer facilitating conditions, develop transference, be non-intrusive, a genuinely real person or whatever. No matter how significant the therapist manages to be, the context of the patient's real life has greater therapeutic punch — with regard to the patient's own experiencing, and from the perspective of experiential psychotherapy.

This means that experiencing is not effectively carried forward when the emphasis is on the therapist-patient interactive relationship, i.e. when therapist and patient are largely attending to and talking with one another. One of the reasons why the patient's experiencing is not carried forward, and is even further suppressed, is that the patient is forced into fulfilling some kind of role. While the therapist plays one role, the patient is moulded into another and a particular role relationship is established (Mahrer, 1978e, 1983a; Mahrer & Gervaize, 1983). The therapist may explicitly or implicitly set out to be kindly and understanding, to be whatever the patient tends to make him into, the strong and reliant one (Haley, 1959, 1973b; Rado, 1962), or a good friend (Schofield, 1964) or a better parent, or one who provides whatever the patient seems to need. The patient is to become the complementary role, e.g. the hurting one, the one who has been mistreated, the one with problems, the little child, the one who values the therapist, the sick one, the combatant. Whether the role is forced upon the patient by the therapist, or whether patient and therapist work together in constructing conjoint roles, the problem is that whatever experiencing is brought forth is largely a function of the role demands. What is left by the wayside is the carrying forward of experiencings unrelated to those attached to the particular roles the therapist's theories, the therapist, and the therapist-patient dyad force the patient to fulfill. Our theory holds that role relationships of whatever kind have the net effect of losing, ignoring, missing, or suppressing virtually all the experiencings which are to be carried forward. That is a serious problem.

If the patient is experiencing a sense of deprivation, of being without parental love and care, it is easy for the therapist to provide caring concern and love, and thereby prevent the carrying forward of the very experiencing in the patient. Attempts to assess what the patient needs and then to provide whatever that is only serve to seal off and counteract the carrying forward of the experiencing. If there is a deeper experiencing of manipulating and controlling the bad parents, of getting them to do guilt-dances, then this deeper experiencing is likewise sealed off as the therapist rushes in to be the good, caring, providing parental figure. In this scenario, the therapist is drawn toward being the really good parent or friend, the one who provides what the patient needs, the helpful one, and this is justified as being growth-promoting, providing facilitative conditions, offering a corrective emotional experience, building a relationship, or whatever. While this serves to build the kinds of role relationships some therapists are intentionally or inadvertently drawn toward constructing, what is expressly ignored is the carrying forward of whatever the patient may have been experiencing.

Many therapies expressly set out to build a certain kind of relationship, to fulfill certain therapist and patient roles and mutual role relationships. Therapist may be parent and patient may be child (e.g., Whitaker & Malone, 1953). Patient may be the scared little baby ego, frightened to come too close or stay too far away (e.g., Fairbairn, 1952; Guntrip, 1969). The therapist may strive to live up to the positive image the patient has of the therapist (e.g. Angyal, 1965). Therapist is to be the all-knowing, healthy, mature exemplar (Jourard, 1971a, 1971b), and the patient is to be the one who values the therapist and struggles to be like the therapist. Many therapies define clear therapist and patient roles and relationships. For our purposes, however, the building and fulfilling of these role relationships ignore, dilute, or seal off the carrying forward of the patient's experiencings.

Even more ominously, whatever kind of interactional relationship is constructed by therapist and patient serves to hide, avoid, deflect, and prevent deeper experiencings from carrying forth. Even when the therapist determinedly fulfills a role of being a neutral screen, or non-intrusive, or letting the patient relate however the patient is ready to relate, the nature of the therapist-patient relationship is counterproductive to the carrying forward of deeper experiencings. "In an analysis, transference has a twofold aspect. We have already stated that it must fundamentally be considered as a form of resistance. The patient defends himself against discussing his infantile instincts by reliving them" (Fenichel, 1953b, p. 326). All in all, the therapist-patient relationship is especially ineffective in carrying forward deeper experiencings hidden by and out of the zone of the relationship itself.

As long as the predominant interactive relationship is between therapist and patient, the consequences tend to exclude the carrying forward of the patient's experiencings. In most therapies, much of what occurs is the interactive relationship (Bordin, 1959; Goldstein, Heller & Sechrest, 1966; Patterson, 1968, 1974), and many methods are used to build and to work within a relationship in which each talks mainly to the other within some kind of relational context. As crucial as this massive enterprise is for many therapies, experiencing is not especially carried forward (and is typically interfered with) to the extent that therapists engage in patient relationships, interact with the patient, implicitly or explicitly fulfill some role relationship with the patient, and use all sorts of methods to engage in whatever they believe are useful ways of relating to and with the patient.

Deflecting the patient's attention onto therapist-preferred data. In order to carry forward experiencing, the patient's attention is to be directed onto a meaningful focal center within the meaningful situational context. Existential-humanistic thinking and its phenomenological methods instruct us that carrying forward of experiencing requires attention focused onto the phenomenologically right center within the phenomenologically right situational context for that experiencing (e.g., Gendlin, 1978; Kondo, 1958; Mahrer, 1975b; Pelletier & Garfield, 1976). In contrast, many commonly used therapeutic methods not only prevent this from occurring but deflect the patient's attention away from its phenomenologically "natural" focal center and situational context. When the patient's attention is deflected onto other data preferred by the therapist, the likely consequence is the relative failure to carry forward experiencing.

In initial sessions, it is common for the therapist to seize the patient's attention, and to direct it into areas which the therapist regards as important. For example, the therapist directs the patient into identifying something as the problem, telling about its background and how it interferes in the patient's life, what the patient has done about the problem, something about the patient's family life, vocation, and so on. If the patient is ready to experience a childlike hopeful trust in the therapist, and to let attention go to appropriate centers, this cannot occur and, instead, the therapist forces the patient to place attention on those topics of importance to the intake-interviewing therapist (Beier, 1966; Davis, 1971; Frank, 1959, 1961a, 1961b; Frank & Sweetland, 1962; Haley, 1963; Labov & Fanshel, 1977; Mahrer, 1983a; Mahrer, Edwards, Durak & Sterner, 1985; Prochaska & DiClemente, 1984; Stieper & Wiener, 1965). The net effect of such a strategy is that the patient's attention is deflected before it even has a chance to go to experientially meaningful centers.

Similarly, the patient's attention is deflected and not allowed to go to experientially meaningful centers in approaches which first try to define the problem (the diagnostic phase) and then apply a treatment program. In most behavior therapies, for example, the therapist explicitly sets out to obtain the relevant data behind the target complaint, and then explicitly applies the appropriate program aimed at altering the behavioral contingencies (e.g., Wolpe, 1976). In many psychoanalytic/psychodynamic therapies, a similar agenda is followed. While such phases make sense in these therapeutic approaches, the methods used deflect the patient's attention from experientially relevant data and are confounding to the carrying forward of experiencing.

Even when the patient is already attending to some center, and experiencing is alive and moving forward, many common methods have the effect of deflecting attention and truncating the carrying forward of experiencing. If the patient is undergoing some experiencing as she attends to her cancer or to the remarks of her sister, attention is deflected as the therapist asks about how the patient felt, wonders about how the patient might have behaved, gets at some historical information, invites the patient to see what all this means in terms of the patient-therapist relationship, tries to relate that to something the patient said last session, pushes the patient into seeing the underlying fears or thoughts, or pursues the checking out of inferences about the patient's pathology. Instead of attending to experientially useful centers, the patient's attention is drawn off to all sorts of topics, and the consequence is the deadening of experiencing.

Even before the therapist says or does something, the way the therapist listens and what the therapist listens for will either further the patient's attention or deflect it away. Suppose that the patient is attending to the remarks of her sister, and experiencing is ongoing as the patient is starting to focus on particular remarks. If the therapist listens through diagnostic ears ("Her paranoid tendencies are showing again"), attention is deflected. If the therapist listens by translating into the therapist-patient relationship ("She is complaining about what her sister said; I know what I said in the beginning of the session was provocative and unnecessary"), attention is deflected. If the therapist listens for the underlying cognitions ("She thinks that whatever she does is OK, and no one has the right to be critical of her"), or the referred-to feelings ("She says she feels hurt by her sister's remarks"), or accompanying bodily postures ("I notice that when she talks about her family, she sits up tall in the chair"), then the patient's attention is deflected.

Most ways of listening to and making sense of what patients do and say tend to deflect the patient's attention. Most kinds of therapist statements and interventions likewise tend to deflect the patient's attention. The net effect of deflecting the patient's attention into topics engineered by the therapist is to prevent the carrying forward of experiencing. It is remarkable how much of what therapists do tends to deflect patients' attention away from focused centering and the carrying forward of experiencing.

Experientially inert methods of illuminating the earlier and the deeper. Carrying forward experiencing calls for methods of getting at earlier events in the patient's life, and for getting at deeper experiencings. In many therapies there are common methods which also aim at getting at earlier and deeper material, but which are not useful in getting at our kinds of earlier events or in opening up deeper experiencings.

Some psychodynamic, depth, or psychoanalytic therapies include a rich body of clinical inferences which provide the "deeper meanings" of patients' behaviors, problems, complaints, and symptoms. The therapist thereby knows the deeper meaning of the patient's headache, ulcer, fear of high places, nail-biting, nose-picking, snoring, skin rash, palm sweating, temper outbursts, tiredness, low back pains, forgetfulness, lip-smacking, joint pains, facial tic, and procrastination. While these deeper psychodynamic inferences may provide therapists and patients with interesting conversation, they are not especially effective in opening up or carrying forward deeper experiencings.

Sometimes the idea is to get at deeper material by direct translation, e.g., of headache into repressed aggression. Sometimes direct translation is replaced by clinical choice among sets of deeper psychodynamic interpretations. For example, there are several different theories of what may be described as depression. What is deeper may be "orality" (Abraham, 1927), or hostility which is turned back onto the self (Freud, 1976g), deeper tendencies to manipulate significant other people (Rado, 1928), a need to suffer and be punished (Beck, 1967), or other notions of the deeper meanings of depression (Mahrer & Bornstein, 1969; Millon, 1981). Inventing new psychodynamic inferences of what is deeper, selecting one from among the alternatives, or using one rather consistently—none of these options is of use for the therapist who seeks to be in touch with the patient's immediately ongoing deeper experiencings.

Nor will clinically sensitive listening to the tell-tale free associational blocks and stops bring the experiential therapist to deeper experiencings or to experientially meaningful early life situations. In some therapies, however, this method is trusted to disclose the deeper and the earlier: "This undirected kind of thinking is a most important means of tapping the unconscious, and of reviving unconscious conflicts and the memories that are related to their origin" (Wolberg, 1954, p. 61).

In many therapies, there is a rather well-defined picture of what all patients are like at a deeper level. For example, all patients are basically developmentally arrested little egos, scared of the outer world of relationships, or all patients are basically organisms whose early conditionings were of the wrong kind, or all patients are basically sexual and aggressive animals, or all patients are basically maligned children waiting for the growth-promoting influence of the good parent. The method of starting with a defined preconception of what is deeper is not at all useful for carrying forward deeper experiencings whose nature, in experiential theory, varies with the particular patient.

If a theory accepts the idea that the deeper and the earlier are linked, then "the earlier the better," and significant events are held as occurring in infancy or possibly early childhood. However, not everyone agrees (e.g., Adler, 1959; Dreikurs, 1948; Jung, 1934; Sullivan, 1953b). Alexander (1963) warns that later events are often much more important than earlier ones, and that the search for constantly earlier material may simply be an error. Furthermore, Alexander cautions that the patient's tempting the therapist with very early memories is frequently an effectively evasive ruse. As a general rule, for purposes of carrying forward of experiencing, I agree with Alexander.

Behavior therapies also tend to reject the "earlier-the-better" guideline for finding significant life events. Instead, they look for particular life events which constitute the learning situations for the unadaptive or maladaptive or problematic behaviors which they seek to modify (e.g., Bandura, 1969; Goldfried & Davison, 1976; Ullmann & Krasner, 1965; Yates, 1975). Accordingly, their theory does not point them in and around the very earliest life situations. It is also understandable that the kinds of early life events of interest to behavior therapists are typically far afield from those the experiential therapist would use in carrying forward experiencing.

While all of these methods are used in other therapies to uncover the earlier and the deeper, perhaps the most heralded method is that the therapist-patient relationship is used to revivify early and deeper material, to open the way for the patient to reveal the earlier and the deeper, or to serve as the stage upon which the patient plays out the earlier and the deeper. If the therapist provides the right conditions, the patient will open up deep material arising from earlier life events. If the therapist fulfills the role of parent, the patient will become the child who thereby opens up the earlier and the deeper. If the therapist negotiates a transference, the patient will live out the earlier and the deeper. As tenaciously as some approaches hold to the uncovering value of the therapist-patient relationship, experiential therapy finds it of little or no use in illuminating deeper experiential material from the patient's early life.

One of the reasons is that the therapist-patient relationship is, from the perspective of our theory of practice, rigorously co-constructed by both participants, a conjointly mutual enterprise (Heidegger, 1963; Mahrer, 1983a; Mullan & Sangiuliano, 1964; Ouspensky, 1949; Wheelis, 1969). It does not matter whether the therapist determines to fulfill whatever role the patient places upon her, whether the therapist is determinedly non-intrusive, " . . . is entirely neutral and simply offers the patient a 'screen', a 'mirror', on which he can freely project the contents of his psyche" (Caruso, 1964, p. 140), works hard at being the good parent or to provide exemplary facilitating conditions. Indeed, since it is the therapist whose methods and theories impose the contours of the relationship, the material which emerges is more than co-constructed; it is predominantly determined by the therapist rather than the patient. In the more emotional peaks of transference, it is, from our view, erroneous to presume that the material which occurs pours out of the patient's earlier and deeper bowels. I submit that such "transference phenomena" are largely a function of the psychoanalytic therapist in mutual co-construction with the patient. In terms of illuminating that which is experientially earlier and deeper in the patient, such material is far from either significant or useful.

A second reason is that the very structure of the therapist-patient relationship sharply truncates earlier and deeper material to an inefficient and ineffective tiny sector. It is inefficient because it is like inspecting a subterranean metropolis with a tiny pen-light. It is ineffective because the therapist-patient relationship opens only a minuscule of early deeper material related to the relationship itself, and thereby misses virtually the whole universe of experientially meaningful early life events. Freud (1976b) was scrupulously careful in acknowledging that the transference relationship admitted a narrow chain of early historical data. Because the patient is interacting with a therapist who is carrying out the professional role of a psychoanalyst, the physical arrangements, the multiple sessions per week, the way the therapist speaks and what the therapist speaks about, the functions the patient is to carry out—all of this pulls in certain chains of early recollections and leaves out the large proportion of other early experiences. Although it is often acknowledged that the psychoanalytic therapist generally fulfills the parental role, the specific kind of parental role will pull in and push out particular kinds of early experiences. Is the therapist to be some sort of "primordial parent" (Whitaker & Malone, 1953), a "trusted good parental object" (Fairbairn, 1943), or some other sort of parental figure? Even if an early event is played out on the therapeutic stage (cf. Bergman, 1949), it is highly unlikely that the narrow chain of psychoanalytic early memories even begins to approach the range of early experiences which would be useful for the carrying forward of experiencings within our approach.

There is a third reason why the transference relationship is essentially useless in opening up earlier and deeper experiential material. In terms of the authenticity of experiencing, in terms of actually existing in the earlier situational context, in terms of actually feeling and being the infant or child one was, in terms of undergoing the actual earlier and deeper experiencing, our proposition is that transference phenomena hold a pale second to a genuine reliving of that earlier event. Regardless of psychoanalytic protestations of the genuineness of transference phenomena (e.g., Angyal, 1965; Guntrip, 1969), the current therapist-patient relationship is incredibly less useful than the actual earlier situational context. Carrying forward the experiencing of having surgery at age two years or of a near-drowning at four years is much more effectively negotiated when the patient is being a two-year-old or four-year-old child, actually existing and fully being in those feeling-filled situations, rather than being a patient relating to a psychoanalytic psychotherapist.

On balance, many common methods for illuminating earlier life events and deeper material are not especially useful for purposes of carrying forward experiencing. This may be extended to include methods which deflect the patient's attention away from experientially meaningful material, methods linked more to the development and use of the therapist-patient relationship, methods of "talking about" rather than experiencing, and methods aimed toward enhancing insight and understanding. On the other hand, there are methods which may be modified and used for the explicit purpose of carrying forward experiencing, and these will be described in the next chapter.

CHAPTER 2

Carrying Forward the
Potentials for Experiencing:
Methods

EVERY SESSION STARTS with the patient getting into an experiential state. This means the patient is reclining in a comfortable chair, feet on a hassock, eyes closed. At least moderately strong bodily sensations are occurring in the patient's body, and the patient's attention is distributed onto some meaningful area or focal center. The therapist is in a symmetrical state, sharing bodily sensations and attentional focus. The therapist is ready to listen experientially, i.e., to have experiencing and to let images and situational contexts occur. This is the first step (Figure 1, p. xvi). From here, the therapeutic process moves to either carrying forward the potentials for experiencing or experiencing the relationship between the patient and the deeper potential.

The purpose of the present chapter is to answer the question: What working methods are used to carry forward potentials for experiencing? Briefly, the answer is that the working methods for carrying forward experiencing fall into three classes. One consists of clarifying and making more real the situational context in which the experiencing occurs. A second includes methods whereby the therapist expresses the experiencing, is its voice and behavioralizing agency. The third class includes methods which enable the therapist to welcome, acknowledge and describe the nature of the experiencing.

CLARIFYING THE SITUATIONAL
CONTEXT

The therapist clarifies and makes experientially real the immediate scene or situational context. The more the patient exists and lives in the meaningful situational context, the more the experiencing carries forward. The therapist accomplishes this by defining its features and characteristics, by finding those critical instances of Kairos when experiencing would have heightened if the situational moment had fully occurred, and by discovering and existing in those situational contexts which occurred earlier in the patient's life and which contain the more powerful deeper experiencings (e.g., Mahrer & Pearson, 1971; Shorr, 1972, 1974; Stampfl & Levis, 1973).

Experiential listening determines that the therapist clarifies the situational context. How does the therapist decide to carry forward the potentials for experiencing (chapter 2) rather than work the relationship between the patient and the deeper potential (chapter 4)? If the therapist is going to carry forward the potential for experiencing, what determines that the therapist does this by clarifying the situational context rather than expressing the experiencing or describing what the experiencing is like? The answer to these questions is that the therapist as therapist does no deciding, makes no determinations. The therapist does not figure out what to do.

Instead, the therapist listens experientially to what the patient says and does. The therapist is passively aligned with and resonating with the patient as the patient is doing and speaking. It is experiential listening that determines what the therapist does. As the therapist listens experientially, saying the words right along with the patient, there will be occasions when the therapist will see some image, some figure or object, some scene or situational context. All of a sudden the therapist sees a person with a sad look, a toy truck being moved by the fingers of a little girl, a tray of food in a dark corner of a kitchen, a courtyard on church grounds. These images and scenes just appear to the passively listening therapist who is being with the patient, saying the words right along with the patient, allowing the patient's voice and way of being to be the therapist's own. The decision is made by passive experiential listening.

When the patient says and does something, not every experiential therapist will be drawn toward the situational context. As indicated in Figure 3, there are other centers of gravity, other places to which the experientially listening therapist's attention may be drawn. Yet most therapists, listening to the patient right now, will be guided into the same center, e.g., the situational context. The principle is that experiential listening determines that the therapist clarifies the situational context; in other words, it is the patient whose immediate way of being leads the therapist to the situational context. If a group of experiential therapists listen to this part of what the patient is doing and saying,

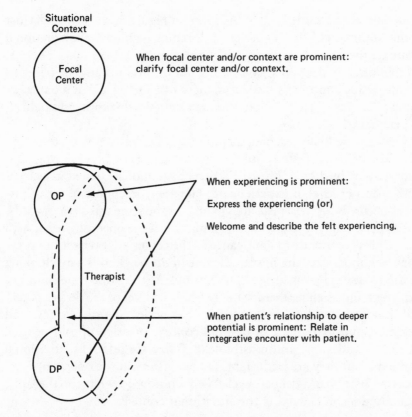

Situational
Context

Focal
Center

When focal center and/or context are prominent:
clarify focal center and/or context.

OP

When experiencing is prominent:

Express the experiencing (or)

Welcome and describe the felt experiencing.

Therapist

When patient's relationship to deeper
potential is prominent: Relate in
integrative encounter with patient.

DP

Figure 3. The Determining Conditions and the Functions of the Experiential Psycho-therapist

most of these therapists will attend to some situational context as their center of gravity.

This is a gracefully natural process. It just happens. According to the theory of experiential psychotherapy, the dominant center of gravity can only be in one place, only be within some kind of experiencing or within some focal center and situational context (Figure 3). If the therapist resonates with what the patient says and how the patient says it, the therapist is either having some experiencing, mainly, or being in some situational context, mainly. So it is natural and graceful that right now the therapist's main center of gravity is on some figure or object, some focal center or scene or situation, some place " . . . where the patient's immediate interest is momentarily centered" (Fenichel, 1945, p. 25).

Then the therapist merely clarifies what is there. Once the situational context is presented to the therapist, the therapist clarifies it, identifies it further, sees it more clearly. As given in Figure 3, the process is just about automatic. When experiential listening highlights the situational context, then the therapist clarifies the situational context. There is no thinking, no decisions, no figuring out of this or that. The patient's words define a mother's face or an ulcer or a graveyard or a party, or some other piece of a situational context, and the therapist automatically clarifies.

One experientially listening therapist may be drawn toward the situational context associated with the operating level of experiencing, and another may be drawn toward a different situational context associated with a deeper level of experiencing. Here is where most of the differences occur. Both therapists are "right." As the patient is saying words, one experientially listening therapist may be at the operating level, with a mild glow of a sense of annoyance as the center of gravity is her pregnant neighbor, standing next to the tree in the neighbor's yard, looking at the budding leaves in the early spring. At the same time, another experientially listening therapist may be at the level of the deeper potential, having a mild glow of the deeper experiencing of coldness and frigidity, and living in a situational context of dried up old people, shrunken and alone and mostly dead. They see different situational contexts, but they are both right, for one listens at the operating level and one listens at a deeper level. We turn now to what the therapist actually does in clarifying the situational context.

Phenomenological Description of the Experiential Scene

The therapist first lives a little bit more in the scene, attends to it a little more, allows himself to exist and be in that situational context. Then the therapist describes whatever part of that scene is at the attentional center. This is called phenomenological description of the experiential scene because the therapist is merely describing whatever is there for him, that part of the scene in which the therapist is already experiencing, the phenomenon to which the therapist is attending.

When the therapist describes the experiential scene, both the therapist and the patient tend to live in that scene a little more, to exist in that situation as if it were present and real. The payoff is that there is a carrying forward of experiencing. In other words, therapeutic experiencing occurs when the therapist describes the scene so that whatever experiencing is present tends to carry forward.

There are a few guidelines for doing this. One is that the therapist is right here in this scene, existing in this actual situational moment.

While the patient is existing in the situation just a little bit, the therapist lets herself be in the scene a lot further, so that it is even more real for the therapist. Second, the therapist uses the Gestalt procedures of speaking in the here-and-now, present tense, and speaking to the figure or entity in the scene. Describing the scene is a matter of talking to the parts which are being described. Third, the therapist welcomes being in the situation, invites the situation to occur and be present. There is a welcoming acceptance of the scene, whether it is pleasant or unpleasant (e.g., Cautela, 1966; Erickson & Rossi, 1981; Erickson, Rossi & Rossi, 1976). These guidelines are illustrated in the following examples.

The threat-filled, fear-laden scene. As patients behave and talk, what often appears to the experientially listening therapist is some kind of threat-filled, fear-laden scene. It is as if the patient and therapist are existing in a threatening situation a little bit. They are witness to it and are present in it, but they are also threatened by it. The therapist lets the threat be, and describes the salient components of the scene. For example, the patient is hesitant and reluctant to go to the committee meeting. He knows that the other eight members are going to engineer his withdrawal from the committee because he severely attacked the committee for a recent action it took.

Pt: This is one meeting I don't want to attend. No way. I hate feeling so uptight inside. They're all going to be there. They have the agenda all figured out. Jack'll be formal and friendly. (The therapist sees Jack. He is getting the meeting ready, just about to start.)

T: He smiles, yeah, but he looks away, not direct. There's the table; it's getting started. The air is charged already. (The therapist describes what is there for her as the patient's words evoke a scene. Now the patient can construct something further, or something new.)

Pt: They all smile. They laugh. They even look at you. (There is a tight, scared, bitterness in this. This way of being and these words now evoke the thoughts behind the laughing, the smiling, and the looking at you.)

T: They're all sitting now, and they are slowly going to bring up the right issue, the one they'll use to get rid of the bad apple.

Pt: Representation! They'll talk about, no, they'll bring up the need for a representative from Montreal. We've been talking about it, and now they're gonna ease me out! I know it's coming! Those lying bastards! It'll be smooth, oh yeah. All nice and aboveboard. Damn! Damn!!! (Here is a carrying forward of experiencing.)

Many scenes are bothersome, painful, laced with fear and threat. What the therapist allows herself to do is to be present in it, to see it, and then to describe the nature of the threatening scene:

Pt: (Referring to her husband and two children) I know I don't mean anything
    to them. Sometimes I think about ending it all, just killing myself.
    Suicide. They wouldn't give a damn. Maybe. I don't know. (The thera-
    pist sees a scene in which the husband and kids really do not care. They
    get along just fine without her.)
T: The three of them are in the kitchen and they're all playing cards. Shit!
    They're happy! Christine's laughing! And they're a real family! They
    are having fun playing cards.
Pt: Rick's a better mother than I am. The kids feel better with him.
T: (These words build a scene of peace. The kids are nestled into good mother
    Rick's chest, his arms around them). He's sitting on the sofa, and the
    kids are nestled, real comfortable, on his chest. What a peaceful scene.
Pt: (Pause. Then the experiencing carries forward.) We were never that way.
    I never . . . we are so busy, and always fighting! I really wish I could
    be a little girl and not worry about anything, just have nothing to do,
    and be a little girl. I wish!

The patient is being a 14-year-old boy helping his mother fold laundry. Soon his words invoke a scene which is surrounded with threat.
The therapist welcomes this scene and describes what she sees:

Pt: I like helping you on Saturdays. You have such pretty hair, thick and
    blonde blonde, white almost. You showered and you're all dressed up.
    You're going to be gone this afternoon. I know where you're going. With
    some guy. Your lover. You're going to be with him all afternoon, the
    two of you . . . (The patient stops here, but the therapist sees an image
    of mother, sprawled out naked on a bed, and the lover. The therapist
    describes the scene.)
T: I see her lying on a bed, clean sheets, a big bed, and she's with this guy,
    and she's naked, nothing on.
Pt: Maybe.
T: Her beautiful thick hair, I see it all over the pillow, and her hands are
    touching her breasts.
Pt: She wouldn't do that! No! No!

While this scene is filled with threat, the therapist allows the scene
to be present, whatever it is, and describes the scene which is here. Daring to see the scene clearly is scaring and threatening, but the therapist
takes this step, lets the scene take some form and shape, and then
describes the parts of the scene which are revealed. The consequence
is the carrying forward of experiencing.

The special listener. As the patient's words invoke images, it is as
if the therapist is aware of some other person, a special listener who

is receiving what the patient is saying. The image of the special listener may be vague or defined. It may appear as a sinister hooded figure, an old grandparent, the therapist, a prototypical wise parent, guru, enemy, deceased older sister, God, the accuser.

He has been talking for about three minutes, carefully explaining his feelings and reactions to a recent conversation with his sister and mother about "what to do" about the way the brother has been "acting" lately.

Pt: (Continuing) . . . So I'm asking myself these questions. Why? Am I completely out of step with the rest of the world? Am I the one who's supposed to be responsible for how he is? I don't think so. I know I did it most of my life, but I can't be expected to come every time they got a little problem. Harry drinks. So let him drink I say. I'm not the one with the answers. Well, of course I'll do whatever I can. I love him, and he's my brother . . .

As the patient continues, there slowly emerges a presence, a figure who is hearing all of these words. It is as if someone were here, receiving and listening. Vaguely indistinct, it is nevertheless present, a figure who is listening, receiving, paying careful attention. The actual content of the words recedes, and the therapist is experiencing a sense of telling his complaints, sharing his troubles. Yet the center of attention is some vague figure nearby.

T: An older person, someone. Listening to me. Somebody is here. (This sparks an immediate image in the patient.)
Pt: My sister used to talk to my Dad. There on the porch. She'd be with him, and I'd be inside. Never felt much. I couldn't . . . they'd listen to the ball games. (These words draw the therapist's attention to the way the two are together on the porch.)
T: She's sitting there with her knees drawn up, and they're both following the game, closely.
Pt: My Dad took me once to a ballgame. All I remember is when he was walking around after. He couldn't find the car. (He is crying, softly. Experiencing is carrying forward.)

Usually the special listener is an almost magical figure, with roots in the patient's childhood. There may have been a precious period of being with such a special listener, but it ended. The wonderful grandfather died when the patient was a young child. Or there was a brief meeting with an old woman who chanced upon the patient in the park when the patient was a young child, and the young child was instantly drawn to this magical old woman who knew everything, and listened. The patient does not talk directly to that person or even talk about that person. Instead, the patient talks, and the experientially listening therapist senses the presence of the special listener in the background, or vaguely nearby, implied, alluded to, but present. Sometimes the special listener takes the form of the therapist. Again, the figure of the therapist is only implied and alluded to, but there is an evoked presence:

Pt: I answer, but I don't talk from me, from what is going on within me. I keep thinking all the time what the other person is thinking about me. I always have some notion or some thoughts about what they think about me. I wish I could get over that somehow. (The therapist sees a therapist-like figure, sitting, observing, having thoughts, and this figure is clarified.)

T: He's sitting in the chair, watching, listening. I don't think I like what he's thinking.

Pt: But that's the way . . .

T: Thoughts, private thoughts, all to himself. They are critical thoughts.

Pt: Well, even if they're bad. I wish I could, just ask about it, know what's going on. Like they have eyes, I know. They look. (These words evoke an image of the eyes of the special listener.)

T: Actually the eyes look all right. They seem all right. (This makes the experiential scene just a little more real.)

Pt: I saw a picture of God, in a book at my aunt's house when I was very little. I sat in the field behind their house and stared at the eyes. I felt hollow and like I was transparent. I knew it was God, God. I sat there, must have been for hours. Not my eyes, that didn't mean anything. His eyes. The way God looked at me. I never felt like that before, or ever again. I wanted to keep that picture. I took it home with me and never told my aunt. I kept it hidden at home, and looked at it, I remember I waited until dark, and I would let him look at me, and I knew, I really knew . . . (starts crying). . . . Oh dear God (more crying). Please take care of me. I feel so bad (hard crying).

The patient's words may define a special listener who sneers at the patient, has no use for the patient, sees the patient as the worthless person that he really is, accuses the patient of this or that. The therapist's attention is drawn toward this figure as the patient defends herself as doing the best she can:

Pt: There is just too much for me to do. And I'm all by myself. I have to take care of my kids by myself, and the house is not small, no one helps me. I can't get it done by myself.

T: (Clarifying the image of the highly disapproving woman whose image is invoked) I don't think that's going to impress her. She still looks damned critical.

Pt: (Angrily) Nothing satisfies you! You had a husband! He was at least home! All you ever do is bitch at me, but you never help! Damn you! Leave me alone!!! (Strong experiencing is carried forward.)

When the patient's words invoke a special listener who has form and shape and presence, the therapist sees this special listener and describes something of what it is like. By describing these images, the scene is clarified, and experiencing carries forward.

Scenes associated with experiential states. As the therapist shares a moderate or strong experiential state, the therapist's attention may be drawn to some scene, some situational context in which this heightened experiencing is occurring. The therapist lives in this scene, describing whatever is here to be clarified. For example, the patient may be in a whipped-up frenzy of experiencing, an experiential state of frenetic fragmentation, of exploding fear:

Pt: What's the use? Of anything! Nothing matters anymore. You can't count on anything! Things change too fast! I don't even care anymore! What the hell are plans? You work and do your best and it's for nothing! (Voice shaking and raspy with verging panic) No one's going to care! Why even try? What for? There's no use for anything! (As these words come from the therapist, as the therapist sinks into this experiential state, the therapist sees flashes of catastrophic scenes, and she describes them.)

T: Someone died. Mother. Father. A house burned down. An accident. Something shaking and falling apart.

Pt: They wanted to do tests, a biopsy or something. Cancer!! Lump in my breast!! What do they know about my body? He said I may have cancer! More tests! Tests! I may have cancer!!! Cancer!!!

Instead of a churned up experiential state, the patient may sink into a dream-like reverie, a hypnogogic flow of fantasies which express an experiencing of lazy drifting, a loose letting go, a trusting kind of floating:

Pt: . . . Soft purple shades, spiraling, faces, clouds and colors inside a rainbow and beads, rain, raindrops glistening, soft, soft and going in, yellows and blues, purples in the sky, lines of soft purples and yellows, and sky. Small, very small little ones, fingers and cylinders, up in the sky, parallel colors of purple and yellow and soft reds, lines across and cool, warm and cool . . . (As the therapist allows these words to come from him, spoken in the same way, easily, the therapist is aware of a situational context, a place where all of this is occurring.)

T: Voices, friendly voices, a few people. Somewhere, hear the voices.

Pt: I slipped on something and got wet. My Daddy and somebody are fishing. Four or five, four. A little river. Nighttime, and there's a fire, a thing around me, warm. I'm tired.

T: And they are talking together.

Pt: (As if a little boy, being and talking as a little boy) It's so nice. All wrapped up in the blanket, and sleepy, my Daddy's hand is on my shoulder, and the sky is purple and yellow, and they're talking, low and friendly, quiet, they're talking together and I'm with my Daddy. Sleeping in the blanket, and the sky is so pretty, so nice being here with my Daddy . . .

The main character. The patient's words tend to illuminate a single main character, alive and present, even though there is little or no background or surroundings or situational context. Generally the main character is a person. Sometimes it is an animal, object, thing. Often, however, it is an agency which is given form and shape, e.g., the patient's anxiety or temper or worries, the problem with which the patient is coping, engaging, interacting, or the external forces which are swirling about, determining things. In any case, the experiential scene is filled with the central main character.

Pt: I feel pushed down. Suffocated, really pushed down. It's like I'm being compressed. I don't know. (The therapist is witness to a force or agency which is doing this. It is a thing which suffocates and pushes down and compresses. The center of gravity is this agency rather than the inner experiencing of feeling and being some way.)

T: Yeah, a thing, some thing, and it pushes me down. It is doing this to me.

Pt: Like iron, it's iron or something, and it grips me, pushes at me, like iron and it won't let go, like it just pushes! (The therapist sees it as grabbing, gripping, and as menacingly unreachable.)

T: There's no reaching it, and . . . and it's like an awful thing!

Pt: Brutal, brutal. Big, yeah, it's big and dark, big and dark and just brutal! It doesn't know anything else! It's brutal and strong, and it doesn't care about anything! (Clarifying its evoked form and shape carries forward the experiencing.)

In the following, the agitated patient is centering upon an external figure who is given form and shape toward the end of her statement:

Pt: Well, he just has to understand. It may be bad, but I gotta do. I gotta. I'm so crowded. I gotta have a little time for myself. That's the way it should be for a while. I'll tell him. I want to go do what I want once in a while. I'll tell him. He has no right. No reason why I shouldn't! I don't know what he'll do! (The therapist who says all of this with the patient sees "him" as furious, as not permitting this.)

T: Well, he doesn't like this. He's furious! There's a look on his face.

Pt: (She stiffens as attention focuses on him.) He hates me! His face . . . the look . . .

T: Tight, and the eyes, and the mouth, tight.

Pt: Why can't you just let me go! I don't belong to you. You don't own me! (She is screaming these words as her fists are pounding the sides of the chair.)

The most powerful and compelling focal center. The patient's focal center may be a powerful entity, occupying the whole scene, compelling virtually all of the patient's attention. It dominates the patient's world to such an extent that the center of gravity lies within that person or thing, and there is virtually no personhood or sense of identity left to be the patient. It may be a bodily event such as the cancer or brain tumor. It may be some external person or thing such as the controlling father, or the orange cat that always stares at you menacingly. It may be some internal or external force, agency, power, or merely "it." Whatever its locus or nature or form and shape, it is the most powerful and compelling focal center which drains the integrity out of the patient and into it.

As the therapist sees it and describes it, it becomes even more real. Significant features of it come into prominence as the powerful and compelling focal center becomes even more real. Then a most curious change tends to occur (Fromm, Suzuki, & de Martino, 1960; Mahrer, 1979). It is as if the patient assimilates into that focal center, slides into being it. The patient literally becomes that powerful and compelling focal center as the therapist clarifies more and more of what it is. For example, most of this patient's attention is poured into the powerfully compelling "faces":

Pt: . . . and I wake up with them. I see the faces on the wall, and behind me when I look in the mirror. When I walk through the market there are people, a guy who has a junk shop, others. They look at me. Just look. Like they are waiting for something to happen to me. I can't tell if they know, what's going to, but they watch me, yeah, watching mainly. I come into the market and they just look at me. They know something's going to happen. They wait. They have blank expressions like they're hiding.

T: (Seeing the faces up close, daring to get close to them) I'm seeing the face
   from about two feet away. Very close to it, just seeing the eyes and the
   blank expression.
Pt: Force. He knows. He's got the power. (The therapist becomes drawn in,
   as if moving into the force of the other one.)
T: (Dreamily) This person knows. Inside this person is the power, behind the
   eyes that are just watching, inside, behind the eyes.
Pt: There is skin and a face, but it is nothing. Everything is behind, and it
   is strong. A power. To know. Watching. Power. Power. (Pause) Feel
   it. Power. Watching. My body is growing . . . feel the force. I got the
   power. I am strong! I see! Feel it. Inside. Oh! Power! In me! Watching!
   My body's bigger! I feel bigger! Strong!! Strong!!

As the therapist increasingly clarifies the compelling attentional
center, experiencing carries forward and the patient enters into the image of the menacing mother:

Pt: You're like a lizard, a gigantic lizard, always there, and evil! You have
   nothing inside, no care, heart. You are evil! Just fat and evil, bloated,
   big, selfish. You are twisted and mean, you do damage, damage, and
   you don't even know about it!
T: (Drawn more and more into clarifying the evil inside all the flesh) Just big
   flesh, fat, fat neck, big fat neck, overfed animal lizard, and evil inside,
   green pussy evil, puss oozing inside all the fat.
Pt: (Riveted on the looming imagery) Smelly fat, sweaty. Big arms, fat, hanging down, soft and swishy, mean, mean inside, a mean inside, all mean
   and evil, fat evil, hurting and doing, fat doing, hurting, smelly, you
   smell.
T: Stenchy smell. Sweaty stenchy body odor smell.
Pt: Garbage, dirty fat garbage, yellow fat, chicken, chicken fat, big, whole
   body is dirty chicken fat, and smelly, and evil, hating, hating children
   and husband and family, quiet, and thinking they are little and think
   they are so good. Hoping they die, die, evil thoughts, lots of evil
   thoughts about the other people in the family, smiling when someone
   dies, gloating when someone isn't pretty anymore, coming down to your
   level, gloating, enjoying the evil thoughts about them . . .

She is now starting to wallow in the experiential process embodied
in the compelling figure. On the other hand, further description of the
compelling focal center may be followed by its easing away, even as
the experiencing carries forward.

Pt: (Moving her head slowly down toward her chest and then raising it
   high) . . . It won't ever go away, never let up. There, all the time. (The

patient has been complaining incessantly about the headache, and what it is like, especially its relentlessness.)

T: Gripping, like iron, a force, all it knows is tightening.

Pt: A band, like a band, iron, and it is an alive, living thing, it is alive and it grips, tightens, and never lets go!

T: (As if slowly assimilating into its relentless gripping) Tightens like a vise, an alive vise, the strength, the gripping strength! It's going to be here forever.

Pt: Yeah, yeah! Forever, never go away, a will, it has a will, alive, and a will, nothing is going to change it ever, nothing is, nothing at all can change it . . . (pause) . . . back of my head is, going away, softening. . . . It's softening . . . going away . . . breaking up! What a thing! Yeah, yeah. But it's been hurting me for weeks, and it's easing away, my head is looser now, hasn't felt like this, like it let my head go, it did what it wanted. It let me go. It just let me go and my head is, it's gone . . . for the first time it's like a friend! It doesn't hurt anymore! What a funny thing. It went away!

Whether inside the body or outside, whether a person or an agency or an "it," whatever its nature or locus, the therapist merely describes and clarifies, moving closer and closer, and the experiencing carries forward.

Spontaneous images and scenes. The therapist will be aware of images and scenes which appear spontaneously, without any effort or work, without thinking or clinical inferring. They are spontaneous because they seem to be unrelated to whatever the patient is doing and saying; they seem disconnected to whatever is coming from the patient; they appear suddenly. Therapists who learn to trust whatever images and scenes appear gain increasing access to the wealth of spontaneous images and scenes that occur as the patient is being and talking.

When these occur, the therapist sees what they are and describes them. In the actual moment of seeing and describing, there are no thoughts identifying the image or scene as spontaneous. They are spontaneous only when the therapist may listen later to a tape of the session, or as others follow without listening experientially. But in the actual therapeutic moment all the therapist is doing is receiving an image or scene and describing it.

The spontaneous image may be a vividly seen old, gnarled, wrinkled hand where moments before the therapist was in a scene with his son, both laughing as they are brushing their teeth in the bathroom. That is, it may be a single object or thing, or it may be a sudden memory from early childhood, quite unrelated to the scene which had been there for some time before. It may be a sudden and unrelated odor, pungent or a sweet flowery fragrance. It may be a weird or bizarre flash of blood spurting or twisted faces or bathtubs dancing with one another.

Whatever the nature of these spontaneous images and scenes, there are generally two interrelated consequences to the therapist's describing and clarifying what they are like. One is that experiencing is carried forward. The second is that the patient welcomes the new realm of spontaneous images, and this experiencing is also carried forward.

The spontaneous image may be mundane rather than weird, and may be somewhat related to the present scene, rather than disconnected from the contents of the scene:

Pt: (Addressing mother) . . . So you nag at me, nag, always nagging, at me all the time about my messy room, and the way I come home late for supper, and I have filthy shirts, and don't get good grades and my friends. Jeez, everything! Your voice whines at me, you whine. I have to wear Jack's (his older brother) shoes, his old running shoes, and you yell 'cause I don't have laces. I never think of it till you start in at me . . . (The therapist sees a man, the father, standing in the driveway, holding a hose, gently watering the lawn.)

T: So there's Dad there, watering the lawn. Holding the hose, smoking.

Pt: (Pause) Yeah. He smokes his pipe and stays out of it. (With the words "stays out of it," the therapist now sees a slight grin on Dad's face, from about five feet away.)

T: A little grin, not much. He grins a bit. And keeps on watering.

Pt: I know she should be yelling at him, not at me! You bitch (spoken quietly, as if through clenched teeth). You damned bitch! Why the hell don't you yell at him and leave me alone? Always talk about him behind his back. If you're mad, tell him! Get off my case! Back off!!

The scene may be kinesthetic, and with odors. In the following, the patient is agitated and flipping from here to there in depression:

Pt: I want to sleep. I want to die. I am scared! Please put me away, anywhere, just leave me alone. I feel hot, so hot, and tired. My head hurts. Maybe I am just sleepy. I have a headache. I'm not getting anywhere, and I just want to sleep. When I get up, all I can think about is getting to sleep. My body aches, my legs ache. I wish I could throw up. Sleep, if I could only sleep. So I can let me bleed, and my head can feel something else. (The therapist is aware of an odor of fresh earth, and coolness, and of a kind of floating of the body, a light hovering).

T: The earth is cool and smells fresh.

Pt: Mother . . . mother (she sobs quietly). I want to get in the coffin and lie next to you. (Her mother is in fact still alive.) You were not dead . . . (Long hard sobbing, deep and anguished. It ends with a moan.) Noooooo! I should be with you, next to your body, with you. Bleeding and bleeding till my body is curled up next to you. (The therapist's attention is on the mother, sleeping, but unresponsive.)

T: I think you're pretending to be asleep, but there are thoughts there, in your head.

Pt: (Smashing the hassock with her legs, beating the arms of the chair.) Ooooooo! (She moans and moans.)

One method of clarifying the situational context is phenomenological description of the experiential scene. Let the situational context occur, and merely describe what is there. We now turn to a second method for clarifying the situational context.

The Altered State: Actually Being in the Real Situation

There are methods of clarifying a situation so it becomes so real that therapist and patient actually seem to be existing in that situation. It is like being in a dream or in a hypnotic state; it is an altered state in which therapist and patient are actually in the real situation. While the methods of phenomenological description of the experiential scene put the therapist and patient somewhat into a live situation, these methods enable the therapist and patient to go further.

Therapist and patient illuminate all the details of the entire situation. The aim is to fill in all of the details of the situation. As more and more of the actual details are illuminated and set into place, a point is reached where the situation is made intensely real. This calls for cooperation between therapist and patient, each helping the other in completing everything, from the specifics of the surroundings to the physical postures of the people, from the odors to the sounds. The therapist allows her attention to scan until the details are filled in. In the following, the patient and therapist have already filled in the more prominent parts of the situation which occurred yesterday as she was walking with a friend and came across a neighbor in the market:

Pt: . . . and the look on her face was happy, just laughing, and I felt like she was thinking about me and Sally (her friend), thinking, yeah, that I was being silly. I'm not that way much, 'cause I was walking and holding Sally's arm when we met.

T: So she sees Sally, and I'm still holding Sally by the arm . . .

Pt: Sally's standing back a little, to my right, back a couple of steps. I think she's looking at the stand.

T: The stand. (The therapist sees a stand of oranges.) Oranges, in rows.

Pt: Flowers, there was a stand of flowers, reds and yellows, a swirl of colors there, to my right, and there are no people around, just us, like, I am on a stage, coming out on a stage and the place is so open, there is sky and sunshine, and I feel so good with Sal, so comfortable with her and walking . . . (She pauses and there are quiet tears. In these instances, the therapist is really here, in this situation.) . . . I love you. I feel so good with you! I feel so close to you, and I love showing you off. . . . The smell of the flowers, and the sunshine and the colors . . .

The more the therapist and patient allow themselves to see and describe the details of the scene, the more they drift into the scene. The more they drift into the scene, the more details are revealed. As this process continues, the two will move into being and existing in the actual, real situation.

Filling in the final, key, obscure elements in the situation. There may be a few key elements which are to be filled in. They are "key" in that they are significant elements in the situation, and they are "key" in that the filling in of the elements places the patient and therapist into the altered state, into the actual, real situation. It is as if these final elements have to remain obscure in order to keep the patient and therapist from actually being in the real situation. When they are filled in, the final barrier is removed and the patient and therapist are really existing in the situation. Generally there is a kind of charge or tension around these final elements.

The scene was from childhood, and it involved an experiencing of heady closeness, an exciting closeness with a man. The patient was about seven years old, living in a middle-class suburb. On a few Saturdays he would get up around five in the morning, ride his bicycle to the old shack on the gravel road, and just sit by the side of the road, listening to the sounds. The situation involved a fascinating spell of being joined by a skinny old man, in tattered old clothing, the two of them sitting by the roadside, talking.

Pt: I know how special it felt there with him, and how somehow I always remember that old skinny guy, like he changed my life. Felt different after that day, but the strange thing is that I can't remember the sound of his voice. (Here a new element is added to the scene, for now the therapist hears this fellow's voice. The scene had included everything, but there was no talking, now there is a voice.)

T: Hey yes! There is talking! Something is going on. Maybe words. I hear his voice. I'm trying to let his voice sound. Strange! He says very little. Like "hmmm" and "yeah."

Pt: Well, we watched the ants in the gravel there, and we listened mainly to the sounds. Birds, there were birds. But his voice was new, I don't remember even what he said. I can't remember anything we said, but I know we stayed there 'cause we were there for a long time, but I know we talked. I don't know what we talked about. (We are almost straining to let the conversation come out of hiding. Somehow the therapist knew that the skinny old man was listening mostly, but then it switched and he was doing most of the talking.)

T: First it seems like he is listening mostly and then it seems like he is doing most of the talking, and about, about things, like how ants live and the birds.

Pt: (With some animation) Oh! I told him a lie! I told him about the family who lived in the shack! Oh yes! I told him that they had a little boy that was sick! (Laughs) That they kept him in the little house in back, oh Christ, that's the outhouse! (Laughs hard) Well, I remember! I told him this whole story about who lived there and the family and the old guy probably lives there himself but he lets me tell it. I told him that the little boy was dying and was sick and they kept him in the little room out back 'cause he would get them sick, and I told him that I saw them bring his food to him and that he liked corn and they raised corn for him, and that the only thing he played with was a little white dog named Ginger, and I'm making up this whole long story about how they're not bad parents, but they had to keep him in the little room 'cause he would make everyone sick if they got his sickness, and the whole thing, and he lets me talk and his voice is real quiet. He asks me questions about the boy and I felt so scared telling him till he gave me a stone. He had it in his pocket! God, I remember now! (Pause) He gives me a stone and it was so pretty and I'm feeling like what I thought was special and . . . oh . . . we go to the little house out back and it's all open and broken and empty, just a little house room, and I'm telling him stories about how I want to fix up that little room and where I'd get the wood. He's smoking a cigarette and I walk like him, with my hands in my pocket. He gives me this stone and no one ever gave me anything. (His voice was low, and everything was real as we were filled with the experiencing of wondrous closeness with this special skinny old man in the tattered old clothes. The scene is real; the experiencing is here-and-now and intensely real.)

By filling in the final, key, obscure elements in the situation, the patient and therapist enter into an altered state in which they are actually being in the real situation. It is alive and present, and there is a consequent carrying forward of the experiencing.

Therapist undergoes the altered state of actually being in the real situation. The therapist allows herself to enter into the situation. By preceding the patient, the therapist then can describe the salient components of the situation, and the effect is that of bringing the patient along. In doing this, the therapist is offering the patient the opportunity to join the therapist in the actual live situation. It is a kind of hypnotism, a suggested invitation to join the therapist. In this method, the therapist does most of the talking after the therapist and patient define the general contours of the situation. It is as if the therapist's stream of talk brings the patient into the altered state along with the therapist.

These situations typically have some common characteristics. Usually they are from early childhood. The experiencing is more pervasive than sharp, more a state of experiencing than a screeching peak. They are usually scenes in which the patient is by oneself rather than a back-and-forth interaction with another person. The therapist enters into the altered state and details the situation, slowly concretizing every element in such detail that the patient is drawn into the experiential state.

At a recent committee meeting, the patient allowed risky perceptions and thoughts to intrude: seeing a third eye on her; having him be naked from the waist down, below the table; slowly raising the end of the table so that the committee members gradually leaned to the downside of the large table. Next, the patient drifted into early childhood experiences. One of these brought the therapist to a very early situation:

T: The year is 1948 . . . 1948. Three years old. Just three. 1948. In Ottawa. The house on Laurier, the nice house. It is sunshiny. On the lawn in front of the house. Three years old. Standing on the sidewalk. The sidewalk in front of the house. Three years old. Going to spread the legs, shoes there, spread the legs and put my head down, down, down, standing with my legs spread on the sidewalk, facing the street, and I put my head down and look through my legs at the house. I turned the whole thing upside down. It is all different. The house is upside down now, and I'm looking at the whole house, I am looking at the steps of the house. All seems funny and different. The steps are different. I look at the steps, and now I see the grass all different. The grass goes over there, and the house is all different. It is strange and I keep looking at

the steps, they seem funny and different, and I'm looking at the steps
and the door . . .
Pt: It's not the same. Everything seems closer. The house is closer to me . . .
(Laughs). It's all funny! (Giggles like a little boy)

The patient has joined the therapist in the altered state of the actual
situation. There are, then, at least three ways in which the therapist
brings the situation into actual reality, and the patient moves into an
altered state of actually being in the real situation. For a few moments
or so, perhaps longer, the patient is living and being in the scene, actually existing in the live situation. It is real. In this real situation, experiencing carries forward. That is the payoff.

The Critical Moment of Peak Experiencing

There are a few rare instances in which a person can recollect the
circumstances in the exact instant when experiencing was peak. In these
rare moments, it seems as if the world stood still during that instant
when the person is filled with the saturated experiencing. It lasts but
a moment, yet the person acutely remembers the bodily sensations, the
exact words being said, the looks on their faces, the details of the room,
everything. It is the critical moment which Kelman (1969) calls the moment of Kairos.

Aside from these rare exceptions, patients ordinarily stray in the
general vicinity of these peak moments, but never cross the boundary.
Patients will spend hundreds of therapy hours talking about incidents
occurring a few minutes ago, a day or so ago, many years ago. Yet
they will never venture into the critical seconds in which experiencing
was peak. They will allude generally to the event. They will describe
in detail what occurred before and after. They will talk roundabout
the critical moment. But they never will pinpoint exactly what occurred
in that critical instant when their experienced feelings were at their
height. Whole chunks of that moment will be cloudy or missing, vague
or lumpy, distorted or twisted. Patients will skip over the concrete par-
ticulars, stay miles above the actual instant, rush over or around the
details, point toward it from nearby. They rarely enter into the critical
moment of peak experiencing.

The method consists of delving closer and closer to the very heart
of the critical moment. It is a process of digging, of opening up, of going
further and further into the specifics of that instant when the experienc-

ing was at its peak. In that instant, what exact behavior was carried out by the patient? By the other person? What are the specific postures, looks, colors, thoughts, flashes, smells, feelings, touchings, sensations?

Illuminating the critical moment is the work of the therapist. Once the therapist smells the critical moment, it is up to the therapist to lead the way. Every session will offer two or three opportunities. It is the therapist who must take the plunge into the critical moment. It is always there. What is required is the conviction that a critical moment is right here, somewhere, and the readiness to do what practically no one ever does, namely, open up the specifics of the critical moment. The therapist actively searches for that critical moment, that defined instant, when experiencing is the most intense. Phenomenological description of the experiential scene is effective. Actually being in the real situation reaches a next plateau. Getting at the critical moment is the jewel.

The following is illustrative of a gradual process of focusing down further and further into the critical moment. She is upset as she tells about the incident yesterday with her two friends, Richard and Mel:

Pt: So Richard gets that way every so often. You can't tell. He just gets in a mood, and then I know, I know. He gets sarcastic, and a little mean, but I understand. You got to excuse him every so often when he gets like that. (Experiential listening reveals a deeper potential which absolutely does not excuse him; indeed, it is quite critical of his being like that. The scene is one in which Richard is out of hand; he is bitter, sarcastic, spewing a hard-edged meanness all around him.)

T: Richard is getting a little out of hand. There is a hard edge to his voice, nasty, and the look on his face . . .

Pt: (Loud) Well, I got mad at him! He goes too far sometimes! God! I don't know why I even let him come over sometimes! I think I've had it with his smart shitty remarks! (One part of the therapist is mobilized to say all of this directly to Richard. But the major attentional centering is something Richard said, some remark.)

T: (Loud) Something happened! He said something! He did something! I don't know exactly what!

Pt: (Very agitated and shouting) He has that damned superior look! I don't know what Mel did! He sat there! Just sat there, innocent like, and Richard and that superior look, hitting the baseball mitt, sneering, icy. Damn! What's so wrong? Acts so damned superior! I hate that!

The patient is alluding to some critical moment, pointing toward its presence. But she is hovering at a charged and strongly feelinged imminence. Patients (and therapists) typically stay at this level of strong feeling and move no closer. Yet the therapist senses the presence of a critical instant of peak experiencing, and the therapist is ready to get down to it.

T: (Matching the patient's level of agitation) Something happened here! Some where! Richard said something! There was a moment when the feeling just skyrocketed. Something happened! I know it! I can feel it, down here! Sneering, I see him sneering and hitting the mitt, hitting it hard! And there is something with Mel, something! Something! I know!

Pt: Well, Mel doesn't get it! He doesn't get it. Richard said something about something. I don't know. Richard made fun of Mel, and he just made fun of him! That's all . . . I don't know . . . he always gets that way. (So far and no further. Now, in typical fashion, the patient veers away from the critical moment, and the experiencing level drops. But the therapist perseveres because the therapist's attention is riveted on the specific critical moment underneath the haze. While the patient drops in the experiential level, the therapist remains at a high level, and, speaking slowly but with feeling, remains prepared to go deeper.)

T: But something is here. Richard and Mel. Something is here. It is happening in my bones. Something about Mel, and Richard did something. He said something or looked some way. And Mel is still hazy, but something's here. (The patient returns and lifts out more of what is occurring in and near the critical moment.)

Pt: Mel doesn't get it. He doesn't understand. Mel's reading the paper. (She is trying to fill it in for herself.) And Richard says something about baseball. He says baseball, I think. (She is straining to identify what happened.) A dumbell. Oh! Oh yeah! Mel says you play baseball with a bat! And Richard says that Mel could play 'cause he's batty, and then Richard looks at him! And then, he, uh, I think, I think that, uh, Mel did something. He was reading the paper . . . (The air is charged. We are closer.)

T: Now it's happening! Now! Richard looks at Mel. At Mel. Richard looks at Mel! He is looking at him. I see a sneer!

Pt: (Low and husky voice, trembling) Richard puts his hand on his penis and looks down at Mel, he's close to Mel, and Mel's scared of him. Richard knows Mel's gay. "Wanta play with my bat?" He is mean! He ridicules Mel, and I . . . I am staring at Mel and Mel's scared and he's quiet, and he looks broken and looks down. (Starts to cry) Like a hurt little child! That no one wants! (She is crying hard now, with loud bawling.) A little gentle boy. (She continues crying and crying as she is experientially energized in the critical moment.)

Many therapists avoid opening up the critical moments, so patients coast through months and years of life (and therapy) without getting down to the critical moments of peak experiencing. In virtually every session, a significant degree of therapeutic movement can occur if the therapist dares to enter into the critical moments and to open up the peak experiencing contained therein. Instead of coasting about in the general vicinity, the method is one of relentless opening of the critical moments which are implied or alluded to or nearby. Exactly when did the peak experiencing occur? Precisely what is occurring in this instant? What are the details which are here as the experiencing is uppermost? It is a matter of probing, of courageous lifting out, of defining the actual instant when the awful feeling is at its zenith. This process of opening up the critical moment is the energy which releases the experiencing.

Patients will come reasonably close and then stop. The therapist can get closer. Patients will veer away or even use dramatic means of getting away. The therapist can stay pointed at the critical moment. The therapist is to persist. Here is where the therapist's readiness and willingness and skill are leverages to enable the patient to open up critical moments which otherwise may remain festering and vague for months or years—or forever.

We have discussed three ways of clarifying the situational context and thereby carrying forward experiencing: describing the situation, undergoing the altered state of actually entering into the situation, and getting down into the critical moment when the experiencing was at its peak. A fourth way consists of going from whatever situational context you are working with now to discovering some earlier situational context. It is a matter of using past events in order to carry forward experiencing. Once we can discover the right events to work with, we know what to do. We can describe the situation, undergo the altered state of actually entering into the situation, or get down into the critical moment. But how do we discover the therapeutically important early life experiences?

DISCOVERING THE IMPORTANT EARLY
EXPERIENCES

Experiencing is carried forward within situational contexts, lived moments, recollected scenes. How can we find the important ones? How do we go from whatever scene we are in now to some earlier one that is even more valuable for carrying forward experiencing?

Freud found a way whereby some past experiences may be brought to life in the transference relationship between therapist and patient. Instead of going back into the past, the past was invited into the ongoing present; " . . . the patient *remembers* nothing of what is forgotten or repressed, but that he expresses it in *action*. He reproduces it not in his memory but in his behavior; he *repeats* it, without of course knowing that he is repeating it . . . " (Freud, 1959, p. 369). In experiential psychotherapy, there are other methods for discovering the most valuable, useful, or significant early experiences.

Using the Experiencing to Revivify the Early Situation

When the experiencing patient goes into the past, the appropriate early situation comes to life. By letting the patient experience fully and strongly, and by allowing the context to be a few months ago or a few years ago or many years ago or when the patient was just a little child, the earlier event is brought to life again (e.g., Bugental, 1978; Rose, 1976; Wyss, 1973). We start with whatever experiencing is here now, full and strong. If this experiencing fills the patient as much as possible, then some situational context will be present and will appear as we enter into the past.

Sheer experiencing pulls for a situational context. If the patient is filled with a strong measure of experiencing, that state of experiencing will bring forth some context, some situation. Once we have the experiencing, we then turn toward the past and the experiencing will act as a kind of magnet, pulling old situational contexts with relative ease (cf. Freud, 1976a). The important point is to describe the nature of the experiencing. It may be disconcerting, hurtful, painful; it may be happy and pleasant (cf. Lankton & Lankton, 1983). No matter how the experiencing feels, the therapist describes exactly what the experiencing is like. As the patient enters into the past, early situational contexts will affix themselves to the experiencing.

Our work started with a recent incident in which her husband bought a new briefcase. Soon the patient was having a measure of experiencing. It consisted of the sense of being overlooked, of being just a piece of shit who doesn't deserve to be regarded, of being a dismissible object. The patient is experiencing this, and the therapist is experiencing this, but the context is the recent incident in which he shows her the new briefcase. The aim is to allow ourselves to be filled with this experiencing, to detach from the recent situation with the husband and briefcase, and to allow an earlier situational context to appear.

T: (With saturated feeling) Some time ago! Many years ago! I am three or six or 11 or 22, some time ago. I am a little girl! A few years ago, maybe just seven years old. And I feel so very overlooked. Overlooked!

Overlooked!!! Oh! I'm just a piece of shit! So overlooked. I don't deserve to be told! No one has to tell me anything 'cause I'm not worth it! I'm not worth it! I'm just a piece of shit who isn't worth it! (The therapist is filled with this experiencing. It is powerful and gripping. But there is no scene. The therapist is being a child or an adolescent, filled with this experiencing, and the patient will live in the scene. Now it is up to the patient. Where are we? Having a full measure of this experiencing, what are the circumstances? She fills in the scene which is revivified for her.)

Pt: (She is crying softly.) Grampa came to play with me on Sundays. And, somebody at the table told me, they looked at each other, he wasn't there last time either. My aunt was holding something up, maybe a glass or something, and she was across the table. The dining room table, on Sundays. My cousins knew that he died. But, my aunt said that he wouldn't be coming. All I felt was that something had happened or something! I remember that it felt they were all far away and my ears were like under water. I didn't hear, I don't even know if anybody said anything. I felt like my head was going to break. (Cries) Nobody ever told me. I . . . don't know. It was just awful! (More tears)

Sometimes the recollected earlier scene is mundane, and sometimes it is dramatic. Sometimes it is a remembered event, and sometimes it appears as if from nowhere. In the following, the patient had been vaguely and generally disconsolate, and then the experiencing crystallized. It emerged as a sense of ending it all, an almost peaceful giving in, an ending of the struggle, a ceasing of all effort. It was like the experiencing of the peace of death. The therapist allowed herself to be filled with this experiencing, but within the context of some earlier surroundings. All the therapist does is to insert herself into the general surroundings of an earlier time; there are no specific scenes or situations.

T: (Filled with the experiencing of ending all the struggle) I don't know how old I am, maybe 10, maybe around 10, or younger? Maybe younger. I have no idea where I am, somewhere, but I am maybe seven or eight, or up to 10 maybe. But I know what is going on in me, and I want to know where I am, what's happening around me, 'cause I am already just stopping, no longer struggling, it's all over. I struggled, I struggled, and now I feel almost peaceful. I stopped struggling! No more! I'm peaceful now, it's all over. Now, where am I? Where am I? (This experiencing pulls an early situational context.)

Pt: (Slumped way down in the chair, legs drawn up tight against his chest. He is shaking slightly.) They pushed me in the refrigerator. It's in the basement of the big house near the trees, the old house. We crawled in through the basement window, and we played in the basement, in the summer, and they put me inside the refrigerator. It was a big one. I couldn't hear anything, and it was black in there. I wasn't crying, I didn't cry. I just didn't do anything, I never even thought about maybe dying 'cause of no air, never even thought of that. I just stopped struggling. I didn't scream or anything, that's the funny part, but never thought about dying. I did the strangest thing. Not relaxed, I think I just gave up, just like an animal that's cornered and doesn't fight anymore. Just lets itself go limp. I went limp. Had no idea I might have died. I didn't even struggle. I never yelled or anything. (As he is saying this, in a low, slow voice, his whole body is quivering slightly, and his breathing is slow and very deep.)

First you uncover the experiencing. Then the therapist allows the experiencing to be quite full and strong, and all of this is to occur within the generalized surroundings of some earlier period of life. As the patient likewise shares in this experiencing, allows it to occur in the generalized context of the past, an earlier situation will be discovered. That is how it works when we start with the nature of experiencing.

Framing the General Contours of the Early Experience

The therapist describes the general contours of an early experience, and the patient fills in the specifics of a particular early experience. It is as if the therapist is describing the shadowy outlines of some early event, and the patient then sees it vividly. In this method we discover the important early experience by framing the general contours of the event.

By starting from the present situational context. When experiencing carries forward and is strong, there is always some situational context, some scene in which this experiencing is occurring. The therapist starts with this situational context, goes to an earlier time frame, and describes the general contours of a scene. This is tantamount to describing some earlier experience without knowing precisely what specific early experience she is describing. The patient then fills in the specific event.

In the session, strong experiencing occurs as a sense of not existing, of blending into the surroundings, of being everything, of no longer having a personhood or identity. It is a feeling of awe. This occurs as she is alone on the flat roof of her town house, with trees nearby, the sounds of birds and an occasional car, no people. She is sitting with her back against the chimney stack, looking up at the lazy clouds in the late afternoon sky, with her arms on her knees, and her legs crossed underneath. It is very peaceful. The therapist describes the contours of this situation, and does so within the context of an earlier time.

T: I am younger now. I feel younger. I feel like I am about five or seven, yes, around five or seven, just five or seven, and I am somewhere, somewhere. I am all by myself, all alone, somewhere, I think, yes, there are trees around, yes, trees, and I'm all by myself, high up, I feel high up somewhere.

Pt: (Interrupting, and talking in a kind of lilting, sing-song voice) I lived in Rochester when I was a girl, and I remember there was a place near my home with a brook and I used to walk on the rocks in the brook. One day I climbed a little hill and got up in a tree. I had never been in a tree, ever, but I climbed, not high, not real high, close to the ground. It was a nice tree. I got in this one spot, and the sun was out. There were so many leaves. That tree was so, just friendly. It was strange. I never was in a tree before. I sat there and looked all around. It was a little like being hidden, yeah, and so nice. I never felt like that before. Just sitting here, in the tree. I wasn't scared of falling. Not at all. It was just the greatest feeling. I just sat there, and pretended, I can't remember. I pretended something, but I guess I just stayed there sitting in that tree. I never told anyone. I never went there with anyone.

The important thing is the "set," the postured vigilance for some scene to appear as the therapist sketches in the general contours. As long as the patient is "set" to see some scene, some early scene will appear regularly as the therapist frames in the general contours. It is the discovered early experience.

The heightening of experiencing occurred as his continual headache eased, and as he was filled with a sense of closeness for his father. The context was just a few days ago when, on a Sunday morning, he stopped in to see his mother, just to say hello. After a few minutes at coffee, she said that father had something to say to him or ask him or something, so he went to see his father in the backyard. His father had fallen asleep in the lawn chair, and the standard sparring distance just washed away as the patient stood quietly by, watching his father breathing slowly. As the patient is in this scene, there is an experiencing of innocent childlike closeness. It is quite strong. The therapist uses this situational context to discover an earlier scene by framing in the general contours.

T: And now all of this fades away. No lawn, no father, no sleep. I am somewhere else, somewhere at a different time, another time. (The therapist is being in the right time posture, the right "set.") It is some time ago, another time. (Now the therapist is ready to fill in the general contours.) This other person is here, someone I don't always get along with, but now things are different, for a moment no fighting. Almost feels close and all right. Something's here, something. (It is important to frame in the significant parts, and to do so with large, easy strokes.)

Pt: I see fire, like in a bonfire, no, like a furnace. A furnace. Seems OK. I remember. Yes. Yes, I remember. I was, I just shivered. I remember the janitor in junior high, in the basement. We were scared of him. I was really scared. I don't know how I got down there, but I'm in the basement, and he's sitting on a chair or something and looking at the fire in the big furnace, and I see the way his face looks. Different. He seems real different. Just friendly. I don't even know what he said. I can't even remember what happened. (Pause) Yes I do! I do. He showed me his hands, and he looked at my hand, he touched my hand and I didn't know what to do. I really felt all kinds of things with him. Yeah, I don't think I said much. That's when I started, with boys I mean. I think.

In this way, the therapist and patient discover the important early scenes, the ones in which some experiencing was quite strong. All the therapist does is to frame the general contours of some early situational context.

By anthropomorphizing the patient's potentials and relationships between potentials. The general idea is that the patient's potential for experiencing and the relationship between potentials are also roles which were carried out by some other persons in the patient's life. The method works like this. When experiencing is carried forward and reaches a peak, the therapist describes the nature of this experiencing as if this were a description of some person from the patient's life. When the strong experiencing involves the relationships between two potentials, these are described as other persons from the patient's life. In effect, we are anthropomorphizing the patient's ongoing potentials and ongoing relationships between potentials.

At the present moment, the patient is in the throes of strong experiencing. It is the experiencing of being hurt, being mistreated, being victimized, maligned, injured. This is the ongoing experiencing. The therapist invokes an earlier scene by describing the experiencing as if it were the description of a role played by some actual figure.

T: And now it is long ago, and I'm somewhere else, some other time, somewhere. I am in some other time. I feel maybe around eight or ten. Yes,
   or maybe a little older. There is someone, maybe me or not, not me,
   someone else. Someone who is the mistreated one, the one who is victimized, the goat, the injured one, the one who is mistreated. Somebody.
   Somebody. Somebody is here now. Who is this? Who is this one?

Pt: My uncle Stan. I'm in the kitchen. I think my Dad is here. My mother
   is here, they're laughing. My mother had three sisters, my aunts. They
   married, and my uncle Stan was the baby. They tell stories about him,
   they're laughing and I don't remember if I laugh, maybe, but I don't
   remember. They tell how he was so dumb, they make fun of him and
   they never invite him. They—I don't like them. He was an alcoholic.
   They told a story that he used to fall off the bed and fall on his head,
   and they'd say that's why he, that explains the way he is, something happened to his head. His head shook all the time, and they said it was
   'cause he drank, or maybe something's wrong with his head. Now it
   seems cruel, just cruel, the way the sisters made fun of him, and I never
   even thought about, I never said anything, I don't think I ever felt
   anything.

   The immediate, strong experiencing is anthropomorphized into some
figure occurring in an earlier scene, and thereby the scene is discovered.
We can also start with the relationships between two potentials. Suppose that we identify two operating potentials which are related together in a negative, disintegrative manner so that the patient is never happy
in either, runs from one into the other, and is never fully either one.
He is sometimes confident, excited, forward moving, and sometimes
gloomy, unsure, depressed, and stuck. Experiencing one, there is
unhappiness from the other, and he rattles back and forth between the
two, not happy in either.

T: There are two people, some two people from an earlier time and some
   earlier place, from some time ago, some other time. I think I know a
   little of what they are like, but I don't know who they are, so I'll try.
   I'll describe them, and I want to catch even a glimpse of who the hell
   I'm describing. Let's see. One is confident and can be excited about
   something, ready to make plans and do things, and the other, they don't
   get along, the other is unsure, holding back, holding back, and . . .

Pt: (Cutting in here) That's my uncle Rick and aunt Bert. I lived with them
   alot 'cause they had a place near school, where I went. I stayed with
   them. He had a plumbing shop, he could fix things. He could, he
   worked places. He, they used to argue. He wanted to have his own
   place, the plumbing shop was in his garage, and it stopped, so he

worked in this antique place, well, it had old chairs and stuff. She was
always mad at him 'cause he didn't, well, she was always worried that
it wouldn't work, I guess she was right. They always fought.

Experiential listening will reveal a relationship between the patient
and the patient's "self." That is, the patient's way of talking and the
content of what the patient is saying invoke in the experientially listening therapist an image of a defined self with which the patient has a
particular relationship. In the following, he is experiencing a sense of
pride in the "self" which is defined as exceedingly tough and resistant:

Pt: (Continuing on) . . . So she's right! I know she's right! I've had that problem as long as I can remember. Been to therapy four years, best analyst
in town. Whew, it cost, and I went three times a week for almost four
years. It didn't work. It's too deep or something. Someone does something, behind my back, a real bad thing, and it gets registered, for life.
Never forgets! I don't like it. I'd be happier without it, I know! Have
a happier home life, be a better consultant, but there it is! It grabs hold
and never lets go, it holds on like a bulldog, keeps the juices up for
decades, and it's going to pay it back eye for eye and tooth for tooth,
no matter now long! (Experiential listening reveals the prideful relationship between patient and the defined part of "self," an image of two persons whom the therapist describes.)
T: (Dreamily) Well I can see these two people, but it's like a dream, like from
some other time. I see two people. I don't know who they are, but I
can sort of see them. Who are they? One is like the avenger, all this person knows is getting even. A crime is committed, some bad crime, and
this person is going to punish the criminal, and nothing is ever going
to stop it, nothing will get in this one's way no matter how long it takes,
ever. And the other one is older, bigger, yeah, bigger, maybe a father,
no, more like a friend or brother. "That's my boy. I'm proud of him!
He's tough and he never forgets." He is really proud of his partner or
his friend or someone. But I don't know who they are. Somebody.
Pt: I don't see people. I see the Easter dinner, at my house. My Dad's family.
Kermit's there. He's about 12 years older than me. He used to take me
walking. He used to walk with me on Sundays when we'd go to church
and then he'd walk with me, and he got in trouble. (He is starting to
cry now.) He was a God to me. He was on the swimming team and he
always knew what to do. But he died. (Crying) He was killed by the
cops, and no one did anything! In my livingroom, and they all felt bad,
and they didn't do anything! I was in elementary school, my father and
the whole family just talked and they acted like no one's supposed to
do anything. My Gramma cried, and my Mom never wanted to talk

about it. I bought it. I didn't do anything, and I told everyone that he was killed by cops. Oh God!

We start with the salient components of the present scene. By describing these features, and by allowing them to frame earlier scenes, the patient will be in the earlier situation. We accomplish this by starting with characteristics of the present scene, and by "anthropomorphizing" the patient's immediately present potentials and relationships between potentials. In effect, we invoke the early scene by framing in the general contours of the present situation.

Early Experiences From the "Primitive Field"

Many therapeutic approaches look for important and significant early events on the basis of particular notions of the furthest and deepest reaches of where to look, conceptions of how human beings are formed and come about, of what comprises human beings from the very beginning. Experiential psychotherapy is tied to an existential-humanistic theory of human beings which accepts the concept of a "primitive field" (Mahrer, 1978a). In terms of psychotherapeutic practice, this concept of a "primitive field" means that a most important and significant class of early experiences occurred in the time roughly approximated by a year or so before conception to three or five years after birth. Keeping in mind the discovery of important early experiences, there are two direct implications for the therapist.

One is that the important experiences in this period need not happen "to" the patient. That is, the key figures may not include the patient. Indeed, the patient may not even have been conceived yet. If the patient is around, it is only as a bit player in the scene. The important people are the other figures in this time frame, generally the parents or key persons who play significant roles in this "primitive field." The second direct implication is that the time frame begins with the year or so prior to conception. This reinforces the idea that the players in the incident need not include the patient as an infant, a neonate, or a fetus. We discover important earlier experiences by going to this primitive field in which the significant players are the important figures around the infant or the neonate or fetus or to-be-conceived patient.

Indications for going to early experiences in the "primitive field." There are at least three indications that the important early experiences may reside or have roots in the "primitive field." One is that the present situation includes some highly compelling person or agency around which the patient's whole world seems to revolve, a person or agency at the very heart of the patient's meaningful world. This person or agency thoroughly dominates the patient's world, and virtually all of the patient's attention is compellingly focused there (Eigen, 1973; Laing, 1975). Most of the patient's concerns consist of father or mother or the evil enemy or the menacing forces out there or alien forces or the people who never leave the patient alone, who plot against him. Under these conditions, it is as if the "center of gravity" of the patient resides out there in the form of the compelling person or agency rather than within the patient. It is the patient whose whole life is centered upon pleasing father, getting free from father, resolving the problem with father, ridding herself of the father who is always at the center of her world. It is the patient who is described in classical recountings of the "paranoid" patient or classical existential descriptions of the externalized self:

> . . . the place of the self is taken by the Mitwelt. . . . For the Mitwelt is not one's own standard but an alien one, and as such it is no longer dependent on myself but faces me as something immovable and foreign . . . the transfer of the center of gravity of our existence from our own self to the judgement of others, experienced as fixed. Thereby the self . . . becomes a state of things, judged by the others and accordingly by me — in other words, it becomes objectified, made into a "fixed" object or thing, with fixed contours, fixed dimensions and weight (Binswanger, 1958c, p. 341).

When the center of gravity is in the external figure or agency around which one's whole life swings, it pays to turn to the important events of the "primitive field." A second indication is when therapy finally reaches the basic potentials. As therapeutic work continues, deeper potentials tend to be brought into the operating domain. This opens the way for the presence of genuinely basic potentials. When therapy reaches that point, the important early experiences reside in the primitive field. Much of the advanced work of experiential therapy goes back to experiences centering upon the significant figures of the primitive field.

The third indication is that the recollected event seems to be plucked out of another person's life, especially someone living during or before the patient's earliest months and years. Patients occasionally bring up scenes and events which almost seem to defy understanding in terms of the patient's own life. Some clinical theorists give them a home in a kind of cultural unconscious; these experiences come from other lives, from other people. An apparently recollected memory of being caught in a cave may be understood as transmitted through some shared cultural unconscious so that the event is rooted in experience far more archaic than one's own actual life (cf. Roheim, 1971). Or, the event is squeezed into experiences surrounding one's own birth. Freud states that some truly early experiences took place before the infant is developed enough to comprehend them:

> No memory of one special kind of highly important experience can usually be recovered: these are experiences which took place in very early childhood, before and they could be comprehended, but which were *subsequently* interpreted and understood. One gains a knowledge of them from dreams . . . (Freud, 1959, p. 368).

What do we do with "memories" of events which are difficult to place within the patient's own early life? Freud struggled with how to explain such memories of early seduction, of sexual arousal, of wishes to get rid of a parent (Masson, 1983). There are memories of birth, of traveling in a foreign country, of being a different person, of having a different existence, memories which almost seem to belong to some other person's life.

In experiential psychotherapy, we open the door beyond the life of the patient and out into the life of the figures who comprised the primitive field. These are the figures encompassing the infant, the figures who defined and gave meaning to the infant, the figures for whom the very idea of the infant-to-be was a meaningful center. The early seduction experience may have involved mother's own experience in the years before and after the infant's conception. The sexual arousal may be what was occurring in mother or father during these earliest years. Wishes to be rid of that person may have resided in the older child, in mother or father. The significance of actual birth may involve mother's own experiential peak. Father's strongest experiencing may have occurred in foreign travels just before the patient was conceived. All of these events occurred, but the time frame includes the few years before and after conception, and they happened "to" the key figures in the patient's primitive world, rather than "to" the patient in the usual sense.

Enabling the patient to discover early experiences from the "primitive field." The patient has to be shown how to discover scenes and incidents from the primitive field. Until the patient learns to have access to these experiences, the therapist has to take the first steps to show the patient what to do and how to do it. The therapist may accomplish this by explicitly allowing figures other than the patient to be the center of gravity, to be the ones the experiences happen "to." The therapist also casts the patient in a role of only a bit player in the scene. In the following, Ellen had been in therapy two or three times a week for about a year and a half. During the present session, a basic potential was beginning to surface. There is an experiencing of being bad, of doing bad things which were so bad that they were hidden from every one, especially from her husband. These were the experiential peaks in the session. She had just finished hard, racking crying in a recent incident in which she had given her husband's favorite antique painting to a friend of hers, and the wrenching railing was accompanied with the following words:

Pt: But I couldn't refuse a friend! I just couldn't (hard crying). . . . How can I ever tell him? It was bad! I can't tell him!

These words were punctuated with full-bodied hard crying. We had gone to a number of significant early events, dating back to when the patient was four and five, and a few when she was about three years old. But now the scope was extended to include the primitive field.

T: In 1945, Ellen's Mommy and Daddy moved away from that wonderful house on Spring Street in Halifax. And that is when Ellen is three years old. But now it is 1943, 1943, and Ellen's Mommy and Daddy have a little one-year-old girl, their daughter, and her name is Ellen. Ellen is a baby, a little baby, one year old. She is in the little bedroom on the second floor of the home, sleeping, taking a nap. Ellen sleeps a lot. I know something about what's happening with Ellen's aunt Pru, or maybe her Daddy or Mommy, or maybe Ellen's Gramma Tibbie. I am going to describe what is going on, and something will appear, some person or maybe two or three persons. Right now it is vague, but I will say some words and then something will appear. Meantime, we can let little baby Ellen sleep, a little baby. Something is happening in the house on Spring Street. . . . Someone is feeling bad. Someone did something bad, really bad. This person did something bad. Can't refuse a friend, cannot refuse a friend, but did something bad. Can't tell what was bad. It was someone's favorite. Can't ever tell . . . (The therapist stops, for now the therapist is seeing shadowy figures which are defined by her words. After the pause, the patient fills in her own scene, and does so in a trance-like way, with a kind of monotone voice quality.)

Pt: Mommy was bad. She did bad things with him. She had sex with him.
Dad adored his boss, had him over for supper all the time. Dad was
a fine carpenter who loved his boss. His boss was his favorite and Mom
had intercourse with the boss, Mr. Gilbert. He had straight gray hair
and he was tall, and Dad was from Hungary. Mother was so pretty and
quiet, and she, I always suspected that she did something. Mr. Gilbert
was distinguished. I never met him 'cause Mom and Dad moved away
after I was born and I was Dad's favorite. He had me and no other
children, and something happened in Halifax. Mother did something
bad and never told Dad about what she did. Dad worked for Mr.
Gilbert almost from the time he came to Canada from Hungary, and
he loved Mr. Gilbert. (Pause) I don't think I ever thought about that,
but it was so clear. Mom did a bad thing and maybe she never ever said
anything about it. They were having fights and thinking about a divorce
when Mom died. She was so pretty in the pictures. Before I was born.
Before she got pregnant. She did something bad. And she got punished
for what she did. (The patient is talking slowly, as if in a kind of trance,
but the whole chest cavity is full of expanding pressure, and the sensations are very strong.)

The most basic and fundamental early experiences reside in the
"primitive field" and may be discovered by this kind of guided search
into that powerful domain.

Experiential Unfolding Into
Earlier Experiences

By working with one situational context, carrying forward the experiencing within that situational context, the consequence is the discovery
of more important early experiences. It is as if experiences or situational
contexts are organized into sequences or packages or hierarchies so
that experiential work in one opens the way to the next.

The method is simply that of carrying forward the experiencing all
the way, leaving open the possibility that the heightened experiencing
will itself lead into earlier situations. This sequential process unfolds
into progressively earlier and more significant events: "If Freud . . . had
encouraged his patients beyond verbal free associations, if he had encouraged them to talk in the present in order to elicit more nonverbal
expressions of feelings and bodily participation, he would have discovered what Janov did—that this emotional flooding of the patient
permitted the earliest memories to surface" (Rose, 1976, p. 81).

By carrying forward the experiencing in one scene, another scene will be opened up. In this way the process of discovering new early experiences takes care of itself. If some experience is a kind of sticking point, we simply carry forward experiencing within the context of that scene. Some patients easily go to some big memory, e.g., the recollection of the father being killed in the car accident in front of the house, the remembrance of mother walking out of the house and out of the patient's life, the early beating by the kid next door, the hospitalization when the left leg was removed, grandmother's kindly look just a month or so before she died. It is as if most hurts end up in the favorite painful experience. These are similar to what Freud described as "screen memories," including pieces of the forgotten earlier memories. However they are understood, they are favorite stopping places, easy to arrive at and difficult to get beyond. Our solution is simply to work with them. i.e., carry forward whatever experiencing is present, and the consequence is the unfolding into the next early experience.

THERAPIST AS THE EXPRESSIVE VOICE OF THE POTENTIAL

As we have seen, one way of carrying forward experiencing is to clarify the situational context. The therapist may also live and be the potential for experiencing, being its voice, giving expression to the potential. As a consequence, experiencing also carries forward.

Experiential listening determines that the therapist is the expressive voice of the potential. Who or what determines that the therapist right now will clarify the situational context or give expressive voice to the potential? Does the therapist determine that right now it is time to do one or the other? The answer is that it is experiential listening that does the determination, that draws the therapist into being the expressive voice of the potential, that places the therapist's "center of gravity" in the potential, and that sets the therapist into motion as the expressive voice of the potential.

By means of careful, sensitive, passive experiential listening, the therapist is induced and activated into clarifying the situational context or giving expressive voice to the potential. The therapist is pulled, drawn, activated into the situational context or into the inner experiencing. When the inner experiencing is more predominant, then the therapist is the expressive voice of the potential. The process is selfless and automatic, and it is determined essentially by experiential listening rather than by the therapist's intention, cognition, or clinical preference. The therapist is merely ready to do what experiential listening induces the therapist to do.

If a group of experiential psychotherapists listen to what the patient is saying and doing, virtually all of them will be pulled toward the invoked situational context or toward the invoked experiencing. The experientially listening therapist will see something, will be aware of the situational context, or the therapist will "have" an experiencing, will sense some kind of experiencing occurring inside. The therapist must learn how to listen experientially, but once the skill is acquired, the therapist's center of gravity will be drawn either toward the scene or toward the experiencing. The therapist is, right now, the expressive voice of the potential because experiential listening sets that into motion.

The Principle: The Therapist Is the Expressive Voice of the Potential

Carrying forward of the experiencing means that the therapist is the one who carries it forward, the one who behaves, acts, expresses, says it, does it, undergoes whatever it is. When experiential listening activates a potential, the therapist is the expressor of whatever it is. It is the therapist who experiences. Then experiencing carries forward in the patient.

There is a kind of rhythm here. It begins with the patient who behaves and says words. The therapist listens experientially. If experiencing is activated in the therapist, the therapist expresses in the act of carrying forward the experiencing. Now it is all up to the patient, again, and the process continues. This is the general principle. How this is accomplished is helped by a number of working guidelines.

The Working Guidelines

For purposes of illustration, each of the working guidelines is described separately. However, in actual work, they go together as a functional package.

The therapist expresses whatever potential is present: operating or deeper potential. As long as the therapist is experiencing something, the therapist expresses. It does not matter whether it is right here on the surface or something deeper. The emphasis is on expressing the experiencing, not in evaluating its depth. Sometimes this means merely expressing what is already occurring at the operating level:

Pt: (In angry disbelief, describing the fellow from the head office who comes to "take a look at" the new facility) He's leaning over the table. For some crazy reason I believe him implicitly. He's some sort of God or something. Or Great Protector. That's what. Jerome T. God! His comment is, "What kind of a place is this?" He doesn't trust me. He says, "Well, who is this Zubin? What does he do?" He's really saying that! He's saying that Zubin's no good and neither am I. (The outrage is welling up in the therapist, and all the therapist does is express this experiencing which is present.)

T: (In a kind of imitation of James Cagney) Just who the hell do you think you are? I'll give you five seconds to get the hell out of here. That's all, just five. (The patient also carries forward.)

Pt: FUCK YOU!! YOU THINK YOU'RE SOME KIND OF GOD OR SOMETHING!!!

As the patient continues, what may be activated is a deeper wimpy fecklessness, a little girlness in her, a deeper sense of being easily discounted:

Pt: (Angrily complaining) . . . I just don't like the way he forces me to explain and explain! So I guess I finally got mad. And it seems like it doesn't matter! He makes me explain that, and explain and explain! I am not a little girl to be treated that way. He doesn't have the right to treat me like that! (The experiencing invoked in the therapist is the little girl, lip out, easily criticized by the adult man.)

T: Just 'cause I'm a little girl, 'cause I'm not grown up enough, no one should treat me like a little girl. I try to pretend that I'm grownup like the big people. That is just not really very fair . . .

Pt: Yeah, well I hate that! I, uh, my hair is down to my ass. (Half laughing but still very annoyed) But he has no right to treat me like that! Oh Jeez! Ha! I feel about five years old! Jeez!!

With another patient, the deeper experiencing consisted of enjoyably wicked nastiness covered up by the apparent "problem":

Pt: One thing as well . . . that's been bothering me over the last few years, and uh, but . . . in my relationships with women . . . I'm so . . . well, it's a double thing . . . they are fairly good in a sense, on one level . . . at least . . . I relate fairly well. I'm fairly open. I'd like to be more . . . I'd like to give of myself more . . . more. Give myself of my emotions more. (The therapist is enjoined to be teasingly, devastatingly distant from women, and relishing every nuance of this.)

T: Ah, you delightful little bitches. Just try to get to me. Don't touch! Ah HUH! Get away!!! Off!!!

Pt: (Bursting into hard laughter) That sounds like fun!!!

Even if the experiencing is at the operating level, it may only be hinted at and implied, again dressed up in problem clothing, somewhat as above:

Pt: Kevin found some list of classics and he showed me. He said he bet that I had read all of them. That did something to me. I looked at the list. I did. (Little snort) He said, "You're smart." I felt foolish, praised. He puts himself down, makes me distant. Sounds like worship, comes out like a ritual, bowing and scraping. Something so empty. (The therapist is filled with the experiencing of being the esteemed one, the God on a pedestal.)

T: Ah, how fitting it is to be here on this pedestal, marble. Kevin . . . (in mock shared secrecy, half whispering) I am God, you know. Always had that something just a little special about me. There's one in every Jewish family.

Pt: But I have feet of clay. I barely read. I feel like a damned failure. Sure! I remember when I broke a window. I hit a foul ball or something and the other kids were happy 'cause they said I was finally gonna get it, and my friend Chuck said that my Mom and Dad would praise God that I had such a strength to hit the ball so far! (Laughs hard)

At the operating level, there is a sense of utter depression, but the deeper experiencing is of a quite different nature:

Pt: Pretty soon I'll be 40, and the kids are too much. They deserve a real mother. He (her ex-husband) doesn't care anymore. (The gloom is getting heavier.) It's too much. I can't do it anymore. It's all too much. I'll never make it. I just don't see any way to take it any longer . . . (Now the scene is vivid. I am a totally withdrawn looney, in the looney bin, staring straight ahead, with my mouth open. And, incidently, I'm no longer taking care of the damned kids.)

T: (In a little girl crazy voice) I don't have any children. Children? What children? I'm sitting here in the crazy ward, staring straight ahead. I don't know how long I've been here with the other nuts, but I'm just a little girl, and my Mommy is going to come visit me this afternoon and bring me a present. I have no children. I'm just a little girl!

Pt: It's worse having the kids! Three kids! Thirteen and nine and seven for Christ's sakes! It's like a damned prison! No! I don't want to have them! I wish they were grown up and gone! I know that sounds awful, but not to me it doesn't! It's a damned prison!!!

There is a welcomed, letting-be in the expression. Whatever the nature of the experiencing, the therapist is the voice and the expressive agency. It does not matter whether the accompanying feelings are constricting, painful, anguished, or exhilarating, joyful, and delightful. There is a kind of welcoming and letting-be for any kind of experiencing, and for any kind of accompanying feeling (Fromm, 1941; Mahrer, 1970a; Pelletier & Garfield, 1976). Even when the therapist's body is tight and shaking, even when there is an icy chill down the back or the whole body feels ponderous or dead, the therapist expresses the experiencing in an enveloping context of welcomed letting-be. This is the extreme of client-centered positive regard as it applies to one's own immediate experiencing. It is as if any experiencing is welcomed, let be, and expressed.

But this means there will be a difference, often, between the experiencing in the patient and the experiencing which is expressed by the therapist. The difference is that the therapist expresses an experiencing which is allowed to occur, which is welcomed and expressed. Even if it hurts, the welcoming or letting-be comes from an integrative relationship with it, and its expression lends a welcoming character to the hurt and pain.

Pt: (Being with her father who is disapproving of her) So what's he going to find fault with now? Oh what's the use? My sister can walk away but not me. I'm always, like a mark on me. He waits and waits and finds something and then talks all day! Waits for me to do something bad. Acts like I'm disgusting. I'm the one who should be different. What's the use? (The therapist senses the sheer badness, the evilness, and allows it to fill her. It becomes a spiteful act.)

T: Here's my middle finger, Edward! Stick it up your ass! (There is a playful aggressivity here.) You found out that I stole money from your wallet? Huh! Grrrrrrr!

Pt: (Lots of energy.) He'd have a heart attack! He'd have an attack right there in front of me!!

No matter what the nature of the experiencing, the therapist lets it occur, welcomes its presence:

Pt: (In a cold, metallic monotone) I have tried. But I am getting discouraged. There is no feeling. None. I just do not feel anything. I feel dull, dead. I am numb. I do not feel. (As the therapist resonates to these words, there is a tone of insistence, as if these are the rules for how her inner state is to be.)

T: (With firm, good-feelinged insistence.) I shall not have any feelings. No one is ever going to force me into showing any feelings. I have decided, and that is just the way it is to be. (And then crisply) And that's that!

Pt: Well, it's 'cause there aren't any! Ha! And no one can make me! I do not feel. I don't feel anything! Shit! Why the hell should I?

Expression is in the form of concrete behaviors. To express the experiencing means to behave, do, act. The therapist expresses the experiencing by means of behaviors. The therapist cries and whines, beats the chair, lifts up the hips, kicks, yells and bellows, yawns and coughs, makes fists and thumps the chest, curls up and stretches, wheedles and sings, whistles and chirps, reaches out and salutes. The therapist lets the body do all sorts of behavings. With eyes closed and existing in all sorts of situational contexts, the therapist engages in flying and falling, running and jumping, setting fires and throwing dishes, having intercourse and eating snake meat, glaring and kissing, walking along and crossing the street. The therapist expresses by moving, acting, interacting, doing, engaging, behaving.

Pt: (Excitedly describing what it is like to walk along with the delightful woman from the office) I want to reach out and affect my own destiny. I can do what I want to do and it's great! We just walked around and around, and we held hands. I love the way she walks, just straight ahead, nice. Yeah. So we're walking together, lunch time, nice, sunny. I never walked like that before. (The experiencing in the therapist is the excited delight of just being with her, spontaneously caught up in all this, and it spills out in behavior as the therapist turns to her.)
T: The hell with going back to the office! Let's just skip it, OK? Let's just spend the whole afternoon together! Let's! Yes? No?
Pt: There's a park down there, a little park! I love this! I just love being here, and being here with you. Wow! Wow, it's wonderful! Sonuvagun! Well then the weeked! I'll do anything with you, I just want to be with you! Ha!

"Behavioralizing" is easy to do when the feelings are those of excitement, vibrancy, aliveness, vitality. But even when they are of a different order the therapist engages in the behavior.

Pt: (In a room with her old aunt whom she visited after many years) I compare her to what she was. Now she . . . she . . . her hair is thin, and her body is so thin, skin is, has no fat, like a little bird, big wide eyes, watery, so fragile. (In the therapist there is an experiencing of enfolding tenderness, a kind of protective holding.)
T: (Reaching out and bringing the aunt against the chest, holding the frail little woman close, patting her back very gently, and very aware of the little bird-like body pressing against the chest.) Oh . . . I have missed you so. I love you.
Pt: (Tenderly) I remember when I was a little girl and I was at your house and I hurt my knee, fell or something. You always smelled so fresh and

nice. You were on the front porch and I was in your lap and you held me. I, you were my favorite aunt, and I always thought you were so . . . pretty.

Expression is directly to and with the experientially alive other person within the experientially real situational context. Experiencing carries forward when the therapist is fully with the other person, actually existing and being with the other person, expressing it to and with that other person, and within the genuinely real situational context. By means of experiential listening, the therapist will literally be in some scene, some situational context, and there will be some figure with whom the therapist is engaged. The therapist expresses directly to and with that figure, and within that situation (Gervaize, Mahrer, & Markow, 1985; Levitsky & Perls, 1970; Perls, 1969a).

What the patient is partially expressing is made alive and real by expressing it directly to the right person. In its simplest form, the patient is but one step away from direct expression to and with the other person, and the therapist ventures this next step:

Pt: (In a childhood scene in the kitchen, playing on the floor, and looking at Mother) . . . She always seemed to be different when she had a fight with Dad. She sat at the table and ate toast . . . (The therapist is wholly interacting with Mom, and expresses the readiness to interact with her.)
T: Mom, I know you had a fight with Dad. Mom, I can see, you're quiet, you get quiet. I see you, pulled in, you eat your toast. I'm going to talk with you, really with you Mom.
Pt: (Softly crying.) Mom . . . I'm sorry . . . Mom . . .

Something very special happens when the therapist and patient directly interact with the other person, and say the words directly to that other person. It is as if the experiencing undergoes a sharp increase merely through the medium of the direct engagement.

Pt: He was my best friend. I remember him just sitting on the toilet. I know that's funny. But that's how I remember him. I'd sit on the floor outside and wait for him. He'd sit there.
T: Marvin, I like you. I really like you. I see your pants, Marvin.
Pt: You're my best friend. I think we had some of our best times with you sitting on the toilet. (Laughs) Remember we planned a long bicycle trip? You kept talking about how great it would be and I wondered if you could ever find a crapper. Well, Marv, you're always on a crapper. I'll bring along the toilet paper. We take potato chips and toilet paper. I like the chips, and you need the toilet paper. Damn, I like you!

When the therapist expresses directly with and to the other person, the patient tends to follow suit, and experiencing takes a step forward. Frequently the patient departs from such direct interaction with little asides, as if the patient is now talking to no one in particular. Yet, to the experientially listening therapist, these apparent asides are more grist for the direct interaction mill, and the therapist uses this material also:

Pt: (In a scene from his early adolescence, talking to his father) You were so, I could never trust you, 'cause you changed. I had to see if you're drunk. You'd be different. Like two people. When you drank, when you got that way, I don't know . . . (Then, pulling back from direct interaction, he gives a sort of side comment.) I thought he acted like an animal. (Here is the loaded statement which the therapist feeds into the direct interactive relationship.)

T: And you really did! You did! You acted like an animal!

Pt: (Staying with this further expression.) I could never trust you! Do you know what you were like? Nobody talked about it! You were rotten! I hated you!!!

As the patient and therapist are in a scene, the patient "talks about" instead of saying it directly. The therapist takes this next step and engages in a direct interaction, saying it directly to the other person.

Pt: Well, he comes in late, really late! I was sleeping! Woke me up! And he asks for some coffee. Then I see the gun! What the hell is that for? He shouldn't be bringing me the damned gun! He's on parole and he'll get into trouble! What a damned fool thing to do. (The therapist aims these words directly at the idiot who comes in late with the gun.)

T: Sam, you idiot! What the hell is that for? You're on parole! What a damned fool thing to do, you damned fool you!

Pt: You're going to get into a shitpot of trouble. And me too! Me too! You're gonna mess me up, damn you! But this time, no way!!!!

"Talking about" is almost saying it directly. When a scene is invoked and the patient comes close to saying it directly to the other person, the therapist takes the next step:

Pt: She was as usual, I mean she was tight. But of course she never would admit it. She seemed restless and on edge. Or maybe I was. I know the feeling, yeah, me, and she gets that way. She said she did nothing. (Then with strong feeling) But I don't believe her.

T: Are you listening, Sue? Sue! I'm talking to you! Listen to me! You said you did nothing, but I don't believe you!

Pt: (Voice quivering) You lie to me . . . (Softly) You never tell me the truth. (Crying)

The patient is in a direct engagement, saying it directly to the other person. Then the patient stops, and does something which seems to be out of the scene. For example, the patient complains of a sudden headache, or starts crying, or has a muscular cramp, or apparently pulls out of the engagement and mentions a fleeting thought or describes an image or has a reaction to what he has just done or felt. The therapist feeds this back into the direct interaction:

Pt: So you find fault with everything about me! I got dandruff, sure, and your hair is always just perfect, Auntie. Whatever you say I take as a personal rebuff, not just on me, but my Mom and me. No I don't stand straight, yes, and I slouch. Sure I do. I should dress right. OK. (Then, in an apparent movement out of the direct engagement with Auntie.) . . . I got a headache. Just started, in the back . . . I could never talk to her like that.
T: Are you listening, Auntie? I don't really have the nerve to talk to you like this! It gives me a headache!
Pt: 'Cause I feel like I don't have the right! I don't know why! I really don't. I feel like I'm dirty and you got, you're supposed to criticize me. Why? Huh? How come? What a helluva way to live! Who the hell are you anyway? Mom's older nastier sister! A flaming asshole! That's what you are! You have the headache! It's your turn! Jeez! Jeez!

The patient may be invoking a scene in which she is a little girl who never gets angry or protests. Soon the patient was quite engaged with the image of herself as a little girl, about eight or nine, being told that she will not be allowed to have a school garden this year. The relationship is between the patient and this image of her self as a child. The therapist makes this very real and alive by taking the next step, and saying it directly to the little girl:

Pt: . . . I think my teacher told me, in the back of the school, by the school gardens. For the summer. I felt bad, inside, but the funny thing, I can see myself, standing, skinny little thing, big eyes, and not saying anything. But the feelings inside. No, no I think that's wrong! She didn't feel anything bad. No, she didn't. She didn't feel anything, nothing. That's the weird thing. She floated. She didn't feel bad. She didn't. She felt nothing. I don't think anything. (In the scene, the therapist is being about six or eight feet away from the image of the little girl. It is as if the therapist is saying these words directly to the little girl.)

T: Little girl, Sharon! I want to talk to you. Can you try to look at me? You
have such big old eyes, but they really don't see much. And you have
such skinny little legs and body. I love you. Right now you don't feel
much of anything. You don't even know what having your own feelings
is like. I don't even know if you know what I'm saying.

Pt: You poor little mutt! You're asleep, and you've been asleep since you were
born. I am going to take you home with me. You belong to me. I'm
going to be with you. (She stopped. There were tears pouring down her
face and on her neck.)

Patients often have the other figure in sight. They are with the friend
from last night, or with a spouse or the enemy from second grade.
Direct expression involves saying it directly to that other person. On
the other hand, it is also common that the experientially listening
therapist is in a "deeper" scene, resonating to a "deeper" experiencing.
The net result is that the patient is seeing one thing and the therapist
another. The therapist, however, is only aware of the immediate experiencing and the immediate other figure with and to whom the therapist
is quite ready to express directly. This occurs especially when the experientially listening therapist is in a scene with a very special listener,
the magical other figure who hears all of this, the kindly and accepting
confidant whom the patient never really had, the perfect parental figure
to whom the most private confidences can be bestowed. For example,
after an initial session, the patient lapses into an almost sepulchral
mood as he spends the first part of the second session reciting the story
of his life. As the therapist shares in this, there is a vivid encompassing
scene of being with a most precious, very special listener, the fully loving, fully accepting parental figure. He winds up one lengthy statement:

Pt: . . . all of the kids loved that kitchen, 'cause we all sat around the big table
and there was always lots of noise. Everyone was talking, and the kitch-
en was the center, well, the room was the place between the kitchen
and the dining room. We moved away from there though. I don't know,
maybe I was nine. Never went back there . . . (The therapist is saying
all of this to a kindly old figure, sitting, listening, receiving. The therapist
talks directly to this person.)

T: It is so nice being here with you, telling you. I feel so good with you, 'cause
I miss you.

Pt: (As if the patient fills in this special listener) I lived in, my Gramma died
when I was 12. She smoked a lot, and I miss my Gramma. Gramma.
You used to hold my hand, put your hand over mine and I would tell
you stories. You would rub my hand. Gramma. Gramma, I am a
middle-aged man and I miss my Gramma. I miss you . . .

What the patient says is often addressed toward this special listener, some special person who receives it all. This person is frequently omniscient or Godlike or all-wise or the perfect parent. The patient tells about so many problems and difficulties in her life, going from one to the other. Slowly the content of what she says is replaced by a scene in which she is saying all of this to some unspecified figure. It is more than a therapist; it is what the therapist stands for. She winds up:

Pt: . . . so Sheldon wants to have me learn golf, but I can't do it. He's good, and I am such a dud in sports. I wish I could but it'd flop. He'd die if he saw me . . . (It is like being in the presence of a special listener who hears all of this and can make it all better, because this person is wise and saintly and cares.)
T: So you will help me? You'll make it all better. You're older and wiser and you know everything.
Pt: Yee Gods! I never had anyone to talk to! I think I was almost dreaming 'cause I had flashes of my Daddy's grave. I never cried, but I used to go to his grave on my bicycle and I'd sit there and tell him everything. I never talked to him when he was alive. He was my Daddy more when he died. I always wanted to talk to him. Tell him everything. I have this diary. My heart is pounding! It's really pounding hard!

There are occasions where the patient is talking directly to the therapist, addressing the therapist, even to the extent of saying "you." From within the patient's world, the therapist merely carries forward the direct expression:

Pt: You know me better than anyone. You know what I'm like. I think about that often. It helps me. If you'd write out what I'm like, then I could read it when I get down. I could read it and have it with me when I am down. It'd help. (The experiencing is that of being passive and allowing myself to entreat the all-knowing therapist.)
T: Please? Would you? Please?
Pt: I want something from you. (Crying) Something special. Just for me. (Silence, sobbing) Something about me . . .

When the patient addresses the therapist, the therapist-as-patient says it even more directly, in even more straightforward engagement:

Pt: (Tight and tense) I don't think I'm making progress. I come here three times a week, and I don't know.
T: You're not helping me, you prick!
Pt: Oh! I couldn't say that! (Laughing) Yes I can! I do my part and you're

not helping me! You . . . prick! (Laughs hard) I'm going to say it again.
You fucking bastard! (Screeches) May your family multiply like weeds!
No! I wish you lived in a dung heap! Go to hell, you fucking bastard.
Damn this feels good! Eat shit!!! (Laughs hilariously) Kiss my ass!

Expression is with a fuller degree of experiencing. As the expressive
voice of the potential, the therapist carries out the experiencing energet-
ically, vibrantly, with feeling. There are two levels of strength or
amplitude to this. At a minimum, whatever the therapist expresses is
at least at what might be termed the "working" degree of experiencing.
This means that there is a moderate degree of bodily sensations such
as a moderate warmth over the face, a moderate tightness in the back
of the neck, a moderate tingling in the skin, a moderate vibrancy in
the genitals, a moderate clutching up in the stomach. If the patient is
already at this moderate level, the therapist expresses with a stronger
degree of experiencing. The therapist stays somewhat ahead of the patient by letting the expression occur with just a little more fullness,
energy, amplitude, loudness, strength, intensity of bodily sensation,
and sheer degree of experiencing.

In this sense, the therapist is the model, the exemplar (Jourard,
1971b, 1976), the teacher who expresses it again and again, more and
more, with greater and greater feeling. Whether the experiencing is
good or bad, pleasant and unpleasant, the therapist expresses with a
fuller degree of experiencing.

Pt: (Breathing hard, her voice raised. She is already at the working level of
    experiencing.) There is no home. It is not my home. I live in Marilyn
    and Becky's home! Just live with them. Like a guest. A thing in their
    house! It's not a home!
T: (Loud and full) A thing! A thing! A thing in their house! In their house!
    A thing in their house! More! More! I'm just a thing in their house! A
    thing in their house!
Pt: (Almost shrieking) WHAT AM I DOING HERE? I DON'T BELONG!
    I DON'T BELONG HERE! I DON'T KNOW WHAT I'M DOING
    HERE!!!

Fuller experiencing includes making noises, exclaiming, groaning,
yelling, moving the body, shaking—somewhat more than the energy
level coming from the patient. He is allowing himself to have sexual
experiencing to a moderate degree as he wickedly confesses to the secret
act he carries out alone in his bedroom on the bed in front of the large
mirror.

Pt: My dick is clenched, tension here, up and down, like deep in the root,
    on my bed, turning slowly and pretending there is a man here with me,

watching me, the yellow panties. I feel good, tight, and seeing myself in the mirror, seeing my body. I am sexual, livid, hot, attractive. Looking at my legs, the v of my hair, the yellow v, hot, my smooth thighs, legs, moving slowly. (With fuller loudness and amplitude, moving his body more, letting himself go with stronger seductive lustiness, the therapist moans.)

T: OOOooohhh. AAAaaaaaaaaa!!!!!!

Pt: (Bursting with feeling. Rubbing his hands vigorously over his genitals, writhing.) Feast your eyes, you MAN! LOOK AT THIS . . . OOOOOO-oooooo!!! FANTASTIC. GO CRAZY WITH MEEEEEEE. AH AH AH AH!!!

The therapist raises the experiential level, increases the intensity by expressing with feelinged energy and vitality. The patient is riding along on a mild level of experiencing as she invokes scenes about what may happen when she visits her folks in Montreal.

Pt: So Donald will come with me. He's almost 50 and we've been living in his place for about six months. With his daughter. She's 19, almost my age. He plays, works. We're all on welfare. He's from Bermuda, jet black. His daughter's got gorgeous skin. I hate to think what they'll do. Well, I know. They'll look at each other. They won't talk. It'll be something.

T: (With high energy) It's OK, folks, we'll only be living here for a year! You'll love it! Just till the baby comes! If it's black we'll leave it with you!

Pt: Oh shit! (Laughs heartily) My Dad'd pee in his pants! (Screeching laughter) Mom'd turn into a statue!!! (Very hard laughing)

These are the working guidelines for how the therapist is the expressive voice of the potential. It all begins with the patient invoking some kind of experiencing in the experientially listening therapist. Given this experiencing, the therapist expresses it, and the consequence is the carrying forward of the experiencing. That is the process. Then the patient talks and behaves once again, and the process is repeated. But this is only one way in which the therapist uses the immediate experiencing. There is another way.

WELCOMING DESCRIPTION OF THE EXPERIENTIAL STATE

As the patient is speaking and behaving right now, the therapist listens experientially. If the therapist's attention is pulled by the scene or situational context, the therapist clarifies what is there (Figure 3). If the therapist's attention is pulled by the immediate experiencing, the therapist may be the expressive voice of the potential or the therapist may welcome the experiencing and describe what it is like. In either case, the consequence is the carrying forward of the experiencing.

Experiential listening determines that the therapist welcomes and describes the experiential state. Experiential listening is a passive process. Yet it determines whether the therapist clarifies the situational context, is the expressive voice of the potential, or welcomes and describes the experiential state (Figure 3). If experiential listening illuminates the therapist's inner experiential state, pulls attention onto the experiential state, then the therapist merely welcomes and describes that state. Rather than activating the experiencing out into some situational context, the therapist's attentional center is drawn toward the inner experiencing itself. It is the difference between being activated to express the anger at the other person and, on the other hand, being drawn toward the presence of the inner anger itself.

The Principle: The Therapist Welcomes and Describes the Experiential State

Carrying forward of (the patient's) experiencing occurs to the extent that the therapist welcomes and describes (her own immediate) experiential state. The therapist is aware that something is present, the therapist welcomes this experiencing, invites it to come in, and the therapist describes the gracious visitor, tells what it is like. To the extent that the therapist does all of this, the experiencing carries forward. This is the general principle. What follows are working guidelines for welcoming and describing the experiential state.

The Working Guidelines

The experiential state is occurring here in the therapist. All the therapist does is be aware of the experiencing which is present right now, in the therapist, welcome and describe the experiencing which is present right now, in the therapist.

The therapist welcomes and describes the behavioral tendencies. It is as if the therapist can sense behavioral tendencies that are here, ready to occur, activated and present inside the therapist. The therapist welcomes these behavioral tendencies, and describes what they are like, their nature, and what they incline the therapist to do. The therapist is not carrying out the behaviors, not expressing them. All the therapist is doing is describing what they are, what they are like.

The patient is living in a scene including her husband and the business associate whom they are entertaining in their home:

Pt: I know he has a toupee. It was a toupee, I thought. It was a toupee. I was just looking at it. My husband's entertaining him and trying to make an impression, and I'm looking at it. (Sharp staccato laugh) (In the therapist there is an inner behavioral pull. The therapist senses her body impulsively reaching out and grabbing the toupee.)

T: (Animatedly) Oh my God! I almost reached out and grabbed the hairpiece! Lifted it up! I could feel myself just about to do it!

Pt: (Laughing hard, almost shrieking) Yeah!! Yeah!!! I shouldn't have stared at it! (Hard laughter)

The therapist welcomes the behavior, even if the accompanying feeling may be scary:

Pt: I can feel the circle, like it's big, big, and I'm sitting on it. It's almost transparent, but whenever I breathe out, it gets bigger, and then if I breathe in it gets a little smaller. It gets larger and larger as I breathe. Now I feel smaller, much smaller. The circle is getting large. I feel smaller, much smaller. The circle is really getting large! I feel very small, very tiny! But I know I won't fall from the circle 'cause I'm attached to it! (The therapist is aware of and welcomes the behavioral sense of falling from the circle, and describes what that is like.)

T: I can feel the falling! It happens as I would keel over to the right, just falling off of it!

Pt: (Frightened, stern) Nothing's going to happen to me! I will stay right here! I will not leave go!

The therapist notices bodily sensations and welcomes them as nascent incipient behaviors:

Pt: (Whining on and on about the unfair treatment at work) . . . So he wasn't even in that job at the time, at least not then. I couldn't cope with all the red tape, all that damned red tape. They really fucked me up, put me in a temporary position and they kept me there for two years. (The therapist is aware of strong bodily sensations.)

T: My hand's clenching into a fist, and my mouth's stretching like it wants to yell. I can feel a big complaining getting ready inside me!!!

Pt: I can't quit. I have nothing to show. I'd like to scream. Can I scream? (He is talking loudly.) OK to scream? (He is screaming.) SHIT!!

The therapist welcomes and describes the "state of experiencing."
The therapist becomes aware of a "state of experiencing", welcomes
this state, and describes what it is like. It is as if the therapist welcomes
an experiential state and simply describes what it is like being scared,
being crazy, being in love, being ponderous, being dead, being in any
kind of experiential state which is present right now (cf. Gendlin, 1961,
1969, 1972, 1978).

Pt: My grandmother made my Mom mean. I could play down in the basement
     where there were all kinds of things. But when Gramma would come
     down and see me she'd always act like I was doing something bad. (The
     therapist is aware of and welcoming of the badness which fills him, and
     he describes this state of badness.)
T: Yeah, sort of like being evil, and, and sneaky, yeah, sneaky. Like I'm up
     to no good, evil, sure, doing secret evil things, bad, I can't, feel wicked.
Pt: I remember! I'm not supposed to touch myself. Yeah! I used to put marbles
     up my hole, and she, she comes down to catch me. I think she wanted
     to see, but she never said anything! She's a dirty old lady! Lady! Ha!
     She wanted to catch me!

Welcoming the state means graciously allowing oneself to be in the
state, letting it happen. Even if the patient draws back in horror from
the deeper state, the therapist welcomes the experiential state and
describes what it is like.

Pt: . . . My father would drag her around the floor, screaming at her, and
     my mother would just lie there, dragged around, limp, like a rag! Not
     doing anything. She would talk to the birds we had, canaries . . . but
     I could never make out what she said, and she'd never let me hear. I
     was scared of her 'cause of that. And I think I was scared of the birds.
     She'd scream like crazy if I'd put my finger in the cage to try to pet
     them . . . worried about my hurting them. . . . She thought my Dad
     was always attracted to her sister. Yelled that she knew about them.
     God! I remember when she died. . . . She hung herself in the garage . . .
     (In the therapist there is the deeper experiencing of utter craziness, com-
     plete deranged looniness. It is present, welcomed, and described.)
T: Yes, well, when I become a complete tutti-frutti, a genuine loony, it's sort
     of like it lets me be free, really free to do what I want. Right now it's
     like I wouldn't do anything, of course, but it's sort of like being on a
     high all the time. Even if I hang from a rope in the garage, sort of dangl-
     ing, twisting a little. It's like taking a whiff of ammonia and everything's
     all clear, like bouncing and playing, inside . . . (The therapist's descrip-
     tion is followed by the carrying forward of experiencing in the patient.)

Pt: Ever since I was, all my life, I never even let anyone ever think that something was wrong with me. So I am a therapist and an administrator, and I even look respectable. No booze, no drugs, don't even smoke. I thought that if I could die someday, a natural death of something, then I'd be able to go to the kind of hell that, a fun hell, and I could do all the things I never did in my life. Always someday. Even my kids are sane. If I could be just a little insane, just a little. (Laughs) Then I coulda joined in with them and danced around the room yelling and rolling around like they did. Ha! What a waste! I shouldn't have just watched! I should have joined in! Hell, they would have gone on! Ha!

The therapist welcomes and describes the strong bodily sensations. The experiential state may be highlighted by bodily sensations such as the right arm suddenly becoming paralyzed, or the feet feeling icy cold, or a shooting pain inside the upper chest, or the stomach now being tight and cramped. If these bodily sensations pull the therapist's attention, if they announce themselves, then the therapist welcomes and describes them.

Welcoming and describing the bodily sensations means that the therapist allows them to be, invites them to grow and to flourish (Mahrer, 1983c; Warkentin & Whitaker, 1965; Whitaker, Warkentin, & Malone, 1959). It is a matter of having a good relationship with them. The bodily sensation is a friend, graciously invited to occur. The stance is not that of a distant observer, removed and objective; it is welcoming. The aim is not to relax the body (Jacobson, 1938; Wolpe & Lazarus, 1966), to get rid of or relabel the bodily sensation, but, rather, to welcome it (Jackson, 1967) and to heighten awareness of the sensation (Lowen, 1972: Simkin, 1977; Zinker, 1977).

Sometimes the bodily sensation may make sense in regard to the situational context. Out in the fields, under the sunny sky of midday, the therapist's face may feel warm. In a cramped position, the back may be tight. Facing the hated enemy, there may be a sense of butterflies in the stomach or a hot ball in the chest. Sometimes the bodily sensations may seem to be quite unrelated to the ongoing situational context. Admiring the newborn baby, the therapist suddenly has a locked cramp in the right calf muscle, or a darting pain in the heart region. Sometimes the bodily sensations may seem weird. There is a warm wet sensation on the left forearm; the right eye feels as if blood is pouring out; the whole body feels like it is being propelled forward at a dizzy speed; the chest seems soft and pussy and gushy. As long as there is a prominent bodily sensation, the therapist welcomes and describes it.

As a consequence, experiencing carries forward. The therapist's description deepens and opens up the experiential nature of the bodily sensations, and they carry forward into behaviors. For example, the welcoming description of tears getting ready, the puffing up of the cheeks, the water there behind the eyes, the softness in the eyes and face — all of this careful description tends to bring forth tears. Yet the overriding consequence is the carrying forth of experiencing.

Pt: Lots of times at night I'd start thinking about my Mom and Dad. I miss them. I wish they didn't die. I was about 16. Both of them. I'd lie in bed and look up at the ceiling and think about them, and I'd have my eyes open, remember what they looked like, really looked like . . . (The therapist is aware of tears getting ready around the eyes and upper cheeks, and the therapist describes these bodily sensations.)

T: My face is warm now, kind of. Puffy. Around the eyes and cheeks. Warm in the face. Like tears getting ready. Puffy and warm.

Pt: I remember Mom's voice when I'd get into bed with them and she'd pat my hand and grin and not wake Dad up. (Tears are running down her cheeks.)

As the therapist listens experientially, a sudden and apparently unrelated bodily sensation may demand attention:

Pt: . . . so my brother, he'd beat up on my sisters and I would shake and blush, I'd blush! He'd take them all on even though they were older, and they were tough. They were tough! They'd hit hard, and he'd take them on. They'd all be on the bed with pillows and wrestling and yelling and he'd fight like a bat out of hell. (At this point the therapist suddenly has a searing pain in the ankle. It is quite painful.)

T: Ouch! Oh! My ankle! Oh! My ankle hurts! (Grabbing and massaging the ankle)

Pt: (Just continuing) He'd grab them and get 'em both down. He was strong! Wiry and tough as can be! He'd use his legs and get one in a scissors and he'd hold the other with his arms and hands! And I'd stand by the bed and rub my penis! I always had the feelings in my penis when they'd fight. Everyone screeching, and me with my penis!

The therapist welcomes and describes the unfolding sequence of experiential states. As the therapist welcomes and describes the experiential state, it carries forward, moves, unfolds. Description of one experiential state allows it to carry forward into another. Accordingly, the welcomed description of one experiential state unfolds into a new experiential state, and as the therapist welcomes and describes this new experiential state there is a continuing unfolding sequence.

He was a little boy sitting dutifully at the dining room table in his grandmother's apartment. The whole family was frightened of her, especially his Dad and Mom. In the scene, with the therapist as "the expressive voice of the potential," his very private inner thought ("I don't like her") was blurted out by the therapist, "I don't like you." Shocked silence.

T: Now it's like the whole table and the people all kind of recede away and instead I am aware of the pressure inside my head. I'm aware mainly of my face. It's very hot, inside and out, and there is alot of pressure from inside, like all I am aware of is what's going on in my body. Now my ears are plugged up, I can't even hear anything. My ears are stopped up, both of them. But the funny thing is that only my face is hot and full of pressure. My arms and my chest and stomach, they feel OK. I'm not going to shake to death or throw up or anything. I feel all right, but my face feels so hot. Now I want to put my hands under the table and hold them together, 'cause my hands are starting to tingle a little. So now I'm holding them together under the table, kind of just holding them against each other. Now my face is not so hot anymore. I am aware of my face, and especially the mouth now, yes, the muscles around my mouth. Why they are trying to get my mouth to smile a little. It's like they're pulling to each side and down. I think my lips are pulling to each side and down. That feels like a smile.

Pt: I think that's the first time I ever talked to you! I spent a whole childhood responding to her. Yes Grandma; thank you, Grandma. If I could have said it, I spent a whole childhood having thoughts that of course no one ever said. You're a hideous old witch, Grandma. You're a tyrant, Grandma. But no one ever said anything to her! Not my Dad or Mom or anyone. Even her sisters deferred to her. I would have led the way! I don't like you, Grandma. Everyone's scared of you, Grandma! But you're not so bad, you're a reasonable soul! Ha! That's a lie! You're a first-class son-of-a-bitch! That's what you are! And you were surrounded by a bunch of eunuchs!

If the welcomed description of one experiential state opens another, and the therapist moves to the next and the next, then the therapist may talk for a minute or two. As the patient accompanies the therapist on this detailed experiential journey, the consequence is the carrying forward of experiencing. On other occasions, the unfolding is more of a back-and-forth process conjointly carried forward by therapist and patient. In either case, the process is one of progressive unfolding.

Welcoming description is with a fuller degree of experiencing. There is an attitude which conveys the way the therapist welcomes and describes the experiential state. It is as if the therapist invites the experiential state to come in, have a home in him, fill him up. The therapist is eager and ready to give in to it. Whatever it is, wherever it is in the body, the therapist is prepared for the experiential state to fill his whole body, spread out as far as it can go. The therapist is eager and ready to pour more and more attention onto it, and to get closer and closer as the therapist details more and more of what it is.

Given this attitude, the therapist almost automatically has a fuller degree of sheer experiencing. As a rule, the therapist stays a little ahead of the patient. That is, compared with the patient, the therapist has a somewhat fuller level of experiencing. There is fuller energy and vitality. This is more a matter of amplitude and saturation than it is a matter of shrillness or loudness or screaming.

This fuller level of experiencing occurs whether the experiential state is pleasant or unpleasant, terrifying or delightful. The therapist welcomes and describes it with a level of experiencing which is always moderately strong (i.e., at or above the working level), and which is a little fuller than that occurring in the patient.

Pt: (Moderately energetic) I'm doing more of what I want. I do it. And she's happier too. She's OK. We're getting along much better now. I'm not scared of her and she's not scared of me 'cause we talk, really talk together a lot now. She seems different and she tells me that I'm different and I suppose that I am. Sure feel better. A load's off, that's what it's like, a load's gone from my back. Free. Yeah. Like free. (In the therapist there is a kind of energizing vitality. It feels as if the body is dancing, and the therapist welcomes and describes this with fuller experiencing.)
T: My body's moving, here and there, like it wants to do a little dance! If I let it go, it will dance around and maybe do a little singing here!
Pt: (Laughs) A little pitter patter, maestro! I feel like I just woke up and I am dancing around with Rita—right after we take showers together and we're naked and dum de dum! Yeah!

If the patient is already describing the experiential state, the therapist continues this, but at the fuller level of experiencing.

Pt: My fingers. The palm is controlling my fingers, without my fingers knowing about it. Like waves. The arms of the chair, they're pushing against my hands and fingers. Something is moving my fingers. (The therapist

welcomes this experiential state, and describes it, infusing all of this with
somewhat fuller experiencing.)

T: Feels like a force coming from the chair, the arms of the chair! Oh! From
outside, a force into my palms and fingers!

Pt: I can't move my fingers! They are . . . are funny! I can't even move them!
But they're buzzing! I'm not kidding! It's like a force getting into them
and I just can't move 'em at all, I can't even move them! Feels like dead
flesh that's . . . that's being radiated or something! Wowee! That's
weird. It feels weird!

These are the methods for carrying forward the potentials for experiencing. Set in motion by careful experiential listening, the therapist may
(a) clarify the situational context, (b) be the expressive voice of the
potential, or (c) welcome and describe the experiential state. As the
therapist becomes increasingly skilled in using these methods, the
passive part of this process is one of increasing trust in experiential
listening, and the active part is the increasingly effective use of these
methods in carrying forward the potentials for experiencing.

CHAPTER 3

Experiencing the Relationship with Deeper Potentials: Introduction

CHANGE OCCURS THROUGH "therapeutic experiencing." Chapters 1 and 2 dealt with one kind of therapeutic experiencing, namely, the carrying forward of the potentials for experiencing. Chapters 3 and 4 deal with a second kind of therapeutic experiencing. In its long form, it is referred to as the experiencing of the relationship between the patient and the deeper potentials. This consists of an encounter between the deeper potential and the patient. It is an encounter that is internal and that proceeds inevitably in the direction of integration between patient and deeper potential (Figure 4). In its short form it is referred to as the internal integrative encounter.

The purpose of chapter 4 is to show how this is done, i.e., to describe the methods. The purpose of chapter 3 is to provide a background, an explanation and rationale for these methods of bringing about an internal integrative encounter.

The General Principle

According to an existential-humanistic theory of human beings (Mahrer, 1978a), we can speak of a patient who operates and functions as an "operating domain," and we can speak of a "deeper domain." There is a relationship between the operating potentials and the deeper potentials, that is, between the operating potential (OP1 in Figure 4) and the deeper potential (DP2 in Figure 4). The key ingredient is the relationship between these two.

Almost without exception, the relationship between the patient (OP1) and the deeper potential is disintegrative. That is, the patient is bothered by the deeper potential, stays away from it, pushes it down,

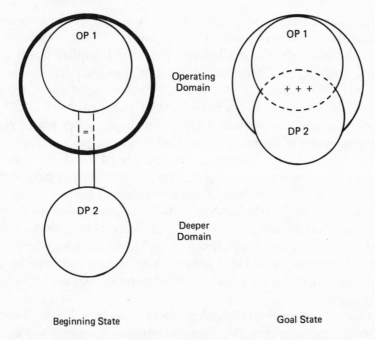

Figure 4. The In-therapy Change: Experiencing the Relationships With Deeper Potentials

keeps distance from it. The relationship from patient to deeper potential is characterized by tension, threat, avoidance, blockage. Frequently, there is sufficient distance so that the patient feels little or nothing of what the deeper potential is, maintains a safe numbing moat of separation with and from it. Occasionally the patient is scared by the deeper potential, is threatened by its imminence, may even be terrified by its menacing presence. This disintegrative relationship is indicated by the two negative signs in the channel between the patient and the deeper potential (Figure 4).

Therapeutic experiencing consists of the wholesale encounter between the patient and the deeper potential, and between the deeper potential and the patient; it is a two-way interactive relationship. The general principle may be framed as follows: *Psychotherapeutic change occurs through therapeutic experiencing of the integratively encountering relationship between the patient and the deeper potential.*

There is an encounter in which the patient and the deeper potential communicate with one another, openly and honestly express to one another, push and shove at one another, have it out with one another. It is a genuine, full-blown encounter between the patient and the deeper potential—as if the deeper potential were a live entity, with its own form and shape and personality. They respond and react to each other, yell and scream, shriek and bellow, touch and fondle, caress and cherish, open up and assimilate, one into the other (cf. Lewis & Streitfeld, 1972; Schutz, 1971, 1973; Whitaker & Malone, 1953). There is, in short, an experiencing of their relationship.

The consequence is twofold. One is that the deeper potential rises up into the operating domain; it is activated and comes closer. Incidentally, this change also occurs as a consequence of the sheer carrying forward of experiencing (see Figure 2, p. 4). The second part of the consequence is unique to internal encountering. There is a softening, easing, opening of the relationship between the patient and the deeper potential. This is the jewel. The relationship becomes friendly, welcoming, harmonious. It is accompanied with feelings of oneness, wholeness, intactness, inner peace and tranquility. This change is indicated by the positive signs in the overlap between the operating and deeper potentials in Figure 4.

As experiencing of the relationship proceeds, there will be heightened experiencing of disintegration. These disintegrative feelings will intensify until a clash occurs, a peak intensity of the disintegrative relationship. Then the change occurs and there is an integrative relationship. The sequence is from disintegrative to more disintegrative and then to integrative. This is the general principle of therapeutic experiencing of the relationship between the patient and the deeper potential.

Intensity and content of the experiencing. In order for the relationship to change from disintegrative to integrative, the experiencing of the relationship must attain a very high level of intensity. The patient experiences this relationship to a moderate degree whenever the deeper potential activates, whenever it even begins to move closer to the patient. But the momentous change from disintegrative to integrative relationships requires the highest level of sheer experiencing; " . . . only in the occurrence of the emotional clash is there provided the firepower to change . . . " (Havens, 1973, p. 158). It reaches the proportions of what Wyss (1973) refers to as an existential convulsion, or what Angyal (1965, p. 224) describes as " . . . the fire of an intensive and persuasive emotional experience."

This intensive experience, this emotional clash, means that bodily sensations are to be intense, and include all or most of the body. It also means that the participants are wholly locked into relating to one another, with the attention of each wholly riveted upon the other.

As the disintegrative relationship heats up, the patient is increasingly saturated with the painful experiencing of the relationship between patient and deeper potential. The patient experiences utter anxiety, the awful imminence of being radically changed into something absolutely alien, the ending of one's whole existence, total collapse, wholesale destruction, dread, terror, being totally in pieces, chaos, wholly disjointed and fractionated (Binswanger, 1958a, 1967, Kovacs, 1965; Whitaker & Malone, 1953; Wyss, 1973). These words point toward the nature of the disintegrative relationship at its zenith. While the peak may last only a few seconds, or perhaps on and off for a longer period, the content is powerful and painful.

Some reasons for the intensity and content of the experiencing. The patient is entitled to have such experiencing to such a degree. There are two interrelated reasons. One is that the very aims and purposes of the operating potential contain the seeds of its own destruction, for the operating potential was born out of a disintegrative relationship with the deeper potential. It was conceived and dedicated to resist the deeper potential, to keep it away, to fend it off, to deny and hide it, to present the polar face (Mahrer, 1978a). If the deeper potential relishes the wicked experiencing, the operating potential has fear, anxiety, embarrassment, guilt, and shame about it (cf. Binswanger, 1958a). If the operating potential is fascinated and repelled by some figure or agency, hypnotically drawn and compelled by it, riveted by it, the deeper potential is the sheer experiencing of utterly being it, losing one's existence in its existence. If the deeper potential accuses the patient, levels the horrible charge against him, the operating potential struggles to defend itself, to prove how unfair and false the charges are. Whatever the nature of the deeper potential, the operating potential struggles against it, must show that he is really not that way at all. If the deeper potential insists on giving up what is so precious to the operating potential, the person must ever more cling to it in desperation, must insure and secure the treasured way of being. While the deeper potential whispers of despair and hopelessness, the operating potential desperately seeks after the wonderful, the precious, the valued, the myth, the illusion. Whatever the nature of the deeper potential, the operating potential must be dedicated to showing, achieving, presenting the opposite face, the polarity.

The very presence of the disintegrative relationship means that the purpose and aim of the operating potential is to oppose, hide, deny, fend off the deeper potential. Accordingly, if the deeper potential gains energy and is activated, if the deeper potential comes closer and closer, if it presses for any kind of closer relationship, it is understandable that the operating potential is entitled to undergo that new relationship with intensity and with an experiencing whose content is powerful and painful.

The second reason, interrelated with the first, is that the core of the operating potential's disintegrative relationship toward the deeper potential is the imminence of the ending of the operating potential's very existence. The closer the deeper potential comes, the closer is the likelihood of closing out the operating potential's existence. The experiencing is that " . . . of being overpowered by this ground and by sinking back into Nothingness" (Binswanger, 1958c, p. 305), of facing the utter certainty of one's own destruction (Caruso, 1964), the absolute futility of further struggle (Angyal, 1965), the ironclad death of everything that I am (Allport, 1961; Schachtel, 1959; Suzuki, 1956).

For psychoanalysis, the intrusive imminence of deeper processes threatens the conscious-unconscious duality of separation (Bowlby, 1969, 1973; Ellenberger, 1970; Knight, 1941, 1952; Mahler, 1968), and brings, for example, the dreaded loss of parental love or the dread of parental punishment: "Repressed feelings, attitudes and fears, and the early experiences associated with them, continue to strive for conscious recognition, but are kept from awareness by dread of repetition of parental loss of love or punishment . . . " (Wolberg, 1954, p. 59). From the existential-humanistic theory of human beings, the intrusive imminence of the deeper process means the sense of final destruction, the ending of one's existence, death, nothingness, the vacuum. There are reasons for the intensity and content of the painful experiencing.

The therapeutic significance of experiencing the relationship with the deeper potentials. Suppose that there are a few moments or more when the patient undergoes an encountering interaction and reaches a state of integrative relationship with the deeper potential. Why and how is this therapeutically significant? What has been achieved? Here are several ways of describing the therapeutic significance of this step:

• The disintegrative relationship is no longer present. As indicated on the right in Figure 4, there are no negative signs in the relationship between the operating (OP1) and deeper (DP2) potentials. This means that disintegrative feelings are gone, or almost gone: the inner turmoil, the inner state of being torn apart, the disjunctiveness, the anxiety of pieces at war with one another, the constant vigilance, the avoiding and pulling away and denying, the hiding and polarity, the feelings of disharmony, inner tension, being in pieces. These disintegrative feelings are washed away (Buber, 1957; Fromm, 1959).

• Disintegrative bodily phenomena extinguish. These are the bodily expression of disintegrative relationships. Broader than what has come to be called "psychosomatic problems," these include the whole range of bodily events, especially those studied by Von Weizsacker and his colleagues (Wyss, 1973), the physical-bodily growths, ailments, events, and conditions which are the bodily expression of the powerfully disintegrative relationships between the patient and the deeper potentials. When these relationships become integrative, these bodily phenomena extinguish (cf. Feldenkrais, 1949, 1972; Mahrer, 1980b; Schur, 1966).

• There is now a good-feelinged, integrative relationship between the patient and the deeper potential. This shows itself in two ways. One is that there are now good, integrative feelings of inner wholeness, peacefulness, togetherness, oneness, inner harmony, a sense of intactness, tranquility (Mahrer, 1967a, 1967b; Buytendijk, 1950). The disintegrative inner struggle against the deeper potential is reduced, and there is a welcoming, accepting, playfulness and fondness toward the deeper potential. Much of the impelled striving and the driven struggling is now over (Angyal, 1965), the watchful vigilance against the inner potential can now end, a state which Whitaker and Malone (1953) refer to as "re-repression." These integrative relationships are indicated in Figure 4 by the three positive signs in the overlap between OP1 and DP2.

• The deeper potential shifts from its bad, disintegrative form to its good, integrative form. Here is an inner alchemy in which the very nature and content of the deeper potential shift as a consequence of the experiencing of the relationship between the patient and the deeper potential, the internal encounter. Gendlin (1964) holds that many theories lack explanatory concepts to account for such a powerful change in what lies within:

> To account for this change in the nature of contents, we need a type of definition (explanatory constructs) which also can change. We cannot explain *change* in the nature of the *content* when our theory specifically defines personality only as content. . . . The theories cannot explain

how these contents melt and lose their character to become something
of a different character (pp. 104–105).

This shift in content occurs as a consequence of the experiencing
of the relationship between the patient and the deeper potential, for
the integrative encounter allows the very content of the deeper potentials to transform from their disintegrative content to their integrative
content. This is a magical consequence of the full internal integrative
encounter.

• The deeper potential moves into the operating domain. In terms
of space, the deeper potential moves from being distant to being right
up against the operating domain, touching the patient, rubbing up
against the person. No longer separated and distant from the deeper
potential, the patient is only a whisper away from actually being the
deeper potential. It is as if the patient can almost sense what it would
be like to be the deeper potential. This change is indicated in Figure
4 by the shrinkage in the perimeter around the operating domain, and
by the movement of the deeper potential right into the operating space.

• The stage is set for movement to the next step (see Figure 1, p.
xvi), in which the patient disengages from the operating domain and
enters into being the deeper potential. It is noted that this consequence
is shared with the carrying forward of the potentials for experiencing.
In other words, as indicated in Figure 1, whether the therapist carries
forward the potentials for experiencing (chapters 1 and 2) or engages
in the internal encounter (chapters 3 and 4), the shared consequence
is a paving of the way toward the patient's actually being the deeper
potential. If you look at Figure 2 (p. 4) and Figure 4, both include the
deeper potential coming so close into the operating domain that the
patient only has to take a slight step toward the deeper potential and
the patient would virtually be inside the deeper potential.

• The patient who has gone through this internal encounter and
who has achieved even a few moments of this sense of integration between potentials has a taste of what it means to achieve the state of
"integration." If you put together the previous six ways in which the
internal integrative encounter is significant, you have a taste of the state
of integration. In existential-humanistic theory, this is one-half of the
grand goal state toward which experiential psychotherapy aspires. The
other half is known as actualization. The internal integrative encounter

provides the patient with a little sampling of what this state of integration is like.

Leverage of the Therapist as Deeper Potential

In this step, the therapist speaks with the voice of the deeper potential. The therapist takes on the identity of the patient's deeper potential and speaks to the patient as if it were the patient's own deeper potential who is speaking to the patient. The whole engagement, the encounter, is between the patient and the therapist-as-deeper-potential. If the aim is to work the relationship between the patient and the deeper potential, if the aim is to bring about an integrative internal encounter between the patient and the deeper potential, then why should the therapist serve as the voice or agency of the deeper potential? For those aims, what are the leverages (advantages, special characteristics) of the therapist as the deeper potential?

The therapist can "be" the deeper potential; the patient cannot. With rare exceptions, patients are unable to get out of the operating domain and "be" the deeper potential (Step 4, Figure 1, p. xvi). Indeed, the disintegrative relationship between the operating and deeper potentials virtually means that the patient cannot do this. Yet, if there is going to be an interaction, an encounter between the two, the deeper potential must somehow come alive and be able to interact in a therapeutic encounter. How may this be accomplished?

Here is a technical problem for a psychotherapy which values an integrative encounter between the patient and a deeper potential, a deeper process, or however it is termed. If we have a good grasp on the nature of a patient's deeper potential, the one which is stirring right now, what can we do to have that deeper potential come alive, have voice, and engage in an integrative encounter with the patient? In experiential psychotherapy the best answer we have so far is that the therapist can take on the identity and voice of this deeper potential, and the therapist-as-deeper-potential can engage in this internal encounter. In other words, the therapist can "be" the deeper potential; the patient cannot.

In order to carry out this step, the therapist must be superior to the patient in the ability to "be" the deeper potential. The therapist must be able to step out of or leave behind her own operating domain and get into the deeper potential which is present. The therapist is entitled to have her own problems, to be far from an integrated and actualized ideal. However, the requirement is that the therapist must be sufficiently friendly, welcoming, and integrated with her own deeper potentials to allow herself to "be" any and all deeper potentials, including the one which is resonating right now as the patient is being and talking. Indeed, this is one of the qualities which distinguishes the therapist from the patient (Boss, 1963; Havens, 1973, 1976; Mahrer, 1978c). While the patient pulls back from, is terrified by, backs off from the deeper potential, the therapist is ready, willing, and able to dive into being deeper potentials in general, and this deeper potential in particular.

The other side of the interaction. When the deeper potential comes to life, acquires a voice, it can interact with the patient. That is a real advantage, for the patient is unable to have a back-and-forth interaction with the deeper potential. The patient may look at her insides, may have insight and understanding of whatever she sees, but the insides will never interact. Suppose that the patient sees a deeper "fear of being overlooked" or a "nasty competitiveness" or a "petty criticalness." Only when the deeper process comes to life and gains a voice can the nasty competitiveness interact back upon the patient, express its own insight and understanding of the patient—"Well, now I can see what you are like too; actually, from down deep in here, you kind of impress me as a great pretender. You act as if you are everyone's friend, loyal, helpful. None of that is true. I understand what you are like." The other side of the interaction occurs when the deeper process can talk back to the patient, have its own say, tell the patient what it thinks about the patient, react and respond to the patient. Only when the deeper process comes alive and does all of this can there be a relationship, an interaction between the patient and the deeper process, and between the deeper process and the patient. Only then can the two of them play and cavort with one another, have mutual insight and understanding into one another, fight and squabble, argue and nag, have it out with one another. The therapeutic leverage is that the other side comes to life and effects an interaction.

The therapeutic leverage is also that the other side of the interaction can occur in its integrative form. The patient avoids the deeper potential, runs from it, sees it as monstrous and awful, hides and denies it, relates to it disintegratively. The disintegrative relationship goes from the patient to the deeper potential. The Copernican switch is that the deeper potential is absolutely free of all that. The deeper potential does not avoid the patient, run from the patient, see the patient as monstrous and awful, hide and deny the patient. Only the patient's side of the interaction is disintegrative. The deeper potential's relationship with the patient is free to be delightfully integrative. In a very real sense, this other side of the interaction is astoundingly free of the patient's disintegrative relationship.

Because the deeper potential can relate integratively, the "other side of the interaction" can include the offering of integrative intimacy. The patient may keep a safe distance from the deeper potential. But the deeper potential can offer what Maslow (1962) speaks of as intimacy love, the I-thou relationship of Buber (1955, 1958), the mature intimacy-love of Fromm (1956), Lewis' gift intimacy (1960), Seguin's (1965) dual shared relationship, Binswanger's (1958a, 1967) duality of communion. From its side of the interaction, the deeper potential can offer the closest kind of integrative relationship.

This other side of the interaction slices right through the problem of "resistance" as it is called in a psychoanalytic vocabulary. "The patient shows resistance against recognizing unconscious content. Overcoming this resistance is one of the primary technical problems of the treatment" (Alexander, 1963, p. 440; see also A. Freud, 1946; Kubie, 1943). The patient's resistance or disintegrative relationship is solved by the single tactic of an end run in which the other side of the interaction is brought to life. While the patient is "resistant" to the deeper process, the deeper process has no "resistance" to the patient, so the interaction is free to occur. The problem of "resistance" is solved by giving the integrative, "unresistant" deeper process a form and shape and voice with which to interact with the patient.

What is more, the very nature and content of the deeper potential shift from the bad disintegrative form to the good integrative form. From the perspective of the patient, the deeper potential is bad, awful, menacing, monstrous, disintegrative. In stark contrast, from the perspective of the deeper potential, it can occur as pleasant, lovely, benign, pure, integrative. The other side of the interaction therefore discloses the good integrative form of the deeper potential.

Harnessing the power of the relating deeper potential. The relating deeper potential has incredible power. The operating domain has far less power. The therapist has far less power. Externalized or "projected" agencies, forces, significant others, groups — none of these compare with the power of the relating deeper potential. According to existential-humanistic theory, it is the relating deeper potential which invests the power in the friend who loves you, the enemy who criticizes you, God who accepts you, the group that ridicules you, the alien force that menaces you, the child who depends upon you, the spouse who trusts you. All of those highly important persons and groups, with all their highly important relationships to you, are powered by the deeper potentials and their relationships with and toward the patient. When the therapist speaks with the voice of the relating deeper potential, the therapist harnesses that incredible power.

When the deeper potential speaks to the patient, when the insides contain that about which the patient is guilty, shameful, defensive, and when these insides rise up and talk directly to the patient, the effects are powerful (Condrau & Boss, 1971; Hora, 1962). That is when the guilt and shame and defensiveness shoot way up. The patient is pierced with the voice of the "existential conscience," reminding the patient of the highest sin against his inner self (Hora, 1962). The therapist who speaks the words of the deeper potential is speaking from incredible power.

The right words from a friend or lover may be quite powerful. They may be strong when they come from a parent or special person or a therapist with whom there is a strong (transference) relationship. They may be stronger yet when they come from the voice of God or the devil. But when one's own deepest potentials assume a form and shape, when they become vividly real and give voice to their feelings and attitudes about you, then the effects are incredibly powerful. This is when the words of the therapist-as-deeper-potential seem to have that ring of truth. They remain with the patient long after the session. They stand out as if they come from the inner core which is the truth about the patient. These are the words which seem to come from some mystical innermost being that has always known everything about the patient.

The relating deeper potential is in intimate contact with every nuance of the patient. It sees and knows everything, every ripple of reaction, every delicate movement. It knows what the patient does not know about himself. It knows every slight detail about the patient's avoidance, denial, cover-up, wicked thought, hidden wish. The relating deeper potential is supremely sensitive to the patient's slightest movement toward or away, back and forth. It is as if the relating deeper potential sees the whole inner workings of the patient under the most powerful illumination of its discerning lens. It is as if the relating deeper potential is so intimately connected to the soft feelinged underbelly of the patient that it sees and knows everything. It knows you more intimately than your mother knows you, or your best friend, or your priest, therapist, God. It really knows.

What is more, only the relating, interacting deeper potential can effect a genuine integrative encounter. External encounters can be powerful when they are between you and mother, your child, your spouse, lover, group, family, enemy, God, therapist. But these external encounters are less able to reach the internal integration offered by the internal encounter with one's own deeper potential. One reason is that the therapist-as-deeper-potential can go further than these external others. The therapist-as-deeper-potential can proceed in and through the peak of feeling and out into the other side, the integrative good feelings. In contrast, relationships with significant others typically magnify disintegrative feelings and get no further. The power lies in going beyond the heights of disintegration and into the integrative relationships.

Secondly, the real resource of the power lies in the relating deeper potential. Whatever power these other figures have is borrowed from, provided by, invested by, externalized by the relating deeper potential. At their most powerful, these external figures can only approach the greater power of the deeper potential.

Thirdly, no matter how strongly felt is the relationship with the other person, no matter how similar the other person may be to the nature of the deeper potential, there is always a large confounding measure of the other person as a unique entity. Father is still a person in his own right. So is the therapist upon whom the patient has "transferred" something of the deeper process. An intensely felt relationship with father or with the therapist can, at best, only approximate the relationship with the actual relating deeper potential.

Finally, the relating deeper potential is quite free to relate integratively—with loving fondness, respect and regard, playful childlikeness, to relate from its good, integrative form. This is virtually impossible for external figures, even for those which engage in a strong relationship with the patient.

Solving the problems of the patient's avoidance and resistance to therapy and to the therapist. There are all sorts of problems posed by the patient's avoidances of therapy and the therapist, so-called "resistance" to therapy and the therapist. Not only are these problems sidestepped, but they are converted to therapeutic advantage by the strategy of the therapist as the voice and agency of the relating deeper potential.

Psychoanalysis has a long history of wrestling with the knotty problems of the patient's negative feelings about therapy and the therapist (Wyss, 1973). Guntrip describes one catch-22 version of this problem:

" . . . until psychotherapy has helped him to become less afraid of relationships, he cannot make much use of the treatment, yet while he cannot effect this relationship spontaneously because of his anxieties, the treatment cannot get under way. The problem is not insoluble or psychotherapy would never get going at all, but it constitutes probably the major difficulty in treatment" (1969, p. 328). At the other extreme, patients who have built an impervious moat around themselves, whose life is dedicated to the erection of massive distance and separation, are often regarded as crazy or deranged or psychotic, and are generally foreclosed away from psychotherapy itself (Federn, 1952; Gendlin, 1972; Rosen, 1953; Rosenfeld, 1954; Searles, 1965; Sullivan, 1953a). Whether mild or intense, whether a general lifestyle or a deep-seated internal conflict, patients' resistances and avoidance of therapy and the therapist are most formidible problems for the psychotherapist.

When the arena is the channel of relationships between the deeper potential and the patient, these problems are effectively side-stepped. While the patient is avoidant, resistant, pulling away from therapy and the therapist, the deeper potential uses all of this to its advantage. The deeper potential pushes the patient, badgers him, ridicules him, encourages him, plays with him, whips him up, goes him one better, attacks him, incorporates all of this in the internal relationship. What is a terribly difficult problem for the external therapist is grist for the internal encounter between deeper potential and patient.

The deeper potential is the underlying architect, organizing the avoidances and resistances to therapy and the therapist. If this deeper potential consists of the experiencing of a controlling tyranny, the patient may withdraw from being a good patient or become silent or probe for the therapist's weaknesses or counter all the therapist's moves with an effective "What's the use of even trying?" or attack the therapist or deftly slide away from anything remotely threatening (Cole, 1980; Mahrer & Kangas, 1970; May, 1968). Underneath is the activating sense of controlling and tyrannizing the therapist. As the relating external therapist there is trouble in coping with these avoidances and resistances. But as the voice of the relating deeper potential, the therapist is faced with no avoidances and resistances. Accordingly, the deeper potential can say, "Great! You got the bastard sweating. . . . He'll never get out of that one . . . keep it up, kid, I think we got the upper hand. . . . Jesus you're an obnoxious sonuvagun. . . . More of that shit and someday someone's going to break your jaw. . . . How the hell do you get away with that shit? . . . I love this; the big doctor is probably trying to figure out how to squirm out of this one . . . "

By being the voice of the deeper potential in relating to the patient, the therapist not only solves many of the problems of avoidance and resistance to therapy and to the therapist, but also converts these to therapeutic advantage in effecting the internal encounter. Indeed, this is only one of the therapeutic leverages gained by the therapist-as-deeper-potential in the internal encounter with the patient.

The Patient Determines Whether the Therapist Carries Forward the Experiencing or Engages in an Internal Encounter

When the patient behaves and talks, the therapist is ready to carry forward the experiencing or to "work" the relationship between the deeper potential and the patient. The therapist is ready to do either one. It is the *patient* who determines which one the therapist does. The therapist does not decide to work this relationship. The therapist does not figure out that now is the time to be the voice of the deeper potential in relating to the patient. All the therapist does is listen experientially, and the patient will do the selection.

The patient will activate the relating deeper potential. The patient will illuminate the deeper potential and the relationship between the patient and the deeper potential. How does the therapist know? The therapist knows by experiential listening. If the therapist is made to be the experiencing deeper potential, and if the therapist's attention is drawn onto the patient, then the therapist is working the relationship between the patient and the deeper potential. All of this is a passive process, for all the therapist does is allow the patient's behavior and words to bring forth a deeper potential which is relating in some way to the patient. Here is an example:

Pt: My daughter respects me. I know she respects me. I've been a good mother, a good example, set a good example. If there's one thing I'm sure of, she respects me.

The experientially listening therapist is drawn into being a deeper potential and relating with the patient. Indeed, experiential listening discloses a deeper experiencing of being a bad mother, one who deserves little or no respect, who doesn't give a damn about the daughter. And this deeper potential is already engaged in a relationship with the patient.

This point is given graphically in Figure 3, p. 53. The therapist carries forward the experiencing when experiential listening makes prominent the experiencing or makes prominent the focal center and situational context. But when experiential listening makes prominent the patient's relationship with the deeper potential, then the therapist engages in the internal encounter with the patient. We already have a deeper part which is a bad mother who doesn't give a damn about the daughter. We already have a relationship where the patient is defensively pulling back from that deeper potential. The other side of that relationship, the one from the deeper potential to the patient, can be that of an integrative encounter.

It is almost as if the patient is illuminating a deeper potential and constructing a relationship of sorts between the patient and the deeper potential. Or, in other words, the experientially listening therapist is just about invited to be a particular deeper potential, and to attend and relate to the patient. If the therapist listens experientially, the therapist's attention is drawn to the patient, and the therapist is drawn toward flatly disagreeing with the patient, ridiculing the patient, loving what the patient is trying to hide or deny, leveling the accusation, telling the patient the real truth, dispelling the clung-to illusion, labeling the effort as silly or fruitless or wrong, naming the truth in what the patient is avoiding or denying or running from, scolding the patient, or generally carrying out an integrative encounter from the internal relationship the patient determines.

Methods of Experiencing the Relationship with Deeper Potentials: Some Soft Hintings

The patient behaves and talks in such a way that the experientially listening therapist senses a deeper potential, and is drawn into expressing the relationship between this deeper potential and the patient. Then, speaking with the voice of the deeper potential, and talking to the patient, the therapist says words, relates in some way. What are the soft hintings of what the therapist says and does? What are some soft hintings of the actual methods and techniques used by the therapist? Rather than an exhaustive summary, what follows is an illustrative foray into some of the soft hintings toward useable methods.

You are the problem, and you must go. Many therapies preserve and maintain the patient himself, and identify the problem as something safely nearby. For example, the problem and the required change lies in your surroundings, your family, your significant others, your group, your interpersonal relations (Adler, 1931, 1969; Bowen, 1978; Caudill, 1958; Minuchin, 1974; Sullivan, 1953b). When these are modified or resolved or improved, things will be better with you. The problem is that you do not have the right kind and amount of insight and understanding. The problem is that your cognitions are mixed up and wrong (Dreikurs, 1947, 1967; Ellis, 1967; Glasser, 1965; Kelly, 1955, 1967; Meichenbaum, 1977; Meichenbaum & Goodman, 1971). When these are altered, things will be all right. The problem is in the lack of certain key behaviors. When you acquire these, things will be better (Bandura, 1969; Rimm & Masters, 1974; Yates, 1975). The problem, and what must be changed, lies in bad insides, faulty early experiences, neurotic patterns, wrong thoughts, poor responses, inadequate learnings, psychopathology, inadequate insight and understanding, and so on. In all this, the patient himself is relatively safe; nothing too drastic will occur in the very core of the patient's precious self. The problem is distal, in selected parts of you. It is not *you*.

But some therapies point the accusing finger right at the patient himself. "You are the problem; and you must go." This is the ominous message proclaimed by the deeper potential, and it is found in some therapies in one method or another (cf. Frank, 1961b). It is the central theme of existentialism, namely, you are the one who must undergo the most extreme of changes, the final confrontation with death, the eternal nothingness. You can no longer stand behind your problems or your sufferings or your behavior, for the problem is you, and it is you who must die (Binswanger, 1967; Feifel, 1959; Koestenbaum, 1978; Park, 1975; Van Kaam, 1966).

The Zen master engages in a direct encounter with the very heart of the patient/student. Everything which is the person is at the very center of the Zen master's work until the person collapses. It is you, the very person who sought therapy, who is to end, die, undergo radical change. You will be frustrated and attacked, relentlessly pursued until you give up and die:

> Time after time he reaches an intellectual solution which is rejected by the Zen master. With increasing despair he concentrates more and more on the Koan until his concentration is no longer voluntary; the problem cannot be put aside . . . the feeling of doubt which emerges is carefully maintained until something like a crisis is reached. . . . Death images like "walking in darkness" or "enclosed in a black lacquer casket" are used to describe this state of mind. In the midst of it, the student "lets go" of his egoistic self, "throws himself into the abyss," and satori follows (Maupin, 1965, pp. 143–144).

In a similar theme, some therapies put the therapeutic fix on the very person of the patient himself. For example, some therapies identify the crux of the problem as the patient's own clinging to the way he is, his own dogged determination to close out other possibilities in a self-defeating self-constriction. The finger points to the final inner sense of I-ness, the very core of my most precious identity, the final wisp of Dasein, the nucleus of the precious self that I am. I am the heart of the matter, and the locus of the change is right here in this sensitive innermost core (Binswanger, 1958a; Boss, 1963; Hora, 1962; May, 1967).

This same idea is found in the methods used to undergo the inner integrative encounter.

The Gestalt "chairs" method. There are various methods which enable the patient to have an encounter, a dialogue, a back-and-forth interaction between the patient and a deeper self or personality process. One method is to have the patient talk to parts of oneself: your headache, your tapping foot, your whispering voice, your clenched fist (e.g., Fagan, 1974; Levitsky & Perls, 1970). Another method is for the patient to carry out a therapeutic regime expressly directed at the objectified self. For example, Haley (1963, pp. 47–49) instructs a 17-year-old bedwetter to punish himself by awakening when he is wet, taking a two-mile wet walk, returning to the bedroom, and sleeping in the wet bed. In psychodrama, the patient or other therapeutic partners play out the role of the deeper interacting process (Moreno, 1959).

Perhaps the most refined method of conducting a two-way interaction with inner parts of oneself is the Gestalt "chairs" method (Finney, 1976; Greenberg, 1979; Levitsky & Perls, 1970; Perls, 1969a). The patient is in one chair. The deeper process is in the other chair, and the patient is to act out both sides of the interaction. As the patient, the patient talks to the deeper process; then, in the other chair, as the deeper process, the patient talks to the objectified patient-self. Here is an explicit method for making alive the two-way, back-and-forth, interactive encounter between the patient and the deeper process.

I regard the two-chairs method as the most prominent forerunner of the internal integrative encounter in experiential psychotherapy. Perhaps the major difference is that in the experiential method it is the therapist who speaks and interacts as the deeper process, whereas in the two-chair method it is the patient who is to get into the identity of the deeper process and who speaks and interacts as the deeper process. As a method of accomplishing what the internal integrative encounter is designed to accomplish, there are several problems in the two-chair method. One is that the patient must be able to truly "be" the deeper process. That is an extremely tall order. Indeed, being the deeper process is itself a separate step in experiential psychotherapy (chapters 5 and 6). Second, the patient must be able to speak as, express as, and behave as the deeper process. That is also a tall order. Finally, in being and expressing as the deeper process, the patient would also have to relate to the substantive patient in an integratively therapeutic manner which attained the clashing encounter and proceeded on to the integrative relationship. That is difficult for the patient to accomplish.

Encountering and self-disclosure. Methods of carrying out the external encounter between therapist and patient have a great deal to teach us about methods for carrying out the internal encounter. The external encounter ordinarily calls upon therapist self-disclosure, and this method also provides some genuine hintings about how to negotiate the internal encounter.

According to Havens (1973), one of the pioneering roots of the encounter occurred when Minkowski, in the 1920s, welcomed into his home a patient with whom, in the course of daily living, he had daily non-traditional, non-professional clashes. There were emotional explosions and fights which somehow seemed to result in welcomed changes in the patient. Existential clinical practice refined and developed this encountering relationship into a powerful method: "Existential psychotherapy prefers, to the use of the psychoanalytic transference, the use of another interpersonal experience, 'encounter'" (Ellenberger, 1958, p. 119). Perhaps the defining characteristic of this encountering relationship is the direct interaction between the deepest processes in the two participants. "The really essential aspect of the relationship is simply the accessibility of the unconscious dynamics of both participants, each to the other" (Whitaker & Malone, 1953, p. 427).

This meeting may or may not involve aggressive confrontations, but it typically includes the full meeting of the participants in the closest and most intimate clashings. Perhaps the most vocal pioneers of this aspect of the encounter were M. Heidegger, L. Binswanger, M. Buber, M. Scheler, and K. Löwith (Wyss, 1973). All of these saw sharp restrictions and problems in the ordinary psychodynamic-psychoanalytic relationship between therapist and patient, and all worked to refine and develop the I-thou, fully intimate existential encounter as the most powerfully useful therapeutic relationship.

Negotiating this powerful relationship requires what Denes-Radom-isli (1977) refers to as the therapist's "presence": ' . . . a full, alive, alert, nontruncated there-ness. It refers to being without hiding . . . presence is that quality of a person which reveals his who-ness with vibrant immediacy" (p. 29). This calls for a refinement of Jourard's (1968, 1971a, 1971b) self-disclosure into a full-blown emotional reaction to the patient (cf. Kempler, 1968). The therapist furthers the encounter, establishes contact between the therapist's deeper processes and those of the patient, by disclosing the therapist's immediately present, deep feelings with and toward the patient: "The therapist's effort is to communicate as fully as possible his feeling responses to the presence of the patient, and his experiences in this relationship" (Whitaker, Warkentin, & Malone, 1959, p. 255).

As a consequence, things happen. The encountering relationship builds up powerful forces of therapeutic change. Perhaps it is because the therapist sees into the very heart of the patient: " . . . once a counter-identification has occurred with the patient, the emotional insights of the therapists in the emotional relationship become more accurate and, when communicated to the patient, are a constructive factor in her therapeutic growth" (Whitaker, Warkentin, & Malone, 1959, p. 242). Perhaps it is because this particular kind of interaction changes something in the patient: " . . . expressing our feelings does not just tell about entities in us. Rather, expressing our feelings toward him is an interactive process and constitutes what occurs in him as much as in us" (Gendlin, 1966, p. 243). For whatever reason, the open communication of deep-seated feelinged reactions within the encountering channel activates deeper processes in the patient who is propelled into therapeutic change.

Existential therapists count heavily on the encounter as a powerful avenue of therapeutic change; " . . . it is in the encounter of two people that each of the participants is altered" (Denes-Radomisli, 1977, p. 26). More powerfully effective than the psychoanalytic transference (Ellenberger, 1958), the external encountering relationship is heralded as exceeding the psychoanalytic transference in opening up deeper processes of change (Wyss, 1973). Encountering and the use of self-disclosure to further the genuine meeting are intertwined roots of the method of internal encountering.

Empathic interpretations as the serendipitous voice of the patient's insides. Client-centered therapists try to get inside the patient's world and to speak from within the patient's own internal frame of reference. Psychoanalytic therapists often use methods which aim at inviting the patient's internal frame of reference to extrude itself onto the therapist as transference, projection, externalization. Whether the therapist tries to get into the patient's insides or tries to get the insides transferred onto the therapist, there are rare and precious moments when the words of the empathic or interpretive therapist almost seem to come from something within the patient. It is as if the therapist speaks with the voice of the patient's insides.

When this happens, when the therapist's words seem to be coming from a deeper process within the patient, the words have a special effect. The therapist says, "You wish that your father really understood, instead of occasionally just coming close," or "Wouldn't it be nice if you really were a precious jewel?" Out of all the empathic and interpretive statements made by the therapist, these special words have extraordinary punch when they seem to come from the voice of the inner depths of the patient, rather than merely from the therapist.

There are many attempts to identify the characteristics of effective empathic and interpretive statements (Adams & Frye, 1964; Bergman, 1951; Hekmat, 1971; Mahrer, Clark, Comeau & Brunette, in press; Wachtel, 1980). My suggestion is that many of these especially effective statements are as if they were spoken by the patient's own deeper potential when the therapist manages to get inside the patient's world or to be made into the (transferred) external agency of the patient's deeper potential. Sometimes the therapist says the words which would be spoken by the deeper potential if it could speak. Sometimes the therapist uses the word "I" as if the speaker were the patient himself, even something deeper within the patient. Whether in restating or rephrasing what the patient said, or in referring to oneself, it is eerie how opportune it is that "I" can refer to the patient, and especially to something deeper in the patient. Then the patient can understandably say, " . . . 'You are all the things I say and don't say, and do and don't do . . . '" (Whitaker, Warkentin, & Malone, 1959, p. 237).

Sometimes the words of the therapist merge into those which would be said by the deeper potential. They seem to come from the deeper potential, and the words bespeak the relationship of the deeper potential toward the patient:

> . . . You are not a plain, fat, disgusting slob. You are the fattest, homeliest, most disgusting horrible bucket of lard I have ever seen, and it is appalling to look at you. . . . You have got the homeliest face I have seen. . . . You have no taste, even in clothes, your feet slop all over the edges of your shoes. To put it simply—you are a hideous mess . . . (Erickson, in Haley, 1973a, p. 116).

Therapists may attack the patient, insult and criticize the patient, berate and ridicule the patient. Yet the words seem to be coming from something deeper within the patient rather than from the external therapist. No matter how the therapist explains or describes or rationalizes the statements, a precious few have that added power bestowed by the "as if" quality of coming from the patient's deeper inner processes. In a haphazard way, perhaps, some therapist statements are thereby quite special, and this special effect may show the power of the therapist as the voice of the deeper potential, relating to and talking to the patient. Here is another significant precursor of the integrative internal encounter.

Components of the "good relationship" which would be useful in the internal integrative encounter. Nearly every therapy has ideas about what kind of relationship is a good one and why that is a good kind of relationship between therapist and patient. It is my impression that a few of these components are also useful in effecting the internal integrative encounter, while most of what comprises the "good therapist-patient relationship" is relatively useless for these purposes. It is a matter of sensitive picking and choosing from many components phrased in many different vocabularies. The question is whether that particular component in the good relationship between therapist and patient also seems to qualify as a good component in the integrative encountering relationship between deeper potential and patient.

Three of these components have already been discussed. That is, in some versions of the good relationship, the therapist relates so as to indicate to the patient that it is the patient himself who must undergo the significant change, rather than some distal aspect or problem or influence. Second, the good relationship includes encountering the patient and open self-disclosing of anything and everything occurring within the therapist. Third, some versions of the good therapist-patient relationship include empathic interpretations of what the patient is like, framed so that they are as if coming from the patient's own insides. These three components of some therapist-patient relationships are also useful in the internal encounter.

In addition, there are two other components which are found in some conceptions of the good relationship and which are especially useful for the internal encountering relationship. One consists of a genuine, full, heartfelt liking of the patient. It is the sense of wonderful friendship between two best friends who have known each other a long time and who unabashedly like one another. It is the feeling you have when you spontaneously touch or hug that special buddy and say, "I like you!" It is a very special, open, fond appreciation (Bugental, 1965; Ofman, 1976; Polster & Polster, 1974; Sagarin, 1973; Wyss, 1973) combined with a good measure of good-feelinged intimacy (Buhler, 1967; Fromm, 1947; Jourard, 1963; Teilhard de Chardin, 1965). This is what is meant by an integrative relationship, and it is found in some conceptions of the good therapist-patient relationship.

It is not the safe little whiff of intimacy that some therapists manage to steal in the sanctuary of the therapy office (Bugental, 1964; Lawton, 1958). It is not the promise of intimacy which some therapists use to entice patients. Nor does it consist of the client-centered warm regard, generalized acceptance, humanistic positive regard (e.g., Carkhuff & Berenson, 1967; Patterson, 1974; Rogers, 1965).

The second component is a tough, hard, invincible commitment, a being-with the patient which has no conditions, no waverings, no ending. As he became increasingly disillusioned with psychoanalytic treatment methods, Fierman (1965) turned increasingly to this aspect of the relationship, to staying in unflinching contact throughout the patient's whole course of defensive twistings and turnings, wrenchings and fightings, resistances and contortions. Proponents of this kind of patient-therapist relationship are ready to see the relationship go all the way in any and all directions, throughout all the emotionally encountering clashes. This is much more than a willingness to see the patient in endless years of psychoanalytic therapy (cf. Milner, 1969). Instead, it is the invincible commitment to stay throughout all the emotional frustrations, the emotional clashes, the full encounter (Berg & Steinberg, 1973; Boss, 1963; Bugental, 1967; Farrelly & Brandsma, 1974; Havens, 1973; Kempler, 1968; Laing, 1962; Mullan & Sangiuliano, 1964; Perls, 1969b, 1976; Whitaker, Warkentin, & Malone, 1959).

This section has illustrated some of the more prominent roots, connections, precursors, and soft hintings for methods of experiencing the internal, integrative, encountering relationship between deeper potential and patient. We now turn to some common therapeutic concepts which are inappropriate for these purposes.

Theoretical Concepts Inappropriate for the Experiencing of Relationships With the Deeper Potential

The existential-humanistic theory of human beings makes it sensible and understandable that psychotherapy would enhance the experiencing of relationships between the patient and the deeper potentials. The theoretical concepts fit; they are appropriate. This means our methods fit, are appropriate, dovetail with existential-humanistic theory. On the other hand, some concepts from other theories are gratingly inappropriate for the very notion of enhancing this internal relationship. Here are a few of these theoretical concepts especially alien to the experiencing of relationships between the patient and the deeper potential.

The lack of deeper processes capable of having a relationship with the patient. Many theories of human beings have no conceptual room for the idea of deeper processes of any kind. In existential-humanistic theory we speak of deeper potentials and basic potentials. Psychoanalysis speaks of an unconscious. Whether referred to as deeper potentials, unconscious, deeper personality processes, or "insides," there is some notion of an inner universe with processes of one sort or another. In contrast, there are plenty of other theories which have no such conception in their picture of what human beings are like. I am not referring exclusively to right-wing behavioral theorists, some of whom have yet to include the idea of a cognitive behavioral conception of human beings (Liberman, 1972; Ullmann & Krasner, 1965). I am also referring to those theories where what is within is still a part of the substantive personality, the functioning, thinking, behaving individual. Instead of genuinely deeper processes, there are faulty learnings, wrong ideas, and all manner of processes which are functioning cogs in the behaving organism without ever having the status of more or less independent organization, of truly deeper internal processes. For all those theories which lack the idea of internal personality processes (e.g., Adler, 1938; Bandura, 1969; Ellis, 1971; Glasser & Zunin, 1973; Kelly, 1955; Mischel, 1968) there is little or no conceptual basis for the therapeutic value of working the relationship between the patient and something which is not there.

On the other hand, some theories do include a conception of genuinely internal personality processes. If, however, these internal processes are not capable of having a relationship with the patient, the other side of the patient's relationship with them, then there is no place for ways of promoting the experiencing of these relationships. Gendlin (1964) points out that many theories conceptualize internal contents which are more or less fixed, static, stable, and unchanging. When the insides are seen this way, there is little or no basis for a two-way, interactive relationship.

Wyss (1973) speaks of psychoanalytic theorists who hold to notions in which the ego can know the unconscious but has no way of engaging in a genuine meeting with it, and in which the unconscious is conceived as containing drives and cathexes and "objects" of its drives and cathexes, but again, without being capable of genuine encountering interactions and meetings with these objects. Psychoanalytic conceptions of the unconscious, as well as many conceptions of inner drives and urges and needs, do not contain conceptual bases for any sort of back-and-forth encountering relationship.

If the insides include unconscious wishes, cognitive thoughts, conflicts, irrational ideas, biological needs and drives, social pushes and pulls, personality traits, or most of the static constituents in most theories of human beings, these seldom if ever include the capacity to interact with the patient, ridicule and badger the patient, have a loving relationship with the patient, interact and meet with the patient. If the deeper processes, whatever their supposed nature, are incapable of having a relationship with the patient, then those concepts are inappropriate for the experiencing of relationships with deeper processes.

Will an "effective" therapist-patient relationship bring about an internal integrative relationship? There are many reasons why a given kind of therapist-patient relationship is considered to be effective. In many approaches, a prominent reason is that the effective therapist-patient relationship will lead to a more accepting, welcoming, integrative relationship between the patient and the deeper processes (Fine, 1971; Kohut, 1971; Patterson, 1974; Rogers, 1965; Schwartz, 1951; Whitmont & Kaufmann, 1973). My contention is that this proposition is tenuous at best. No matter what kind of "effective" relationship the external therapist constructs with the patient, there will be little or no change in the direction of an integrative relationship between patient and deeper processes. There will be no internal encounter, no back-and-forth interaction between patient and deeper processes, no internal integration.

One kind of effective therapist-patient relationship is constructed out of the patient's projections from childhood relationships with significant figures. Whether understood as classical psychoanalytic transference or broadened to include particularized lines of projection (e.g., Flugel, 1945), whether the transference relationship is held as constituting a powerful two-person encounter (Condrau & Boss, 1971) or as lacking these constituencies (Wyss, 1973), the transference relationship does not bring about an internal integrative encounter between the patient and the patient's deeper processes, however they are described.

The same holds true for virtually all other relationships that therapists regard as effective. No matter how the therapist is to the patient, it does not follow that there will be an internal encounter, a two-way internal interaction, or an integrative relationship. These particular changes are especially impervious to the relationship between external therapist and patient, however "effective" that relationship may be shown to be for other purposes. "This point must be emphasized because of the common error in many circles of assuming that the experience of one's being will take place automatically if only one is accepted by someone else. This is the basic error of some forms of 'relationship therapy'" (May, 1958, p. 45). An effective therapist-patient relationship is not followed by an integrative internal relationship.

Therapists may value a relationship in which the therapist is open, self-disclosing, transparent, free of defenses. This may approach the radical wing in which the therapist tells the patient erotic dreams stimulated by the therapist's feelings for the patient (Whitaker, Warkentin, & Malone, 1959), or the more conservative wing in which the therapist offers calculatedly periodic glimpses into the outer impersonal boundaries of the therapist's thoughts. If the therapist is openly transparent to the patient, will the patient engage in an integratively encountering relationship with the deeper personality processes? Probably not (Mahrer, Fellers, Brown, Gervaize, & Durak, 1981).

Nor will the internal integrative encounter occur when the therapist offers the patient an egalitarian relationship, relates with trust and confidence in the patient, is friendly and helpful, offers nurturance and succorance, provides love and warmth, is unconditionally positively regarding, relates with strength and firmness, gives the patient the gift of a new and wonderful outlook on life, is ready to go through hell with the patient, bestows upon the patient whatever was missing as a child, or a " . . . reality relationship of a supportive, growth-promoting and finally personally liberating kind" (Guntrip, 1969, p. 316).

Regardless of the nature of the "effective" relationship, regardless of the supposed therapeutic consequences of any kind of good relationship, relationships from the external therapist to the patient will generally fail to bring about an internal integrative encounter between the patient and the deeper personality processes.

Conceptualizing deeper processes as dangerous and powerful, and the patient as vulnerable and fragile. Many therapies begin by seeing deeper processes as very dangerous and very powerful. With deeper processes as monstrous, crazed, out of control, uncivilized, explosive, the patient is seen as vulnerable and fragile, weak and needing support, in danger of being overwhelmed and crushed, overrun and shattered. When therapies start out by conceptualizing patients and deeper processes in this way, there is little or no room for an internal integrative encounter.

Psychodynamic-psychoanalytic therapies are perhaps the best outfitted with this way of regarding patients and their deeper processes. Interpretations must be properly timed lest the patient be overwhelmed by interpretations which are premature, and for which the patient is not yet ready. Build a good relationship to help the patient withstand dangerous inner material which might be stirred up by premature interpretations. Word interpretations carefully to avoid arousing deeper threatening material. Do not push the patient too much; be careful not to overload the patient with too much stress. Be vigilant for signs that the patient is falling apart, showing symptoms of psychosis, requiring emotional support. Make sure that the patient is intact, has sufficient ego strength. Gauge whether the patient is regressing in the face of excessive opening up of deep material. Assess the patient's ability to tolerate instinctual material, the patient's intactness and state of defenses. There is a whole litany growing out of the delicate patient and the dangerous deeper material.

What is deeper is instinctual, primitive, dangerous. It may overwhelm the patient. Unconscious material must be handled carefully. The patient should not act out. Impulses must be held in check. If deeper material comes out, the patient is in danger of doing strange things, falling apart, losing control, no longer having contact with reality, becoming beserk, crazy, psychotic. "The view of 'latent psychotic contents' leads to two dangerous errors: either one decides that the individual's feeling of difficulty and trouble had better be ignored (lest they 'blossom into' full psychosis), or one 'interprets' them and 'digs' them 'out'" (Gendlin, 1964, p. 143). Watch out for the monstrous instinctual material.

Given the situation, there is a way out. Effective building of the right therapist-patient relationship strengthens the patient's ability to tolerate instinctual material. The therapeutic alliance adds the therapist's weight to that of the patient, and thereby the patient is better enabled to cope with the exigencies of deeper processes. As the patient gains insight and understanding of the unconscious material, it is rendered less offensive and menacing. "By understanding the unconscious we free ourselves from its domination" (Jung, 1962, p. 122). This whole litany reinforces the theme of the patient as fragile and the deeper processes as dangerously powerful.

It is the therapist's own personal conceptualization which imposes and maintains the patient as vulnerable and fragile, and the deeper processes as dangerous, powerful, and overwhelming. The patient may or may not be this way, regard deeper personality processes that way, or maintain such a relationship with deeper processes. However, when the therapist conceptualizes the patient and the deeper processes in this manner, it is virtually impossible to consider internal encounters which move in the direction of integrative relationships between the patient and the deeper personality processes. Our therapeutic avenue is more than alien, more than hard to understand; it is drenched with danger.

Psychodynamic and psychoanalytic therapists are not the only ones who hold such a conceptualization of the patient and the deeper processes, but they are perhaps the most prominent holders of this view. In order to conceive of an internal encounter, a back-and-forth interaction which moves toward the achieving of a newfound integrative relationship, psychodynamic and psychoanalytic theory would have to accept wrenching changes in the conception of human beings and personality structure. All in all, those therapies which see patients as vulnerable to dangerous and menacing inner processes will tend to shy away from welcoming the idea of an internal integrative encounter.

These are some prominent theoretical concepts which are inappropriate for working the relationship between the patient and the deeper processes. I have only mentioned three such theoretical concepts, but the general idea is that the therapist will have a place for the internal integrative encounter only to the extent that the therapist's theoretical conceptualization includes appropriate concepts of deeper personality processes, their nature and relationship with the patient. We now turn to some therapeutic methods which, although they may appear useful for these purposes, are inappropriate for the experiencing of relationships between the deeper processes and the patient.

Methods of Experiencing the Relationship
With Deeper Potentials: Some Learnings
About What Does Not Work

What methods might the therapist be drawn toward using to "work" the experiential relationship between the patient and the deeper potential? There are methods which might appear to be useful, but which are generally ineffective.

Methods which constrain the interactive relationship to that between patient and external therapist. There are two categories of methods which are so inclusive and so common that they encompass a large proportion of what most therapists do most of the time—and both big categories of methods almost insure that there is little or no experiencing of the relationship between the patient and the deeper potentials. One category includes the many methods for constraining the patient to attend to, talk to, address the external therapist. In most therapies, the therapist uses methods of communication which force the patient to talk to the therapist rather than the insides, to interact and relate with the external therapist instead of the insides (Mahrer, 1980c, 1983a, in press; Moustakas, 1962).

When the communication methods enforce a dialoguing interaction between patient and therapist, what is foreclosed is the dialoguing interaction between patient and deeper processes. Patients may talk about their insides, they may find their deeper processes intriguing, but the channel of interactive communication is that of therapist and patient. It is therapist and patient who talk with one another about the patient's insides. All of the very common methods which therapists use to talk to patients, to insure that the interactive relationship is between therapist and patient attending to one another and talking to one another—all of these methods have little or no genuine usefulness in the experiential working of the relationship between patient and deeper processes.

The second category includes the range of blatant and subtle methods therapists use to encompass themselves in one role and patients in another. With rare exception, psychotherapy may be described as the use of methods of fulfilling one role and encompassing the partner in a complementary role (Bugental, 1964; Greben, 1977; Halpern, 1965; Lawton, 1958; Mahrer, 1976b, 1978e, 1983a; Mahrer & Gervaize, 1983; Towbin, 1978). Before the patient even arrives for the first appointment, most psychotherapists are ready to enact one role and outfit the patient with another. For example, I, the therapist, shall be your parent-protector against great anxiety. You are to be a drowning person without a lifeboat, sinking in an ocean of swarming anxiety: "First, he needs a parent-figure as a protector against gross anxiety. He may recognize or resist this, but either consciously or unconsciously he feels like a drowning man without a lifeboat" (Guntrip, 1969, p. 336).

Virtually every therapist tends to surround herself in some role, and the patient in another. The object-relations approach may have three or four, just as every approach has its own appropriate set of favorite role-relationships. This calls for effective methods to establish and maintain these roles. Indeed, a considerable proportion of the methods therapists use is instrumental in establishing and maintaining these important therapist and patient roles. The problem is that the net result is to constrain relationships to those between patient and external therapist, the one who is drowning and the parent-protector, the one who is so misunderstood and the great understander, the confused one and the mature exemplar, and dozens of explicit or implicit role-relationships. What is lost in all this is the relationship between the patient and the patient's deeper processes. In general, the methods used to establish and maintain therapist-patient role-relationships are irrelevant and confounding to the experiencing of relationships between patient and inner processes.

Reflective and interpretive "talking about," and the promotion of self-exploration, self-understanding, and insight. A great deal of psychotherapy involves the therapist making interpretive and reflective statements so as to promote the patient's exploring of self, understanding of self, and insight into what is held as deeper. Even when the desired consequences occur, little or nothing is done to heighten the internal encounter between patient and whatever is deeper, little or nothing to promote the experiencing of the relationship between patient and deeper processes. For our purposes, reflective statements and interpretive statements do not work.

Whether the therapist reflects or interprets, the prominent interaction is between therapist and patient rather than between patient and deeper processes (Mahrer, Brown, Gervaize, & Fellers, 1983; Mahrer, Durak, Lawson & Nifakis, in press), between the therapist who does the reflecting and interpreting, and the patient. There is virtually no integrative meeting of deeper potential and patient, no strong experiencing of the relationship between patient and deeper potential. Instead, there is typically muted experiencing as the therapist reflectively and interpretively talks to the patient about something inside the patient.

When therapists reflect, is there a consequent deeper exploration of the patient's inner self, as is held in client-centered thinking (Rogers, 1958, 1970a, 1970b, 1975)? Some researchers say yes (e.g., Highlen & Baccus, 1977; Hoffnung, 1969; Kurz & Grummon, 1972) and some suggest maybe not (e.g., Auerswald, 1974; Barnabei, Cormier, & Nye, 1974; Hill & Gormally, 1977). My impression is that reflections in large part draw interactive attention to the therapist who does the reflection, little or no exploration of what lies deeper in the patient, and a valued interaction for the patient who likes to talk about herself in the company of someone who is quite willing to do so (Mahrer,

Brown, Gervaize, & Fellers, 1983). While talking about oneself is valuable and treasured by many patients, it is a far cry from having an encountering relationship with deeper processes.

Nor will insight and understanding bring the patient into a strong-feelinged encounter with the deeper processes. The patient may learn all sorts of things about his genetic history, avoidances and defenses against some inner processes, the nature of supposedly internal conflicts, interesting attributions of deeper characteristics inside the patient, inventive explanations of how these characteristics arose and how they operate and function (e.g., Alexander, 1963; Arieti, 1962; Fenichel, 1954a; Whitehorn, 1959). The problem is that the internal encounter is not brought about " . . . by the therapist making inferences which become increasingly plausible when they are seen to fit more and more instances" (Angyal, 1965, p. 288). Understanding does not lead to the patient's becoming " . . . integrated within himself. . . . This synthesis can be achieved by experience and seldom simply by understanding" (Whitaker & Malone, 1953, p. 424). Insight and understanding have little or no bearing on the experiencing of the internal, back-and-forth integrative encounter between deeper process and patient.

Indeed, insight and understanding tend to keep the patient safely away from deeper processes. A little knowledge about what is deeper, a reasonable summary about what the insides are like—this makes for a comfortable safety moat between the deeper insides and the patient who has little or no desire to get any closer to whatever the deeper insides are like. At base, the operating domain of existential-humanistic theory (or the ego of psychoanalytic theory) have a great deal invested in refusing to get too involved with deeper personality processes (cf. Lacan, 1953, 1977).

Instead of this internal encounter, the patient typically gets involved in coping with the therapist's efforts to get the patient to see things the way the therapist does. The therapist's interpretive activity invites or pressures the patient to adopt the therapist's notions about what the patient is like. It is a struggle for control, a battle in which the therapist uses all the professional muscle he can garner, all sorts of tricks, seductive methods, authority, logic, guided questioning, threats and warnings, and incredible patience (the therapist may apply quietly relentless pressure for five to ten years)—all to get the patient to adopt the therapist's notions and ideas about what the patient is like (Claiborn, 1982; Labov, 1972; Labov & Fanshel, 1977; Searle, 1976). When the patient succumbs and adopts the therapist's notions about the patient's insides, these therapists like to speak about the therapeutic improvement which is thereby evidenced. From my perspective, the major change is in the therapist for whom it is very important that the patient value his words, cherish his ideas, look up to the therapist as a knowing person, a person to be respected, a person with special insight and understanding into the patient, a person whose statements are of real worth (Mahrer, Durak, Lawson, & Nifakis, in press). But the patient's adoption of the therapist's interpretive statements has little or nothing to do with the experiential relationship between deeper potential and patient, and between patient and deeper potential.

Even if the therapist is successful in the patient's achievement of insight and understanding, that which the patient sees and understands is not something with which the patient engages in an interactive encounter. Within psychoanalytic-psychodynamic approaches, the patient is to have insight and understanding into such topics as why and how the patient's "symptoms" arose and occur, how and why the patient interacts with the therapist in a particular manner, personality characteristics the patient is supposed to have, how and why the patient avoids and resists whatever the therapist believes the patient avoids and resists, why and how the patient came to be the sort of person the patient is, how and why the patient affects the therapist and others in particular ways. Other approaches try to get the patient to have insight and understanding into the guiding life philosophy, world view, cognitions, religious concepts, warping influences of culture, the effects of intrauterine life, the effects of society, and so on. Even if the patient has the sense of having achieved the desired brand of insight and understanding, it is virtually impossible to have a two-way encountering relationship with the idea that your attraction to exotic women comes from your attraction to your light-skinned, blonde mother, or with your inner wish to dominate your brother, or with your implicit notion that you must be loved to be of worth, or with your newfound memory of enjoying having your feet tickled when you were a child. The nature and content of that which the patient comes to understand and have insight into do not lend themselves to having an internal encountering relationship. Even if the patient gains insight and understanding, there is little or no experiencing of the relationship between the patient and the deeper processes, and there is little or no internal, integrative encounter.

In all of this, the patient is to have insight and understanding into whatever the external therapist says is there. While the external therapist may be quite accurate in seeing or inferring the warping influence of the patient's culture, repressed anger, or sexual wishes toward mother, all of this comes from the external vantage point. Accurate observations and inferences from the external vantage point may have little to do with accurate observations and inferences from the internal vantage point. Regardless of how accurate the external therapist is, the internal therapist will likely sense a different inner, deeper process. Accordingly, an internal encounter between the patient and her deeper personality processes cannot be achieved by the external therapist's observations and inferences, regardless of their accuracy from the external perspective.

Indeed, the very logistics of reflective and interpretive statements, of exploring the self, gaining insight and understanding, are geared to keep the patient from any genuine meeting or encountering of whatever is deeper. As long as the patient is attending to the reflecting-interpreting therapist, as long as the relationship is between the patient and the external therapist, there is little or no likelihood of a genuine encountering meeting between patient and deeper potentials. As long as the patient explores the self, maintains a stance of getting insight and understanding of the insides, that very posture is one of safe distance and separation. The whole strategy and its logistics work against an inner encounter.

Finally, from the experiential perspective, insight and understanding of deeper personality processes *follow* the internal encounter. Insight and understanding are frail means of promoting the internal encounter, but they are helpful signs that the internal encounter has occurred and has moved toward some degree of integration. From the experiential perspective, once the patient has an open, friendly, integrative relational channel with the deeper potential, then the patient is able to play with it, see it anew, describe what it is like, understand what it is and how it works. In experiential therapy, patients frequently express statements of knowing, seeing, and understanding their inner and deeper potentials after a richly effective internal encounter.

Methods of distancing, twisting, avoiding, manipulating the patient; being further removed from the patient than the patient is from the deeper processes. Instead of bringing about a close, integrative relationship between the patient and the deeper process, there are many commonly used methods which effect the opposite kind of relationship between the patient and therapist, one characterized by distortion, twisting, separation, distance, avoidance, control, manipulation. Indeed, if the patient (instead of the therapist) used these methods in ordinary relationships (instead of therapy), the patient would earn the right to be called deranged and lunatic, crazy and out of contact. As a means of bringing about an integrative internal encounter, these methods are supremely ineffective.

Many therapists take what patients say, and translate it into a substantially different system of meaning, decoded and changed from one set of symbols to another. When patients think they are saying one thing, the therapist asserts they are saying something altogether different. The real meaning emerges when the therapist rearranges it, imposes the therapist's translation system to it, and then comes out with the decoded meaning of what the patient is really saying. Yet if the patient were to reverse the process and do to the therapist what the therapist does to the patient, the therapist would accuse the patient of using all sorts of "mechanisms" indicative of "psychosis." Patients' statements

> . . . might just begin to be made to make some sense, if we change around what they say, cutting it up, taking it apart, joining what is separate, turning it around, upside-down, inside-out, back to front. The curious thing is that psychoanalysts ascribe these and other operations, viz. depersonalization, objectification, reification, scomatization, disavowal, denial, lack of understanding, lack of sympathy, lack of empathy, lack of affective rapport, undoing, condensation, projection, introjection, reversal, etc. to the objects upon whom they themselves employ them (Laing, 1982, pp. 48–49).

When therapists relate to the patient in this way, it is justified as being therapeutic; when patients relate to therapists in this way, it is called being psychotic. This way of relating to patients is not an effective means of promoting the close and integrative relationship between patient and deeper processes.

But these therapists go much further. Their way of listening to patients, of grasping and making sense of what patients say, rests upon a cognitive system which is exceedingly private and personal. Indeed, if the patient's cognitive system were equally private and personal, the therapist would regard the patient as "autistic." What is more, the therapist's highly personalized, highly private system of cognitive ideas is also exceedingly rigid and fixed. To what degree is it open to change? To what degree is it open to modification by the other person or by "reality"? If the patient's highly personalized, private ideas were so rigid, so fixed, so impervious to change by and from the therapist and "reality," the therapist would call the patient "paranoid." In a careful examination of the verbatim interchanges between a psychoanalyst and a patient, Laing (1982) concludes that the therapist equals or exceeds the patient in so-called "psychotic" distancings, twistings, avoidances, manipulations:

> It is difficult to imagine what the patient could say that could tell Bion anything he does not think he knows. . . . It is difficult to imagine anything anyone could say which would possibly reveal to Bion that his constructions could be wrong, or that they are a grinding machine which reduces any sense to total nonsense. It is difficult to fathom the difference between Bion's psychoanalytic phantasies and what is usually called a psychotic delusional system. . . . Change the way of listening to these interchanges, and the analyst's remarks seem to be coming out of the mouth of someone who could well be diagnosed as an extremely disturbed paranoid schizophrenic, hounding one of his persecuting victims to the ground. Honors for craziness are evenly divided (p. 52).

Many therapeutic methods are gross examples of such distancing, avoiding, maintaining of withdrawn and private thoughts, transmuting what the other does into one's own rigidly autistic conceptual system. Therapists observe the patient from afar, engage in private thoughts, and calculatedly put on a social-professional face. If the patient were to be this way, it would be called being withdrawn from affect, being split-off, psychopathic, paranoid.

Therapists commonly use methods which involve private clinical inferences about the patient, diagnosing the patient, assessing the degree of psychopathology and emotional illness. Therapists watch and observe the patient, note this and that, come to private conclusions about the meaning of this gesture, the significance of that pause, how this statement of the patient relates to that earlier statement, what psychodynamic is indicated by the piece of information, how these bits of data add up to a given psychodiagnostic inference. Such a relationship inflicts the most menacing distance between therapist and patient, behind which the therapist treats the patient as an object. This is the screeching manifestation of the same disintegrative relationship between the patient and his deeper processes, and such methods only reinforce the disintegrative relationship instead of promoting an integrative internal encounter.

Therapists use a host of methods to construct and maintain this disintegrative distance between themselves and their patients. Once the therapist arrives at the private inference that the patient is off-the-beam, sick, psychopathological, psychotic, the therapist keeps the patient at arm's length. The therapist is enjoined not to ask too many prying questions, to have private thoughts which must not be revealed to the patient, to avoid having a close relationship with the patient, to maintain a position which is impregnable and unwavering, to stay out of dangerous material lest the patient become delusional, to avoid threatening topics, to maintain a vigilant suspiciousness about patient ploys (cf. Bullard, 1960). Yet, if the patient were to relate to the therapist in precisely these ways, the therapist would call the patient psychotic, paranoid, sick.

Even when patients are not regarded as crazy, therapists maintain incredible masks and moats between themselves and the patient. Therapists listen to what the patient says and they observe what the patient does. Then therapists engage in private weighings, analyzings, clinical inferrings, removed plannings. On the basis of this private and withdrawn assessment, the therapist decides to say something to the patient (Banaka, 1971). The therapist decides that now is the time to offer the interpretation worded in this way; then the therapist carefully detects the response and decides to press a little further or to drop the effort. Yet all of this careful executive planning occurs far removed from the patient. Indeed, all the patient sees is what the therapist chooses to show. It may be a carefully preprogrammed script in which the therapist acts out the role of the good parent or treats the patient as if the patient were an adult or normal instead of a child or crazy. If the patient were to engage in removed private calculations and to present a distal mask to the therapist, the therapist may call the patient all sorts of pathological names.

Therapists generally rely on methods that place incredible distance between therapist and patient, that twist virtually everything the patient says and does, that avoid and pull away from the patient, that are highly controlling and manipulative. Whereas these methods are rationalized and justified in many ways, and whereas these methods may be useful for many other purposes, the overall conclusion is that they are grossly inappropriate for bringing about the integrative internal encounter. Central as these methods are for many therapists and therapies, for our purposes they do not work.

Methods of complicity with the patient in fighting against the deeper processes. Many therapies share the idea that the therapist is to join with the patient in fighting against the deeper process. There are many methods for joining in the patient's struggle to bury what is deeper, to push it down, get rid of it, keep it under control, overcome and conquer it, alleviate and reduce it, seal it off and keep it from making trouble. Such methods serve to reinforce the deeper process as bad, awful, dangerous, menacing, explosive, powerful, overwhelming. For our purposes, such methods act against the experiencing of the relationship between the patient and the deeper processes, and virtually insure that there will not occur an integrative relationship with the deeper processes.

Across the various therapies, deeper processes are represented in many vocabularies, from maladaptive habits to neurotic structures, from irrational beliefs to archetypes, from unadaptive learnings to instincts, from complexes to cognitions. However they are described, the methods are aimed at fighting against the bad deeper process. It is in the concrete methods used that therapies differ widely from one another. Yet they are commonly engaged in the good struggle to do something about the bad deeper process.

There are methods to extinguish and decondition it, to gain control over it, to attack it and replace it. There are methods of gaining insight and understanding into it. We can assuage the guilt and reduce the anxiety from it. We can relax ourselves against it, or use methods to strengthen defenses against it. We can learn methods of getting away from it or coping with it. We can redefine, relabel, redescribe it, and acquire new philosophies about it.

The problem is that when the therapist is complicit with the patient in fighting against the deeper process, the relationship is locked in as negative, hateful, menacing, oppositional, disintegrative, and the deeper process is locked in as bad, powerful, awful, something to be distrusted and conquered, overcome and sealed off. It does not matter if the methods are successful or not. There can be no encountering, no meeting, no genuine intimacy. There can be no friendly relations, no welcoming, no integrative relationships. All of the methods of complicity with the patient in fighting against the deeper process lose the opportunity to bring about an experiential encounter, an integrative relationship.

All in all, there are loads of methods which therapists use which are either inert, neutral, ineffective, or counterproductive in the work of experiencing the relationship between the patient and the deeper potentials. Leaving aside these methods, and building upon other methods which hold promise, we turn now from the introduction to the actual methods for experiencing the internal integrative relationship between the operating and deeper domains.

CHAPTER 4

Experiencing the Relationship With Deeper Potentials: Methods

WHEN THE PATIENT BEHAVES and talks, and when the therapist listens experientially, one of two things occur. The patient may activate or illuminate an operating or deeper potential within some meaningful situational context. When that occurs, the therapist uses methods which carry forward that experiencing (chapter 2). Or, the patient activates or illuminates the relationship between the patient and some deeper potential. When that occurs, the therapist takes on the identity of the deeper potential and relates directly to the patient. The process is one of furthering the experiencing of the relationship between the patient and the deeper potential, to engage in the internal encounter and to achieve an integrative relationship between the patient and the deeper potential.

The present chapter describes methods to accomplish the internal integrative encounter and answers this question: When the patient illuminates the relationship with the deeper potential, what methods are effective in achieving the internal, integrative encounter?

The first answer is that the therapist speaks to the patient with the voice of the deeper potential. This makes alive and real and exceedingly present the relationship between the patient and deeper potential. The second answer is that in speaking with the voice of the deeper potential, the therapist relates in very particular ways which result in the internal integrative encounter. Each of these will be described in turn.

THE DEEPER POTENTIAL TALKS TO THE PATIENT

Therapeutic magic occurs when the deeper potential actually comes to life and talks to the patient. Now the patient hears the voice of the insides, speaking directly to the patient. This is the magic, for there is now an alive experiencing of the relationship between the patient and the deeper potential.

Through experiential listening, the therapist senses a deeper potential, resonates to it, and lets it occur in her. Then she gives voice to it in speaking to the patient. What the therapist says is effective if it makes more alive the experiential relationship between the patient and the voice of the deeper potential. "The purpose of therapist responses is not being right; therapist responses aim to carry the client's experiencing further" (Gendlin, 1968, p. 212; see also Holt, 1968).

Existential-humanistic theory and experiential listening recognize that the patient will take some kind of disintegrative posture against whatever deeper potential is constructed. It is as if the patient pantomimes a defensive posture against an unseen inner antagonist. All the therapist does is make the inner antagonist come to life by stepping into its identity and saying and doing what the patient is already inviting the antagonist to do. In brief, the therapist speaks with the voice of the deeper potential and says what the patient invites the deeper potential to say. That is the method.

As a consequence, the relationship between patient and deeper potential springs to life. The deeper potential is now real, present, relating. This means that the patient will be caught in disintegrative feelings of tension and disharmony, of fear and fright, of being torn apart and invaded, of losing existence. The clash is on its way. When the deeper potential comes to life and talks to the patient, the relationship is given a strong dose of experiential life.

In what follows, I am organizing deeper potentials into three large categories merely for purposes of organization. While this organization makes some sense of the way most patients construct deeper potentials, the therapist in actual practice pays no attention to this threefold division. All the therapist does is to become the voice of the idiosyncratic deeper potential the patient constructs, and to speak to the patient who is postured against the relating deeper potential.

The Bad Deeper Potential

The patient is in a disintegrative posture against a deeper potential which is related to as bad (evil, menacing, animal, fiendish, crazy, wicked, craven, uncivilized). The therapist steps into the identity of the bad deeper potential and talks to the patient. Here are a few common postures the patient assumes in relation to the bad deeper potential, together with some examples of the therapist as the voice of the bad deeper potential.

Opposing the inner accusation. The patient assumes the posture of opposing (denying, fighting, assembling arguments against) some inner accusation. It is as if the patient is being accused by the bad deeper potential. In effect, the patient is saying "I am good" or "I am not bad" and the inner bad deeper potential says, "But I know that you really are bad." The patient says, "There is nothing wrong with that; that is an all right thing to do; I was justified in doing this; most people would have the same reaction, doing that is normal," while the accusing deeper bad potential is to say, "That is terribly wrong; that is an awful thing to do; there was no justification at all; no one would be that way; only people who are mad or bad would behave that way."

The therapist gives voice to the bad deeper potential which levels the accusation, as if the bad deeper potential were alive and actually leveling the accusation. As a consequence, the relationship is given experiential life, and the patient is now engaging in a very real relationship with the accusing, bad deeper potential.

Pt: (Indicating that he left his father and mother recently, after being their caretaker for years) I have to think of my own future. Never can tell, no. They'll get along. Sure they will. My aunt can take care of them if anything happens. (The inner voice puts the accusation into live words.)
T: If anything happens to them, it'll be your fault, you ungrateful, selfish, uncaring, lousy son!
Pt: I have to take care of my own future!
T: Bullshit!

She is describing a recent incident and then, at the end, she defends herself against an inner accusation of being cruel, vengeful, and vindictive:

Pt: She threw a pillow at me and I got hit in the mouth and my lip started bleeding from the zipper. It hit me. I was crying and I don't like her doing that. So I got mad at her. I called Chuck and asked him out. That always gets her hurt and serves her right. . . . (Here it comes.) I wouldn't have done that if she'd been nice to me!
T: How mean! How cruel! How awful!
Pt: No!
T: YES!!! CRUEL! MEAN! TERRIBLE PERSON!!!

He tells about the masturbation, and then defends himself against an accusation which no one had leveled at him:

Pt: Just about every day it happens. Secretly. We have sex and then I, well,
    it's been a long time, masturbate. . . . (In a defensive voice) Well, one
    thing. It doesn't mean I'm a pervert . . .
T: (Crisply) You are a pervert. That's the first sure sign.
Pt: (Taken aback) Huh?
T: And that's the second sign. That proves it. Pervert!! Pervert!!

*Fear and fright, shame and guilt, suffering and pain, rejection of
the bad deeper potential.* The patient constructs some bad deeper
potential and assumes a posture of rejecting it, suffering painfully with
it, having fear and fright toward it, having shame and guilt about it.
These and similar kinds of feelings are testimony to the presence of
a bad deeper potential about which the patient is entitled and justified
to have such feelings. For example, feelings of guilt and shame evidence
a kind of surreptitious alliance with the inner badness about which the
patient feels the guilt and shame (Boss, 1963; Buber, 1957; Fingarette,
1962; Mahrer, 1977):

> shame shows to the other precisely what it wants to hide from him. . . .
> Whether I blush because I myself have touched the inner border of sin,
> or because another has touched it, I always show him by blushing
> something which at bottom I do not wish to show at all, namely the
> "point" where the inner border of sin "in me" is touched (Binswanger,
> 1958c, p. 337).

The patient may have all kinds of fearful reactions to the deeper processes, which are constructed as powerful inner forces pressing to overwhelm the patient and to discharge into the external world:

> This is the model which psychoanalysis sets up for psychic processes
> in general. The situation always is that relatively primary biological
> needs — "instincts" or "drives" — are pressing for discharge, while oppos-
> ing trends develop and make themselves felt under the influence of the
> external world, and check the discharge or put it off . . . (there is
> a) . . . constant interplay between the instincts and the instinct-inhibit-
> ing or instinct-modifying institution . . . (Fenichel, 1954c, p. 25).

Suppose that the bad instincts or drives came alive and interacted
directly with the patient who is fighting against them, trying to inhibit
them and to keep them in check. Suppose that the patient is actually
confronted with the live form of that which the patient rejects as bad.
Suppose that the patient is actually confronted with the bad deeper pro-

cess about which the patient has fear and fright, guilt and shame. As the therapist speaks with that voice, and speaks directly to the patient, giving that bad deeper potential flesh and blood and presence, the consequence is the heightening of the relationship, an experiential enlivening of of the internal relationship.

Patients will suffer, have pain and anguish, all in relation to some deeper potential. I suffer in my aloneness. I hurt in my being a failure. I have anguish in my being unappreciated. I wallow in the pain of my not being a good parent. These postures construct and illuminate a deeper potential which is handed the role of validating the suffering. It knows that the patient absolutely deserves to be alone, has earned the right to be an abyssmal failure, is thoroughly entitled to be unappreciated, is even a worse parent than he believes (Bach & Goldberg, 1974; Hora, 1962; Pasternak, 1974). As the deeper potential comes to life, there is heightened experiencing of the relationship between the patient and the exceedingly bad deeper potential.

He is racked with guilt and shame as he tearfully confesses:

Pt: I have no idea what came over me. Crazy. Some impulse. She's my niece! She's 13 years old! I was a different person! What came over me? Oh my God! I'll never get over this. (Cries) My whole life, nothing like this. I can't face her. No one. Oh God. (There is a mischievous bad sexuality, an inner experiencing of sheer bad sexual enjoyment.)
T: Well, you ought to suffer! It's starting, isn't it? The wonderful sex is oozing out, oozing from every pore. Sex sex sex . . .
Pt: THAT'S ENOUGH!! (Here is the live relationship.)
T: IT'S JUST STARTING! THERE'S LOTS MORE ON THE WAY!!!

In the following, the patient defines and constructs a deeper potential which is simultaneously rejected as some way the patient would not be or as something the patient would not carry out.

Pt: My project is progressing, but I don't care. I guess I'm holding the fort. Tidying over situations. Swaine is doing all right. I can't complain about him. I mean I wouldn't put the blame on him. Not really. I couldn't do that. (If the deeper potential would love to complain, to put the blame on Swaine, to revel in the experiencing of attacking, assaulting, destroying, and if it were to speak to the patient, what might it say?)
T: It would be dee-lightful to complain about the son-of-a-bitch! C'mon, let's put the blame on him! It sounds like fun!
Pt: I couldn't be that way!
T: Wanna bet?

If the patient feels sufficiently bad about it, the inner, wicked deliciousness is voiced:

Pt: (Slowly and heavily, in a mood of depression) I know I'm to blame. A homewrecker. I told May (a friend of hers) about Gail (another friend) and Richard (May's husband). Started their marriage on the skids. Divorce. Everybody, like the rest of us. Ended it for them. I know it's my fault. (The therapist melds into a deeper experiencing of the malicious wickedness.)
T: (Lilting voice.) Yeess, you sly thing you! Veery clever!
Pt: (Silence) I didn't mean to . . .
T: (Connivingly, half-whispering) All the better, dearie, all the better. He-He-He!

Here are the opening steps of the experienced relationships between patient and bad deeper potentials. The bad deeper potentials are alive and talking to the patient. The relationship is now present, and the encounter is on its way.

The Deeper Void of Death

Some deeper potentials are responded to as if they were an inner void of death—a state of forever nothingness, the utter despair of inevitable hopelessness, the final giving up of everything, the illusionary nature of everything. The patient takes up some posture in relationship to the inner void of death, the vacuum, hopelessness. In order to give this relationship experiential life, the therapist speaks with the voice of the deeper void of death, and talks to the patient. All the therapist does is bring experiential life to what the patient postures against and thereby constructs. Here are some common ways that patients relate to a deeper potential of nothingness, vacuum, illusion, death, and here are ways in which the therapist talks to the patient as the voice of the deeper potential.

Struggles against the inevitable inner destiny. The patient struggles against the inevitable awful inner destiny, and the very struggle only validates the absolute certainty of the end, the awful state, the inevitable destiny. All efforts to ward it off are in vain. In the end, the patient must give up, must succumb to the inevitable inner destiny, the endless void of death. Whatever the concrete nature of the awful destiny, in the end there can only be its brand of death.

The patient struggles against insanity, derangement, madness, craziness (Esterson, 1978; Laing, 1975; Laing & Esterson, 1970). The patient struggles against aging, against the inner hatreds, the grotesque mediocrity, the ravages of the cancer, the twisted inner perversity. All struggles are in vain. In the end the patient will be overtaken. The inner destiny is intractable, inevitable.

He is compelled by the crippled, the twisted, the deformed, the handicapped. He is compelled by those who suicide, those who are down and out, the bums and bag ladies, the alcoholics sleeping in the alleys. He is compelled by his mother who went crazy, and all those who end up utterly mad. He is compelled by the insidious condition which slowly eats away at the flesh, at the brain, the nerves, the soul. Deep within, the inner voice whispers that it is only a matter of time. This is the way the patient is going to end up. This is the ineluctable destiny (Binswanger, 1958c; Tillich, 1952).

The therapist inhales the deeper potential and speaks with its voice and being. It is as if the deeper potential comes to life and says its words out loud, directly to the patient. Give up. The struggles are in vain. There is no way of avoiding the inner destiny. It is going to happen. The menacing inner state is intractable. The terrible inner condition is going to happen. There is no hope.

When the therapist gives voice to the inner inevitable destiny, the experiential relationship between the patient and the deeper potential comes to life. There is an experiential explosion. It is the beginning of the internal encounter.

He is struggling against the sensed inevitable aloneness, the terrible inner destiny of being utterly isolated:

Pt: I've always tried, wanted someone to be with me, special. I want that. I'm getting older. Never works out. I try to be . . . good. I always wanted someone close. (The therapist is the inner aloneness.)
T: Well, it's beginning to dawn. There'll never be anyone!
Pt: (Crying) No.
T: Finally sinking in. It's been coming the whole life. Alone!
Pt: (Crying) Oh no, no, no. (More sobbing)

The spectre of the homosexual life is returning as he battles against the terrible possibility:

Pt: My wife, she understands what happened to me before. I got a wife now, and my son. I have a right to live, going to get better. It'll be all right.

Everything passes. I'll be all right. Everyone gets scared, a relapse, every so often. I have a garden, owe it to my family. I have friends. No more of that anymore. We accomplished a lot, a house, family, I have a kid . . .

T: I give it about two months maybe, and then "the return of the queer." The right guy, a beautiful guy and back into the gay life!

Pt: I'd kill myself!!!

T: (Laughing) Boy would you miss a lot of great sex!!

The patient and inevitable inner destiny are now alive and engaged in an interactive relationship. The deeper potential is talking openly and directly to the patient, and the encounter is starting.

The inner futility of "efforts after." The patient makes efforts after, searchings for, strugglings for, workings toward, seekings after, hoping for, dreaming about. The assuming of such postures constructs and illuminates the inner void of death. All is in vain, hopeless, fruitless. In the end, success and attainment are impossible.

The patient's efforts rest on the idea that change can occur, things can get better, there is hope, he can be different, the awful state can be resolved, the problem can be alleviated (cf. Franks, 1974). In throwing himself into trying, he trusts that a desirable change will occur. In this " . . . excavation of the past" he hopes "for some 'archeological find' to bring about a miracle" (Angyal, 1965, p. 206). Such efforts and hopes construct and illuminate the inner futility. Nothing will work. There will be no change.

The patient is caught in the impasse, stuck in the dilemma, pulled this way and that way, trapped between this and that. The state is awful. Surely there is some way out. Such "efforts after" only construct and illuminate the inner futility. There can never be any way out, no relief or solution. It is the inner absoluteness of foreverness, of no change.

Efforts are directed after being with special others. It is the reaching out after oneness and intimacy, the searching for closeness, the fingers outstretched to the other one, the strugglings after closeness. It is searchings after the caring therapist, the long journeys to find the special one with whom the I-thou relationship can be achieved. Yet the very "efforts after" betray the inner futility. It is all in vain. The searchings are for nothing. There is really no one like that. It is all fluffy dreams.

There are thinning hopes of becoming someone really special, of having that wonderful feeling of having made it, of having the most important person in one's life return again, of realizing all the potentials which are there inside, of being transformed into the wondrous new personality, of being admired and respected. Yet all these "efforts after" have a soft festering underbelly. One will never become special. There will be no success. It is all over. Those are groundless illusions. You are a failure. There will be no change.

There are almost desperate efforts to have some impact, to have an effect on someone. The patient must be acknowledged, loved, cherished, renowned, prized, feared, respected, coped with, dealt with. All of these efforts have in common the yearning and urgency to have an effect, some impact. Even if it is painful, there is a validating that one is a person, with presence and effects. But the inner futility is that one is a cipher, a zero, a nonentity. One does not count. Basically you are invisible, a nothing, without impact or effect, a vacuum. Even if "they" plot against her and have evil intent toward her, still " . . . the ideas of reference are used by her as proof that others are still interested in her and paying her some attention. . . . Although such attention is unpleasant, it assures her that she is not totally meaningless to them" (Fleischl, 1958, p. 26). But the inner voice pronounces that she is totally meaningless, invisible and without impact, nothing.

As the therapist gives voice to the inner futility of all the "efforts after," as the deeper potential comes to life and talks to the patient, there is a galvanized experiencing of the relationship between the patient and the deeper potential. It becomes alive and real. The experiencing of the relationship has wrenched forward.

In her efforts after life and freedom from the gluey muck of problems, her insistence on life constructs and illuminates the deeper potential of death, utter depression, despairing futility:

Pt: (Depressed) I don't want to end it all. . . . I don't know . . . (pause). There are times when I get out of it. I'll get out of it. I know I have a lot to live for. . . . A lot to do. I have things to do. I have to! I gotta keep thinking of these things. I'm young yet . . .
T: There's no use to struggling. It doesn't matter. It won't be long now. It'll be all over. Quiet and peaceful. All over.
Pt: (Whispering) I can't think that.
T: Sure! It's easy. Listen. There's no use to struggle anymore! It's useless! It'll be over soon! How's that, pretty good?

There is the groundless hope that everything will now be better, that this is the turning point, and the illuminated deeper potential voices the grim truth:

Pt: My father doesn't affect me anymore. That's the big difference. I know I'm cured. That's the turning point. I know I'm going to be all right. Sure. Things will be good now. Sure. I know that. This is the change I've been praying for. I'll be better.

T: Never. Silly dreams. All lies.

Pt: What's wrong with you? You have no faith in me! Is there something wrong with you? What do you know? What the hell's wrong with you? How can you say that? Damn you!

T: Never. Silly dreams. All lies.

Desperate clingings to the precious. Patients may desperately cling to precious basic truths about the world, about life, about the way things are, about themselves. The very desperateness of the clinging constructs and illuminates the deeper void, that these precious truths are groundless, ephemeral, illusory, wrong, empty.

Patients desperately cling to precious relationships, essential others. The precious other may be the spouse or parent whom the patient cherishes or with whom the patient has fought for years. It may be the family, the child, the lover, the enemy. Yet the desperate clinging constructs and illuminates the iron inevitability of giving it up, and with that comes the gripping incursions of death, suicide, giving into utter depression and numbness.

The precious may consist of the carefully maintained recriminations against the awful parent, hurtful but precious justifications for the way one has led the whole life. Mother really is hateful and vindictive; father really is an irrational maniac. These festerings are kept alive through careful nurturing over decades, and they justify the way you have always treated your mother, the way you act toward your father. Yet underneath the desperate clinging to the precious recriminations is the yawning emptiness to the charges, the essential fruitlessness of having fed the recriminations for so many years.

For some patients there is a pressured urgency to invest their selves with preciousness. There is an almost desperate clinging to their selves as precious. They must bathe the self in loving attention, discover wonderful nuances about the self, be unendingly fascinated by their self. It is this desperate clinging which betrays the inner voice of the deeper potential. The inner voice expresses the utter futility of it all, the emptiness, fruitlessness. It is all so groundless. There is no real self. It will not last. It is an illusion.

There may be a desperate clinging to the precious idea. Job security is the most important thing in life. Dedication and devotion to God and the Church are the precious essentials. Faith in the government, the movement, the revolution, the industry; it is this faith which keeps one going. The most precious thing is pleasure in a job well done. There are all sorts of preciously maintained ideas that are the essential keystones of one's life (Dreikurs, 1967; Ellis, 1962, 1971). But the very desperation and unyielding clingings to these ideas construct and illuminate the deep void of death: The idea is wrong, mistaken, groundless, no longer appropriate, illusory, ephemeral, fluff.

As the therapist breathes life into the deeper potential, gives it immediacy and presence, the relationship between the patient and the deeper potential comes alive. It is given a charge of experiencing. Here is the beginning of the interaction between the patient and the deeper potential.

Pt: Well, my mother and I fight sometimes, but when she comes and visits for a few days, I cry when she goes. I know I depend on her. She's so important to me. It's so good being able to tell her things. That's . . . she's my best friend. I've always had her to talk to. I'm lucky. Others don't get along with their parents, and I'm lucky. I don't know how I could ever . . . well, I need her. Couldn't get along. Nice just knowing she's there. I should call her more. (The deeper potential is the other side of all this, the limbo of being without her, the emptiness of life with no mother.)

T: Better get used to being without her. She'll die soon. It'll be all over, or, say, maybe the kid'll grow up and . . . and . . .

Pt: I'll always be with my mother! Always! Nothing's going to be any different! Ever! I need her! I have to have her! I don't know what I'd do if anything happened!

T: Drop the bitch!!! Who needs her!?!?!?

His desperate clinging to the truth of the guiding life principle illuminates the deeper potential which solemnly pronounces its utter uselessness:

Pt: So in maybe eight years, then I'll retire. I've been faithful to the party. Whole life. Since maybe 15. No, 16. Do what the superiors want. Serve them. I've always been someone to count on. Worked hard, yes sir. Real hard. They could always count on me. Faithful. Someone had to do the ground work. They needed someone and I was the one. Lived it, from the day I was a man. Been there to do the work, serve the party, faithful. It's worked well. Paid off. Satisfied.

T: Very sad. What a fool. Another sucker.

Pt: You think I wasted my life? Think I've been a fool? Think I threw my life away? They stand by the ones who worked for them! They are good!

> That's how things work. Serve them right and they stand by you! I
> believed that all my life!
>
> T: Oh shit, here it comes. Another fool who wasted his life and now it's too
> late.

Here are instances where the patient constructs relationships with
a deeper emptiness, fruitlessness, nothingness, void of death. As the
identity of the deeper potential, the therapist gives voice, talks to the
patient, and thereby promotes the experiencing of the relationship between the patient and the deeper potential.

The Dreaded Polarity

The third category of related-to deeper potentials contains all those
deeper potentials which are polarities of what the patient is. As psychoanalytic psychology typifies the roots of bad deeper potentials, and as
existential psychology typifies the roots of the deeper void of death,
it is Jungian psychology which typifies the dreaded polarity.

The way the patient operates and functions and behaves may constitute one pole, with the deeper potential being the other pole. While
the operating domain is kindly and considerate and sweet, the deeper
potential is brutal and sadistic and violent, or perhaps oozing with
grotesque sexuality, or stoic and cold. Ordinary logic helps very little
in getting at the nature and content of the deeper polarity. What does
work is careful experiential listening. What works even less than ordinary logic is some predetermined polarity firmly implanted in the deeper
personality processes by the force of some theory. Existential-humanistic theory takes the position that there are no universal deeper or basic
personality processes (Mahrer, 1978a) and that the best way of knowing this particular person's deeper potentials is by knowing this particular person's deeper potentials. Many theories, on the other hand, give
us ready-made universal polarities of maleness and femaleness, good
and bad, topdog and underdog, homosexuality and heterosexuality,
yearnings for closeness-intimacy and independence-distance, social interest and personal interest.

Whatever the nature of this particular deeper potential, the therapist
merely gives it voice, and expresses this in direct interaction with the
patient. When this happens, the experiencing moves ahead. Patient and
deeper polarity become engaged in the encounter.

Humanly impossible existences. One of the saddest and most painful
polarities is that in which the patient has no other way than to pursue

an existence which is humanly impossible. Whatever the nature of the deeper potential, the patient is caught having to be an operating potential which is humanly impossible. In an eloquent analysis of such a person, Binswanger describes a patient who must attain the polarity of a deeper flawed humanness, with its taking up space, having to eat and sweat and react and defecate. The polar existence is to be free of all human, bodily, creature characteristics, to be invisible. It cannot be done. "A person who wants to lead such a humanly impossible existence we have every right to call deranged" (Binswanger, 1958c, p. 339).

The quest is impossible from the outset, for the patient must attain a state whose very nature is unrealizable. For example, in order to shoot away from the dreaded inner polarity, the patient is forced to be totally free of being born of parents; one must become God, or right and correct about everything, or unaffected by the passage of time, or totally free of the effects of others, or unsurpassed by anyone, or the source of all creativity, or not having to sleep or eat or take up space or defecate or breathe or die. This is what Binswanger refers to as the Extravagant Ideal in which the person is impossibly caught:

> The Dasein now stakes everything on "maintaining" this stance, on — in other words — pursuing this ideal "through thick and thin." The ideal is Extravagant in that it is completely inappropriate to the total life situation and does not, therefore, represent a genuine means. On the contrary, it sets up an insurmountable wall in the path of existence. The Dasein can no longer find its way back out of this Extravagance and instead becomes more and more deeply enmeshed in it (Binswanger, 1967, p. 254).

In the following, the young man must be pure of mind, absolutely clear of thought, perfectly logical, free of conceptual error:

Pt: Dreams would be a good therapeutic vehicle. I have been collecting my dreams for the past two years. When I wake I record the dream as is, and work on them daily. Then I meditate for two hours. Let my thoughts flow and I stand aside and contemplate them as they pass. The day is just play for me. I do it mechanically. Like now, for example, I am observing the words I am saying, and cataloguing the thoughts. It is pure awareness of the flow of thoughts. Even as I speak, I am cataloguing the thoughts and selecting out the interesting ones. I save them by a form of mentation in the evening. They are never lost. I review them all each evening as I enter into pure awareness of the thoughts during the day. (The therapist is filled with the deeper pole underneath this humanly impossible existence, and speaks to the patient directly.)

T: Well, what do you expect from a brain-damaged, confused little kid. Basically a dumb, forgetful slob.
Pt: No!!! Not me! My father was! He was a low-class drunk!
T: Ah, the old story! Like father, like son. Worse, the kid's worse!

She speaks in a child's voice, and is driven toward being the most prized little jewel:

Pt: What I like most of all is getting older. Really! I don't age! I think the way I did when I was five, and my body is ageless. Nothing happens to it, and I'm nearly 40. I'm so fortunate. I don't think I'll ever die. I know I won't. Oh . . . they adore me. Everyone does! Everyone wants to, they wait for me, and they study me. Ha! I know I lived before! I know! I've had existences for 500 years. More! Always the same. I've been the same for 500 years. Perpetual. Ageless. I am an angel who lives each century, and I've known my secret from the time I was born. Even when I was a baby I knew I'd been here before and I will keep on existing for all time. (The therapist voices the dreaded deeper polarity and the impossibility of the polarity she pursues.)
T: When you're in the ground, all the worms'll eat your old dirty flesh, the sagging dry skin, the dead body, bloated and . . . the worms'll eat you. They don't care.
Pt: (An even more pronounced little girl voice) Nothing's gonna happen to me . . .
T: (Interrupting) The dead body, old and sagging, dry dead flesh, no eyes, 'cause the worms ate the eyes, and you can pretend all you want, go ahead, keep it up. You're aging right now, and it's only a matter of time, time, time, aging, aging, coming closer to being old, old, old, and dying, dying, dead, dead . . .

In being the dreaded deeper potential, the therapist illuminates the human impossibility of the operating polarity the patient pursues. While the patient clings to the humanly impossible pole, the therapist gives voice to the inner dreaded polarity, and the relationship is moved into heightened experiential life.

Presenting the polar face. The patient shows one pole, and that betrays the deeper other pole. There is a kind of insistence in being this way, a having-to-be this way, and often the patient may be quite successful in being this polar way. It is the press, the need, the having-to-be that distinguishes this operating potential as one pole of a dreaded deeper other pole. Another distinguishing feature is the social desirability of the face. The patient must be sweet and kind, youthful and attractive, warm and understanding. What is shown is valued and welcomed, is good and fine. But there is something not quite right about this, a superficial thinness and hollowness. He is kind and sweet, but it is as if there is something more, something added. She works at being youthful and attractive, yet something is missing, it does not ring quite true. There is always some hint of a deeper polarity. It is as if one would not be surprised by witnessing the dreaded inner polarity to this presented, forced, socially desirable outer pole.

In his early sixties, thick white hair contrasting with a ruddy face, he is celebrating his attractive virility with the young women:

Pt: I'm more sober now, more rational. More solid. These young kids today! The women, they take to me. Look up to me, admire a man who's solid, made it, takes care of himself, yeah. They want to entertain me. Can I entertain you? (Laughs) But I shouldn't, by all the rules. I'm older. There's this girl Kelly. Just beautiful. Lovely the way she walks. What a peach. But she's married. (The experientially listening therapist is filled with the inner polarity, the sexless aloneness.)

T: Well, you live it up with the pretty young girls. I know what it's like to be alone, really alone.

Pt: No! That's not the way to live. That'll kill you! Gotta get that out of your head! There are lots of girls just waiting to be with me! Blondes, lovely ones! I love these young girls! (The encounter has started to take shape.)

T: So enjoy them! I'll just sit here, all by myself, all alone, and watch the old fart make a damned fool out of himself.

She is a private practitioner who is celebrating her mental soundness:

Pt: I really don't know why I started, but four years of analysis was what did it for me. I don't get caught in problems and I know I'm solid now. I offer my patients a rock, a solid reality. It's nice being grounded. Like, really knowing what's what, not getting myself caught. The nice thing is feeling solid. Knowing I'm on top of things now. My life is in order. I like that. (There are bubblings of a polar crazy wildness, a free spirit, a delightful freneticness. It emerges through the voice of the therapist.)

T: OK! Now can we take off our clothes and screw like hell?

Pt: (Erupts into very hard laughter) You're crazy! (More hard laughter)

T: Not as crazy as you are, you flake!

There is the celebration of feeling and closeness and intimacy. Yet it is but a thin forced veneer, hollow, and illuminates the inner polarity:

Pt: When I was in Manchester I stopped over to touch base with Gart. A marvelous fellow, warm and human. I treasure the openness and the intimacy, one touching the other. We met each other and communed. I think my best friends are my feelings. I'm open to my feelings. I treasure my friends. It's connecting, really connecting with each other. My insides are open. (As the therapist allowed these words to come from her, there emerged a deeper polar coldness and hardness, an unfeelinged smooth metallic surface.)

T: What a beady cold fish you are.

Pt: (In direct hard threat, voice crisply surgical) We'll have to talk about this.

T: What's to talk about? You're a cold fish now. You always have been a cold fish, and you're always going to be a cold fish.

The patient is already at one pole, defensively postured against the other deeper pole. By speaking to the patient with the voice of the deeper polarity, the therapist enlivens the patient's experiencing of the relationship with the deeper potential. The internal encounter is begun.

In this section I have placed deeper potentials into three large categories: bad deeper potentials, deeper potentials which are the void of death, and dreaded inner polarities. This threefold division is merely for the sake of convenience. What is uppermost for the therapist is to listen experientially for those occasions when the patient is engaged in a relationship with a deeper potential, and for the therapist to give voice to that deeper potential. As the therapist speaks to the patient, interacts and relates with the patient, therapeutic magic occurs. There is a deepening experiencing of the relationship between the patient and the deeper potential. That is the method and that is the consequence.

But talking to the patient only starts the internal integrative encounter. The balance of this chapter shows how the therapist talks to the patient and what the therapist does to move the experiencing relationship into an internal integrative encounter.

THE DEEPER POTENTIAL ENGAGES IN AN INTEGRATIVE ENCOUNTER WITH THE PATIENT

The deeper potential (or rather the therapist as the voice of the deeper potential) talks to the patient in very particular ways designed to fuel the experiential relationship, intensify the disintegrative relationship, and bring it to a state of integration. In other words, the therapist engages in an encounter with the patient in such a manner as to achieve integration between patient and deeper potential. How does the therapist do this? What does the therapist say?

Merely having the deeper potential come alive and talk to the patient is not sufficient to bring about the integrative relationship. It is necessary, but it is not sufficient. The therapist must relate along integrative lines which culminate in the integrative relationship.

What does the therapist do? The therapist is the integrative, good-feelinged form of the deeper potential, engages in a wholesale encounter which culminates in a clashing peak, and proceeds on to an integrative relationship. There are at least six interlocking threads comprising the internal integrative encounter: (a) The therapist openly and freely expresses her deeper truth about the patient. (b) When the patient runs from the encounter, the therapist attends fully to that avoidance. (c) It is as if the patient is divided into two persons or "I's", with the patient as one and the therapist as another, and the therapist regards each as separate and equal. (d) The therapist talks to the inner I-ness as distinct and separate from the rest of the operating domain. (e) The therapist likes and loves the patient. (f) The therapist is tough and steadfast in going through the encounter. Each of these six components will be described as illustrations of how the integrating deeper potential relates to the patient.

By Expressing the Deeper Potential's Truth About the Patient

Traditional psychotherapy has three referential meanings in the game of insight. One involves the external therapist's seeing the truth about the patient and telling (interpreting) this to the patient. A second is when the patient has insight into the way he acts and behaves, functions and operates, relates to others, including the therapist. A third is insight into his own deeper personality processes. The patient sees inside, down into the bowels of the intrapsychic inner psychodynamics and deeper processes.

There is a fourth referential meaning of insight, one which is essentially outside the bounds of most traditional psychotherapies. It refers to the way in which the deeper personality processes see and understand (have insight into) the patient. Some psychoanalytic theorists conceptualize the ego as a more or less intact entity, with some of its own intrinsic characteristics, as not wholly a derivative of the id, as having its own intrinsic processes such as memory and perception (Erikson, 1950; Hartmann, Kris, & Loewenstein, 1947; Rapaport, 1958). In a symmetrical conceptual shift, Ouspensky (1949, 1957), Wilber (1979, 1980, 1981) and Perls (1969b, 1970, 1976) represent those who are illuminating the deeper processes as their own centers of gravity, as having their own consciousness, their own ways of seeing and understanding the patient, their own personhoods. Here is a radical switch whereby insight, understanding, and truth can go either way!

In this conception, the deeper potential knows the patient far more intimately than the external therapist, the patient herself, the patient's mother or grandfather or God or the devil or ex-spouse or childhood best friend or closest enemy. The deeper potential knows the patient because the deeper potential developed the patient, was there before the patient, and is always there with the patient (Mahrer, 1978a). The deeper potential knows what the patient is like from inside out. It knows the repulsive truth about the patient, every little frailty and weakness, every nasty and petulant inclination. No matter who or what the patient is like, the deeper potential can dare to speak the truth: "Good God, you really are off your rocker! . . . You are so ugly, so very, very ugly! . . . What a free-loading parasite you are, just living off your sister! . . . You are such a baby, always getting others to make decisions for you!"

While the deeper potential gauges the patient from its highly limited perspective, the assessment is sensitive and accurate. All the deeper potential knows is what it is, its own experiential vantage point, and nothing more. If the deeper potential is the experiencing of not caring, leaving go, rejecting, then it has microscopic insight into the patient from that perspective alone. It is supremely sensitive to the patient's not caring, everything having to do with leaving go, the whole literature on rejection. It will accurately see what it is present to observe. This is the incisive but narrow vector of the truth expressed by the deeper potential.

What the deeper potential sees is accurate, narrow, and restricted to what the deeper potential is capable of seeing. If the deeper potential is the experiencing of not caring, leaving go, rejecting, it is accurately and sensitively on target in sniffing that out in whatever the operating domain does. Accurate from its perspective? Yes. But the deeper potential is also free to be (from the perspective of the operating domain) far-fetched, wild, ridiculous, outlandish. What the deeper potential sees is its truth, and its truth may be expressed in extreme and absurd ways, as exaggerated, caricatured, burlesqued, enlarged, overstated (Farrelly & Brandsma, 1974; Greenwald, 1974; Kopp, 1974; Poland, 1971; Searles, 1963; Whitaker, Felder, Malone, & Warkentin, 1962).

In expressing its truth about the patient to the patient, the consequence is the heating up of the relationship. What the deeper potential says is true, uncannily true, and that juices up the relationship. In addition, the deeper potential is attacking the patient with its truth, with the truth from the deeper potential to the patient. This truth is different from that sensed by the patient, for it is a truth which is not soaked in the patient's disintegrative relationship toward the deeper potential. Free of that disintegrative sheath, the deeper potential's truth has a qualitatively different grain. As a consequence, the internal encounter becomes more intensified.

Let us pick up with the patient who defends herself against the inner accusation of being cruel, vengeful, and vindictive:

Pt: She threw a pillow at me and I got hit in the mouth and my lip started bleeding from the zipper. It hit me. I was crying and I don't like her doing that. So I got mad at her. I called Chuck and asked him out. That always gets her hurt and serves her right. . . . I wouldn't have done that if she'd been nice to me! (The relationship with the deeper potential is invoked, and the deeper potential hurls its truth at the patient.)

T: How mean! How cruel! How awful!

Pt: No!

T: YES!!! CRUEL! MEAN! TERRIBLE PERSON!!!

Pt: No I'm not!

T: Of course you are! You got a mean streak a mile wide.

Pt: That's not true!

T: OK, how wide? Wider than anyone in the family! You're a mean, cruel, vindictive bastard.

Pt: No! I can't let people walk all over me!

T: You're the one who walks all over people. Look what you did to poor little Ruthie! An innocent little pillow fight and you walk all over her! What you did to her was mean, mean mean mean! You are mean! Really mean! Mean mean mean!

Pt: (Sullen silence) I don't want to talk about it.

T: (Deflections have no effect.) Ha! I must be doing pretty well. How about it, you vindictive bitch, is it OK if I go on, or are you going to start being mean to me for telling a little bit of the truth about you?

Pt: (Lightening up a bit) A little bit?

T: Damned right. I know how tight and hot and angry you can get. I know how you can hold a fucking grudge for years and how you'd like to destroy people who did you wrong. I know, and so do you!

Pt: YES I AM! (Nose-on-nose encountering)

T: Stop screaming! That's mean!

Pt: Yes I'm tough . . .

T: (Interrupting) Mean, not just tough, mean, and cruel, not just tough, cruel, really cruel, a really cruel mean tough sonovagun!

Pt: I'D LIKE TO WIPE 'EM OUT!

T: DAMNED RIGHT YOU WOULD, AND YOU'RE THE KIND OF PER-
SON WHO CAN DO IT!

Pt: WELL WHAT'S WRONG WITH THAT! I HAVE A RIGHT TO!

T: You don't even need a right to!!! Cause you are basically a cruel kid! Why
I know that every wonderful little nerve in your little body was on alive,
exciting edge when you got Chuck to go with you. I know that!

Pt: Serves her right! I wish I did more!

T: Oh! More! More! She's capable of doing lots more! Lots more! What do
you expect from a terrible person like you?

Pt: OK! YES! I AM A ROTTEN DAUGHTER!

T: THE WORST KIND OF ROTTEN DAUGHTER! A MEAN CRUEL
ROTTEN DAUGHTER! (Whispering) You don't have to admit everything, you know.

Pt: I WANTED TO DESTROY THEM! IF I HAD A CHANCE I ALWAYS
WANTED TO MAKE THEM COME CRAWLING TO ME AND
BEG MY FORGIVING. AND I WOULD NEVER! NEVER! I WANT-
ED TO MAKE THEM SQUIRM! SAY THEY WERE SORRY! I
WANTED TO MAKE 'EM CRAWL!!!

T: See! You're the worst kind! Mean and cruel and you never really were good
at it! You'd never win the award! You're just full of great possibilities
but no do!

Pt: OH FUCK!!!!!!

The encounter has heated up and has moved toward some degree
of integration. As the deeper potential splashes out the truth, the relationship locks in and moves toward integration. Sometimes there is
a high-feelinged explosion of integration between the patient and the
deeper potential:

Pt: My Dad's real sick, headaches, turned out, a tumor. Going to die of it.
I know I should go back to Edmonton to visit. Got a letter. No call,
they don't call. Like I'm not part of the family. I been thinking about
my Dad. Haven't seen him in three years, maybe more, no, three years.
He maybe's going to die. I should go home. He's my Dad. I should,
ought to. (There is an invoked deeper sense of distant coldness which
speaks its truth.)

T: Good show! Good act! I mean, for a cold-hearted kid, you sounded pretty
convincing!

Pt: (Sudden hard burst of laughter) I wonder what it's like to be honest. (Continued gales of hard laughter)

T: May I have a try? See how this goes over. You are a cold-hearted, nasty
critter who lies to yourself about how much you care about some guy
who claims he's your father. Basically you don't give a damn!

Pt: My heart is pounding! It's pounding!! Damn!! It's going a mile a minute!

T: Hey! Maybe I'm getting close to the truth!

Pt: I hate hearing those words! My God, it's like my chest is going to burst!

T: Take it easy! No! I'm wrong! I'm sorry I said it! I take it all back! You're a loving son! I was just kidding!

Pt: It sounded like it came from right inside my chest! "You don't give a damn about him. You are cold." Yes, shit! I am cold! Yes I am! I don't have any feelings about him at all! Except my chest feels like it's going to burst! (Laughs hard) What the hell is so wrong with being cold! It sounds honest! I think I'm having an honesty attack! Cold! I am cold! Yes! I am cold!

The therapist speaks with the identity and voice of the deeper potential and merely expresses the deeper potential's simple truth about the patient, saying it directly to the patient. Here is one component way of engaging in an integrative encounter with the patient. The charged, incessant leveling of the truth heats up the internal encounter and moves it increasingly in the direction of an integrative relationship.

By Feeding the Avoidances Back Into the Encounter

Because the deeper potential is so very ready to engage in this full relationship, what is magnified and illuminated is every movement by the patient to get away, to escape from the encounter, to pull back from stronger experiencing of the relationship. Indeed, once the deeper potential and patient lock horns, any avoidance by the patient is thrust into bold relief.

When the patient and deeper potential engage in the relationship and the relationship starts to heat up, what can the patient do to avoid the looming encounter? Whether the encountering relationship is just starting or reaching a peak clash, patients will use a number of methods to avoid and get away. Five of these are especially common:

• The patient will leave the encountering relationship and go to other involvements. The patient will slide into some other scene or situational context. Instead of grappling with the therapist-as-deeper-potential, the patient will remember what it was like with her little puppy when she was a little girl, or she will fret about the low back pains she is getting lately, or she will be so pleased about the new neighbor who finally wants to get the yard looking nice the way it should. This is one avoidance ploy.

• The patient will try to disengage the therapist from being the voice of the deeper potential and to place the therapist into the role of external therapist. As the encounter is building, the patient says, "Could you tell me what this is for, what good it will do? . . . Do you really mean that, Dr. Hogan? You sound like you're just kidding me. . . . Did you say that just to upset me? Is that what a therapist does? Dr. Washburn never did anything like that." The patient avoids the encounter with the deeper potential by trying to engage with an external therapist.

• The patient shuts down, withdraws, envelopes himself in silence, sleep or a trance-like state. These are not filled with strong feelings. They are not characterized by anger or hurt or anguish or intense longing. Instead, they are benumbing states designed to cool down the encountering relationship. The patient drifts into a lazy flow of ideas, thoughts, images, and associations. Or the patient falls asleep. Or the patient enters into a low-feelinged silence or a trance-like state of muted experiencing. Sometimes the patient slides into a state of slow, heavy depression and gloom.

• The patient uses crazy ploys designed to place safe distance between patient and the encountering deeper potential. Each patient has favorite crazy ploys for such an emergency. They are bizarre, weird, lunatic, deranged, and thereby aimed at severing the relationship with the therapist (cf. Haley, 1963). The ploy may consist of becoming absolutely uncomprehending or confused or falling to pieces, all aimed at cutting off the encountering relationship (Angyal, 1965; Caruso, 1964). The patient hears voices, becomes his dead mother, talks in jumbled words, has crazy images, is a screeching infant, is attacked by alien creatures.

• The patient falls into dramatic bodily states where attention is wrenched away from the encountering deeper potential and onto some compelling bodily event. Suddenly the patient has a splitting headache or searing chest pains, shakings and tremblings and fits and seizures and muscular cramps. The patient vomits or becomes paralyzed. There are spells of dizziness, incredible heat or cold, skin irritations, loss of bodily integrity.

When the patient avoids the internal encounter in such ways, the therapist merely targets the encountering interaction upon the avoiding patient. It is as if the deeper potential were to play with the patient's attempts to escape ("There you go again, trying to sneak away!"). Or the deeper potential takes it over and joins the patient in the avoidance ("Ah! The old 'crazy ploy.' May I join you? I'm not as good as you, but I do a pretty good job of 'word salad.' Step aside my son, and watch me put on my routine."). The therapist may bathe the avoidance in the light of the deeper potential ("Little children are always able to have temper tantrums. If you're going to be silent, at least be honest, you little child. Hold your breath! C'mon, do it right. Hold your breath!"). The therapist may anticipate the avoidance and get it ready for the patient ("Oh oh, here's where your stomach gets churny and you may vomit. This is the place. I accused the little darling of being a manipulating wizard, and she generally throws up. So let's get it over with and then we can get back to the important business."). The therapist weds the patient and the avoidance forever ("When the angel of death comes to take away old Pierre, 87 years old and creaky, and says, 'Now's the time, Pierre, I'm taking you to heaven,' you'll say, 'Yes, I love apple pie, and my sister is an apple, and everyone has sisters, but I prefer motor scooters."). The therapist playfully attacks the avoidance ("If you ever run away like that again, if you ever stop and turn to silly memories like that, I'm going to tell your wife that you ran over her cat and lied to her about it, and then I'm going to steal your whole gun collection.").

Instead of getting away, the patient is thereby more deeply enmeshed in the internal encounter. In effect, avoidances of the encounter are used to fuel the encounter even further.

We pick up with the patient who is racked with guilt and shame as he tearfully confesses:

Pt: I have no idea what came over me. Crazy. Some impulse. She's my niece! She's 13 years old! I was a different person! What came over me? Oh my God! I'll never get over this. (Cries) My whole life, nothing like this. I can't face her. No one. Oh God. (There is a deeper mischievous sexuality, an inner experiencing of sheer sexual enjoyment.)

T: Well, you ought to suffer! It's starting, isn't it? The wonderful sex is oozing out, oozing from every pore. Sex sex sex . . .

Pt: THAT'S ENOUGH!! (The internal encounter heats up quickly.)

T: IT'S JUST STARTING! THERE'S LOTS MORE ON THE WAY!!!

Pt: (Silence. Four seconds. Six seconds. Eight seconds of avoidance.)

T: Ha! Listen to the sexy pervert trying to run away!

Pt: I'm not running away. (Hurt, as if lower lip is shoved forward.)

T: Of course you are! All you perverts are the same.

Pt: Get off my back!! (The initial avoidance ploy was used to fuel the encounter.)

T: Wow, that's sexy! If I get on your back can we fuck? I'm not a 13-year-old niece!

Pt: LEAVE ME ALONE!

T: NEVER!

Pt: I said drop it!!! I'VE HAD ENOUGH!!! (Pause) OOoooh. My head. My head hurts. I got a splitting headache. Oohh! It really hurts. (Ploy number two.)

T: You want someone to hold your head? Massage it?

Pt: (Silence)

T: I know someone, great legs. You could stick your head between her legs. She's eight. Just right. None of those old broads, 12, 13.

Pt: (Little laugh) You got a one-track mind.

T: (Quietly) Well, my head doesn't hurt.

Pt: I can feel it easing. It's going away. It came like that and now, just about gone. Funny. Feel calm.

T: Think sex.

Pt: I do. I do. I think about sex all my life. Like the great secret. I wish . . . my problem is sex. I feel good! That's funny! I feel different. I think about sex all the damn time. That was an awful thing I did.

T: Unforgivable. (There is a moderate infusion of integration in the relationship.)

Pt: It was. I wish I could just have sex every day. Any kind of woman. Just who will have sex. I want that so much. I could become a sex pervert. It came out of the closet, the pants. Maybe if I'm crazy, a pervert, it'd be OK to have sex. I love sex. It's nice to say it. Nice to hear me say it. I love sex. With anyone. She's 13, and I shouldn't done it, but she's got a body. She's 18 in the body! Hmmmgh! She'll be fantastic at 18! She's fantastic now, who am I kidding!

Sometimes a patient will slide into weird and bizarre states to avoid experiencing the encounter with the deeper potential:

Pt: (Indicating that he left his father and mother recently, after being their caretaker for years) . . . I have to think of my own future. Never can tell, no. They'll get along. Sure they will. My aunt can take care of them if anything happens. (The inner voice is leveling the accusation.)

T: If anything happens to them, it'll be your fault, you ungrateful, selfish, uncaring, lousy son you!

Pt: I have to take care of my future!

T: Bullshit! (That does it. The patient slides into a crazy avoidance state.)

Pt: My uncle is a doctor. He said it was all right to go down the stairs. He has blood in his eye. He knows the evil in me when I have thoughts. I am just waiting. It doesn't matter. The end is coming. It doesn't matter. What does anything matter? I was born and my uncle knows. I have blood in my eye. I see guns. I see black guns. The blood is the beginning because nothing really matters. Just blood. The blood matters. It's the blood of the eye. Blood, lots of blood. There is lots of blood! (The therapist-as-deeper-potential dances right along.)

T: Hey, that sounds like fun! Can I have a piece of that? Blood, blood all over, pools of blood. Red blood. That's the only real. Nothing else is real. . . . How am I doing? It's easier than I thought. . . . May I go on? Blood in my uncle's eye, red blood in the eye. He knows about me. He knows the evil in me, the black evil in me. If I go through the blood there is black evil. I think I got the knack of this. Your turn.

Pt: You're crazy.

T: Well, I learn quickly. Besides, it beats feeling shitty 'cause you ran out on your dear old Mom and Dad. You rotten kid . . . I know, "I have to think of my future."

Pt: I just don't have enough nerve to stand up to them.

T: Wait'll they both die. You can piss on their graves.

No matter what kind of avoidance ploy the patient uses, the therapist-as-deeper-potential merely feeds the avoidance back into the encounter. Avoidances are thereby used to fuel the internal encounter.

By Being the Deeper I-Ness Who Relates to the Patient as Another I-Ness

As the deeper potential, the therapist speaks as "I" just as legitimately as the patient speaks as "I." Just as the patient speaks of the "I" of the operating domain, the therapist speaks as the "I" of the deeper domain. If we were to ask who is the patient, who speaks for the patient, both the patient and the therapist would say, "I do." The patient speaks for the operating domain, and the therapist speaks for the deeper potential.

This makes for an intriguing interaction, for the patient has always spoken for the whole personality structure, all the potentials comprising the operating domain and the deeper domain. The patient may say, "I am always firm and solid. Sometimes I can sense a little wavering of purpose, but I shake it off and go on just as before." Suppose that which he refers to as "a little wavering of purpose" were not only to come alive but to speak with a sense of I-ness equal to that of the patient? In speaking to that little portion which is the operating domain, the deeper part says, "So you are the screwed up asshole who is interfering in my life! I see. I have been ready for years to get on with my life, and you are still the immature little kid, loyal to the party — the little kid who never quite grew up. Well! I'm glad to meet you." The question of who is the patient is replaced by the question of which I-ness speaks for the operating domain and which I-ness speaks for the deeper potential.

As a most legitimate I-ness, as the I who is quite entitled to speak as I, the therapist-as-deeper-potential talks to the patient. The integrative encounter is brought forward when the deeper I-ness relates to the superficial operating I-ness in two ways.

Letting-be and the freedom of independent being. The deeper potential relates to the patient in this way: "I am one person; you are another. I am the way I am; you are the way you are. You do your thing; I'll do my thing. I let you be however you must be; I am free to be what I am." There is an integrative mutual respect of each other's freedom and autonomy (Binswanger, 1958a; Buber, 1955, 1958; Perls, 1976; Van Dusen, 1957). This means that the therapist-as-deeper-potential can do and think and feel and experience whatever its nature is.

If the deeper potential is the experiencing of open sexual attraction, then the deeper potential can talk to the patient in this way: "I like women! I just like women! You like being married to Rachel. Great. I wish you well, old boy. We are into different lives. But I love you. Kiss Rachel hello for me!" The deeper potential has a sense of I-ness just as the patient does; the deeper potential has its experiencing just as the patient does; and the deeper potential relates to the patient along the lines of mutual letting-be and the mutual freedom of independent being. Here is the patient invoking the deeper potential, and relating to it in a disintegrative way:

Pt: My Dad would be proud of me. I'm a good father now. I mean I spend time with the kids, and Rachel. Good husband. I work now. Have a regular job. Come home after work. Things are different. I turned over a new leaf and I've been out of trouble for years. No more fooling around. That's done. No more. (The therapist sinks into being the deeper potential, experiences the sheer delight in being with women, speaks as the I-ness who lets the patient be.)

T: Well, you go home tonight. Be with the kids. And Rachel.

Pt: Yeah.

T: There's this woman, Jean. She turns me on. I'm going to give her a call. You understand.

Pt: (Silence)

T: There's something fantastic about Jean. I don't know what the hell it is. Something exciting about her. I can't wait to just be with her. We click together. I like your life though, but, no, not for me. Just thinking of Jean turns me on!

Pt: Unnn. That's no good. (The interaction is alive.)

T: What do you mean?

Pt: You get into trouble.

T: Sure I get into trouble. The old man never liked me. Shit, he screamed
for years at me. Your life is better. For you! You got a good marriage,
solid job, a front yard, TV, kids. Not me. I got an apartment, a car,
and women. What the hell. It's the life that fits me.

Pt: You're asking for trouble that way. (The two I-nesses are conversing.)

T: Listen, Jean is great. Last night she called me around midnight, asked me
to come over. She was hot. It was a fantastic night. I could hardly keep
up with her. What a woman! Oh what a great woman.

Pt: I don't like that! There's just trouble!

T: I like women! I just like women! You like being married to Rachel. Great.
I wish you well, old boy. We are into different lives. But I love you.
Kiss Rachel hello for me!

Pt: When are you going to grow up? That's just an irresponsible child! (The
deeper I-ness lets the patient be; the patient cannot let the deeper I-ness
be.)

T: You're right! Of course! Except when I'm with Jean, I am excited and . .
. . I like her! Three months ago I didn't even know her. Three months
from now, I don't know. I'll see.

Pt: That's an irresponsible child! GROW UP!

T: OK. Whatever you say! Want me to come into the business? I'll do it.
Whatever you say. It's really all right. I love you. I can like women and
still love you. It's OK.

Pt: (He is crying lightly.) I wish I could be like that. . . . I always fought with
him. . . . I want to be like you . . . (hard crying).

T: Aw, Jerry . . .

Pt: (Still crying hard) I never did anything 'cause, for me . . . always did it
wrong . . . mistakes . . . (hard crying). . . . The way you talked, always felt guilty . . . always got into trouble. . . . I love Rachel and the
kids . . . (long hard sobbing).

T: I know you do. I know. And you're a good man. My life is different. I'll
go my way and you can go yours. All I know is how wonderful it is
to be with Jean, and lots of women. Maybe you and I can be real friends.
Hell, I like you, Jerry. We just lead different lives.

Pt: (Silence) I feel strange.

T: Yeah, I know.

Pt: I need you.

T: Yeah.

Pt: I feel calm. Real calm. Feel different. (Pause) Never felt like this. Things
feel different.

T: Yeah.

There is something integratively special for the patient to be engaging with another part which acts as if it has fully as much right as the patient to refer to itself as "I," to live its own life, and to relate to the patient in the integrative spirit of live and let live, a genuine letting-be. It is like interacting with another you who allows you to be whatever you are while it lives and exists as a different person. Feelings are typically lifted out and the patient becomes quite giddy and silly, or starts crying, or enters into a new state of internal integration.

Frustrated anger at being shut off. There are occasions where the patient activates the deeper potential, almost promising the deeper potential that it has a good chance of actually being expressed. If the deeper potential were a person, there are grounds for excitement and hope. But suddenly, at the last instant, the patient says no, slams the experiential door shut. The deeper potential has been tapped on the shoulder, told to get ready, and then the patient says no. The patient may do this by going into a frozen state, by turning away, by somehow slamming the door in the deeper potential's face. When this occurs, the deeper potential is entitled to be filled with frustrated anger at being shut off. As the deeper potential, the therapist turns on the patient and expresses this frustrated anger. The therapist speaks as one I-ness to another, venting the outrage at being activated and then shut off by the patient. Regardless of the content of the deeper potential, its relationship with the patient is one of frustrated anger.

Pt: So finally he spent the night with me. I loved being with him. I know I shouldn't have called and . . . I guess I begged to have him come over. A washrag. In the morning he made a phone call. I barely was awake. Maybe seven, something. Ah, he called Charlene.

T: Oh oh. (There are sharp jabs in the therapist's chest. Danger signals of some activated deeper potential.)

Pt: He asked me if he could use the phone. I wanted to know if he wanted coffee. Before he phoned. He just phoned. Well, I knew I shouldn't have begged him to come over. I waited three days. He stayed with me the night. I know it wouldn't work. What's the use? I, he, well I listened and he asked her if she wanted to have breakfast with him. (Low voice, gloomy) What's it all for anyhow? Life goes, people go to work, doesn't matter. (The therapist's attention is riveted on the sonovabitch, and the therapist's whole body is charged with violent explosiveness. But the patient drifts away.)

Pt: Things are a little better at work. I'm glad about that. Yolande and I went to lunch. (Bam! The activated deeper violent explosiveness is suddenly left hanging. With the door slammed in its face, the deeper I-ness is filled with frustrated anger directly targeted upon the patient.)

T: My God! I want to shove my fist down his fucking throat!!! I want to kill that bastard! WHAT THE HELL IS WRONG WITH YOU?

Pt: You want me to yell at him? (She is energized almost instantly.)

T: Not you, you depressed spineless lump! I WANT TO!! I WAS READY TO TEAR HIS GOD DAMNED THROAT OUT AND YOU . . . YOU STOPPED ME!!! WHO GAVE YOU THE RIGHT TO STOP ME? WHO DO YOU THINK YOU ARE? (Here is the deeper I-ness yelling at the patient as another I-ness.)

Pt: Why are you yelling at me???

T: 'CAUSE YOU DRIVE ME WILD! WILD! DAMN YOU!!! DAMN YOU!!! I WANTED TO YANK HIS PRICK OFF AND THROW IT OUT THE WINDOW!!!

Pt: (Screaming at the top of her voice.) I'LL NEVER SEE HIM AGAIN!

T: STAY OUT OF THIS! YOU GOT ME INTO ENOUGH TROUBLE! I WANT TO TEAR HIS BALLS OFF!

Pt: (She starts to laugh quite hard, almost shrieking.) SO DO I! WE'LL DO IT TOGETHER!! WHO THE HELL DO YOU THINK YOU ARE ANYWAY! I'M THE ONE WHO OUGHTA RIP HIS HEAD OFF!

The therapist is a legitimate "I," who talks to the patient as another "I." One "I" is the deeper potential who is quite entitled to become furious with the patient, or who is equally entitled to have and express her experiencings while letting the patient be whatever she is. Whether being frustratedly angry at the patient or relating with a sense of letting-be, the deeper potential speaks as "I" in relating to the patient as another "I." The consequence in both cases is the heightening encounter and the shift into an integrative relationship.

By Differentiating the I-ness From the Patient's Operating Self

Existential-humanistic theory describes human beings in terms of a center of I-ness, the very core of that sense of I or self. The operating domain is comprised of potentials for experiencing and an I-ness which has the sense of innermost identity. By isolating that I-ness, everything else which comprises the operating domain is differentiated. Accordingly, there can be an "I" who experiences this or that, who behaves this way and that way, but who can be differentiated from that experiencing and that way of behaving. When the therapist speaks with the voice of the deeper potential, and when the therapist locates that I-ness and talks to it, the therapist has thereby differentiated the center of I-ness from the rest of the operating domain.

The center of I-ness is the Dasein in Daseinsanalysis. Boss (1963) differentiates the I-ness or Dasein in talking to this component about the rest of the way the "patient" is, the way the patient feels and acts and structures his life, and the limitations and restrictions the Dasein has imposed upon itself. In practice, this means that the therapist zeros in on the very core of the I-ness, and talks to that I-ness about the patient's operating self.

The consequence may be explosive. Once the very core of the patient's I-ness is indeed isolated and separated from the operating domain, there may occur an explosive cracking of the operating personality. The I-ness is free. It is made free by this relationship, and it is free of everything else which is the operating domain. It is liberating, freeing, and it is panicky and frightening, for the operating domain is cracked apart and made into a separate entity which can be entered into or disengaged from.

Pt: (She is attending to her companion-lover.) She gets that way when she gets tired of me. Goes and finds someone, someone to get it on with. I followed her to Sue's apartment. Waited, night, sat in the street near the alley, and when it got dark I started wondering about the hospital. I'd have to go back. Could feel the whisperings inside my head. Loud. Whispering, but real loud. For minutes I didn't know why I was sitting there, which apartment was Sue's. Still not sure. Don't even remember getting home, or what I did the next day. But the voices are coming back and I'm going to have to go back to the hospital.

There is the operating potential, the experiencing of controlling threats to go crazy. There is also an I-ness. The therapist addresses the I-ness, and thereby takes the first step in differentiating the I-ness from the experiencing of controlling threats to go crazy. This is done by talking directly to the I-ness, and talking to that I about the operating potential.

T: Hey Gail. You there somewhere? Did you hear her talking? She's saying the voices are coming back and she's going to have to go crazy again and go to the hospital. Did you hear her? I think she's going to do it. What do you think? Were you listening to her? Did you hear her? (The very wording of the statements differentiates a sense of I-ness from the operating self. Is the I-ness willing to accept the invitation, or will the I-ness remain merged with the operating potential?)

Pt: I'm getting worse. (The I-ness stays within the operating potential. But the therapist-as-deeper potential still sees and addresses a differentiated I-ness.)

T: Gail, did you hear that? She said, "I'm getting worse." She's working herself up. And she's very good at it too. Look, you know her better than I do, but I think she's going to go beserk and go back to the hospital. She uses that damned hospital like a weapon. What do you think? (Now the I-ness steps out. There is a new voice.)

Pt: Well she's mad. (There is an I and another entity, a she.)

T: Quiet, not so loud, she'll hear you. How do you mean "mad"?

Pt: (Laughs) She gets mad. She is pissed off at both of them. At lots of people.

T: (In fond wickedness) And she goes beserk, depressed, and they all feel bad.

Pt: Yeah.

T: (In a friendly, conspiratorial whisper) Keep it to yourself, but I think it works. She bludgeons the right people on the noggin when she gets that way and lands herself in the hospital. I got to admire her. Ssshh!

Pt: Me too!

T: Notice the way she talks when she does it, that dead metallic voice? And the way she sits on her bed, for hours. And the way she waits just about ten seconds before she answers anyone? That's skill!

Pt: You noticed. (Little laugh) She got that from her mother, the one who hung herself in the garage.

T: Yeah, mother hung herself. Good material.

Pt: She reminds everyone of that. She uses that. I think she's clever.

T: Yeah, she doesn't bombard people with it, just drops it like a stink bomb, and it lays there smelling for months. No one ever forgets. Ssshh, we're telling her secrets.

Pt: (Laughing) Sometimes I feel sorry for her. Sometimes. Like that's all she knows. She just does it, I mean like she can't do anything else. She's a sad sack.

T: No, I think she does a pretty good job of keeping everyone in line that way, no?

Pt: Yes! Well, she tries. Yes! She is good at it! I'm getting chills in my back. But good, and I'm floating. Just floating nice and easy. Drifting, lazy. I like this. I get glimpses of her like from far away, way above her. Like I'm above her and watching her. I get dizzy. Just glimpses of her, and she's . . . memories of her. She's a little girl, just a little girl and she's unhappy. Real unhappy. I'm shaking. My arms are cold and shaking. But it feels so light. This is funny!

The integrative encounter occurs in part because the therapist relates to the center of I-ness distinct and separate from the patient-as-operating-domain. It is as if there is a wee little I-ness there, quite apart from the person who is the operating potential. By interacting with that differentiated I-ness, the therapist moves in the direction of the integrative encounter.

By Expressing Integrative Fondness for the Patient

The therapist who enters into being the deeper potential and who relates to the patient-as-operating-domain can do a number of things which the patient cannot. One is that the therapist can enter into being the deeper potential. That the patient cannot do, yet. Second, the therapist can be the good, integrative form of the deeper potential. The patient cannot. Third, the therapist-as-deeper potential is able to relate integratively toward the patient. The therapist can like the patient, can relate in a genuine sense of fondness for the patient. This is beyond the patient.

As the internal encounter moves along, and especially when it culminates in an integrative relationship, the therapist will be filled with a warm liking, a joyful fondness for the patient. These are the moments when the therapist expresses this: "I like you. . . . I think you're a wonderful person. . . . You're great. . . . What a delightful person you are. . . . I love you." Here is one way in which the integrative fondness occurs and is expressed.

There is another way. It is when the patient's behavior is center stage, and the therapist's fondness is laced with a playful sense of the silly, absurd, whimsical (Ansell et al., 1981; Farrelly & Brandsma, 1974; Grotjahn, 1966; Mindess, 1971; Rose, 1969; Rosenheim, 1974). The fondness shines through as the interaction takes on a playful ridiculousness. It is this relationship which is present as the therapist says, "Hey, aren't you going a little too far?. . . . Oh, you're going to get it now. . . . That's naughty; you shouldn't be that way. . . . What are you trying to do, be different? . . . That doesn't sound like you; what happened to the passive slob?"

In the following, the internal encounter has been moving along, and takes on the style of integrative fondness:

Pt: What do you mean I'm just a sucking little baby? It's not easy to give up one job and go to another!
T: Come on! You'd love for Selma to hold your head and stroke you and tell you everything's going to be OK.
Pt: Never! I don't need that! What are you talking about?
T: See! Your voice is starting to crack! You're probably going to have tears in your eyes in a second!

Pt: Just shut up will you!?

T: No! God, you're a child!

Pt: I HATE YOU!

T: I LOVE YOU!!!

Pt: WHAT!?

T: I don't know. I forget! What did I say?

Pt: (Laughing) You said you loved me for God's sakes.

T: I did not! You're making it up. All little kids lie.

Pt: DAMN YOU! THERE YOU GO AGAIN.

T: WHAT THE HELL DID I DO NOW?

Pt: YOU'RE DRIVING ME CRAZY!

T: YOU'LL NEVER GO CRAZY! LITTLE BABIES DON'T GO CRAZY! THEY JUST PEE IN THEIR PANTS!

Pt: I'M WARNING YOU!

T: WHAT ARE YOU GOING TO DO LITTLE BABY? FALL DOWN THE STAIRS?

Pt: EEEAAAYAAAWWRGH!!

T: Wait a minute! That's a very peculiar noise for the executive director of a big company! That sounds more like a frustrated little kid who can't have his way!

Pt: (Laughingly) Want to hear it again? AAAAAaaaaaaaaak!!!!!

T: Sounds like you just got sucked into a powerful vacuum cleaner.

Pt: I'd like to piss all over you!

T: That's childish!!

Pt: So what's so fucking wrong?

T: I don't know.

Pt: Sometimes I do feel like a kid.

T: Watch out.

Pt: I'd like to scream and yell like a kid.

T: Now just a minute! You do that and your whole life'll get all turned around. Just be grown up and sober. That's the way.

Pt: Sometimes . . . sometimes. Not always. I really liked screaming. Oh hell, sometimes I get so mixed up, and I want to tell Selma. Just tell her. Not her fault. I don't let me. I remember . . . yeah . . . when I was a kid I had fun with friends. I really had fun. It's July and when I was a kid, we used to play. Chuck and Lou and Art. We were a bunch. I loved summers. I didn't scream and yell, but I sure was silly and we all were. I used to get up early in the morning, about six, and Chuck lived next door. We'd just hang out, play ball, and go skating and ride our bikes.

T: You're a helluva guy.

Pt: Yeah.

T: I like you.

Pt: Well I'm all right.

T: There's something so candid about you; you're honest.

Pt: Yeah. I think so. Yeah. I am.
T: Boy do I feel good! My whole body is . . .
Pt: Yeah! I'm tingling. Like electricity in me.

Throughout the encounter, the therapist expresses an integrative fondness for the patient. It occurs in a playful silliness, an appreciation of the playfully absurd, and even in a straightforward expression of open fondness. This relationship permeates the internal encounter and is one of the effective ingredients in the experiencing of the integrative relationship between patient and deeper potential.

By a Relentless Commitment to the Integrative Internal Encounter

The therapist remains in the internal encounter all the way. This is an unwavering commitment. Once the therapist-as-deeper-potential is locked into the relationship with the patient, that relationship is fixed. In practice, what this means is that the therapist is programmed to stay in the internal encounter as it heats up, as it reaches its peak, and as it opens into a newfound state of integration. This is the single-minded quality of being and staying which Hellmuth Kaiser (Fierman, 1965) highlights in the relationship between therapist and patient. It is the same quality of "being and staying" flagged by Havens:

> . . . the therapeutic power of the existential method springs from this being and staying. But the therapeutic power is not the power of education, suggestion, surgery, or injection; nor is it the power of the transference interpretation of the infantile neurosis and analysis of its resistance, now from within the patient's world, vulnerable as the patient then is. . . . *Being and staying is the goal in itself*. No aspect of the existential method is more difficult than this, to center the effort in being and staying and avoid action, explanation, emotional reassurances, and all the "rational" responses that the patient's desperation must evoke from us (1973, p. 299).

This chapter has identified six components to the integrative encounter, six methods carried out by the therapist-as-deeper-potential. For example, the therapist expresses the deeper potential's truth about the patient, and the therapist feeds the patient's avoidance ploys back into the encounter. In effect, the sixth component potentiates the other five, gives the other five methods their therapeutic punch. The therapist does any or all of the five methods within a context. If that context were to speak, it would say something along the following lines: " . . . and I am going to continue relating to you in these ways relentlessly. I am fully prepared to go to any extreme or to any length. The only direction this relationship can go is toward a state of internal integration. There is no alternative."

Generally, the internal encounter heats up to peaks of strong experiencing and then opens into a state of integration. Occasionally, however, there are dramatic superpeaks. These may consist of exceedingly powerful clashes between patient and therapist-as-deeper-potential. While these are exceptions to the general rule, the therapist is quite prepared to rise to any level of feelinged encounter in the emotional ups and downs along the way toward the final integrative relationship.

The therapist-as-deeper-potential may carry out any or all of these methods. In speaking as the voice of the deeper potential, the therapist may merely express the truth—the deeper potential's truth—to the patient, and do so with a relentless commitment to continue until the encounter reaches a state of integration. On the other hand, the therapist-as-deeper-potential may use all five of the methods in promoting the internal integrative encounter, again with a relentless commitment. In either case, the direction is always toward the state of internal integration, and the encounter ends only when the encounter attains this state.

This is a resounding change. It means that relationships between the patient and deeper potential are now qualitatively new and different. They are integrative: mutually friendly, mutually welcoming and open, harmonious, tranquil, peaceful, close, loving. But it also means that the patient and deeper potential are much closer, much more intimate, in virtual touch with one another. As indicated in Figure 4 (p. 107), and also in Figure 2 (p. 4), the deeper potential is now partially inside the operating domain. Indeed, the symmetry is that carrying forward the potentials for experiencing (chapters 1 and 2) and the internal integrative encounter (chapters 3 and 4) share the same consequence, namely the deeper potential is now well within the operating domain. Patient and deeper potential are close to one another, contiguous. We have accomplished a great deal in bringing together the operating domain and the deeper potential. Indeed, the natural next step is for the patient to "be" the deeper potential, to undertake the momentous step of disengaging from the operating domain and to enter into being the deeper potential. This is the topic of chapters 5 and 6.

CHAPTER 5

Experiential Being of
the Deeper Potentials:
Introduction

WHEN THERE IS A CARRYING forward of the potentials, the patient and the deeper potential are pushing up against and into one another. The next step is for the very heart of the patient, the sense of I-ness, to disengage from the operating domain and to enter into being the deeper potential (Figure 2, p. 4). When there is an integrative encounter between the patient and the deeper potential, the relationship between the two is open and inviting and integrative, and the patient and deeper potential are pushing up against and into one another. Again, the next step is for the I-ness to move out of the operating domain and into the very being of the deeper potential (Figure 4, p. 107).

The purpose of chapter 5 is to give the background for the actual methods (chapter 6). Background includes a little of the underlying theory of personality, as well as a discussion of related therapeutic methods.

The General Principle

Existential-humanistic therapy conceptualizes human beings in terms of a sense of I-ness, the very heart/core of the patient's sense of identity or self (Mahrer, 1978a), the Dasein of Binswanger (1967) and Boss (1963). Almost without exception, this innermost I-ness stays within the boundary of the operating domain. As indicated on the left in Figure 5, the patient is being OP1, is existing in OP1; the center of I-ness remains in the operating domain. Indeed, throughout the day or week or decade, the sense of I-ness may move in or out of all of the operating potentials, and rarely if ever leaves the operating domain.

In the existential-humanistic theory of human beings, I-ness refers

177

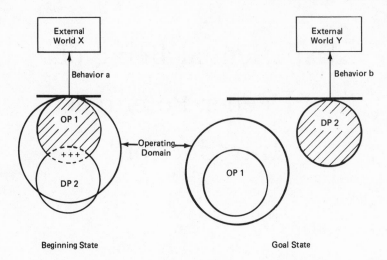

Figure 5. Disengaging From Operating Domain and Being the Deeper Potential

to that which speaks as "I." That inner core which can proclaim "I" may experience as one operating potential after another. The domain of the I-ness includes everything it is, everything it knows or thinks or senses about oneself. That domain falls short of the deeper potentials, but it includes all of the operating potentials. Indeed, it includes nothing but the operating potentials. That is what makes this therapeutic step so radical.

The general principle may be framed as follows: *Psychotherapeutic change occurs through therapeutic experiencing of the radical disengagement of the I-ness from the operating domain, and the wholesale being of the deeper potential.* Quite literally, the center of I-ness is no longer the ordinary person he had been. He no longer experiences as that person, feels as that person, behaves and acts as that person, no longer constructs and builds and lives in the same world. Equally as literally, the patient is now being the deeper potential. The patient, the center of I-ness, is now a qualitatively new person or personality with his or her own experiencings, feelings, ways of behaving and acting, and his own constructed world in which it lives and exists (Laing, 1975; May, 1958; Naranjo, 1969; Ouspensky, 1949; Wilber, 1979). As indicated on the right in Figure 5, the patient is now a qualitatively new person.

Once the center of I-ness enters into the deeper potential, the experiencing is radically new and different. The person who lives inside the operating domain does not experience as the deeper potential. Now the person is this deeper experiencing. In Figure 5, the patient experiences as the striated operating potential 1. The radical change is that the I-ness now experiences as the striated deeper potential 2. The former, continuing person existed in external world X, while the radically new person exists in external world Y. Here is a momentous shift, a wholesale change in what the external world is, what it consists of, how it feels and looks and is with the person. It is the new world of the deeper potential. Similarly, there is a wholesale shift in the accommodating behaviors. By shifting from the operating domain to the deeper potentials, whole packages of old behaviors are left behind, and whole new packages of behaviors are set in place.

In every momentous way, the person is a qualitatively new person. New experiencing means that the person feels different feelings, has different inclinations, different thoughts and ideas, different ways of seeing and perceiving, different attitudes and outlooks, different streams of history. This new person has access to new vistas of memories. It is as if the operating domain has access to its memories and no more. As more and more clutter is removed from the operating domain, the patient may remember more and more of its own cache of available memories. Often depth therapy just shines a little more light on the dim memories which were available (Bucklew, 1960; Freud, 1976; Greenson, 1967; Wolberg, 1954), without stepping outside its assigned store of memories:

> The emergence of repressed memories is a spectacular event which usually has important effects, but it is neither common nor a therapeutic "must"; many patients go through analysis quite successfully without experiencing it even once (Angyal, 1965, p. 262).

In contrast, the deeper domain seems to have its own storehouse of memories, access to whole avenues of early events which were not accessible to the operating domain. It is as if the new person has her own associated cache of memories, fittingly appropriate for a qualitatively new and different person.

Problems are resolved by no longer being the person with the problems. The patient is the operating domain. That is the territory which defines the patient. All of the problems take place in and of the operating domain. Bothersome ways of behaving and responding and acting are of the operating domain. All sorts of unpleasant feelings are of the operating domain. It is the operating domain that has the bad thoughts, the problematic ways of seeing oneself or others or the world.

The existential-humanistic way out of problems is to disengage from being the person with problems. If the problem is some kind of unpleasant or bothersome way of behaving, the solution is to no longer be the person who has those behaviors. If the problem is some sort of feeling which ties the person up in knots, the solution is to step away from being the person with that feeling. If the problem is living in such a world, then give up being a person who lives in such a world. Solve the problem by no longer remaining inside the person who has the problem. Let that person go, together with her way of being and her problems. The I-ness is not confined to the operating domain. There is no law that the I-ness has to stay inside that operating domain. Leave, step away, disengage from the entire operating domain.

You stutter, especially when you are a little excited or nervous. You still bite your nails and don't like eggs. There is always that sense of being not quite fitting in your world of acquaintances, your work, your family. Most of the time you feel exposed and vulnerable. To be honest, much of the time you feel awful. Your mother picks at you, compares you unfavorably with your cousin, and often gives you a headache right behind the eyes and forehead. The "you" behind the "you" includes an inner core, a sense of I-ness. This I-ness can deftly walk out of the whole person, the entire operating domain with all the lingering, plaguing, persistent problems. In one radical exit, the problems are solved when the I-ness leaves go of the person who has all those uncannily clinging problems.

When you die, you will not stutter any longer, nor will you bite your nails. You will be free of that plaguing sense of being exposed raw. There will no longer be that feeling of not quite fitting in. Problems are resolved by no longer being the person with the problems, and that state occurs when you die. This is the way out. Indeed, forthrightly facing one's own death is the keystone of existential change (Binswanger, 1958a; Bugental, 1976; Camus, 1961; Heidegger, 1949; Jaspers, 1955; Kierkegaard, 1944; Mahrer, 1975a). In experiential psychotherapy, facing one's own death is the exiting from your whole personality, the operating domain, and leaving behind the baggage of all of your problems, agonies, restrictions.

With rare exception, most psychotherapies do their work on the operating domain. They try to relate to the operating domain, to have encounters with it, to place it in groups and couples. Psychotherapies try to change its behavior, cleverly force it to change the way it behaves and acts and responds and thinks, have a different way of looking at the world and at oneself. They try to get the operating domain to see all sorts of things about itself, from the way it grew up to hundreds of different variations on what it is really like. But the commonality is that the target is forever the operating domain, whether it is referred to as the patient, the behaving organism, the person, self, or whatever. It is this myopic restriction, this little target of psychotherapeutic pushes and pulls and efforts which is perhaps the foremost difference between virtually all the psychotherapies and the large body of eastern thought (Byles, 1962; Chang, 1959; Herrigel, 1956; Kondo, 1952; Maupin, 1965; Suzuki, 1949, 1956; Van Dusen, 1979; Watts, 1961; Wilhelm, 1962). In eastern thought this thing we call the operating domain or ego or patient or substantive personality is utterly let go. Problems of the person are transcended by disengaging from being the person with the problems.

So many patients are caught between two operating potentials which relate together disintegratively. It is a life of frozen impasse. Never really being free and independent, and never being really close and intimate. The patient is stuck, hemmed in, at the impasse, partially loyal to the spouse and children and the social life, and, on the other hand, living the life of crazy spontaneous wildness. When he inclines toward heterosexuality there is screaming and kicking from the other homosexual side; when he moves toward homosexuality there is criticism and berating from the heterosexual side. The solution is to exit from being the person with the impasse, no longer being the person who is caught on the horns of the dilemma. Simply disengage from the whole operating domain with its impasse problems. Guntrip sees patients as caught and stuck between the fundamental poles of the object relations basic problem: "All through his treatment he will be tossed about between his fears of isolation and his fears of emotional proximity" (1969, p. 289). Our solution is to leave go of the personality for whom it is important that it be tossed about. Patients agonize about this and that decision; having a baby or not having a baby, leaving home or remaining home, having or not having the surgery. The agony and unhappiness of being enmeshed in the decision are solved by no longer being a person with the terrible racking decision.

This step of experiential psychotherapy is marvelously audacious. There is a domain outside of virtually everything you are. In existential-humanistic thought, this new domain is the deeper domain which has been activated by carrying forward the (operating and deeper) potentials for experiencing and by means of the internal integrative encounter. By disengaging from the entire operating domain, from your whole personality of what you are, the problems of that personality are let go, left behind, set free.

The external world is transformed by no longer being the person with that world. When the patient disengages from the operating domain, he leaves behind the external world of the operating domain. All the real problems in that world, all the terrible parts of that world, all of the strained situations, all of the real pressures and traps of that external world—all of this is left behind as the person leaves go of the operating domain. The external world (see Figure 5) is transformed by no longer being the person with that world.

The patient's external world can be exceedingly real. The job market is the way it is. Uncle Henry really left his wife and hasn't seen her in six months. There really are four children. The car really needs a lot of expensive work. The operating domain has its real world. But so does the deeper domain. When the patient steps out of the operating domain and its real world, and when the patient steps into the deeper domain and its (other) real world, the shift has transformed one real external world to another. Most psychotherapies assume that there is to be one external world of reality, and the patient has greater or lesser contact with it, one way or another of seeing and construing it. In existential-humanistic psychology (Mahrer, 1978a) and its experiential psychotherapy, the operating domain has its external world, and the deeper domain has its external world (External World X and External World Y in Figure 5), and each may be quite real. Being the deeper potential means transforming the former, quite real, external world.

There are at least four ways in which that external world is radically altered. One has to do with those parts of the external world which are comprised of the patient's own deeper potentials. The operating domain, struggling against its own deeper potentials, will face them in the form of appropriate parts of the real external world (e.g., Condrau & Boss, 1971; Ellenberger, 1958; Farber, 1966; May, 1953; Ouspensky, 1957). There will be something or someone who is cold and and hard and impenetrable, just as your deeper potential is. It is hideous and feeds on tormenting you, just as your deeper potential does. Once you leave go of being the person with that external ogre, and once you enter into being the deeper potential, the harsh, cruel, tormenting ogre extinguishes. "If you are pursued by an ogre in a dream, and you *become* the ogre, the nightmare disappears" (Perls, 1969a, p. 178). If you are pursued by your ogre who is your older sister, harsh parents, wicked husband, organized opponents, terrible colleagues, relentless enemy, and you disengage from the operating domain which has that ogre, then that ogre is no longer in your very real external world.

A second way in which the external world is utterly transformed has to do with the disintegrative relationships. The operating domain has a world in which there is always painful disintegrative relationships between the patient and some quite real part of the external world. There is always someone who hates you, withdraws from you, makes you tense and bothered, someone with whom relationships are characterized by distrust and distance, strain and pain, disharmony and disjunctiveness. It may be a set of specific persons such as parents or colleagues. It may be more general groups such as those who depend upon you or those above you or those with opposing beliefs. It may be virtually the entire external world. When the patient steps out of the operating domain, what is also left behind is that world of disintegrative relationships. Lifelong efforts to repair or cope with such painful relationships are achieved in an instant when the patient no longer is the person who has the external world.

Third, the patient will no longer live in an external world which supports the operating potentials. In order for those operating potentials to be experienced, the external world must be organized into the right kinds of situations, contexts and involvements. Existential-humanistic theory holds that the operating potential organizes and constructs the external world, and this is the reversal of the principle underlying most psychotherapies wherein it is the external world which organizes and constructs the reacting and responding person. Accordingly, in experiential psychotherapy, an operating potential as the poor, unfortunate victim must organize and construct appropriate contexts such as menacing tyrants, cold-hearted victimizers, people who pillage and rape and take advantage of you. If the patient disengages from the operating potential, that external world loses its meaning; it is likewise disengaged from. Perpetual experiencing of being misunderstood and unappreciated by the bad parents require appropriately bad parents who provide the necessary and sufficient situational context. The parents are exceedingly real, and are really bad, not understanding and not appreciating. As the patient steps out of that operating domain, there is no further need for such an external world. Accordingly, the parents stand disclosed as not misunderstanding and unappreciating, or as having other, apparently new, qualities and characteristics, or as having their own quality and characteristic of being misunderstanding and unappreciating.

The fourth way in which the external world transforms is for those unfortunate persons for whom the very foundation of their personalities lies in the archaically powerful external figures. The central axis of their personhood revolves around critical figures who are the only and most significant centers of their world. Everything revolves around Mother or Father or some other figure who lends meaning and significance to their lives. Levy-Bruhl (1923) refers to this as the "participation mystique" between the person and the external world. Jung (1962) describes this state as without a sense of self: "Insofar as the difference between subject and object does not become conscious, unconscious identity prevails. . . . Plants and animals then behave like men; men are at the same time themselves and animals also, and everything is alive with ghosts and gods" (p. 123). It is the state of being caught in the primitive personality, where the determining axis of the personality lies outside oneself and in other marvelously powerful primitive figures who determined and developed you in the first place and in whose lives you still exist (Mahrer, 1978a). When the patient finally leaves go of that operating domain and disengages, in that instant the whole primitive world vanishes. Those primitive figures lose their archaic power and stand revealed as the human beings that they are. The external world is transformed.

In these four ways, existential-humanistic theory and its experiential psychotherapy accommodate transforming changes in the very real external world in which the former operating domain had existed. Our general principle of disengaging from the operating domain and being the deeper potential is merely one principle of psychotherapeutic change, but it packs a powerful impact on the very nature of the external world.

Being the deeper potential versus preserving-strengthening the self. Being the deeper potential means sacrificing the very sense of self. It is much more than giving up a home, a profession, a family, or a kidney. It is a letting go of one's very personhood, one's own identity, the "ego," one's essential self. The patient comes to an end, dies, no longer is anything that one was. Instead of being preserved, the person stops existing. Instead of helping the patient to cope with inner problems or behave differently, the therapist helps the patient to let go of his very self. Instead of being strengthened, the ego is left to die. Instead of maintaining the self, helping it with its problems, trying to do therapy with it, making it feel better, the therapy moves toward disengagement of the inner core of I-ness from the entire self as it enters into being the deeper potential.

In experiential psychotherapy, the person (self, identity, ego) who enters therapy will close out its existence and no longer be. The persisting sense of self is extinguished. This is the meaning of "existential death." Disengaging from everything which is "I" and emerging into a radically new existence as the deeper potential means undergoing death; " . . . a man has to suffer the ordeal of despair and 'existential anxiety,' i.e. the anxiety of a man facing the limits of his own existence with its fullest implications: death, nothingness" (Ellenberger, 1958, p. 119). You die, you extinguish, you are no more; " . . . the transformation process is seen as one of death and rebirth, where the outer man with his unnecessary ways of manipulating the world must give way to the manifestation of the inner . . . " (Naranjo, 1969, p. 101). You will pass out of existence, and some other person will take your place; you will die, and there will be a new life who is not you; everything which is you will end, even your sense of self, and something else will replace the you who is about to die.

This destiny for the self is in contrast to one in which the implicit aim is to retain and preserve the self, to give it greater consciousness, and even to "realize" this conscious ego-self: " . . . the goal of analysis is self-realization. This requires an increase in consciousness; and to achieve this, new material must be related to the ego . . . "(Wheelwright, 1956, p. 129). Many approaches aim at maintaining the person or self by giving it insight and understanding into the bad deeper personality processes: "The ideal human condition toward which Freud's therapy aimed appears to me to have been a state of freedom in which a person could, through understanding, hold himself inwardly free from the coercive prohibitions of society and free also from the coerciveness of blind biological impulses" (Whitehorn, 1959, p. 5). The ego's autonomy is to be shored up against the dangerous inner impulses (Allport, 1960; Fenichel, 1954b; Wyss, 1973) in the continuing struggle to preserve its stability: " . . . psychodynamic theory is changing its orientation from 'release and/or control of instinctive impulses' to the 'maturing of the ego in adult personality.' Perhaps we should put it in an even more elementary way as 'the individual's struggle to achieve and preserve a stable ego'" (Guntrip, 1969, p. 173). The stable ego is preserved by, for example, increasing its consciousness and awareness: "Therapy, of necessity, consists of restoring to consciousness that which was removed by repression . . . " (Wolberg, 1954, p. 59). The self (ego, identity, consciousness) is good. It is to be preserved against the bad insides.

Preserving and strengthening the self rest on the ideas that what is deeper is mostly trouble and should be allowed into the continuing self in small doses of insight and understanding, and that the seeds of a wonderful personality lie in the self, the ego, the person one is. Existential-humanistic theory and its experiential psychotherapy hold to the opposite idea. What is deeper is more sound and solid. It is the deeper domain which contains the seeds of what the person can be. The operating domain is a lot of excess baggage; it is trouble, it is expendable. Our existential-humanistic position is also shared by theorists such as Rank (1929, 1945), Jung (1933), and Angyal (1965). According to Jung, the seeds of the person the patient can become lie in the unconscious psychic constitution. As Angyal states, "The healthy pattern must be sought and uncovered, not within the pseudonormal surface personality where its vestiges serve merely to disguise the neurotic assumptions, but within the depth of neurosis itself . . . " (1965, p. 287). In general, however, the conceptual foundation for our position lies in existential thought.

Being the deeper potential means disengaging from and no longer being the person you are, the self, the operating domain, the ego. That is one destiny; it is the direction of change of experiential psychotherapy. Many other approaches choose to retain the person, enhance and preserve the self, strengthen and uphold the ego. There is quite a difference in the two destinies, in the two theories, and these differences are shown in differences in the methods which are used and the consequences which occur (Budge, 1983).

The radical transformation: Explosive or quiet? When the center of I-ness leaves go of the operating domain and enters into the being of the deeper potential, is this an explosive step, a quiet step, or does it seem to depend upon a few key factors? Most writers describe the transformation as explosive. There are emotional fireworks of utter terror or incredible despair or similar kinds of powerful bad feelings. It is typically described as the most wrenching ordeal. Passing from "inauthentic" to "authentic" existences means the suffering of intense "existential anxiety," a matter of passing through critical despair and screeching terror (e.g., Angyal, 1965; Ellenberger, 1958; Wyss, 1973): " . . . with severe neurosis, if one aims at a fundamental cure, there is no other way to recovery than the way that leads through despair. . . . A sweeping experience of bankruptcy must come if the person is to break out of his neurotic enclosure . . . " (Angyal, 1965, p. 225).

There are many descriptions of explosively powerful feelings of terror and despair as the patient, desperately clinging to the operating domain, faces the imminence of the encroaching deeper potential. The scene is one in which the patient faces the terrible certainty of having to plunge into the catastrophic abyss of the looming deeper domain. It is " . . . the fear of having no relationship at all and losing one's ego in a vacuum; and the fear of entering into a relationship and feeling that one's weak ego wil be overwhelmed" (Guntrip, 1969, p. 340). This transformation is construed as the final shattering of what one is, the plunge into neverending limbo, the final death, being out there in vacuum space of blackness. Many therapists and patients conceptualize this transformation as necessitating the undergoing of violent paroxyms of utter pain, of complete madness, of plunging into absolute death, of reaching the peak of suffering. Wholesale transformation into a radically new being is pictured as a catastrophically explosive state in which the patient willingly submits to madness or death or agonized suffering or electric/chemical shock or the iron will of God, the devil, the guru, the supreme one. The picture is of some massive conversion or transformation or transmutation accompanied by explosively powerful feelings.

Following the shift into the deeper domain, there often is indeed an outbreak of powerfully explosive feelings. When the center of I-ness disengages from the operating domain and enters into being the deeper potential, the radically new person might well cut loose in intense feelings. It is understandable that the deeper potential will undergo experiencings whose strength and intensity exceed that of the operating potentials. But this is experiencing of a different order than that of the patient who is in the process of disengaging from the operating domain and heading toward the domain of the deeper potentials. Boss (1963) describes this heightened plateau of strong experiencing as the patient completes the process and enters into the being of the deeper potential:

> To be allowed to be a little child for once, this was the "open sesame" that flung wide the field-gates which had so long stemmed back her own true potentials from expression. It was as if she had been waiting her whole life for precisely this permission. The entire façade of her former mode of life—the excessively conscientious, work-oriented, goal-striving patterns hammered into her so long—burst asunder, and with the full force of her prodigious vitality, there broke through all the small child urges to suck thumbs and to kick and squeel . . . (p. 15).

The center of I-ness that is in the operating domain has little or no idea of what the new deeper person will do. The waking person has little or no idea of actually who she will be in the dream world.

Therefore, the person who faces the disengagement from the operating domain may have powerfully explosive feelings as she confronts the possibility of utter transformation. It is understandable that the radical transformation may be accompanied with explosive feelings, but that does not mean they are necessary.

In fact, most of the time the shift from the operating domain in the deeper potential is quietly unobtrusive. It does not follow a convulsive peak of explosive feeling. Instead, it generally follows a silence of a few seconds or more. Frequently, the patient will report falling into a drowsy state, or gliding through a charged state, or going through a state of drifting. Sometimes the patient will catch herself before falling into the deeper potential, and this will be a literal falling: "Oh! I fell! I caught myself! I felt like I was falling!" The transformation from being in the operating domain to being in the deeper domain can be as graceful and quiet as the transformation from wakefulness to sleeping and dreaming.

There are two reasons why the radical transformation can be quiet rather than explosive. One is that the stage is set by the previous steps. To the extent that operating and deeper potentials were carried forward, the way is prepared for a quiet change. To the extent that the relationship between patient and deeper potentials is now integrative, the stage is set for a quiet change. The previous steps in the session make the situation ready for a quiet transformation. Indeed, the purpose of the previous steps is just that of paving the way toward the disengagement from the operating domain and entrance into the deeper potential. The explosive turmoil tends to occur in the two previous steps rather than here.

The second reason for the transformation being quiet is that the experiential therapist uses methods designed to effect the transformation effectively, smoothly, and quietly. By using the right methods, the transformation can be a smooth and quiet one. Becoming an entirely new and different person is a matter of being in the deeper potential, and the methods of negotiating this change can be deft, effective, and pointed rather than being grossly explosive or crude.

The radical transformation: Eash session or after years of groundwork preparation? The theory of experiential psychotherapy holds that disengagement from the operating domain and being the deeper potential requires (a) the right preparation, and (b) effective methods.

"The right preparation" means that the patient must be cheek-by-jowl with the deeper potential. They must be touching one another. This occurs when the patient and deeper potential are overlapping somewhat, when the deeper potential has pushed its way into the operating domain (see Figures 2, p. 4, and 4, p. 107). When there is some measure of carrying forward of the potentials, especially the deeper potential, then this state is attained (see Figure 2). When there is a measure of encountering integrative relationship between patient and deeper potential, then this state is attained (see Figure 4). Whether this state is attained by carrying forward the potentials or by an integrative relationship or both, this first requirement is met. The end-state of both procedures (see Figures 2 and 4) is the beginning-state of the radical transformation (see Figure 5).

The second requirement is that effective methods are used by both therapist and patient. Without these methods, and without persons ready for and competent in using them, patient and therapist will not be successful in negotiating this change.

Once patient and deeper potential are intimate with one another, touching and experientially involved, then the patient is in a position to disengage from the operating domain and enter into the deeper domain by means of the methods to be described in chapter 6. The key point is that these requirements are to be met each session! As given in Figure 1 (p. xvi), each session of experiential psychotherapy goes through this fourth step. It may be for a few seconds or it may be a half-hour or longer, but the patient is invited and enabled to leave the ordinary operating domain and to be the deeper potential. The work of experiential therapy makes it understandable and expected that the patient will undertake this step each and every session. According to humanistic-existential theory, the patient undertakes this step each evening of dreaming (Mahrer, 1978a); it can also be undertaken during each and every therapy session.

It is to occur in the middle sessions. It is to occur in the early sessions. It is to occur in the initial session. It is to occur in the final session. It is to occur each and every session. Indeed, it must occur if the session is going to proceed on to the final step in each and every session (see chapters 7 and 8).

In contrast, many other therapists have conceptual and praxis reasons for expecting that such a change, if it is to take place at all, can only occur after considerable groundwork preparation. Only after years of proper groundwork could and should patients be expected to negotiate such sober change. Angyal is representative of those who hold such a position:

> A great deal of work has to be done before the patient can be mobilized for the process of change. His reliance on a neurotic pattern of living

has to be broken and the latent healthy pattern has to be unearthed and cultivated before it can be restored to its rightful dominant position (Angyal, 1965, p. 222).

In many therapies patients are not to disengage from their substantive personality structures and to enter into being their deeper processes. In a few therapies, such a shift is to occur—but only after years of groundwork preparation. In contrast, experiential psychotherapy is based upon a theory of human beings which enables such a shift to occur each session, a series of preparatory steps (steps 1-3 in Figure 1) that sets the groundwork each session, and effective methods (chapter 6) for enabling this shift to occur each session.

The limits of the radical transformation. Compared to the aims and purposes of most western psychotherapies, disengaging from the operating domain and being the deeper potential is a profound transformation. In the conceptual boundaries of most western psychotherapies, changes occur in the conscious self, between the conscious self and the external world, and between the conscious self and the deeper processes. Yet in all this the center of I-ness remains within the operating domain. In contrast, disengagement of the I-ness from the operating domain or conscious self and entry into the deeper potential is a radical change.

There is a transition state, a kind of limbo. It occurs as the center of I-ness leaves go of the operating domain and passes through a limbo state in which the I-ness is no longer within the operating domain, nor is the I-ness yet within the deeper potential. I know very little of this transitional state, except that the patient goes through this limbo state each time there is passage from operating to deeper domain.

Some have written about this limbo state. In some Buddhist and Taoist bodies of thought, for example, it is here that the sense of I-ness is to be (e.g., Wilhelm, 1962), free not only of the ordinary operating domain, but free also of the deeper domain. Where experiential psychotherapy offers the person freedom from the sense of self in which one has continually existed in the operating domain, others go beyond this in aiming for a state of " . . . selflessness, the absence of any permanent self . . . the reduction of self to zero" (Byles, 1962, pp. 190–191). This is a state of being neither in the operating domain nor the deeper domain. It is akin to a state of samadhi, the trance-like state described in yoga (cf. Dalal & Barber, 1970).

The limits of our radical transformation consist of the deeper domain. We go no further. There are eastern bodies of thought that seem to be free of our limits and that seem to open a new universe that we merely brush by (Anderson, 1980; Byles, 1962; Chang, 1959; Herrigel, 1956; Kondo, 1952; Maupin, 1965; Pelletier & Garfield, 1976; Suzuki, 1949; Van Dusen, 1979; Watts, 1961; Wilhelm, 1962). Compared to most western psychotherapies, our changes are qualitatively new and different. Compared to some eastern bodies of thought, our changes may be regarded as merely an initial baby step toward even more profound changes.

The therapeutic significance of being the deeper potential. Why is this step so important? What is the therapeutic significance of disengaging from the operating domain and entering into being the deeper potential?

• The patient has achieved the profound state of being free of the old operating domain. No longer is the patient the person she had been. Disengaging from the whole former personality means leaving go of all of the problems, disintegrative relationships, painful ways of being and behaving, and external world of the old operating domain. All of the problems are resolved by no longer being the person with the problems.

• The patient is now a qualitatively new and different person. Potentials for experiencing are new and different, behaviors are new and different, and the world in which the patient exists is new and different. The deeper potentials are different from what they were when the patient was inside the operating domain. That is, from the vantage point of the operating domain, what was deeper was monstrous, evil, animal impulses, sexual cravings, violent aggressiveness, uncivilized biological urges, awful stuff. Freed of the disintegrative patient perspective, the deeper potentials are free to occur in their own integrative form and shape and content. All in all, the patient is indeed a changed person. From the perspective of existential-humanistic theory, this is an exceedingly better and more valuable new personality than the old operating domain. In effect, the patient is now the deeper domain.

• This new state is a closer approximation of actualization and integration. It is the state of actualization in that the deeper potentials are now actualized, present, functioning, alive. What was deeper is now the patient and the patient is now the deeper domain. It is the state of integration in that the patient is now able to manifest one of the hallmarks of the state of integration, namely being able to have graceful access into and out of neighboring potentials.

• Finally, the stage is now set for the last step in each session, i.e., new ways of being/behaving in the extra-therapy world. In this sense, the in-therapy, functional purpose of each step is to pave the way toward the actual tasting and sampling of actual changes in ways of being and behaving.

Each of these points is illustrated on the right in Figure 5, and constitute the reasons for this step, the therapeutic significance of disengaging from the operating domain and being the deeper potential.

It Is the Therapist Who Determines That We Undertake This Step

Whether or not we carry forward the experiencing of potentials (step 2, Figure 1) is determined by the patient. Whether or not we work the relationship between patient and deeper potential (step 3, Figure 1) is likewise determined by the patient. It is the patient who activates some operating or deeper potential. It is the patient who activates the relationship with some deeper potential. All the therapist does is to be passive to what the patient initiates.

Occasionally the patient will move almost naturally into the present step. As the patient is experiencing the carrying forward of a deeper potential, there will be occasions when the patient will almost naturally slide out of the operating domain and into being the deeper potential. When the encounter between patient and therapist-as-deeper potential moves along and gains integration, occasionally the patient will slide into being the deeper potential. These are more or less natural consequences. The therapist used no additional methods to enable the patient to disengage from the operating domain and to enter into the deeper domain.

However, it is more common that carrying forward the potentials or engaging in the encounter will simply accomplish its work. Finished with this or these steps, no longer resonating within the patient's personality, the therapist drifts outside, and now the therapist is an external therapist. In this locus, the therapist has thoughts. What do I do now? What is the next step? It is here in this external locus that the therapist determines to undertake the next step. Unlike the previous steps, it is the therapist who makes this determination.

Methods of Disengaging From the Operating Domain and Being the Deeper Domain: Some Soft Hintings

A point is reached where the deeper potential is carried forward or where there is a good measure of integration between patient and deeper potential. The way is clear for the patient to undertake the momentous shift out of the operating domain and into the domain of the deeper potential. How is this accomplished? There are methods used by therapists both within and without the larger experiential community, but whose methods are appropriate. While chapter 6 describes the actual methods, this section illustrates some of the soft hintings toward these actual methods.

Addressing one of a number of "I's." Long before there was a science and profession of psychology, there was acknowledgment of multiple "I's" floating in and out of various selves or personalities. There is one "I" when awake and conscious, and another "I" who occurs in dreams. Within the dream world itself, I may be two separate and distinct personalities in the dream. However, the notion of multiple "I's" entered psychology and psychiatry under a cloud of psychopathology. There was something ominous and suspect about a person or I who floated from one distinct personality to another. In milder form in what was called amnesic conditions or fugue states, multiple "I's" gained notoriety as multiple personalities through the early work of Morton Prince (1905), and remained an intriguing but infrequent entity in the history of abnormal psychology and psychiatry (Taylor & Martin, 1944).

The concept of multiple personalities rested on a firm position that the "normal" person maintained a single, continuing, ordinary personality or self or sense of I. Against this base, sliding from one to another was different, suspect, pathological. In contrast, another conception of personality allowed for ordinary, typical, everyday persons as having multiple centers of consciousness, multiple selves or personalities. Ouspensky (1949, 1957) is perhaps best representative of theorists who conceive of human beings in terms of multiple "personalities" and who grant the very center of I-ness the conceptual right to float in and out of these centers of consciousness. Indeed, many therapies accept this implicit structure of personality while rejecting it explicitly. Consider the implicit personality structure in the actual wording of therapist statements wherein the therapist talks to the patient about a presumably separate and distinct self. This is implied when therapists say things such as, "Don't *you* see what *you* are doing? . . . When are *you* going

to snap out of this? . . . How do *you* feel about what *you* just did?"
It is as if the therapist is dividing the patient into one "you" who is doing
and being, and another "you" who is aware of that other you, has
thoughts and feelings and awareness of the other you. Many therapists
carry out a theory which is more sophisticated than its textbook form.

The organizing of a person into multiple "I's" or personhoods or
selves is of a different order than ordinary talking to a single "I" about
a static personality. Therapists who talk to the single "I" about static
qualities and characteristics of that I's personality will tend to maintain
a dialogue with that single I: "How do you feel about your relations
with your husband? . . . When did the spells first become serious? . . .
What do you think about your temper outbursts?" There is only one
"you" and the therapist talks to that "you" about "your" relations with
your husband, "your" spells, "your" temper outbursts. It is a matter
of talking to the patient about static characteristics of the patient.

It is another matter to bypass the person who is right here, being
and doing and interacting, and to search out another I-ness who is
available there, somewhere. Gendlin (1972), for example, distinguishes
between the patient who is right here, a silently withdrawn and unresponsive self or I-ness, and a deeper separate personhood who is seen
by the therapist. Gendlin can elect to go beyond the presently interacting person, and to search out and talk " . . . to the person I imagine—a
sad person, silent, broken, given up, hurt by those he cared about, in
a state hospital, not cared for enough or not understood" (p. 352). Here
is a conceptual granting of multiple selves.

In hypnotherapy, the method is refined in such a manner that the
other, inner, deeper I-ness is invited to come to life in its world in place
of the ordinary, continuing, conscious I-ness or self. Erickson explicitly
organized the personality into parts and addressed the inner deeper personality thereby free to come to life in its own right (Erickson, 1980;
Erickson & Rossi, 1981; Erickson, Rossi & Rossi, 1976; Zeig, 1980).
Accordingly, the therapist can address a deeper "I" who is a little girl
living and being in her world. In this method, the therapist is directly
addressing the little girl rather than talking to the patient about the
little girl in her: "And maybe you might like to wonder what you will
be when you grow up. Maybe you would like to wonder what you will
be when you grow up. . . . Would you like your favorite candy to eat
right now!" (Erickson, in Zeig, 1980, p. 87).

Erickson divides the person into, for example, a "conscious" part
and an "unconscious" part. In talking to the "unconscious" part, the
therapist has thereby invited an I-ness to shift from the ordinary contin-

uing conscious personality into the unconscious personality. It is as if the therapist explicitly allows there to be several persons, living and being in several parts of the whole personality. Then the "person" or I-ness to whom Erickson talks is enabled to be free to disengage from one personality domain and to be in another. The I-ness is free to be the "conscious" person or the "unconscious" person. Here is a sophisticated and refined method for enabling the very center of the personhood or I-ness, in our vocabulary, to disengage from the operating domain and to enter into being the deeper domain. Do you wish to be the conscious person? Do you wish to be the unconscious person? I can talk to you in such a manner that you will be either one, and thereby I can move you into and out of the various domains which comprise your larger personality.

From these roots comes a newfound set of options for the simple question of whom the therapist addresses. Experiential psychotherapy accepts the idea that each potential is a home for its own sense of identity and self. Many therapists address the patient as if the core sense of I-ness and the operating domain are coterminal, but in experiential psychotherapy the chosen option is to distinguish the core sense of I-ness from the potentials for experiencing. The therapist rivets her eye on the inner sense of I-ness, no matter what potential it puts on, and thereby allows that sense of I-ness to disengage from the whole operating domain and float easily into the deeper domain.

Standing off from and seeing oneself. One kind of ordinary insight has the patient looking down into deeper personality processes. She sees (has insight into) her own intrapsychic structure, unconscious material, inner workings. There is a second kind of insight in which the patient sees the way she is behaving, functioning, operating, rather than looking down into deeper intrapsychic personality processes. It is the difference between psychodynamic-psychoanalytic insight and Gestalt "awareness" (Enright, 1970; Levitsky & Perls, 1970; Naranjo, 1969; Perls, 1969b). She sees the way she laughs every time she talks about this, or the way she tends to try to be this way with particular persons, or the way she denies the aggressive thoughts toward her sister, or the way she clears her throat when she is rattled. She is standing off a bit and seeing her more superficial, substantive, operating surface self.

If we extend this more superficial meaning of insight-awareness further, the patient is less and less in the operating domain, seeing oneself, and is more and more moving outside the operating domain, seeing the whole operating domain. Instead of being in the operating domain (Angyal refers to this as the "unhealthy pattern"), the patient has moved outside the very operating domain and sees it from an "outside vantage point":

> To gain insight means to look *inside* the functioning of one's unhealthy pattern. While doing this, one stands *outside* one's neurosis; one gains an outside vantage point. . . . At the moment of insight one sees one's neurotic problems in perspective, instead of being utterly buried in them (Angyal, 1965, p. 228).

Where is the person located in doing this? In our vocabulary, the patient has backed out of the operating domain in order to see all of it. If we then take an even further backward step, the patient would be outside the operating domain and would be seeing an image of oneself. It would be as if the patient is seeing a movie or portrait or videotape or picture of oneself. Many therapies use this method. For example, Bandler and Grinder (1982) invite the patient to do this in observing oneself being in a bothersome, feelinged, traumatic incident. They aim at distancing or dissociating by seeing oneself in that incident, or even by going a step further by seeing oneself seeing oneself. There are, then, three patients. Patient 1 is in the incident; patient 2 watches patient 1; and patient 3 watches patient 2. While their aim is to divest the patient of strong uncomfortable feelings, the method also manages to get the patient out and away from the confines of the ordinary continuing identity or self or operating domain.

The commonality in these methods is that of disengaging from oneself in seeing oneself. For our purposes, the more the patient separates from oneself in seeing oneself, the more the very center of I-ness is backing out and away from the operating domain. This is the nub of Mead's (1934) brilliant analysis of the self wherein self occurs as one can take the attitude of others toward oneself. When I can see myself, I am thereby backing off from and out away from that operating domain which I see. All in all, the enterprise of seeing oneself (the operating domain) is tantamount to disengagement from the operating domain, and this constitutes a most useful soft hinting toward actual therapeutic methods.

Succumbing to the catastrophic awfulness. The situation is that the deeper potential is so intrusive, so right up against the patient, that the patient can either hold onto the continuing sense of I-ness or succumb to the menacing invasive deeper potential. The decision is between remaining the person you are or succumbing to a totally alternative existence of being the catastrophic awfulness. This is not a decision between how you shall be or how you shall behave. It is a matter of succumbing to the catastrophic awfulness and thereby closing out your very existence, identity, and sense of self. It is giving in to the terrible state you are struggling to avoid.

Typically, the patient is in a catastrophic situation which presses in on every side, and the situation is so powerful, so demanding that the monstrous danger is falling into the highly active, dangerously imminent deeper potential. What is more, the ordinary ways out are unavailable in this catastrophic situation. Instead of allowing for ordinary avoidances such as becoming ill or falling asleep or going mad, the situation exerts a compelling pull for the deeper potential; " . . . the experience has a tendency to arise in situations of total extremity or despair, when the individual finds himself without any alternative but to surrender entirely" (Watts, 1960, p. 443). The context pulls the patient to succumb to the catastrophic awfulness.

Angyal refers to this as the "struggle for decision" which is " . . . directed against facing the bankruptcy of his way of life and against being plunged into despair; it is the life and death struggle of the neurosis" (1965, p. 275). In this decision, the existential option is to plunge into utter despair, give in to yawning depression, let the evil ooze into you, stop struggling against the inexorable destiny that has been stalking you forever, surrender to the madness in you, succumb to your catastrophic awfulness. If the tortuous fate is to be wholly vulnerable to the menacing people who have been spying on you, just let it happen:

> How would it be if you were to allow everything there is a right to be, and to hold yourself open to all that wants to come to you, even though the erstwhile structure of your existence were to turn out to be too small and have to be broken asunder and to die? Let the spies come and give them full power to do as they wish, and just see what happens (Boss, 1963, pp. 13–14).

The theory and the methods of existential approaches offer the possibility of a wholesale surrender to the catastrophic inner processes. It may be the absolute terror of death, of madness, of nothingness, of limbo, of structurelessness. The content does not matter. What does matter is that there is some inner catastrophic awfulness to which the patient succumbs. This is an essence of death and rebirth, of metamorphosis, of wholesale change in one's very depths, as enunciated by the existential body of clinical thought (Binswanger, 1958b, 1967; Boss, 1963; Ellenberger, 1970; Esterson, 1978; Heidegger, 1949; Laing, 1975; Mahrer, 1978a; May, 1958).

In friendly contrast are those approaches wherein the patient is to face and touch the catastrophic, but without endangering the existence of the self. That is, the patient is to dip down a bit into the catastrophic, to have injections of tiny doses, to move gradually closer and closer. Yet the patient is never to plunge wholly into it, never to be wholly invaded or overcome by it—only face it and touch it so that he can deal with it better, without ever wallowing helplessly in it. These are behaviorally grounded flooding therapies, desensitization therapies, implosive therapies, and others (Brown, 1973; Hogan & Kirchner, 1967; Lowen, 1958, 1965, 1967; Olsen, 1976; Rose, 1976; Shorr, 1972, 1974; Stampfl, 1977; Wolpe, 1973).

The critical distinction is between those therapies and methods which retain the patient as patient, while exposing the person to doses of uncomfortable situations, and those existential therapies and methods which close out the whole existence of patient as patient. It is the difference between still being you or no longer being you. If you succumb completely to the catastrophic awfulness, then you will no longer be you. It is quite a different matter for the patient to remain as the patient while sampling a desensitization hierarchy. It is quite a different matter when the patient remains the same person but manages to survive the incidents which were arranged for him:

> All I did was arrange a restaurant trip and make arrangements with the waitress and manager for a beautiful quarrel . . . and Will found he could live through it. . . . He could live through a divorcee, six-times divorced. He could learn to dance from that pretty, six-times divorced girl. . . . All Will needed was to find out he could cross the street, go into a restaurant. He would drive several blocks out of his way so he couldn't see it. I showed him all the good places to faint. He couldn't do it. I gave him every opportunity to faint, to die . . . (Erickson, in Zeig, 1980, p. 102).

Our aim is for the center of I-ness to disengage from the entire operating domain, and to enter into the deeper domain. This aim is not accomplished by a therapy and by methods which preserve the patient, and gradually expose him to bite-sized samples of the deeper catastrophic awfulness. On the other hand, methods which involve the wholesale plunge into the inner terror serve to close out the ordinary, continuing personhood and to effect the profound transformation of the person into the deeper domain. Here is another soft hinting, namely, *succumb to that which you are struggling to avoid in you, give in to the inner catastrophic awfulness.*

Letting the deeper process enter into the patient. One of the central ideas behind Wolpe's (1958) "reciprocal inhibition" is that if you can get the patient to do and be some way that is (a) adjusted, healthy, adaptive and non-neurotic, and that (b) is antagonistic or inhibitory to ways which are unadjusted, unhealthy, maladaptive or neurotic, then the probability of the latter kind of behavior is reduced. This idea becomes a soft hinting for our purposes when the invited new way of being and behaving comes from the deeper processes, rather than from the therapist's notions of what adjusted, healthy, adapted, non-neurotic behavior is like. The new way of being and behaving must come from somewhere. When it comes from the deeper domain and it is antagonistic or inhibitory to the ordinary ways of being and behaving, then the consequence is a soft hinting toward being the deeper potential. When it comes from the therapist's notions of what is normal and adjusted and is antagonistic or inhibitory to the ordinary ways of being and behaving, then the consequence is normal and adjusted behavior.

There are many methods, used in many therapies, where the patient is invited to allow something from the deeper personality processes into the way the patient now acts, behaves, and functions. Often the aim is to dislodge or replace or reduce the typical behavior which is regarded as unadjusted, unhealthy, maladaptive or neurotic. Often the aim is to enable the patient to take on the way of being that came from the deeper personality process. Whatever the therapy regarded as the gain, the procedure accomplishes what we wish to accomplish, namely to enter into the being of the deeper personality process.

Erickson (in Zeig, 1980) relied on the same idea used in Wolpe's reciprocal inhibition. A patient's aggressive bullying behavior was nudged aside by means of a more socially adaptive gentleness toward a woman. However, unlike Wolpe, Erickson took the new behavior from his conception of what lay deeper in the patient, i.e., a gentleness and loving feeling toward the woman. Nevertheless, the problematic behavior was "reciprocally inhibited" by the gentleness and loving. And, in so doing, the patient was backing into being the deeper potential.

The key is selecting the new way of being and behaving from the patient's own deeper processes rather than from the therapist's notions of what is normal or adjusted. The therapist may create double bind paradoxes, incompatible messages, but such that the way out or the choice forces the patient to act on the basis of their own deeper processes (Bateson, Jackson, Haley, & Weakland, 1956; Watzlawick, Beavin, & Jackson, 1967). The therapist may invite the patient to take the role of another person, and to carry out a way of being and behaving that comes from the patient's own deeper resources (Casriel, 1972). The therapist may provide the patient with the right script, words, and behavior in some scene or situation, and the script, words, or behavior are taken from the patient's own deeper processes (Dusay, 1970). What is common across so many of these methods, regardless of the conceptual approach, is the use of new ways of being and behaving that are incompatible and inhibitory to the current ways of being and behaving and that are taken from the deeper personality processes.

By taking the new way of being from the deeper personality processes, one can go back into recent or remote situations and, this time, renegotiate them by being the deeper personality process. Again, many therapies use these methods and identify all sorts of therapeutic accomplishments. Yet the common consequence is that the patient is being the deeper personality process. Bandler and Grinder (1982) specifically use such procedures and refer to them as "changing history." In Gestalt therapy, the therapist hands the patient a concrete way of being and behaving, one generally extracted from the patient's own deeper processes:

> F: Can you do something phoney? Yah?
> M: Yes.
> F: Go on playing Papa, and then go back and each time you answer, "Fuck you!"
> M: Each time I answer my father, I say, "Fuck you"?
> F: Yes, Right. He is sermonizing, isn't he? So let him preach, and each time he tries to bullshit you into something, tell him "Fuck you" . . .
> M: Nyahnyanhyah. I'm getting sick and tired of being treated like a child!
> F: Well, your voice doesn't tell it, doesn't say so. Your voice is a voice of a petulant child. Try my medicine. Tell him "Fuck you."
> M: Fuck you, you old bastard (Perls, 1969a, pp. 146–147).

The commonality across all of these methods is that of letting pieces and bits of the deeper personality enter into the patient. As this occurs, the net result is the transforming of the patient into being the deeper process, and that is what our methods are aimed at accomplishing.

Letting the patient enter into being the deeper process. The idea is to locate and identify the deeper process and then to invite the patient to be it, live it, become it. Of all the therapies, perhaps this idea is most refined in the methods and techniques of Gestalt therapy. How do Gestalt therapists figure out what the deeper process is? They have a number of methods of accomplishing this.

One is the method of polarities. There are several favorite polarities which are held as common in Gestalt therapy. For example, there is the top-dog/under-dog polarity which is regarded as occurring in most people, with one generally seen as on the surface and the other buried deeper. Accordingly, patients who manifest the top-dog are invited to play out and be the under-dog; patients who exhibit under-dog behaviors are told to enact the top-dog polarity.

The "reversal technique" is a variation on this theme. Whatever way of being seems to be uppermost and manifest in the patient, the therapist reasons that the other side of this lies deeper within the patient, and accordingly the patient is asked to act out the opposite:

> One way in which the Gestalt therapist approaches certain symptoms or difficulties is to help the patient realize that overt behavior commonly represents the reversal of underlying or latent impulses. We therefore use the reversal technique. For example, the patient claims to suffer from inhibition or excessive timidity. He will be asked to play an exhibitionist. In taking this plunge into an area fraught with anxiety, he makes contact with a part of himself that has long been submerged. . . . Or, the patient may be unassertive and overly sweet; he will be asked to play the part of an uncooperative and spiteful person (Levitsky & Perls, 1970; pp. 146–147).

Another method is based on the principle of externalization or projection. According to Perls (1969b), virtually all of one's world is populated by externalizations and projections. As a method of re-owning or getting these projections back into the person, the patient is to be or take the role of that externalized or projected part. Accordingly, the patient is to be or take the role of the untrustworthy neighbor, the parent whom the patient feels is not really interested or caring. The patient is to take the role of and "be" the menacing alien forces or the snake of which you are terrified. The patient is to take the role of the tall building, the broken stop sign, or the license plate — anything which has meaning as the externalized, projected part of the patient:

> . . . the therapist suggested she respond as though she were now her
> mother. . . . As she began to explore, she found herself at first apologiz-
> ing by pleading ignorance, and as she continued, now as her own
> mother, she began defending her own right not to listen; then, in tears,
> explained how inadequate she felt as a mother so she dared not listen
> (Kempler, 1968, p. 90).

> Fritz: Okey, be this incomplete house . . .
> N: . . . I'm open and unprotected and there are winds blowing inside
>   (voice sinks to a whisper) and if you climb on me you'll fall. And
>   if you'll judge me . . . I'd fall (Perls, 1969a, p. 102).

These methods locate and identify the deeper personality processes,
and they point the way for the patient to enter into being these externalized or projected deeper parts. In addition, there are Gestalt refinements
for enabling the patient to "be" these externalized parts fully and with
feeling. For example, when being the other part, the patient is to speak
literally as and from the other part. The words and grammar are to
be as and from the other part:

> F: . . . So you can play a train. "I'm a train . . . "
> C: I'm a train and I'm going somewhere, but it's nowhere. It has direc-
>   tion—
> F: *I* have direction.
> C: I have direction. I have *enormous* direction (Perls, 1969a, p. 98).

Another refinement is for the patient to exaggerate the being and
doing, to act it out, dance it out, celebrate whatever it is. If the person
tends to clench her teeth, she is to celebrate that by clenching much
harder, to growl and make sounds appropriate for rigidly tight clenching. If he hides a secret, put the hiding on the stage: "Each person thinks
of a well-guarded secret . . . (and is asked) . . . to boast about what
a terrible secret he nurses" (Levitsky & Perls, 1970, p. 146).

These are featured methods developed within a Gestalt therapy and
useful for enabling the person to get out of the person one is and to
enter into the experiential being of the deeper personality processes.

Doing to the other what the other does to you. Many theories hold
to one or another version of building external worlds out of one's own
deeper personality processes, of externalization, of projection. The notion is particularly useful when the other person does something especially meaningful to you. It is especially meaningful because it comes from

the other person as the externalization or projection of your own deeper insides. Accordingly, the method of reversing the action and doing it to the other person serves to take the patient out of his ordinary operating domain (in our vocabulary) and to allow him to enter into being the deeper domain.

Perls used this method as a variant of his ways of working with projection. The patient is enabled to "own the projection" by what was termed "reversal," that is, by doing to the other what the other did to the patient. If the other rejects or controls the patient, then the patient rejects or controls the other:

> One technical means by which Perls worked with projection involved what he called "reversal"; for instance, the patient who expressed concern with the therapist's possible criticisms of him is asked to become the *criticizer* and to actively criticize the therapist (Shaffer, 1978, p. 90).

This method is open to description from several different vocabularies. Yet the method works in the same way. Within a psychoanalytic vocabulary, it is described as the principle of converse consequences:

> . . . the principle of converse consequences states that experience is mastered by repeating in an active role what one has previously experienced in a passive role; one must do what one has suffered. What alter has done to ego, ego must do to alter (Loevinger, 1966, p. 435).

As a representative of its use in other therapies, Shorr (1972) describes his way of applying this method within the context of his psycho-imagination therapy. For example, doing to others what they have done to you may take the form of "accusing the accusers":

> Here the person who has been under a barrage of self-hate and powerlessness from certain accusers is told to imagine himself in a witness box, and to imagine the accusations that certain people are directing toward him. I then ask him to accuse the accusers. I urge him to scream at them . . . (Shorr, 1972, p. 57).

Open to several different vocabularies, the essential method consists of doing to others what they do to you. It is one way of getting the patient out of the ordinary, continuing personality and into the deeper personality. Interestingly, patients are frequently struck by the thunderous bizarreness of doing to them what they do to the patient. It is as if some grand rule would be violated. It is frequently inconceivable that

I can do to my mother, enemy, boss, grandfather, aunt, father what they do to me. My role is to be on the receiving end, and it is giddily preposterous for me to do it to them. Yet this is precisely the method which effects the radical shift into being the deeper potential of which the other person is the agency. Perhaps that explains in part why doing so is utterly inconceivable.

It is a momentous step for the very heart of the patient to disengage from the operating domain and to enter into being the deeper potential. Many theories of psychotherapy have no place for any sort of change such as this. Some theories are cordial to such a step. What is more, it appears that there are methods for negotiating such a change. In the subsequent chapter, our methods beg and borrow from the methods illustrated in this section. These methods are soft hintings to which our methods are indebted, and out of which our methods are developed.

Methods of Disengaging From the Operating Domain and Being the Deeper Domain: Some Learnings About What Does Not Work

Are there methods that might appear suitable for effecting the change into being the deeper potential, but that do not work or are not useful within the context of experiential psychotherapy?

One of the problems here is that most therapies do not consider it an important goal to invite the very core of the patient to get out of his personality and "be" inside a truly deeper domain. Even if the theory accepts the idea of a deeper domain, it is rare that theories will see therapeutic value in a wholesale being of that deeper domain. Accordingly, there are not that many methods which are useful in accomplishing what most therapies do not aim at accomplishing.

Indeed, in many approaches, the patient's genuine being of a deeper personality process, especially some really alien deeper process, is regarded as awful. The patient is understood as being psychotic, as having lost his mind, as wallowing in "primary process" material. These states are understood as states of craziness, as states to be avoided at all costs, as catastrophic, regressed, monstrous, without reality contact.

Instead of dealing with profoundly deeper personality processes, many therapies confine their work to knowing or being aware of material which is somewhat disturbing, but generally within the zone of comfortably consciousness. It is material which hovers around the edges of what we would term the operating domain. It extends to material which is "pre-conscious" or not quite in awareness. In client-centered therapy, this is the range of work, the somewhat further periphery of what we are to explore of our selves (Rogers, 1959, 1970b, 1975). Methods of empathic reflection, set within the context of the right facilitating conditions, provide for this exploration of what I am. But the workhorse methods of client-centered therapy do not entail the patient ever abandoning the domain of who and what he is, merely stepping to the edges of the self and exploring a little more. There is no wholesale being of any qualitatively different and deeper universe so distant from what one is. Methods in and around those of empathic reflection are not designed or useful for disengagement from the continuing personality and transformation into being deeper personality processes.

The field of psychotherapy is filled with methods of interpretation. Therapists are frequently riveted upon a course of single-minded interpretation of one kind or another. Indeed, many psychotherapies differ from one another in terms of the favorite content of what they interpret at and to the patient. Patients are given the therapist's interpretations of the patient's real feelings, the goal of their immediate behaviors, their essential life philosophies, the sexual or aggressive explanations of the way they are, the real reasons for the way they interact with the therapist, the archetypal influences on their life, the particular ways in which their families have caused them to be, the kinds of early traumas which set their life path, the mistaken ideas they believe in, the wrong values to which they hold, the grand explanation of their problems, the influence of early seductive events, peer relations, birth events, infantile relations with mother, attachment to and loss of early parental figures, and on and on and on.

The family of interpretive methods is not especially useful in effecting the patient's disengagement from the substantive personality in which the patient exists, and in effecting the being of deeper processes. Indeed, for these purposes, the family of interpretive methods is counterproductive, for it tends further to lock the patient into the substantive personality.

The field of psychotherapy also is rich in methods of building therapist-patient relationships that are held as therapeutic. There are all kinds of methods to construct relationships that are helpful, caring, facilitative, corrective, reality-enforcing, managing, parent-replacing, friendly, growth-providing, transferential, bonding, influencing, encountering, childifying, and so on. For each favorite therapist-patient relationship there are many methods aimed at building the relationship either quickly or gradually over years. However, relationship-building methods are not designed for or useful in effecting the patient's disengagement from the continuing personality and entrance into deeper processes. This whole large family of methods is not useful for our purposes. Indeed, as with many common methods, they are counterproductive, for they tend to lock the patient into the substantive continuing personality.

In a similar fashion, the behavioral methods further entrench the patient into the substantive personality. These methods are based upon a conception of human beings without deeper personality processes and have no intention of serving to free the person from their functioning personality and of serving to enable the patient to enter into being the deeper personality processes. There are methods of feedback, modeling, behavioral rehearsal, desensitization, assertiveness training, motivational stimulation, social reinforcement, contingency management, relaxation training, self-control, aversive control, covert sensitization, and more. Although these methods are common, they were neither designed nor effective for enabling the patient to disengage from the ordinary, continuing personality and to enter into being the deeper personality process.

These methods are not the soft hintings of our own methods. They are not effective for our purposes. In general, the purposes of this chapter have been to provide a conceptual basis for methods of enabling the patient to disengage from the operating domain and to enter into the being of the deeper potentials. We now turn to the working methods themselves.

CHAPTER 6

Experiential Being of the Deeper Potentials: Methods

CARRYING FORWARD OF experiencing means that the experiencing is heightened, the deeper potential is made alive and is touching against the patient (Figure 2, p. 4). The carrying forward of experiencing has gone as far as it goes, and now the therapist drifts out of the patient and into the external relationship. We are ready for the patient to be the deeper potential.

Or, the therapist is speaking with the voice of the deeper potential and the encountering process moves ahead to a point where there is now a measure of integration between patient and deeper potential, which is touching against the patient (Figure 4, p. 107). Internal integration has accomplished a fair measure, and the therapist drifts out of the patient and into the external relationship. We are again ready for the patient to be the deeper potential.

The purpose of this chapter is to describe the methods which may be used to undertake the radical disengagement of the patient from the operating domain and into the very being of the deeper potential.

The Therapist Shows the Patient What to Do and How to Do It

From outside, the therapist is the teacher or guide who shows the patient what to do and how to do it. This is what the therapist does in the initial step of each session (Figure 1, p. xvi), and this is what the therapist does in the present step also. Most experiential therapists will give more or less the same instructions in more or less the same ways for just about every patient. The emphasis is on showing the patient what to do and how to do it. There is no two-person interactional conversation, no being of a human being who engages in any sort of therapeutic relationship, no providing of a general rationale or background, no wanting or urging or trying to get the patient to undertake this step, no attempts to get around the patient's unreadiness or unwillingness to do this now. But there are considerations in the therapist's showing the patient what to do and how to do it.

Identifying and describing the method the patient is to use. The therapist starts by identifying and describing the method so that the patient knows what to do and how to do it. Suppose that the therapist elects to use the method of reversing the interaction so that the patient does to the significant other figure what that figure is doing to the patient. Or suppose that the therapist selects the method in which the patient goes back into some early situational context and, this time, goes through the scene as the deeper potential instead of the way she actually went through the scene. Whichever method the therapist selects, it is described in sufficient detail so that the patient has a good grasp of the task, of what to do. It is important that the patient understand what is to be done, for it is the patient who is to undertake the method and carry it out.

Suppose that therapeutic work brought patient and therapist to a point where they were existing in a scene where the patient's deeper experiencing was disclosed as a sense of tough coldness, rejection, the strength of having all the cards. In the scene, however, it is mother who is the agency of this experiencing. As always, mother is removed, cold, rejecting, and the patient is tearfully trying to be good, to gain a crumb of acceptance, forever panicky about mother's stern withdrawal and rejection. Now it is time for the patient to do the incredible by reversing the process by doing to mother what mother has always done to the patient. The therapist shows the patient what to do:

T: All right, Ann. We now know something, something we've touched on again and again. There is something in you, a possibility in you. It is something that knows what it is like to be tough and hard and cold. To hold all the cards with regard to mother. There is something in you that knows what it's like to be strong *to her*! It senses what it is like to reject *her*, to be the strong one over *her*! It knows what it's like to have *her* pleading, to make *her* cry! *It* can be cold and hard and rejecting! It is ready to do the impossible—to treat her the way she has always treated you! It is ready to reverse the whole thing and to be the way she has always been. It can look down on *her*, it can make her crawl to *you*, it can be cold and hard to *her*. It has all the power to make *her* plead for *your* little crumbs! *You* can walk away if she isn't good! Ha! That's the task. That's the thing we're ready to do next.

The therapist proceeds to outline what the patient is to do in being this way with mother. This may include specifying the exact words to use, how to say the words, the voice quality and the bodily stance. The therapist may model for the patient, carrying it out as and for the patient. Proper instructions may take time, but the therapist must detail whatever is necessary in showing the patient what to do and how to do it.

Consider the patient whose deeper experiencing was uncovered within the context of early scenes in which his father tries to convince the family that he is a witty and cultured man for all seasons, superior to those with money and big houses and power. The family went along with his pretense, appreciated his long sermons, dutifully laughed on cue. Opening up this scene, the patient was nagged at by inner voices which insisted something was wrong here. No one mentioned his father's drunkenness and his bouts of hurtful depression, his long mysterious absences, and his utter dependence on the money provided by their grandfather. Later in the session, there emerged the deeper potential for experiencing a kind of straight-arrow honesty, a candid openness to reality. Given this deeper potential, and given the early scene, one method of being the deeper potential involves going back into the early scene and living it through as the deeper potential. While this method will be discussed later in this chapter, the important point is that the therapist identifies and describes what the method is and how to carry it out. The patient is to know what to do and how to do it in sufficient detail to do it competently.

T: Here is a being honest, saying it straight, coming right to the point, There is a kind of "and that's the way it is" quality to it. A real characteristic. There inside. And we always have those scenes with your father. He goes to a dinner, someone always invites him, and he always manages to go. He gets drunk, comes home, and starts lying. He's better than the others. None of them can even change a washer in a faucet! The family laughs. André laughs. That's the way it was, over and over. Now suppose that this deeper thing in you were there instead of you. Just suppose. No one in the family was like that. But something in you would have been much different than you were. It knows what it's like to be honest, straight honest, really honest. It knows what it's like to cut through the bullshit and tell it like it is. If that part had been there, if that part had been André, it would have said things and done things and felt things — its way. That's what's waiting. That's what we can do.

The therapist will continue describing what to do and how to do it until the patient knows exactly what to do and how to do it. It is a matter of teaching, instructing, guiding, showing, demonstrating. The patient is learning a skill, and the therapist is the competent master of the skill and of how to teach the patient the skill. Over a series of sessions, the patient acquires these skills, and learns how to follow the methods which will carry him out of the operating domain and into the being of the deeper potential. In all of this, the therapist is the instructor. When the therapist is "outside" the patient, the therapist is the instruction-giver, and these are the instructions the therapist gives at this point in the session.

Emphasizing the patient's readiness, willingness, and full responsibility. While the therapist knows what to do and how to do it, success in this step depends immeasurably upon the patient's readiness and responsible willingness to undertake this step. The therapist is teaching the patient a skill, the learning of which depends upon the patient's voluntary readiness, willingness, and full responsibility (cf. Rose, 1976). If the patient is ready to undertake this next step, fine; if not, fine. The patient is the one who is to undertake the step, and the patient is the one with full responsibility for doing it or not, for doing it well or not. This must be emphasized and it must be meant.

There are two reasons why the patient has virtually all of the responsibility, willingness, and readiness. One is that this step will not work unless the patient is ready, willing, and accepts full responsibility. The other reason is that all of the instructions from the therapist express the value system of experiential psychotherapy, namely, that full choice and responsibility lie with the patient—for undertaking the step or not, for doing it now or not, for doing it a little or a lot or not at all, and even for doing it for a second or a minute or however long the patient wishes.

Throughout the instructions, the therapist repeatedly cedes to the patient full choice and responsibility:

T: What do you think? Do you feel ready to do this? Would you rather not?
      Would you rather wait a while or go to something else? Is this all right?
Pt: I want to. Yeah. I want to do it . . .
T: OK. I'll tell you how to do it. But if you want to stop at any time, just say so. It's up to you.

Usually patients will be ready and willing, especially if the therapist is honest and forthright in ceding all the responsibility to the patient, all the right to be ready or not, and to be willing or not. But what does the therapist do if the patient declines? The answer lies in the nature of the ongoing experiencing as the patient is declining. Suppose that our work thus far has brought the patient to the near vicinity of a deeper experiencing of openness, bondedness, closeness with her mother. The mother's brother had died of cancer when the patient was a child, and he remembers his mother lying on the sofa, face to the wall, gloomy and depressed. The therapist framed in the scene and opened the possibility of being this new way, this new experiencing, in the scene. The therapist gave full instructions, and allowed himself to be in that childhood scene, expressing that experiencing. He then came out of the experiencing and out of the scene, and asked the patient if he were ready. The patient is now curt, tight, and snapping:

Pt: No child of 10 would ever be that way! He'd be pretending to be an adult!

When the therapist is not outside giving instructions, the therapist is inside, aligned with the patient. These words, spoken in and through the therapist, were accompanied with a sudden and powerful clenching of the muscles in the chest wall, with a hot metal shield in the chest cavity. Everything was charged and hurt and angry inside. We are now back at carrying forward the potentials for experiencing, and the therapist does so by describing the compelling bodily sensations.

T: (Quietly, carefully) My chest is suddenly tight, really tight. And it feels like a hot metal shield.
Pt: (Tight and bristling) When you were there with her, you reached out and touched her shoulder. I never touched her! She . . . I saw something all right! She turned on me! She went like this! Pushed me away. Get away! Like I was an animal! That's reality! See! That's what happens! I fucking know! I spent my whole life trying to be the loving one in the family. No, Dad did too, for a while. Then he gave up. No! I damned well don't have the slightest desire to get into that anymore. My whole life I spent making sure that I could live decent without opening myself up to any hurt from anyone! That's a closed chapter. No one is going to dig at me any more, not you, not any woman, and NEVER MY FUCKING BITCH MOTHER! DO YOU GET THE POINT???

There are two therapeutic morals here. One is to respect that patients have choice, responsibility, and the right to undertake this step or not to. If they say no, if they indicate no, then it is no. The second therapeutic moral is that the instructions to be in the significant scene and to be the deeper potential may well activate something very deep and

very powerful, something which is fully justified to come to life under
the radical possibility of the patient's being the deeper potential. Honor
the patient's declining the invitation; accept the new material which
is thereby activated. Flow with what comes from the patient in carrying
forward this new experiencing or in working the internal encountering
relationship.

Generally, however, the patient accepts the invitation. Then the
therapist describes precisely what the patient is to do, step by step.
These precise instructions will of course vary with the identified method. However, a few instructional guidelines apply to all of the methods
for disengaging from the operating domain and being the deeper potential, and the balance of this section deals with the instructional guidelines.

Attaining the state of strong bodily sensations. One guideline is to
say it and do it and be it until strong bodily sensations are present.
Keep going until this happens. The patient is to be the deeper potential
meaningfully and really, and one mark of having attained this meaningfulness and realness is reaching a state in which there are strong bodily
sensations. This means the patient is to "be" the deeper potential, carrying out its behaviors and feelings with loudness and fullness. It is as
if the patient is pumped up with the deeper potential, and what it is
and does comes forth with an intensity which is accompanied with
strong bodily sensations. Here is what the therapist says to Ann, who
is ready and willing to reverse the tables and be to her mother the way
mother has been to her:

T: If you say and do things to mother, and nothing much happens in the body,
   you haven't gotten there yet. Even if there is a little fluttering in the
   stomach, that's not it. You have to be with her and do it to her so that
   things really happen in your body. Really get going. You might be
   laughing and your whole chest is light and tingling, or you may be crying
   with all those feelings. Your heart'll pound and pound or your whole
   head will be light or your whole body will be charged up. It has to be
   strong in your body. So move your body around if that helps. Make
   a fist. Move your arms and legs. Laugh or cry or scream or bellow or
   say it very quietly, as long as there is real feeling in it. That's when you're
   being cold and hard to *her*, you're making *her* crawl and feel shitty.
   That's when you're looking down on *her*! Things will happen in your
   body; it'll feel it.
Pt: OK! Yes. I see!

Sometimes the patient will do it a little, stop, and pull out. Something
began to happen in the body, perhaps, or maybe nothing occurred.

Now that therapist and patient are out of the scene and out of the being of the deeper potential, there is the option of returning for more work—or not:

T: Well! Something happened.
Pt: My heart is really beating and my hands are shaking!
T: Me too. Like a light charge of electricity. My heart is still going.
Pt: Yeah. That's something!
T: Are you ready to go further—till even more starts to happen in your body? Rather not? Yes? What do you think?
Pt: I think I can, yes! That was good!
T: OK. Let's go back. Talk to her, right at her, and keep on. And then things will start up even more in your body. You can go further. Maybe all over the body, all over. Sensations and feelings all over the body.

The therapist really means that the patient has full and honest choice, full readiness, willingness, and responsibility. While the therapist shows the patient what to do and how to do it, it is the patient who must undertake this step herself. There is no doing it to the patient. The therapist is not clever. Nothing is held back or kept private inside the therapist's head. Once the patient and therapist know what to do and how to do it, the readiness, willingness, and full responsibility lie with the patient, and the patient is the one with the choice to indicate yes or no.

The propulsion of continuous expression. When the patient gets inside a deeper potential, fully being that deeper potential means continuously saying and behaving and doing. Say it more, say it a little differently. Do it again and again and again. There are to be no silences, no exits of inaction and unexpression. What is necessary is a groove of continuous expression.

Frequently the patient will say the same words again and again, as if to fill the gap and to keep going. Then there may be a slight change in what is said, or some new words may be added. There is a pulsating rhythm, punctuated by changes in the words, and the rhythm then continues: "You're suffocating me, suffocating me, suffocating me. . . . You're doing it to me, doing it to me, doing it to me . . . and I don't want it. I don't like it, I can't stand it. I can't stand it! It's too much for me! Too much for me, too much for me, too much for me, too much for me. . . . YOU'RE KILLING ME! MY GOD, YOU'RE KILLING ME!!!" All of this is contained in the instructions:

T: When you are in the scene and when you are letting yourself be this way, this other way of being, just keep talking. Keep saying whatever comes

out of you. Say it again and again, over and over, repeat it again and
again, over and over. Just keep making sounds and saying and doing.
Make sure there are no pauses, no silences, even if you must say it again
and again, over and over, changing what you do and say a little or a
great deal. Over and over, with no pauses and no silences . . .

The patient is not to fall into prolonged silences. Neither is the patient to fall into his ordinary ways of exiting from being the deeper
potential. When the student of meditation focuses attention on the
flame of the candle, he is told by the master how to anticipate and avoid
standard kinds of deflections which entice everyone. He is to expect
to imagine tiny explosions, or to be enticed by sleep, or to experience
burning sensations in the spinal cord. The master teaches the student
how to be alert to these interfering deflections, and the student learns
to avoid them. Similarly, the therapist knows the patient's favorite ways
of deflecting from the work, and he is told to not give in to these
distractions:

T: And when you are starting to be that way, you may find yourself pulled
    to become very dizzy and nauseous and you will feel like vomiting. You
    are to keep on with your work and to let all that go by. Do not give
    in to it. Just continue.

Often the patient will proceed up to a point, and then an effective
distraction will stop the work. As therapist and patient pull away, and
they consider reentering, they discuss the importance of going beyond
that point without falling into that distraction:

T: If you are ready to go back, this time, you know that you may again come
    to a point where you feel incredibly lost and alone and panicky. That
    state pulls you away. You are to let it go, let it pass you by. Do not
    fall into that state. It is a good and effective way out which is helpful
    in many ways, but not now. This time do not give in to it. Just keep
    going. Go through it or around it and keep on being what you are.

The patient is to get into the propulsion of continuous expression,
saying and being the deeper potential over and over again, more and
more, modifying and refining what is said and done, but always continuing on and on with no breaks, no pauses, and no giving in to the
favorite exits, avoidances, interferences, or distractions.

*Instructions for showing the patient how to be in the scene and how
to be in the deeper potential.* The therapist may have identified that

the appropriate method is for the patient to reverse the action and to do to the significant other that which the significant other has done to the patient. Or the therapist may identify the method of self-encountering, or succumbing to the catastrophic, or undergoing the critical moment as the deeper potential. Whatever method is identified, there are always two parts to the task. One consists of getting wholly into the scene or situational context or critical moment, and the second consists of being the deeper potential and doing what it does. The second part varies with the actual method which is selected, and this will be discussed later under each of the methods. The first part, however, is standard across all of the methods, and the therapist gives instructions as needed.

Being in the scene means being ready and willing to live wholly in that scene or moment. The therapist instructs the patient to describe everything that is here in the scene: the surroundings, the interactions, the colors, the sounds, the details of the situation, everything.

T: If you are ready, here is what you must do to live completely in this scene, this moment with your father. You must go back to being a little boy of nine. It is 1946. Winter. Cold outside. Your father is sitting in the big chair in the kitchen. Now you are to describe everything about him, and talk to him, or talk to yourself about him. Talk as the little boy of nine. Tell what he looks like, everything about him. Tell what you are thinking and feeling, and where you are and what it feels like right here. And look around the kitchen, describing everything about the kitchen. The colors and the sounds and the smells. There are others here too and you will start to see more and more of them, in 1946, how they are and how they look and how they are dressed and how they are talking and how they are thinking. As you see and feel and smell more and more, and as you describe more and more, you will have more and more come to you, and you will describe more and more until you are now all inside this moment, living here and being here in this moment . . .

These instructions enable the patient to get into the scene more and more, and as the patient enters more and more, new material will come forth. There will be more and more disclosed of what is occurring right here and now in the scene, and each little bit will open up more little bits until the patient is existing wholly in the scene.

Not only does the therapist show the patient how to paint himself into the situation, but the therapist also describes in detail how the patient is to be the deeper potential. The instructions include describing what the patient experiences as the deeper potential, and what the deeper potential feels like, thinks like, experiences. The instructions also include careful and precise description of what the patient-as-deeper-potential does, how he acts and behaves, the movements he carries out, what words he says, how he says the words and carries out the movements. Examples of these instructions will be give under each of the methods.

Demonstrating how to be in the scene and how to be in the deeper potential. When the instructions are over, and if the patient is ready and willing to undertake this step, the therapist does it right along with the patient. In fact, the therapist should be more competent at this than is the patient. The therapist should be an artisan at entering into the situational moment and also at being the deeper potential. Even before the patient begins his work, the therapist's instructions may well include a demonstration of being in the scene and being the deeper potential in the scene. Demonstrating for the patient is just doing beforehand what the therapist will be doing alongside the patient. The therapist typically demonstrates when the patient does not seem to know how to do it or needs a picture or model or demonstration of what he is to do and how he is to do it. Typically, the patient learns the skills with practice and experience, so that there is less and less need for demonstrations.

Here is the therapist demonstrating how to get into the scene with the father, and family, in the kitchen.

T: I'm sitting right here with the wall behind me. Ginny, my sister, is to my right. Hi, kid! You have you . . . something on . . . can't tell . . . jeans, yah, I see them now, and your sweater that's kind of crinkled, and you are getting sleepy. I'm looking around. Hello Mom, hello Richard. And now I see the walls. They are bright yellow. Dad painted them this summer, but now it's cold. There is a clock hanging on the wall. It is a round clock, about a little over a foot in diameter, with wood around it . . .

Sometimes the patient will be drawn in, taking up where the therapist left off. The patient is now existing somewhat in the scene along with the therapist. Sometimes the patient will attend to the therapist and, when the therapist is done, the patient will begin describing the scene. The therapist describes what she sees, building on whatever picture she has of the scene and going on from there. Frequently the patient will attend to what the therapist is describing and, half-existing in the scene, correct what the therapist has described or proceed onto other components:

Pt: Walls, the walls are green, light green, and there's a calendar on the wall, can't remember where. Where? Can't remember. Dad always got a calendar from work. Pictures of outdoors, hunting, fish, geese. Shooting. Always smelled nice and warm. I like the kitchen. We always eat in the kitchen. Mom sits over here, and I have my place. I like my place . . .

When the therapist demonstrates, she details whatever comes forth, whatever she sees and feels and smells, everything which comes to her as she allows herself to be in the scene more and more. Of course, if she keeps on going, she will paint herself into the scene. Instead, she merely does this enough to show the patient how to do it. The same holds for the demonstration of how to be the deeper potential, including what to do and say and how to do and say it. For this patient, it means demonstrating a straightforward open honesty, a realistic candidness. This is the deeper potential which now has a chance to live again in the scene with father in the kitchen. Father is still a little drunk as he is boasting about his superiority over the other men at the dinner he attended. Father has just told a joke, both masking and expressing the hurt-angry feelings at the other men who are successful and stable. The therapist slides into the critical moment of the scene and demonstrates what to do and how to do it.

T: (After describing the deeper potential, what it is experiencing and what it wants to do. The therapist pauses, and during that time he sinks into the scene and into the deeper potential.) I love my Daddy, but I know he is drunk and no one is talking about his being drunk, and I know that you are, Dad. I'm reaching out and now I have your hand. You look at me. I got your attention. Dad, you're still a little drunk, Dad. And no one is saying anything about it. Dad, Dad! And you sound like you don't feel OK with those other men, Dad. Is that it, Dad? Hey, I'm pretty good, 'cause I'm saying what everyone's thinking, even you, Dad. Right? Now don't get mad, 'cause you have a temper when you feel bad and get drunk and try to put down the men you're with. But I feel more like I know how you feel . . . Dad . . . now take it easy, Dad! I could pretend to laugh, but I'm the one who found you crying one day in the basement, remember, and you really cried when you were telling me about Grandpa, remember, Dad? . . .

Demonstrating how to do it means being and expressing the deeper potential, living and being it wholesomely and wholly. It means being the actualizing, integrating form of the deeper potential.

These are the components of the instructions. The therapist uses these as guidelines, with the aim of getting the patient ready to undergo one or another of the actual methods for disengaging from the operating domain and entering into the deeper potential. When the patient is ready, and when the patient knows what to do and how to do it, then therapist and patient undergo one of the following methods.

SELF-ENCOUNTERING

When the therapist is promoting an integrative encounter between the patient and the deeper potential (with the therapist as the voice of the deeper potential), the therapist is seeing and attending to the patient, and the therapist is engaging in an encountering relationship with the patient (step 3, Figure 1, p. xvi). There is a certain symmetry here, for the patient likewise sees and attends to the patient and engages in an encountering relationship.

There are three components to this method. One is that the patient must actually see herself. That is, the patient literally sees an image of herself over there. She disengages from being herself and, instead, sees that other person who is herself. The patient may be five or ten feet away, closer or further. The patient may see that other figure from today or recently or when she was a child. That other figure is the operating self, the operating domain.

Secondly, the more the patient is separate and truly disengaged from that observed figure, the more the patient is in or near the vicinity of the deeper potential. While it is possible to stand off and see oneself, as in a mirror, and still remain in the operating domain, the more one is removed from that observed figure the more one is gliding into the perspective of the deeper domain.

The final component is encountering. This means that the separated, removed, disengaged patient interacts with and encounters that other figure. The patient talks to her, plays with her, expresses her feelings toward her, cares for her, welcomes her, berates her, and generally engages in an integrative encounter with her. These are the components of the self-encountering method for disengaging from the operating domain and being the deeper potential.

Describing the Operating Self

When the patient actually separates from the operating self and describes what the disengaged operating self is like, there are several valuable therapeutic consequences. For one, sheer experiencing goes up. Also, as the patient gets out of the operating domain and takes a look back at it, there is typically an opening up of new memories and new perspectives on how the patient acts and behaves in her current life. But most importantly, the patient is backing into the deeper potential. Free of the operating domain, free of the patient's continuing disintegrative relationship with the deeper potential, the sense of I-ness is now moving into the deeper potential. By means of careful, persistent, feelinged description of the disengaged operating self, the very center of one's I-ness is becoming the deeper potential.

The therapist instructs the patient to describe the disengaged self and demonstrates how to do it. There is instruction, telling how to, and there is demonstration, modeling. Whether instructing or demonstrating, the main thing is to stand apart from the ordinary, continuing, operating person or self and describe everything about that person: "Act as if the whole thing is a scene from a theatrical play, or as if the action can be frozen and you can move out of being the person and can stand off and describe him. Leave that person over there, and come on over here where we can see him. Pretend that we are invisible or as if the other person cannot hear us. Describe him, and describe him in detail. Describe everything about him, everything about the way he is, the posture, the looks, the way he talks, everything. As if you were the director of the play, or even one of the audience, let yourself have feelings and reactions to him, and describe what they are too. But make sure you do a good job of describing that person over there, that other fellow in the scene."

The therapist slowly and carefully gives the above instructions, going over and over them, filling in more of the parts that are vague or that do not make sufficient sense to the patient.

The therapist also demonstrates how to do it, carrying it out for the patient. As the deeper potential who is separate and distinct from the operating self, the therapist gives his description of the scene, of the operating self, of the way the operating self is and behaves and has thoughts and inner feelings.

The patient is a woman who is scared by angry feelings toward her companion, another woman with whom she lives. In one scene, there was an angry outburst at the companion, after which the patient verged toward tears and then came to a rest in silence. The experiencing of anger was quite intense. But that is now over. The therapist is now out of the scene, and she gives instructions to the patient:

T: Well! That was something! My whole body was charged up, and I felt the snarling!
Pt: You bet! I felt like steel, snapping jaws.

T: Yeah! Now I want to ask you something. There for a few seconds you
   were mad, really mad. The jaws did feel like steel and the snarling was
   like an enraged monster. Something strange came over you.

Pt: It sure as hell did. That's not me. Yeah, did.

T: Yeah, I know. Suppose that we freeze that instant, just hold it there. You
   know, like if you and I were directing a play, and we could stop the
   action, and you and I were maybe ten feet away and watching the actress. She looks like you. Hell, she could be your twin sister, but there
   she is.

Pt: OK.

T: Do you think you could stand about, oh, five or ten feet away from her
   in that moment, just that exact moment when she is mad, really mad,
   and could you describe her? Everything about her? Everything? Her
   posture, the jaws, the body, every little detail as you see them, what
   she's thinking, everything?

Pt: Oh! Uh huh. I think maybe. It's not so easy. It's not, haven't done any
   thing. Yeah, I think so? Like what I see when I look at myself?

T: Sure. Listen. I'll show you what it's like. Give me a second to get over here,
   about maybe six or eight feet away. All right. OK. There. She's . . . I'm
   drawn toward her face. There's a look on her face, no! I am pulled by
   her teeth. They are metal! Yeah! Metal teeth, clicking. She's clicking
   them! (Therapist snaps her teeth together hard.) Sounds like that! Those
   are dangerous teeth! They are in her jaw. There's regular flesh on her
   face and jaw but inside the jaw is also metal. God, she's like a monster!
   . . . OK, I'm stopping. There, that's a little bit. What do you think?
   Possible? Would you be willing to do that? Do you feel ready, or maybe
   not ready?

Pt: When you were talking, I was seeing her eyes. Yes, I can. Yes.

T: All right, but it means really seeing her, really like you and I are about
   five or ten feet away, seeing just her, frozen maybe, in that moment.
   The action is stopped.

Pt: Yeah.

T: And when you describe whatever your attention goes to, just let the sensations in the body, let them get strong, whatever. And keep describing
   in detail, keep describing, no pauses. Out loud.

Pt: Sure, OK, I'm ready.

T: OK, I'll stop now, and now I'm over here with you, and we're looking,
   looking, and you start describing whenever you're ready.

Pt: She's crouched. No, she's on the bed, a big outsize bed, and she's sitting
   back, she's barefoot, and I see her from the side. This is really strange!
   I see her! I was just saying things but now I see her! It's weird! (Vivid
   seeing of oneself in moments of strong experiencing is rare. Accomplishing this is exciting.)

T: It's sort of like being invisible and really seeing her. I see the left side of
   her, and I'm looking at her head, face.

Pt: Yeah. Left side. I'm standing and she can't see me.

T: But she's very much alive!

Pt: Her head. And now I'm coming closer, like a zoom lens, now I'm about four feet from her. This is weird! Her body is wiry, tough. It's poised and she's on her haunches, dangerous, she looks like she could leap out, just attack. Yeah, that's it, she looks tough. Hard! She could, uh, explode at someone. Talons. I see talons. Jesus! I really see them! Her hands are up front, and they're going like this, in and out, and the hands are vicious! Vicious!

T: I see them long and wiry.

Pt: In a second she could leap at Jan and grab her. . . . Her body is like metal strands. Coiled, that's it, she seems coiled. This is strange! I really see her, and I know her! But she's over there! And she's . . . got rage! I hear noises, low gutteral, like a rattlesnake, mad, noises, animal noises. AAaaaaaaaa! She's snarling! Her jaws are clenching and unclenching. I see them. Clench, unclench, hard, unclench. Tightening up. Tight. Unclench. She's like a monster. Yes!

T: A monster! I see her! Yes! All she knows, that's all she is!

Pt: (With full feeling, as if riveted by the image.) NOTHING CAN REACH HER. NOTHING CAN REACH HER. SHE IS MAD AND THERE ARE NOISES COMING FROM HER. SHE COULD KILL! GOD! SHE COULD KILL AND SHE COULD DO IT! SHE'S SHAKING! AND SHE COULD KILL!!! GOD, SHE COULD KILL!!!

T: SURE SHE COULD! SURE SHE COULD! SHE COULD KILL!!!

Here is a deeper experiencing of cold rage, a powerful, murderous violence. By describing the disengaged operating domain, by seeing and describing that ordinary self, the patient has moved closer and closer into being inside the deeper potential. Within the operating domain, there were occasional instances when she experienced a sense of anger, an outburst accompanied with hurtful righteousness. By separating out from that operating domain, by seeing and describing it, she is now undergoing the sheer, energized deeper potential.

It is a back and forth process. The more the patient describes of that former operating self the more is seen, and the more is seen the more is here to be described. As this process moves ahead, the patient is increasingly filled with the deeper experiencing.

Generally, the nature of the deeper potential is no surprise. Earlier work in the session disclosed the nature of the deeper potential by carrying forward the experiencing or by working the relationship between the patient and the deeper potential. But there are times when surprises occur. Disengaging from the operating domain frees the sense of I-ness, and there will be occasions when the floating sense of I-ness will glide into some new deeper potential. But in either case, the I-ness has moved into being the deeper potential, for the act of disengaging from and describing the self is powerful.

Indeed, something rather unusual occurs as the patient really sees her operating self. Especially if the image of oneself is caught in some meaningful moment, the achievement of actually seeing oneself is surprisingly singular. It is like watching a movie or videotape of you, exclusively of you, in a moment of higher experiencing. Patients will often exclaim as they see this image.

As you describe, the very process of finding the right words starts experiencing. You are soon caught up in some kind of (deeper) experiencing as you describe more and more of that image with the right words. Many words will not do it. But some key words will, and when the patient slides into that experiential state, the experiencing in turn gets stronger and stronger. The patient has backed into the being of a deeper potential.

There is something else, something quite distinctive about disengaging and seeing the image of the operating self. The disengaged I-ness sees all sorts of things about her self that would otherwise be left outside of therapy. She has reactions to both gross and subtle behavioral ways of being which observant others might be aware of, but which the patient typically leaves outside the therapy room:

Pt: I'm listening to Harvey talk to the waiter. I see the way I sit there. I'm attractive! I like my hair! I guess I must be bored. Seems like it. Looking off a ways. To the right. Hmmm. She's posing. Ugh. (Sighs) She tilts her chin up a little. Oh this is not very flattering. She looks like a model. Beautiful hair, thick. I feel like I'm sitting at another table, watching her, and she's posing. She looks vain, yeah, she looks like a spoiled brat, uh, sort of, cheap, no, not cheap. There's a word. She looks like there's not much to . . . not a wife. She looks affected. That's it. Posing. I do feel funny. Grim. I don't feel good. Even the table! She selected it, and it's the table where most of the people in the restaurant can see her. Oh! She seems like a vain cheap woman, trying to pose. It's almost a little sad. Up close. She's almost old. She's too old to look like that. Old. She's almost 50 for God's sakes, and she dresses like a 20-year-old! It's embarrassing!

But all of this is only what happens when the patient disengages from the operating self and describes it. The second component of self-encountering includes having an interactive relationship with that described self.

Encountering the Operating Self

As the patient describes the operating self, a moment is usually reached when an actual interaction begins to occur, a relationship between the patient or sense of I-ness and the operating self. This is when the therapist enables the development of a genuine interactive relationship, an encounter with the operating self. The therapist instructs the patient to interact and relate further with the operating self, or the therapist does this for the patient and demonstrates how to engage in an interactive encounter with the operating self.

Encountering means to be with, to interact and relate with. It means saying words directly to that other operating self: "You are old, you're trying to pose; for God's sakes, you're almost 50 years old!" It means reaching out to and touching the operating self, physically contacting that other being, caressing her face or slapping her shoulder or enfolding her in your arms or shaking her in frustrated annoyance. Encountering means interaction, relationship, contact, involvement, presence, impact, reaction.

When the patient actually engages in an interactive encounter with the operating self, with that distinct image, then the major therapeutic consequence is that the patient is more fully being the deeper potential. Describing the image of that operating self accomplishes this to a fair degree; actual encountering of that operating self heightens this even more. Now the patient is almost wholly being the deeper potential as she talks and touches and encounters the operating self.

A distinguishing common feature of this step is the sudden rush of powerful experiencing. Often the patient will suddenly fall into almost uncontrollable wailing, an outpouring of archaic hurts, frustrations, longings, the pent-up explosion of lifelong anguish. There is hard racking crying. Often the body will undergo powerful paroxysms, wrenchings, convulsions, lurchings, fits, seizures, loss of bodily integrity, clonic and tonic contractions.

When the therapist is outside, giving instructions, the therapist tells the patient to talk to the operating self, the described self, or the therapist demonstrates this for the patient: "All right, now, if you're ready, go ahead and talk to him. Say what you wish to him. Touch him. Reach out to him. Be here with him. 'You seem so sad, you seem such an unhappy little boy, like you never know how to be nice for them. You poor baby. . . . '" When the patient is in the scene, seeing and describing that operating self, the therapist takes the next step and says the words to the operating self, or the therapist reaches out and touches that other self.

Pt: I see myself just standing there, clean clothes, 'cause I always did what
    Gramma wanted, and I never really said anything. I see myself maybe
    about five, waiting for Gramma, it's Sunday afternoon, on the front
    porch. I see him sitting by himself on the swing. He liked the swing.
    He was a good boy. He took a bath and washed himself and he's all
    dressed just the way Gramma always wanted.

T: His face looks nice, hair combed. (The therapist is participating.)

Pt: Little hands. He'd sit in the middle of the swing. Clean. He's so clean,
    his hair is combed and he has a nice white shirt on. 'Cause he wants
    Gramma to like him. He never thinks about why he's living with Gram-
    ma, 'cause his mother, she is too busy.

T: He doesn't think about that. There are no thoughts like that.

Pt: (So far the image is a little cloudy, but then it becomes clear and present.)
    He is a good boy and he really looks nice. . . . His face is shining! I see
    him! He has his mouth open like when he's excited 'cause he really likes
    the swing! Huh! It's like watching a real movie! I could, uh, I could be
    on the porch with him . . .

T: (The therapist is now on the porch with the little boy.) Hi little boy. Say!
    I can talk to you.

Pt: I'd like to tell you to wake up, wake up finally. You're a nice kid. (There
    is crying, and the crying is quiet but strong. He sobs more like a little
    child than an adult, with sounds like helpless wailing. Then, after
    perhaps 25–35 seconds or so he continues.) You try so hard, and you'll
    spend the rest of your life trying to get them to approve of you. (The
    therapist is drawn toward reaching out and enfolding the child.)

T: If I reach out . . . (arms outstretched) . . .

Pt: Take my hand. I'll take care of you. (All the while the crying continues.)
    . . . Come with me . . .

There is now a deeper experiencing of bondedness and loving care,
of protecting and nurturing. As the patient engages in the encounter,
the patient enters more and more into the deeper potential. In the above
excerpt the patient was seeing the operating self as a child. Often the
center of I-ness disengages from the operating domain of today, with
its current situational context. For example, in the following excerpt,
the patient was describing the ongoing operating self sitting at home
just a few days ago:

Pt: So he gets mad 'cause he can't find the telephone number of the investiga-
    tion agency. He's got shaking hands. They started since they booted him
    out a couple of years ago. He is depressed and he never smiles, look
    at him! Sixty-two and a bitter old man! Jesus! Look at that sad sack!
    He drinks too much and he never did! His face is lined and old, and

he won't even call his son and daughter-in-law! He's mad at everyone, and his hands shake. He's sitting there by the telephone and he thinks about nothing but that huge fucking file that he has been filling for two years! He is drunk! A depressed old bitter angry drunk! (The therapist is drawn toward saying these words to that operating domain, to move into a more encountering interaction.)

T: I can talk to you, you sad old bitter drunk!

Pt: You're killing yourself! Don't you see? (This is said half-pleadingly and half-angrily, and there are tears. The crying started as soon as he talked directly to the old man. Then his whole body wrenched as if it were bolted by a powerful charge of electricity. This lasted a few seconds and the crying continued.)

T: My God, you pitiful old man, you're going to die!

Pt: You got no health! No job! Practically no money! You've had 35 years with a woman you shouldn't have married in the first place. Hell, you're a drunk. You're in great shape! (He is still crying, but there is a tearful lightness as he continues.) You're wasting your life and you only got a few years. I don't know whether to hit you or . . . I don't know. Maybe stick you in some place. Put you in a wheelchair and . . . do something with you. You're a mess, you know that? You're a real mess. (He is still crying, but the mood is quite different.)

T: You need a spanking!

Pt: You're a spoiled baby! You're a crybaby! You're out of the job and they aced you out, and you have never even liked your wife, and the only thing you are proud of is your kids, now that they're grownup, and you were a lousy father. So GET OUT! And stop beating yourself! You got about another five years of that and you'll die! How about coming with me and we'll find some women? Come on! 'Cause (he started laughing amid the crying) . . . I'll leave you here and go do it myself! You want that? I like you, sort of . . . I'll go off by myself, you drunk! I never thought much about your life anyhow! You're a stupid idiot! (There is a lightness and a sense of freedom, a playfulness in his voice.)

His direct encounter brings with it a being of the deeper potential, an experiencing of freedom and liberation, of striking out on one's own. While this movement into the deeper potential comes in part from sheer disengaged description of the operating self, it comes even more surely from the integrative encounter. And with this being of the deeper potential there occurs the being of the good form of this deeper potential, actualizing it in actual interactive behaviors, in its own integrative form. This is the bonus added to that of sheer disengaging from the operating domain and being this deeper potential.

Describing and Encountering
the Primitive Self

Yolande's world revolved around her father. He was the central and significant figure in her past and current life. Indeed, her whole world was mere decoration around him as the keystone. In one session, therapeutic work brought Yolande to a scene which seemed to occur before she was even born, a scene in which her father still owned the little restaurant, and he was doing a little cleaning up before closing. The "primitive self" refers to those patients who have an axial figure in their world, a figure so central that their world only has meaning in relation to that figure. Self-encountering consists of disengaging from the patient whose world swings around that axial figure, and encountering that figure within the context of that figure's own world in the period from a few years before to a few years after the birth of the patient.

Instead of seeing the operating potential, that self, the patient sees the primitive self who is the significant figure. The patient's primitive self, in this theory (Mahrer, 1978a), originated in those figures for whom the patient was a meaningful center and occurred in that period a few years before and after conception and birth. Standing off from and describing those figures, actually having an encounter with them—this is having contact with the primitive self. The consequence is the being of the most basic potentials. Truly profound therapeutic work which deals with the most basic potentials will get us to the primitive field and to the meaningful events in that early period. When the patient's world revolves around some axial figure, the consequence is the washing away of this bond. Indeed, the patient's whole world changes as the patient describes and encounters the primitive figure during that period. It frees up, it loses the axial figure around whom her whole world depends. It is an incredible liberation and freedom.

The therapist gave Yolande instructions for how to start by describing her father:

T: I know you weren't even born yet. In maybe two or three months you might be conceived. You never saw him there in the restaurant. He sold it just before you were born, and they moved to a place a little larger. Two kids, they needed a larger place. What you have is a half-picture of him. You see him from the side, cleaning the counters before closing. Now just describe him. Every little detail that comes to you as you look at him. It is as if you are seeing him before you were even born, watching him. It is 1947. It is inside the little restaurant, and it is about one in the morning.

Pt: He is alone, and I am looking at the hand, the hand that is holding the cloth. It is hairy, black hair. He is quiet. There is no one with him here. I know what that is. I am alone too. Not human. Being by myself all the time and not human being alone. (She had a flash of the hand, but mostly she is having her usual feelinged reactions to her father, the sharing of a deep pool of aloneness, a gloomy separation from others. If Yolande could only "reach" her father, everything would be all right, but her whole life has been spent trying to reach him or to live a life without him, and the net result has been no change; her whole life swings around him.)

T: Wait a minute! Just describe him! You had a little flash of him at the place before closing. Just describe.

Pt: He's much thinner. He's about 22, and he's just a young kid with a wife and a baby daughter, and I'm going to come along in a couple of years. I'm seeing him! I see a shirt! Isn't this strange! I really see a khaki shirt and brown pants! Baggy. They are baggy on him 'cause he's slender. His shoulders are narrow, and he has a serious look on his face. He has black hair, and he is delicate. Works hard, but he's delicate. This is really strange! I see him! He's all by himself. But I really see him! The khaki shirt is too big on him. But not on the arms. He has long arms, and he's slender. My daddy. I am really seeing you. (She stopped suddenly after addressing him. The therapist says this is OK.)

T: I am really seeing you. Sure. I can talk to you. Go ahead.

Pt: Daddy, you really love this restaurant? Do you? Do you love it? I'll bet you spend long hours here. You sure have a lot of hair, and it's black, and you are slender. You are going to be bald and you're going to put on a lot of weight. I like the way you look. You look good. I like your face. You can hear me. But you seem just sad. You know, you seem sad. Your body. You have a body. You have the things that are important to you. Are you going . . . oh!

T: Oh?

Pt: He looked at me! What do you know? He looked right at me! He wasn't mad or anything. He just looked at me with the saddest look. That was peculiar. It's like that look, like he was pleading to keep his restaurant and not have to get a job in the typewriter shop fixing typewriters and getting fat and pulled in and angry all the time. He wanted the restaurant! You really did? Did you? You loved this restaurant! You love it! Uh! (She is talking rapidly and in little gasps.) This was your place. You are making a mistake! Hey, don't get rid of this place! Dad! (She is starting to laugh, but it seems to come more from the rush of things.) You never shoulda got married! Not yet. And for damned sure you never should have had kids. You managed to scrape together for this little place, right? Dad! Hey you! Don't look sad, you can get out of it! (Laughs) Who am I? I'm a pal! I'm the one who sees where you're blowing your life! This is your life, and not scraping away from one typewriter place to another, old and bitter cause you should have enjoyed your life in the restaurant. Or at least tried. Dad, say no! Say no once, then again and again. See! It's easy. Now again. Yeah, it's easy now. Now say, "I want to keep my restaurant!" Ha! It's getting easier isn't it? That's the way, Dad. God, I feel like I'm floating around the place like a tiny little thing with wisdom and trying to tell you how to let yourself be happy. That's happy, you can be happy, Dad!

Here was an experiencing of "doing what *I* want," a sense of *my* wishes and wants, a sense of *my* own rights. This came actualizingly and integratingly alive for the first time in this description and encountering interaction with the primitive image of her father. In this situational context came the flickering of this archaic potential and the taste of what a life could be like freed of revolving around having to please the angry, bitter, depressed father as the very axis of her whole world.

The specific case is when the external figure is the axial center of one's entire world, as with Yolande. The general case is working with basic potentials. Whether specific or general, being the deeper or basic potentials carries us into the events of the primitive personality, in that critical period a few years before and a few years after conception and birth. By describing and encountering those special figures who constitute your primitive self, you are able to "be" the most fundamental potentials within your personality—and evolve into its actualizing, integrating good form.

DOING TO THEM
WHAT THEY DO TO YOU

In this method, the patient becomes the deeper potential by a clean reversal of a lifelong relationship. Throughout one's whole life, from the very beginning, the parental figures may stand as some compellingly significant agency who always holds all of the psychological cards. The primitively powerful figure relates to you in this particular way, and you are the passive recipient of the parental actions. Our theory holds that the deeper potential resides in that way of being to you, in that way of acting and relating toward you. Our method says that when you finally reverse the process, you are being the deeper potential. When you can be that way to the primitive figures, when you can act and relate toward them the way they acted and related to you, then you are being the deeper potential. To accomplish this, there are certain requisite conditions.

Conditions Under Which
This Method Is Invited

Therapeutic work up to now has consisted of carrying forward potentials and/or working the relationship between the patient and the deeper potential. When this work has brought about a certain set of conditions, we are ready to reverse the process and to do to them what they have done to the patient. One of these conditions is being in a scene with the primitively powerful figure. For example, the patient is a young adolescent who is tight and scared as he tells his father that his swim coach has selected him for special lessons because he is really becoming proficient. Father snaps out a few undermining shots, and the patient is decimated. It is important that the patient exist in this scene and that father occur as a powerful significant figure around whom the patient's world revolves. The center of gravity in the patient's world must reside in father.

The scene may be from childhood, and the primitive agent may be the parental figure. The scene may be from today, and the primitive figure may be someone other than the parent. Indeed, the deeper potential may emanate from the hated enemy, the monster beneath the cottage, the alien creature from another planet, the secret foreign agent, the neighborhood dog with the penetrating eyes.

A second condition is that the interaction is a lifelong theme. Throughout the patient's life some figure or agency is always doing to the patient, e.g., alien creatures, external forces, the companion with whom he lives, a boss. Someone or some agency is always there to undermine him, undercut him, sabotage him, or whatever is the nature of the deeper potential carried out by the external figure or agency onto the patient as the passive, helpless, victimized receiver.

The third condition is that it is quite unthinkable to reverse the process and to do to them what they do to the patient. So ingrained and entrenched is the one-way process that it is inconceivable to reverse the action. It is as if the patient were born under the inviolate law that these primitive figures and agencies do this to the patient. To reverse the process is simply beyond comprehension. When these three conditions are present, then we are ready to invite the patient to be the deeper potential by existing in the scene and doing to them what they have always done to the patient.

There is a variation on these conditions. In this variation, instead of some compellingly significant other figure, there is a body phenomenon such as cancer or asthma or ulcerative colitis. There is no scene or critical situational context, but the other conditions are present. That is, the bodily phenomenon is compellingly significant and it is absolutely unthinkable that the patient might reverse the process and do to the bodily phenomenon what it does to the patient.

When these conditions are present, they invite the method of doing to them what they have done to you. In this sense, as is typical in experiential psychotherapy, the therapist more or less just flows along with the therapeutic method rather than making thoughtful conscious decisions about what to do. A few examples will illustrate the conditions which invite the use of this method.

Jeremy was always the victim of his father's hatefully rejecting looks and actions. Father held all the cards, for without father's acceptance, Jeremy would be nothing. His whole life consisted of wooing his father, trying to be accepted a little bit, never offending his father. In the recollected scene, Jeremy comes home in the evening, after playing baseball. He remembers the look on his father's face, the cold eyes, impassive dead expression. Already his heart is pounding and he is in danger of exclusion. It never enters his mind that he could have that same facial expression and turn his father into a terrified pleader for a crumb of acceptance.

Esther had always been the one who was on the outside. There were her mother, father, and older brother. She was not part of that gang, and they all regarded her as an outsider. In the scene, they were merely talking together in the kitchen, and she wasn't even bothering to try to join in; what's the use anyhow? Her whole life was spent cultivating the hurt of not really being one of the family. It was unthinkable that she should ever be the inside one, and that she could keep them away, shun them as outsiders.

Tom's mother and father were competent at everything: being married, maintaining a home, having friends, tennis, knowing how to repair things, being physically attractive. Tom was the failure who tried. In their eyes he was worthless, a kind of stumblebum who had no talent of any kind. Living in this world, Tom remembers watching his parents play tennis, and an aunt asked him if he wanted to hit a few balls. His insides churned as he mumbled words, keenly aware of the looks on his parents' faces as they said nothing but just looked at him. It would be inconceivable for Tom to be the competent one who made his parents feel like stumblebum losers.

Lisa remembers scenes in which her parents would tear at her for keeping things in, having private thoughts, even hiding things in her room. When she was very young they would make her feel awful for putting a pretty little rock in a drawer—without telling them about it. She was not even to look like she was having private thoughts. When she was hated for being "at it again," the "it" consisted of trying to have anything of her own or even venturing outside the family for anything. It was unthinkable that she could accuse her parents of holding private thoughts, keeping things to themselves, daring to venture out of the region of her mandate.

The incontrovertible rule is that the significant early figure does it to the patient, and the patient is the victim, the bad one, the receiver. When this is illustrated in some explicit scene, and when it is unthinkable to reverse the process and to do it to them, the conditions are ripe for this method.

The subclass is when the early parental figure is replaced by a bodily phenomenon. Clearly the cancer is going to kill him. It is beyond medicine and surgery and prayer and everything because it is cancer. The patient is the helplessly passive victim who is going to be killed by the powerful cancer (cf. Mahrer, 1980b). The scenes are waiting for the patient to see the cancer doing its work. It would be folly for the patient to do to the cancer what the cancer does to the patient. That would be as ridiculous as Lisa's reducing her parents to quivering, slobbering, frightened little victims for having the audacity of having private thoughts. These are, however, the appropriate conditions for doing to the other what the other does to you.

The Consequences

The main consequence is that the patient moves into being the deeper potential. Like "self-encountering" and like the three methods to be described subsequently, this method has this main consequence. But there is an additional bonus to this particular method, a bonus which is singular and deserves some discussion because of its very singularity. Reversing the process is often accompanied with a rush of exhilaration, a dizzifying sense of freedom. There is a surge of exciting power, a "high." Patients describe this as " . . . the wildest 'high' I ever had . . . it was like going straight down on a giant roller coaster. . . . I was filled with so much energy. . . . I never felt so free, it was incredible. . . . I couldn't stop; first time in my life I ever felt like that; it was wonderful, like a huge battery inside. . . . " There are some reasons for this added bonus, this consequence of exciting freedom and power.

One reason is that the patient has disengaged from a very particular kind of operating domain. It is one of constraint, of being the victim, the one who is held in and constrained. The primitive external figure has the power, pulls all the strings. Mandate lies inside that external figure. It is the external figure who has the power of determining, structuring, setting the ground rules. Disengaging from that operating domain is like flinging open the doors to a lifelong prison cell. You are suddenly no longer the imprisoned pawn, the victim, the one who is passively done to. This alone is energizing.

Another reason is that the reversed process has been in place from the very onset of the patient's life. What the primitive figures have done to the patient is the story of the patient's entire life from the very beginning. Small wonder that the astounding act of reversing this process is accompanied with such an incredible surge of power.

Third, the content of the deeper potential always includes power, archaic and primitive power. The primitive figures have all the power, and the primitive patient has only that which is invested by the primitive figures. It is the complete power of ownership, of total control and determination. This is the archaic power which is compressed into the primitive parent's setting the rules for how the patient is to be, or being the all-powerful rejecter, or being the one who determines that the patient is being good or bad. Being the one who dares to reverse the process and do to them what they did to you is taking on massive power.

Finally, in reversing the process, the patient is cracking apart the fundamental laws of the universe. It is quite unthinkable that I should be the one who determines that father apologizes to me, that I am the one who decides whether or not mother is lovable. Patients who exist in this primitive world cannot conceive of violating the laws of the universe. To do this is to endanger everything. The very structure of the world cracks wide open. The patient is risking the very end of the world.

All in all, the main consequence for the therapeutic process is the patient's entering into being the deeper potential. But reversing the interaction and doing to the primitive agency what that agency alone is entitled to do to the patient is a method which releases incredible power, freedom, excitement. It is a most singular bonus.

A Few Illustrations

The instructions include all the elements discussed at the beginning of the chapter. In addition, they include a description of the roles the patient is to fulfill and the other figure is to fulfill. The therapist is careful to ascribe the other figure's power to the patient and the victim's role to the other figure.

T: (Following the standard instructions) OK, if you're ready, then it's time for *you* to do it to *her*. This time, you are to be the one who won't let her into *your* life. She has to stay with her new husband and his little baby daughter, and *she* is the one to feel what it's like to be the odd one out. *You* have all the cards now. She is the one who has to come to *you*. *You're* the one with the strength, *you're* the one *she* has to come to. Ah, I'm inhaling it. . . . Are you ready?

Pt: (Starting out a little hesitantly but eagerly) I do not want to eat the cereal, and if I don't want to eat the cereal, that's the way it is! You have to figure out what *I* want, and if you don't get it right, then you can feel shitty. That's the new rule around here. I'm setting the rules from now on! I'm the strong one! (The therapist positions herself alongside the patient to allow all of this to flow through the therapist, and she carries forward this experiencing.)

T: Come to me! If I don't accept you, you're dead. Zap!

Pt: (Typically, if the patient slides partially into reversing the process, whole vistas of appropriate words and ideas come to the patient, and the patient literally becomes the deeper potential with a genuine script.) Mother! Hey lady! I'm over here, with the shitty cereal! I got something to tell you! Up till now I've been the bad one, right? The bad one 'cause I don't fit into the new family! Huh? Well, that's *shit*, mother!! You really ran a number on me, didn't you! The pretense is over! Go ahead and surround yourself with a new man and a new kid. But the truth is *my daddy left you*!! You never would admit that! You made it like *I'm* bad 'cause I won't accept this new family! My daddy left you 'cause he was stuck with you and he wanted out. From me and from you, and he left you! He left you! He said goodbye to you! He didn't want any more of you! Who's the one who doesn't belong, doesn't fit? IT'S YOU! YOU! YOU! DON'T TRY TO PIN THAT ON ME!!! Can't you get that through your damned head? You can't spend your whole life pretending that he didn't exist or that you weren't married for 11 years or that I don't exist or that your man didn't want to be with you anymore! I'm not going to be your rejection goat! He rejected you!!! So now it's time for all three of you to pack up your rejection game and go play some where else. You're going to have to get out of here, all three of you! All three of you are going to have to lie to each other about the lives you didn't have before. No! None of your little twistings anymore! Face the truth kid, he didn't want you anymore, and I don't want you any-more either. My daddy and I are saying the same thing to you now!! We've had enough and now get out!! Go away! We don't want you anymore . . . !! WOW! WOW WOW WOW!!! WHERE THE HELL DID ALL THAT COME FROM? I'm buzzing!!

Lisa's whole life was spent being accused of pulling in, having private thoughts, hiding, not being open and sharing. Attempts to have a

private diary were evidence. Not telling her mother everything that happened at school was evidence. Having a faraway look was evidence.
When she was in her twenties, she spent two bouts in the mental ward
of a hospital after acquaintances found her sitting alone on the bed.
She had been there for three days, not eating, not being with anyone.
In the hospital she remembers having peculiar thoughts about the
thoughts she was having, and hearing voices which warned her against
revealing anything to "them."

Therapeutic work arrived at the early scene in which she was sitting
in the living room reading a novel, and her mother wanted to know
what the book was about. Lisa gave a few offhand vague answers and
her mother began criticizing her for being pulled in and withdrawn.
The highlight was when her mother tried to trace where Lisa got the
book. When she found that Lisa had been given the book by a friend,
and especially a friend whom mother did not know or condone, mother
was furious. Lisa was "peculiar" and "something was really wrong"
with her. The therapist details the reversal:

T: (After citing the basic instructions) . . . This time it's *your* turn. Make *her*
   feel bad for having private thoughts, especially private thoughts about
   maybe wanting to go outside the family! She keeps things to herself.
   She spends time and you don't even know how she does it. *She* is to
   feel rotten because *she* doesn't tell *you* everything. *She* is bad because
   she never tells *you* where *she* is and what *she* does and . . .
Pt: (Explosive laughing) I couldn't! I just couldn't!
T: OK.
Pt: (Still laughing) I've never, in my whole life! She wouldn't stand for it! No,
    no, I want to. (Here is a stirring of readiness.)
T: (Firmly) She spends her mornings when you're in school, and she doesn't
   read, but she has thoughts, and she has the audacity to keep them to
   herself.
Pt: Yeah! This is crazy!!
T: What does she say to Gramma? Gramma and she live so close! She damn
   well should tell you everything; otherwise, otherwise, she's bad! I'm
   warming up. Ready? I see her. See her. Look at her.
Pt: I got the book from Gramma! (Laughs) No I didn't, but Gramma has
    books. I remember reading when I'd stay at Gramma's . . . I liked her
    books. (It starts now.) You never read those books. You never did
    anything at Gramma's. And you only live a few blocks away from
    Gramma! How come? No one does that! I could crawl from here to
    Gramma's. You never got more than a few blocks away! How come?
    You don't read! You never did read! Your mother reads! Gramma used

to read to me! Why didn't you ever read to me? Did your mother ever read to you? Mama? Mama, what's the matter, no answer?

T: STOP THINKING MAMA!!

Pt: Yeah? (And here it comes.) You have a package of letters in a box of your stuff at Gramma's. Love poems! From the guy you married when you were 17!!! Ha! And you were in love! And he was Jewish! Jesus! Grampa had it annulled, and Grampa died a year later. He died of a heart attack! TALK ABOUT ALL THAT MAMA! (Screaming) YOU'RE CRAZY MAMA! YOU NEVER TALK ABOUT THAT!!! (Explosively) I could kill you! You want to read! I'll have a party, with Gramma and your older brother and all your church friends and Daddy, and I'll read the love poems. Jesus, we all will. I'll invite the sucker. How old is he now? 50? Jesus, I'll invite his wife and children. You won't ever talk about your teenaged escapade. Did you get pregnant? DID YOU? TALK!!! TALK!!! What did your mother say to you? Where did you get married? One of the poems was about you two and the motorcycle. It lasted four months. What happened, Mama? Did you get pregnant? DID YOU TELL GRAMMA AND GRAMPA EVERY LITTLE DETAIL? TELL ME MAMA. DON'T HAVE PRIVATE THOUGHTS, YOU BITCH! GOD DAMN YOU, YOU'RE SICK! YOU'RE OUT OF YOUR MIND! YOU OUGHT TO BE PUT AWAY! (She is breathing fast and hard, and then she starts mild laughing, and slowly comes down.) Mama, you're a mess. Too bad. You mighta been a good friend. But you're not . . .

This method succeeds in enabling the patient to enter into being the deeper potential. But it succeeds when the method is used under the right conditions. What the patient reverses must be the deeper potential, and that means the other figure or agency is to be the externalization or agency or primitive manifestation of the deeper potentials within the patient. The right conditions also refer to a significant scene in which the other figure is expressing that same old process, the patient is caught in the same old reaction, and reversing the process is quite unthinkable. Under these conditions, this method will succeed in opening the way for the patient to be the deeper potential.

SUCCUMBING TO THE DEEPER POTENTIAL

The patient becomes the deeper potential by giving up the struggle against it, all efforts to avoid, deny, hide or stay away from the looming deeper potential. Instead, the patient gives in, surrenders, and succumbs. This is the essence of the method.

Conditions Under Which This Method Is
Invited

The most common condition is simply the consequence of therapeutic work so far. That is, carrying forward the potentials for experiencing and working the relationships between the patient and the deeper potential both bring the patient to a point where she is right on the edge of being the deeper potential. In this sense, therapeutic work does the opposite of what the patient has been struggling against her whole life. In being the operating domain, the patient has been working hard to preserve and to maintain herself as the operating domain, and thereby to insure that she does not become the deeper potential. Being the operating domain means denying, opposing, hiding, blocking, pushing away, avoiding the deeper domain. Carrying forward the potentials for experiencing tends to activate the deeper potential and to bring the patient very close to succumbing to the deeper domain. Likewise, working the relationships between the patient and the deeper potential also has the same effect. So sheer therapeutic work brings the patient to the point of succumbing to being the deeper potential. This is one condition under which the patient is simply invited to succumb.

In addition, there are some quite specific ways in which therapeutic work provides the right conditions. One is when the work highlights crisis situations in which the patient's whole world is collapsing and everything pulls the patient to surrender into being the deeper potential. In crisis, the collapse of one's entire world throws the patient into being the deeper potential. These may be immediately current crisis situations or remote traumas, but they are ripe for the surrender.

Therapy will also uncover conditions in which the patient slides away from the awful roles significant others have tried to force onto her. Peers have always seen Joanne as a phony, one who cannot be trusted. Ex-husbands and lovers regard Stella as a self-centered spoiled brat, whose world turns in upon itself and whose center consists of nothing but the patient. Fred has played the family role of the one they consider a little peculiar; something is a little different about little Fred. His whole life has been spent under the spectre that there is something wrong with him. Even recent critical moments are characterized by puffs of terror that there is indeed something wrong with him. Stella becomes tight and hurt and angry whenever anyone verges near the vicinity of accusing her of being a self-centered spoiled brat. Joanne hides the terrible moments when she is an untrusted phony, and she carefully cultivates the role of friendly big sister in her relations with nearly everyone. A condition for succumbing to the deeper potential is when the patient's back is pressed against the wall of the deeper potential.

There is also the condition in which the patient is losing the struggle against the verging awful state. He is terrified of giving in to being the alcoholic bum or the degenerate loser. He is engaged in a last-ditch effort against the catastrophic homosexuality which threatens to tear his whole life to pieces. Or he is clinging desperately to the last hope of really being a well-known archeologist before caving into the fate of being a third-rate academic.

Another special condition is when the circumstances are occurring in the primitive field, in that period a few years before and after conception and birth. The person who struggles against falling into the deeper potential is one of the primitively significant figures rather than the patient herself. When her mother was pregnant, there were some perilous episodes when she nearly gave in to the deeper sexual craving for her stepfather. Just before the patient was conceived, his father lost his job, his father's sister was killed in a terrible accident, and his father almost gave in to the suicidal depression which dogged him throughout the rest of his life. The spectre of succumbing occurred in these primitive figures in the period a little before and after the patient's own conception and birth.

The final special condition is when the patient is on the verge of being assimilated into the compelling other person, when one's center of gravity lies in that powerfully compelling other person and the patient is one slight step away from being and becoming that compelling other figure or entity. It may be the hated grandmother, the devil, the lifelong enemy, the cancer, ulcer, or those who are plotting against him.

The commonality among all these conditions is that the patient is already partly eaten by the deeper potential. All the patient has to do is to stop struggling, surrender, and he will be taken over by the deeper potential.

The Instructions

In effect, the patient is instructed to exist in the appropriate scene and to succumb into being the deeper potential. The scene is to be described in detail, especially the components of the critical moment. The therapist concentrates on describing what the deeper potential is like and how the patient is to allow himself to enter into being the deeper potential. All of this is done in whatever detail is necessary.

Detail is helpful in showing the patient what the deeper potential is like, how it would be in that situation. Detail is necessary in showing the patient how to succumb, what it is like to surrender to that deeper potential.

It is frequently helpful for the therapist to model all this for the patient. The therapist illustrates how to get into the critical moment, how to slide into the deeper potential, and how to be the deeper potential.

Sometimes this requires a great deal of talking by the therapist. When the patient and therapist are out of the scene, careful and detailed instructions may take five or ten minutes or so, especially if this is one of the early sessions. On the other hand, if the patient is experienced and if the therapist and patient are still soaking with the scene and the imminent succumbing into the deeper potential, the instructions may be relatively brief. In the following, the instructions are about average, for the patient has had a fair number of sessions and is rather skilled in the methods of being the deeper potential.

T: So someone had taken some cash from the register. You are 11, and you had access to the cash drawer in the restaurant, just like maybe three or four others, including your brother and sister. And mother just said, "Did you take it?" and she is mad, 'cause she suspects you, right, and she considers you a bad boy, the one who would take it, and the one who would lie to her. She's mad at you. In fact, you really did take it, but she can't prove it. The thing you're trying so hard not to be is a full-blown, defiant, bad kid. That's the deeper thing in you, the thing you try so hard to never be, never show. So now you maybe are willing and ready to give in to it, just to see what the hell that's like. The bad one, the hated one who deserves being hated because you are bad, you did steal the money and she is right. Bad, the bad one. Letting yourself be the bad one. She's looking right at you with that look, that look of anger because she knows that Ken is the bad one and Ken did take the money from the cash register. Letting yourself be the bad one. Letting the bad boy ooze into you. Yes, I am the bad one. I am the bad boy. I stole the money. Maybe I'll never let her know. Maybe I'll lie 'cause I am bad, I am the bad one, and I lie. Should I be bad and lie or should I just let myself be bad and be bad and be bad? I am the bad one, mother! I am evil and sneaky and awful! Yes, I am, I am evil, evil, bad, bad, bad . . . (coming out of it slowly) . . . Whew! Well, how does that feel to you? Ready and willing to go ahead, or not? OK, if you are, then set the scene and the moment and then go ahead. (That is all. Now it is up to the patient, provided that the patient is ready and willing.)

A Few Illustrations

The patient allowed himself to succumb to the deeper experiencing of being that which he had spent his whole life avoiding, namely being a fully evil, wicked, nasty, bad person:

Pt: My uncle won't look at me. He's sitting in the kitchen, and he won't look at me. My sister's here, but my brother's out cleaning the bar. Mom's really mad. "Did you take it?" Did you take it?" Jesus, I did. (Then, screaming) I TOOK THE MONEY! YES, I DID! GOD DAMNED RIGHT I DID! AND YOU KNOW WHY . . . 'CAUSE I'M THE BAD ONE. KEN'S THE BAD ONE! I DON'T EVEN BELONG IN THIS FAMILY! I'M BAD, I'M BAD. RIGHT! EVERYONE KNOWS IT! I'M THE BAD ONE! I've always been the bad kid. If something goes wrong, I did it. Shit! I probably did! I lie too! I won't ever come clean. Come clean? Who slopped dirt on the kitchen floor, mud? Me! I DID IT FOR GOD'S SAKES! I got wet and dirty and never bothered to take off my shoes! And I'm the one who threw the firecracker in the garage and set fire to it. Yeah! Me!!! 'CAUSE I'M THE SHIT ASS AROUND HERE. KEN'S THE BAD ONE!!!

T: AND THAT'S JUST FOR OPENERS MA!

Pt: Oh yeah! I stole money from your purse mom! Jesus, I must have stolen $200 over the years! No I wouldn't tell you. I never ask. I just take. I'm bad, that's why! I'm the bad boy in the family! I'm the one you all dump on, like some sort of rat, somehow, a rat that's stuck, in the family. And damn, I do it, I'm good at it, you couldn't a got a better one, a bad one, except that I'm sneaky, real sneaky, 'cause I never do it right out in the open. I stole Dad's watch, the one he thought he lost when you went on the vacation. Shit! I got 50 bucks for it. What a bastard I am huh! Shit! (Almost chuckling now) OK Mom, do what you want to me. Get mad, come on, Mom, get real mad, I mean what the hell do you want to do to me, beat me? I'll beat you back. You want to throw me out of the family? I deserve it! Go ahead! Throw me out. Go ahead. I'm not going to change! You're not going to suddenly steal things from Gertrude (the neighbor). So what's all the fuss? Huh? Come on, let's dance? Come on, Mom, be happy! You raised the local bad boy. Enjoy me, I'm special!

Fred is a lawyer. All his life he felt that the family regarded him as a little peculiar. They told family stories about his bed-wetting and the way he blamed it on his unseen private friend. They "understood" his sitting alone for hours in the garage. They made him leary of any sports because of his unspecified "condition." He was held back from starting school until he stopped those peculiar rolling hand movements which seemed to frighten the other children. Fred has been in and out of therapy for years on the unspoken terror that if he were without help an unspecified lunacy would take him over. Recently he was removed from being on a committee of the local bar association. They never told him why, and he never inquired. He was fearful that they would allude to his "peculiarity." The deeper potential was the experiencing of utter lunacy, wild craziness, full-blown derangement. The therapist and Fred painted in a scene where he receives a letter of dismissal from the committee and shows up at the committee meeting, uninvited, unexpected, wild-eyed and deranged.

Pt: You got rid of me 'cause you found out I'm a nut, huh? Did my Daddy tell you? Did my Daddy . . . sit down! Haaaaa! SIT DOWN! No one moves when Fred talks! (He shrieks again and again.) NO MOVING! I'm walking around, see my hands move? You were in my elementary school. Remember Mrs. Cushion? She saw me in the bathroom and she told you all about me, my Daddy didn't, you're all a bunch of liars 'cause Fred knows!

T: I'm a deformed crazy!

Pt: There's something wrong with the wiring in my head! I was born that way 'cause the wiring in my head's peculiar. I'm peculiar. Little Fred is peculiar! I'm peculiar! I won't be a lawyer anymore! Will you guys visit me in the hospital? I ought to be locked up in the crazy ward, 'cause I'm PECULIAR! That's the word, peculiar! Pee-culiar! I peed in my bed and I blamed it on my friend. He's my best friend and my only friend. He is the world's greatest high jumper and he can sail over things! He runs with pillows and falls on sand and sails through the air. He takes me with him and we eat leaves, we have long necks and things that can stretch. They get longer and bigger and water pours out of it through the teeth at the end. They are round and long and we play with them together. He's my best friend . . . (He starts to cry.) My friend. (He sobs long and hard.) We played together by the tree. . . . We used to get tiny and go down the ant hills and into the rooms and it was cool and quiet. We'd be tiny, littler than the black ants and we'd be the king and play together inside the palace . . . (Silence and quiet crying) . . . I don't think I've ever cried, and my head feels light and my arms are . . . relaxed. Something funny happened, yes. Damned funny.

T: Peculiar.

Pt: Strange. It felt like lightning went through me there. And I feel strange. Like I don't even want to open my eyes, yes, I'd like to be me now and not Fred. I wish, I don't want to open my eyes. I don't want to live in

Ottawa and be a lawyer and be the guy I've been my whole life. Actually, I wish I could be a little boy playing with my friend. I liked that. (Big sigh.)

The final illustration grows out of an early scene which had appeared several times in different sessions. At first there was a fragment scene in which she was in a state of terror on the bed, and something or some one was "after" her. Gradually, pieces were added until she recollected being four years old and her older sister had tried to suffocate her with a pillow. She recollected the whole episode and opened up the deeper experiencing of giving in, being utterly passive, completely at the mercy of anything and everything. With careful instructions, a fair measure of demonstration by the therapist, and a willingness to try letting herself dip into this for a moment, she began:

Pt: She is quiet, on top of me. She's strong. God she's so strong. She's 12 and I'm only four, and she killed herself when she was 17. Hung herself in the attic. She was crazy; she was always funny. She tried to kill the neighbor's dog by taking scissors and jabbing it in the throat. It almost died. (Now she is crying.) Angie! What did they do to you? I was just a little girl, and you tried to kill me. (All of this is spoken loudly, with tears) You stuffed the pillow in my face and I couldn't breathe! You were suffocating me and I remember I was twisting. Twisting. I remember thinking that I couldn't stop, and I didn't even know it was youuuu. (She is crying very hard.) I remember thinking that I'm going to die, four years old and I had some idea already, going to die, couldn't make a sound, no one to help me . . . (She is becoming passive.)
T: And letting it happen, just giving in, in, giving in, no more struggling!
Pt: I feel limp, pushing in on me, just limp, limp, limp, drained, weak, weak, just so weak, yes, not fighting anymore, limp, my whole body's limp, not breathing anymore. I'm going to die, and I am aware of your face, the eyelashes and your eyes, the eyes of a crazy person, drowning, limp, going down, skin, cool skin, soft, soft, quiet, just floating now . . . smells, water, heavy water, cool, and just my body. I have no legs. Just feel like a tiny baby, without legs, dizzy, I feel dizzy, floating, floating like on water, floating and I have no body, just floating on water, water, drifting . . . getting sleepy . . . I see fires, matches, sand, trees, way above, far away, a beach and dark, fires, lots of little fires, a face, old woman's face, big face, all over the sky . . . drifting, a kindly look, she's looking at me, and there is sunshine, a clear sky and her face . . . she looks so peaceful, an old woman . . . peaceful . . .

If the patient knows what to do and how to do it, and if the patient is ready, then succumbing to the deeper potential means that the patient has disengaged from the operating domain and is being the deeper potential. We know the scene or situation, and we know the deeper potential which is being pulled or activated. It is a matter of just succumbing to the awful deeper potential which is present and lurking in that situation.

The process usually starts out with anguish and hurt and pain. Then, as the patient fully succumbs into being the deeper potential, the transformation occurs. Actualization occurs in the good integrated form of the deeper potential. Free of the disintegrative relationship of the operating domain, the fuller and fuller being of that deeper potential means that it emerges as its good form, actualizing and integrating. Full being of the deeper potential allows for these bonuses as the patient continues being and behaving from within the increasingly good form of that which had existed as the catastrophic awfulness.

NEW EXPERIENCING IN REVIVIFIED CRITICAL MOMENTS

The idea behind this method is straightforward. In previous incidents in your life, there were critical moments when you acted the way you did, but there was at least a possibility of acting on the basis of some other, perhaps deeper, potential. If we know a deeper potential in you, we can return to those critical moments and, this time, be and behave on the basis of this deeper potential. In effect, this method enables the patient to relive special past moments, to have another chance. The easier part is discovering the deeper potential; the harder part is locating the critical moment and then living it through, this time as the deeper potential.

It is easier to discover the deeper potential because therapeutic work has disclosed the nature of the deeper potential. Carrying forward the experiencing brings forth the deeper potential. Working the relationship between the patient and the deeper potential both illuminates the deeper potential and opens the channel between the patient and the deeper potential. We generally have a fairly good idea of the nature of the deeper experiencing. The problem is how to select the critical moment in which that deeper potential is to be experienced.

Selecting an Appropriate Critical Moment

Perhaps the most straightforward way of selecting an appropriate critical moment is to use one which is already present. Therapeutic work carries forward experiencing within the context of a critical moment, or the therapeutic encounter takes place within the encompassing context of some critical moment. It may consist of that critical moment when the patient's father defensively lied to the patient. For a brief instant, the patient was shocked, and then she froze in numbness and let the moment go. This is the critical moment in the immediate background of carrying forward of experiencing or the internal encounter. This incident may have occurred yesterday, recently, a few weeks or months ago, or when the patient was a child. The option is to be the deeper potential within that critical moment. If the deeper potential consists of warm loving intimacy, the opportunity is to return to that critical moment when father's baldfaced, defensive lie was front and center and, this time, to let the deeper, warm, loving intimacy do the experiencing.

A second option is for the therapist (and patient) to identify those critical moments when the particular deeper experiencing was slammed shut. These are highly significant turning points when the deeper potential almost occurred, could have occurred, but was effectively blocked. When mother brought her "friend" to come live in the apartment, there was a critical moment when the seven-year-old patient might have screamed out her rage as she was awakened by noises from mother's bedroom, but instead she fell back to sleep and awoke in a pool of urine. Our work flagged that scene as critical for the deeper experiencing which was rumbling below but did not occur. Having identified the deeper potential, we can go back into the critical moment in the bedroom.

A third option is for the patient to be the deeper potential within critical moments which constitute the truly "problem" moments of ongoing life. He has never gotten along with his father. Problem situations always involve aggressive clashes in which all the old hurts and abrasions scream aloud as the two tangle. Whatever the nature of the deeper potential, the fertile field consists of these problem clashes with father.

The fourth option consists of critical moments signifying territory which is forbidden. In such critical moments the gate is slammed shut with a fierce look, a warning glance, a forced topic switch, a pressure silence, a proclamation, a direct attack for venturing too near. "That's enough! . . . We do not talk about that. . . . Why do you talk about that? What kind of a person are you? . . . Forget about that!" In many effective ways the patient is told that it is wrong or bad or dangerous to probe into this topic, and the patient suddenly is confronted with stone walls, warning signs, guarded gates, posters to stay out. Accordingly, the patient is left with a trail of forbidden conversations behind critical moments in which the patient ventured dangerously close.

Many of these forbidden conversations relate to events occurring during the patient's own memory. Many of them occurred in the primitive period from a few years before and after conception and birth. There are yawning lacunae in the patient's knowledge and understanding of events and circumstances in his life, all surrounded with danger signs.

What really happened to your father's older sister? All you know is that she killed herself a few months before you were born, but no one ever talks about that, and the whole topic is behind a closed door. Mother was in a mental hospital right after you were born, yet you have no clear picture of what happened, and the topic is surrounded with flashing red lights. When you were six years old you found a small package of photographs in your mother's dresser drawer. The pictures were of women doing all sorts of bizarre sexual and aggressive things with one another. Yet you never mentioned the pictures, and no one ever alluded to them. Who was that couple who stayed in the basement for a month or so? There was a lot of yelling and arguing and crying, but no one was ever allowed to ask or even talk about it afterwards. How come Daddy would never mention his older brother, and he got so mad if anyone even alluded to the brother? Why did the family suddenly move away from the small house where the patient grew up? No one ever talks about it, and whenever the patient broaches the subject, all sorts of warning and danger signs appear. There are all sorts of forbidden topics, hidden events, secret circumstances, tabooed conversations.

Here are four options for reentry. Once we have the deeper experiencing, we can get inside the deeper potential and undergo those critical moments in significantly new ways. These selected critical moments constitute the situational context for the new experiencing.

The Instructions, the Procedure, and the Consequences

Once the therapist and patient have selected an appropriate critical moment, the standard instructions are used to invite the patient to be the deeper potential and to go back into that critical moment. Then the patient is to undergo the new experiencing in the revivified critical moment. In the session, Edward started with a recent incident in which he felt intimidated by the older plumber who came to install a radiator in the dining room. Soon therapeutic work led to an early incident when he was ten years old and he was being bathed by his barrel-chested father. Further work illuminated a deeper potential for experiencing a sexual swooning, a passive homosexual seductiveness. The critical moment was signaled by a memory of his father's bawling him out for never bathing properly and telling him that he is now old enough to have his own showers instead of playing in the tub like a little kid. The incident was sealed and never opened. The point of the instructions was mainly to enable Edward to go back to that incident and to undergo a new experiencing as the deeper potential.

T: If you're ready, then it means being ten years old, being in the tub, with the water just about at the level of your belly. You have the black toenail on the right big toe, see it? From the brick that fell right on that toe. The nail's still on, but the nail looks black under the water. And you're aware of your Dad, sort of behind you, washing your back and your arms. He liked to hold your hand tight and shake it sort of hard. He'd be kidding and you'd be laughing. You like this. He liked you. He's in his green bathrobe, and he's got his underwear bottoms on. His chest is real big. Powerful Dad. Big chest. Black hair all over the chest. He's got soap on your right arm, and he's using the wash rag. You're not saying anything. He's saying that you're old enough to stop playing in the tub like a baby, and that's the moment. That's it, 'cause you're having feelings, you're sort of shy and embarrassed, mainly 'cause you're aware of him, drawn to him, and you're having funny feelings. Now it's starting, it's starting. Slowly you're transforming into being a very sexual boy, breathing deeper and deeper, heart is beating fast, fast, and now you're being a very sexual fellow, well beyond your years. (The therapist is describing the being of the new deeper potential which is ready for new experiencing in this moment.) Sure of yourself. Confident. Sexual. Swooning. Sexual. The sexual feelings are filling you and you are starting to have heavy hard balls and your penis is now harder, longer, longer, harder, and the sexual feelings are spreading over your whole body, through your chest and your back and arms, and your legs. Lithe, wiry, slender body, moving, moving, straightening and moving and moving, sexual . . .

Once the patient starts, the therapist goes through the experiencing along with the patient, being the deeper potential in that scene. Both therapist and patient are the deeper potential, saying and doing what the deeper potential says and does to open up this new experiencing. Therapist and patient push one another in this process, with the therapist a little ahead in terms of being the wholesale, full-feelinged, good form of the experiencing.

As the patient continues, there are at least three important consequences. Perhaps the main one is that the patient moves more solidly
into being the deeper potential. By being truly in the scene, and by
behaving more and more from within the deeper potential, the patient
finally becomes the deeper potential, and that is the name of the
method. Secondly, the more the patient experiences through the medium of the deeper potential, the more the patient experiences the good
actualizing and integrating form of the deeper potential. The body will
shimmer with the solid sensations of integration and the louder and
noisier sensations of actualization as the good form of the experiencing
takes over. There is a third consequence. As the patient is being the
deeper potential, behaving in ways which are new and different, each
moment is an opportunity for the patient to allow the other person
likewise to be new and different. Indeed, it would be difficult for the
patient to be the deeper potential when the other person is maintained
as the same old person, with the same old looks, thoughts, mannerisms,
ways of being and behaving, and personality. By living the scene
through as the deeper potential, the invitation is for the other person
to accommodate, and that means both patient and other person are
engaging in change. By being the deeper potential, the patient is releasing the other person from the old role, and the patient is inviting the
other person to take up a new role.

A Few Illustrations

The instructions tell the patient what to do, how to do it, and they
begin the process of actually being the deeper potential in that critical
moment. It is hypnotic-like both for the therapist, who must dip into
being the deeper potential in that moment in order to give the instructions, and also for the patient who is thereby invited into being the
deeper potential in the scene. The therapist describes what it is like
being the seductively teasing little boy in the bathtub and invites the
patient to continue from within this deeper potential.

T: (Quietly) If you're ready, go ahead.
Pt: Well, I could lay here in the tub and I could put my legs over here, I mean
    one leg over here and the other leg over here. If I lift up just a little,
    then you can see my ass and cock, see, right here, yeah and now you're
    seeing it. Actually I feel kind of naked and cool and sort of nice here,
    doing that, and I am (starts to laugh) lifting my little asshole up and
    down so you can see it lifting up and down, there and there. My little

asshole, and I'm showing it to you here and here. See my little breasts Daddy? See how they are sticking out of the water a little bit? See them? You can, go ahead, see you can stroke my breasts and my balls. I'll spread my thighs and my balls and see them? Spread them, I'll spread them. You can spread them and you can stroke them. Run your hand over my balls and my ass. Stick your finger into my asshole.

Then the change occurs. Until now, only some of the patient was existing in the deeper potential. But now most of him spoke from inside the deeper potential. His voice is husky, tantalizing, and he continues:

Pt: Aren't I pretty? Sweet, white, tight, white and soft. My thighs are so nice. Rub them with your hands. Touch them, They are white, tight, soft. Heat, feel the heat of my thighs. Your face is tickling, tickling. Skin feels so good. Touching my balls. Touching, rubbing lightly against my penis, rubbing . . . aaaahhhh! . . . You like it too . . . you do. You do. I do. Something refreshing. I feel, strong, yeah, strong . . . and very sexy.

Edward started from an operating potential in which there was an experiencing of tense intimidation with certain gruff, tough, burly men. From within the operating domain, the disintegrative relationship disclosed a deeper potential of sexual swooning, a homosexual seductiveness. As he became this deeper potential, beginning with the critical moment in the bathtub, the potential deepened and emerged as a full-feelinged sexuality, an all-over, sensual carnality which incorporated the figure of father in its experiencing. The increasingly saturated experiencing of the deeper potential is accompanied with its increasing transformation into its good actualizing and integrating form.

For Helen, problem situations centered about her weight and her family. She was about 60 pounds heavier than she was before her now four-year-old child was born. Her family consisted of her aunt and her aunt's second husband. Helen was raised by her aunt after her mother left to go back to Venezuela soon after Helen was born. Five years ago, when Helen was 24, she became pregnant and again returned to live with her aunt, who agreed to take care of Helen's daughter while Helen worked as an x-ray technician. Helen has been terrified of her aunt as long as she can remember, and she becomes so upset that she vomits nearly every day after being docile to the old tyrant. The recent critical moment was when she returned from work to find the aunt cutting the child's hair in the same way she cut Helen's hair when she was a child, and Helen's daughter had that same vacant expression on her face that Helen remembered. The sight of her child churned up Helen's stomach, and she vomited so intensely and wrenchingly that she became limp and collapsed in the bathroom. Helen's therapy began a week later, and she was in her fourth daily session. In that session, a deeper potential bubbled up. It consisted of a sense of audaciousness, a silly and playful openness and transparency, a sense of daring, a willingness to risk. Would she be ready to be this deeper potential in that critical moment with the aunt and her child? The therapist framed in what the deeper potential would probably say and do, and how Helen would experience as that deeper potential. Then it was Helen's turn.

Pt: Oh my God! What have I done? I've unleashed you on my poor wonderful Kim and you went ahead and did it to her. Same thing you did to me!! Aunt Sophie, try and listen to me. It's not your fault. It's mine. I know you're a perfect tyrant. Shit! I watched you perform for years! And you're good! You're really a peach! But we are leaving. Kim and I are going! Tonight! Thank you for fucking up my life just like I asked you. No! No explanations. I asked to live with you. I made all kinds of good reasons to return to your concentration camp. Not your fault. My fault. Kim, if your hair ever grows back to normal I'm going to let you see real people, and I'm going to put a little money away each month for your therapy, 'cause, kid, you're ripe. Oh yes!

T: 'Cause Kim, Aunt Sophie did the same damned thing to me!

Pt: Aunty! Tell Kim! Go on! You can tell her! Come on, you were there! Remember? You cut my hair the same way, and I really let you know. I think I had a thought, I don't even know what. And you just kept chopping away. You are one lousy hair stylist. But what's worse, oh this is embarrassing, I put my head on the chopping block! And you dear old woman, you went ahead and chopped it off! I asked you to let us stay! (Strikes herself on the forehead) What a dummy! What a real dummy!

T: Aunty, would you have time for me? I'm next. Now that you finished Kim — and I do mean finished . . .

Pt: You poor old sucker, you'd probably go ahead and do mine too! What a dummy I am. (In good spirits) Come on, Kim, let's both go into the bathroom and throw up. You may as well learn the next step. Start your career. Did you know that I threw up just about every day? Oh my God, if you didn't, how come? There I was, throwing up my guts, and I couldn't have been that quiet. And if you did know, then how come we never talked about it? There I go, blaming you. That's something. If I vomited every other day, how come I didn't tell anyone, aunty or friends? Oh, I'm beginning to come out the worse in this whole thing . . .

Here is a different person, an experiencing of playful and risky audaciousness. What is more, the patient is being this new experiencing rather well, even from the critical moment of seeing her aunt cutting Helen's daughter's hair in a revival of an early event in Helen's life. The therapist had been accompanying Helen on this experiential trip, and now becomes a little more active as the new experiencing becomes comfortable.

T: (With strong feeling) All right, aunty, that's the question. Did you know that I tossed my cookies with disgusting regularity in your bathroom? You have ten seconds to answer. Try to think!

Pt: Of course you knew! My God, no one was deaf. You could hear! I sounded like a wretching elephant! It was a daily routine for me. No wonder I work in x-ray!

T: OK aunty, so how come no mention of it? It must have happened maybe three or four hundred times, baby!

Pt: 'Cause I wouldn't let it! Good old Helen lived in her own crazy world and you went right along with it, aunty. Like you're doing now. We will call you on your birthday. We will visit you every so often, like in the fall, maybe. We're getting out of here. 'Cause we shouldn't have been here in the first place. You old dinosaur, you let us stay with you. If I'm so damned stupid, why didn't you tell me no? Never mind! Never mind! I don't want to hear!

T: I know! I know! It's cause Helen is a big fat asshole with an illegitimate kid!

Pt: (Shrieks with explosive laughter) Right! Right! That's right!

T: Wow! Has she fucked up her life!

Pt: (Animatedly, in high spirits) Helen can do what the hell she wants! Kim, come on, Kim. Let's go find a place to live. Just you and me baby! Just us! Just us! Bye Aunty! I should have done this years ago, and now's the time for me! Goodbye Aunty! So long Sophie! Have fun!

This is a new person, the deeper potential. This is a new person who started with the recent critical moment and lived through that event as the playfully audacious experiencing, the openly candid willingness to risk. Yet the underlying theme in this method occurs throughout, namely to disengage from the operating domain, to be the deeper potential, and to undergo this new experiencing in revivified critical moments selected from the recent or remote incidents in the patient's life.

This method is quite powerful and, in one sense, quite optimistic. It allows the patient to go back to previous critical moments and to reexperience as the new deeper potential. It gives the patient an optimistic chance to rewrite history, to redirect the course of one's life experience, and to go back to those critical moments to do and be what therapeutic work discloses as the available possibilities. It is especially powerful and holds especially powerful implications, when therapist and patient discover those very special critical moments in one's life when operating potentials were locked into place and deeper potentials sealed off. These are the powerful turning points or developmental epochs when the patient first became the operating potential and turned her back on the deeper possibility (Mahrer, 1978a). Those significant choice points are not lost; they can be renegotiated through the method of new experiencing in revivified critical moments.

AUTOMATIC ENTRY

In each of the above four methods, the therapist starts from an external locus. Therapeutic work has carried forward the potentials or achieved an internal integrative encounter. That much has been done, and now the therapist is "out," external to the patient and ready to give instructions for how the patient can be the deeper potential.

Why is the therapist external to the patient, separated from the patient, attending mainly to the patient? Generally, the reason is that a point was reached where the therapist pulled out or drifted out. There was a fair measure of carrying forward of the experiencing, and then the therapist moves away, into an external locus. Or, there was a fair measure of internal encountering, and then the therapist likewise exited into the external locus. But suppose the therapist remained in or with the patient, and therapeutic work just moved ahead? What would occur?

The answer is that the patient would naturally and easily move into being the deeper potential. There would occur an automatic entry into being the deeper potential. The principle may be framed as follows: Beyond a given intensity and fullness of experiencing either the carrying forward of potentials or the internal integrative encounter, the consequence is that the patient disengages from the operating domain and automatically enters into being the deeper potential.

There are no new or special methods. All the therapist and patient do is to continue with the carrying forward of experiencing or the internal integrative encounter. The series of steps given in Figure 1 was not deduced from an existential-humanistic theory. It was developed from observing what seemed to occur in patients whose sheer experiencing moved ahead. When patients were undergoing heightened carrying forward of potentials or the internal integrative encounter, and when that sheer experiencing deepened and broadened, what seemed to occur was the dramatic shift into being the deeper potential. The four methods described earlier in this chapter were added as refinements when this automatic entry did not occur, and when the therapist moved back into the external locus.

Sheer carrying forward of experiencing resulted in the patient's being the deeper potential. When the operating potential was increasingly experienced, the patient drifted into being the deeper potential. When the therapist expressed the deeper potential, a point was reached where the patient likewise drifted into being the deeper potential. When therapist and patient attended increasingly to the compelling external figure or internal entity, a point was reached where the patient took on the identity of that externalized or internalized deeper potential. When the bodily sensations swelled to envelop the whole body, a point was reached where the patient also became the deeper potential. In general, each method of carrying forward the experiencing of potentials resulted automatically in patients' entry into being the deeper potentials.

Similarly, as the internal integrative encounter attained the peak clash and moved beyond into a newfound, wholesale integration between patient and deeper potential, the consequence was that the patient moved into being that deeper potential. Steps 2 and 3 of experiential work will open the way for the patient to enter automatically into step 4, the being of the deeper potential.

Movement from the operating domain into being the deeper potential generally occurs in one of three ways. Which of these three ways is taken is a function of a number of determinants. It depends in part on the degree to which the therapist expresses the good integrated form of the deeper potential. The more the therapist is the good form of the deeper potential, the easier is the automatic entry. It depends upon the sheer strength and intensity of the experiencing. The more powerful and intense, the better. It depends also on the degree to which the therapist is successful in the work of carrying forward the potential or opening up the integrative relationship between patient and deeper potential. As a function of determining factors such as these, the automatic entry into the deeper potential will occur in one of the following ways.

• It occurs in little steps. The patient dips into the deeper potential part way, and for a few seconds or so. Yanking back into the operating domain, the patient generally takes another little step of dropping partially and momentarily into being the deeper potential. It is a matter of little steps, each time going a little further into being the deeper potential and staying there a little longer.

• It occurs explosively. It is as if the patient suddenly bursts full-blown into being the deeper potential. Typically, this transmutation is accompanied with a sudden heightening of feelings, either good ones or bad ones. Experiencing is likewise strong as the patient shifts from operating domain to deeper potential.

• It is a quiet transition. Without emotional fireworks, without dramatic fanfare, the patient glides into being the deeper potential. While feelings and bodily sensations may be saturating, they are nevertheless gentle and solid rather than raucous and turbulent.

This third kind of automatic entry occurs especially when the nature and content of the deeper potential are likewise quiet, and when the situational context is one which is also quiet and occurs in childhood. For example, if the deeper potential consists of the experiencing of wholesome trust, there are situational contexts wherein the patient is a little child, resting on his grandfather's lap, aware of the kinesthetic cues, the warmth, the odors, the gentle sleepiness, the soothing sound of his grandfather's voice. Automatic entry into this quiet deeper potential is gentle and peaceful. If the deeper potential consists of naive curiosity, the situational context may be that of an infant, lying comfortably in the crib, exploring the wonders of mother's face, the way the lips move, the eye lashes, the teeth and tongue and nostrils. Experiencing is quiet, and the automatic entry into this deeper potential is likewise gentle and easy and quiet.

Being the deeper potential ends the "work" of experiential psychotherapy. The patient has undergone the carrying forward of potentials (chapters 1, 2), the internal integrative encounter (chapters 3, 4), and the shift into being the deeper potential (chapters 5, 6). We are now approaching the final step in the session, the tasting and risking of changes in ways of being and behaving in the extratherapy world.

CHAPTER 7

Being/Behavioral Change: Introduction

THE FINAL STEP IN each session of experiential psychotherapy is risking of meaningful changes in the patient's ways of being and behaving in the extratherapy world. Everything which has occurred so far in the session is preparation for the experiencing of what it is like to be a new and different person who samples what it is like to be and behave in the new and different ways which were opened up in the work of the session.

This chapter provides the theoretical background or rationale for this step. Chapter 8 then presents the methods.

The General Principle

Each of the previous steps enabled the patient to sample what it is like to be a new and different person. The carrying forward of potentials brought the patient into fuller and more saturated experiencing of both operating and deeper potentials. The internal encounter gave the person a taste of what it is like to have open, integrative channels with deeper potentials, and to be and behave and experience in a new and different way in these internal relationships. Being the deeper potential introduced the patient to a qualitatively new way of being, behaving, and experiencing as the deeper potential. In effect, therapeutic work provided the patient with a taste of what it is like to be a different person, with new ways of being, new ways of behaving, and new ways of experiencing. Therapeutic work took lower-level potentialities in the patient, and converted them to higher-level possibilities (Bandler & Grinder, 1982; Johnson, 1971; Naranjo, 1969; Walsh & Vaughan, 1980; Welwood, 1979).

But none of the previous steps in the session included the risked possibility of actual being/behavior changes in the imminently available extratherapy world. Each of the previous steps required their own situational contexts and their own ways of being and behaving. The final step in the session comprises the final kind of therapeutic experiencing, where the situational context is the extratherapy world of the immediate future and the merchandise consists of the risked possibility of actual new ways of being and behaving in this new world.

The general principle may be framed as follows: *Psychotherapeutic change occurs through therapeutic experiencing of new ways of being and behaving in the imminently present extratherapy world.*

Will therapeutic work automatically result in extratherapy being/ behavioral change? The need for explicit methods. I do not believe that the behavior therapies have contributed a set of new psychotherapeutic methods. Long before a formalized field of behavior therapy, people were getting other people to behave differently by using methods which were later designated with such technical jargon as desensitization, covert sensitization, progressive relaxation, behavioral rehearsal, assertiveness training, contingency management, token economies, aversive control, self-control techniques, and so on (Goldstein & Wolpe, 1971). The methods have been around for centuries; the vocabulary is new. Nor do I believe that a major contribution of the behavior therapies is their vaunted rigorous connection with one or more of the various theories of learning. The actual techniques were embedded in common sense long before there were learning theories to offer their particular brand of sense-making (cf. Lazarus, 1971; London, 1972; Yates, 1975). Nor do I believe that a major contribution of the behavior therapies is their supposed effectiveness in changing their targeted behaviors. From the perspective of an existential-humanistic theory of human beings, the targeted behaviors which behavior therapies set out to modify constitute a spuriously small proportion of the being/behavioral changes which are of concern to us.

Instead, I consider a major contribution of the behavior therapies to be the pioneering emphasis on effecting new ways of behaving, explicitly framed within the immediate extratherapy world. In general, the behavior therapies reject the position that therapeutic work will automatically result in behavioral changes in the patient's extratherapy world. Rather, the behavior therapies have taken the lead in demonstrating the importance of direct therapeutic work aimed at effecting new behaviors in the extratherapy world.

The counter-conditioning of anxiety includes in-therapy approximations of the actual extratherapy conditions, and the active generalization of new behaviors into the real world (Wolpe, 1958, 1973). Relaxation training includes sessions of home practice as well as use in designated real life situations. Assertive behaviors to be tried out in designated actual situations (Goldfried & Davison, 1976; Rimm & Masters, 1974; Wolpe, 1973). Contingency management methods, whether based upon operant principles of positive reinforcement or punishment, include baselines measures from the external world, naturalistic observations, changing explicit conditions in the extratherapy world, use of token economies in actual settings, the charting of actual stimulus conditions, mutual control techniques involving selected others, homework assignments in the real world, and the use of covert sensitization procedures in target situations (Ayllon & Azrin, 1968; Azrin & Holz, 1966; Cautela, 1967; Sherman, 1973). Cognitive techniques frequently emphasize the use of new cognitions within the context of relevant actual life situations, whether the technique is biofeedback, thought-stopping, rational restructuring, self-instructional training, or effective problem-solving (D'Zurilla & Goldfried, 1971; Goldfried & Davison, 1976; Kanfer & Phillips, 1970; Meichenbaum, 1977; Osborn, 1963; Rimm & Masters, 1974; Wolpe, 1973).

In general, behavior therapies have shown the importance of using explicit methods which involve the extratherapy world in their direct efforts to modify behavior. Behavior therapies work directly upon changing behavior within the context of the immediately present external world, and experiential psychotherapy follows in the track laid down by the behavior therapies.

Most other therapies either explicitly or implicitly presume that therapeutic work will automatically be followed by being/behavioral change in the extratherapy world. They have few if any therapeutic operations which explicitly are aimed at bringing about being/behavior al changes in the immediately present world of the patient. The general principle in the majority of other therapies is that sooner or later there will be consequent improvement and change in the patient's extratherapy world, provided that therapeutic process moves along. "Significant changes cannot be enforced on the behavioral level. . . . One changes significantly in one's roots, not in one's branches" (Angyal, 1965, p. 205). Change the patient's personality structure and the patient's way of being and behaving in the extratherapy world will follow more or less automatically.

Experiential psychotherapy flatly disagrees. It joins with these therapies only in highlighting the importance of intrapsychic change. We aim at carrying forward the experiencing of potentials, at bringing about an internal integrative encounter, at disengaging from the operating domain and being the deeper potential. But these steps are regarded as paving the way for the final step of explicitly working for being/behavioral change within the context of the extratherapy world of the immediately present. Where behavior therapies emphasize behavior change in the immediately present extratherapy world, experiential psychotherapy agrees; however, where behavior therapy tends to omit or deemphasize intrapsychic personality change, experiential psychotherapy explicitly focuses on intrapsychic personality change. Where most other therapies emphasize intrapsychic personality change, experiential psychotherapy agrees. Where most other therapies presume that being/behavioral change in the extratherapy world will follow automatically, experiential psychotherapy disagrees and focuses on methods explicitly dedicated to achieving such being/behavioral changes.

Some therapies work toward providing a good relationship with the patient, toward providing conditions in which the patient feels understood and accepted and prized, and toward getting the patient to engage in inner exploration of feelings. Yet the silent presumption is that if this therapeutic work is done well, it will lead automatically to actual being/behavioral changes in the patient's world. According to experiential psychotherapy, in contrast, such changes benefit from explicit therapeutic work directly aimed toward such changes.

In a systematic critique of Jung's approach to therapy, Wyss (1973) discusses the same buried presumption, viz., if the Jungian therapist carries out proper therapeutic work, there will be intrapsychic changes, and it should automatically follow that the patient's ways of being and behaving, as well as the patient's external world, should all change in a proper direction. Instead of accepting a presumption of automatic changes, experiential psychotherapy favors direct work toward explicit changes in the patient's new ways of being and behaving.

Many therapies count on a natural biopsychological healing process where the therapist's contribution is mainly to assist in its action. The therapist may provide the right condition for healing, or the therapist may remove obstacles in the path of the healing process. Guntrip (1969) is representative of this position:

> . . . a healing process which is a regrowing *process* just as much when it concerns the mental life as when it concerns the body, cannot be artificially hurried, however much we may wish it. All that we can do is to discover the obstacles to regrowth, provide a relationship in which the patient can come to feel secure, and leave "nature" to prosecute her healing work at her own pace (p. 288).

This makes sense in a biologically grounded theory of psychotherapy, but it does not make sense in an existential-humanistic theory of human beings and its experiential theory of psychotherapy. Instead of presuming a biologically grounded natural healing process which will slowly lead to the right changes in the patient's ways of being and behaving in the external world, we favor use of straightforward therapeutic work aimed at such changes.

Psychodynamic-psychoanalytic therapies believe that when the therapist gets the patient to remember forgotten or wrongly recollected traumatic events, changes in the patient's ways of being and behaving will follow automatically. Similar changes will occur if the therapist's interpretive statements resolve unconscious conflicts; " . . . to the extent that a resolution of unconscious conflict occurs via the expressive-interpretative aspects of therapy, there is an at least proportional change in symptoms, character traits, and life style" (Wallerstein, 1968, p. 595). In contrast, experiential psychotherapy accepts the proposition that changes in the patient's ways of being and behaving in the external world occur more effectively, more broadly, and more quickly through therapeutic work explicitly directed toward such changes, and rejects the presumption that such changes automatically follow from remembering early traumas and from the therapist's interpretive statements.

Similarly, many therapies presume that changes in the patient's extra-therapy behavior will follow automatically from proper insight or understanding. This is a hallmark of most psychodynamic-psychoanalytic therapies, and it is central to other therapies which offer their own brand of insight and understanding. I reject this proposition. "A patient can see his personal patterns clearly and discuss their antecedents and consequences intelligently without the slightest change taking place" (Angyal, 1965, p. 271). I am aware that the issue may be complicated by interpretations which explicitly aim at extending the traditional thematic connections to include possible behavioral changes in the patient's life performance and adaptive tasks (Alexander, 1963; Alexander & French, 1946, 1948; Rado, 1956, 1962). Nevertheless, I favor a position in which behavioral changes are far more a function of therapeutic work directly targeted upon being and behavioral changes in the external world than an automatic consequence of all the favorite kinds of insights and understandings.

All in all, experiential psychotherapy sides with the behavioral therapies in favoring direct therapeutic work on being/behavioral changes in the external world, and sides with most other therapies which emphasize the importance of preparatory intrapsychic personality change. The whole stage is set for the final step in each session, a step explicitly dedicated toward opening the possibility of actual changes in the patient's ways of being and behaving in the external world, a final step built upon the foundation of internal changes in the patient's deeper personality structure.

Trying and readiness for considering new ways of being and behaving. Experiential therapy turns to the considering of being/behavioral change after the patient has gone through the being of the deeper potential. That is the guideline in the standard session where the patient reaches a significant level of experiencing in each of the steps. There are two reasons for this. One is that the patient is ready for considering changes in ways of being and behaving only after a high degree of experiencing has been achieved, and the other reason is that the way is best paved for considering these changes when the patient has achieved a carrying forward of potentials, an integrative internal encounter, and an experiential being of the deeper potential. In other words, the steps of the therapeutic process get the patient ready for being/behavioral changes.

This means that the considering of being/behavioral change occurs at the end of each session. Because the therapeutic process takes the patient through a sequence of experiencings each session, the patient is ready for a consideration of being/behavioral change each and every session. In this connection, we join with Ericksonian hypnotherapy, wherein the final part of each session is likewise aimed at actual new ways of being (Lankton & Lankton, 1983).

In many approaches, the initial series of sessions is not used to get to the consideration of sober changes in one's world and in one's ways of being and behaving in that world. Instead, the common model is to consider psychotherapy as a career. It may be only 10 to 30 sessions or so, or it may be a long career of five to ten years. The actual consideration of specific changes in the patient's real world tends to occur toward the end of the whole therapy career. Typically, this career is organized into a beginning phase in which the problem is laid out, a long and extensive work phase in which the therapy aims at doing something about the problem, and a final ending phase in which dissolution of the therapeutic relationship is coupled with an expectation of more or less automatic changes in the patient's functional adjustment (Cashdan, 1973; Cormier & Cormier, 1977; Craighead, Kazdin, & Mahoney, 1976; Gottman & Leiblum, 1974; Osipow & Walsh, 1970). In contrast, the experiential method carries the patient through these three steps in each session, starting with attention-centered getting ready for work, then moving on to the middle phase of experiential work, and ending with a consideration of what these experiential changes imply for a new and changing patient in a new and changing world.

The timing, then, is after the patient has achieved a high level of experiencing, especially in being the deeper potential. With regard to readiness, something very interesting happens when the patient is the deeper potential, after the deeper potential has been activated and carried forward, and after relations with the deeper potential are significantly integrative. What is very interesting is that it is quite natural to turn to the consideration of being/behavioral change. Once patients go through the preceding steps and are being the deeper potential, patients tend quite naturally to turn to the extratherapy world and to new ways of being and behaving in that world. It is as if the patient spontaneously turns to the actual world waiting out there: "Well! That would certainly surprise Bob and the kids." . . . "It's funny. I'm practically never like this." . . . "My life would sure be different if I felt this way." . . . "But nothing like that ever happens in my life." . . . "There'd be lots of changes, for sure." . . . "I'd straighten out a helluva lot with the family." . . . "Oh, would this be great. What a big difference!" . . . "I always thought things could be different with Ma, and now I know it's up to me." . . . "I see colors. Pretty colors. Things I never felt before. What a life it could be!". It is as if the sheer being of the deeper potential, within its own context, opens the way for a turning to the immediate, available, real, extratherapy world.

All in all, a good measure of being the deeper potential seems almost naturally to lead to the invoking of the extratherapy world and the possibility of new ways of being in the world.

The locus and functions of the therapist. Where is the therapist in the work of considering and tasting the possibility of new ways of being and behaving? The answer is that the therapist is inside the deeper potential, looking out onto the extratherapy world. The therapist is not external, separate from the patient. Instead, the therapist is still dripping with what it is like being the deeper potential, the living, breathing deeper potential who is now turning to the extratherapy world.

From within the deeper potential, the therapist is able to see what the good integrative form of this deeper potential would be like in the extratherapy world. This is a desideratum for being an experiential psychotherapist who negotiates this final step. This is what the therapist brings to the patient; this is what the therapist has that the patient does not. It means that the therapist can be and behave as the integrative good form of the deeper potential in the immediate real world out there. The therapist can take that magnificant next step of actually being and behaving in entirely new ways, some little and some big, but all new in a newly unfolding world. Where the patient is somewhat ready, the therapist is exceedingly ready. Where the patient may have a muted flash, the therapist has a vivid picture of the way the external world can be. Where the patient stands on the verge of new ways of being and behaving, the therapist can and does behave in quite new and different ways.

Another function of the therapist is to lead the patient into actual tasting or sampling of these new possibilities. The therapist is the leader in carrying out the new ways of being and behaving and in activating the patient into doing the same thing. Of the many therapies which exemplify this step, perhaps Ericksonian hypnotherapy is one of the more vocal in ending each session with the active promotion of new ways of being and behaving (Erickson, 1980; Erickson & Rossi, 1981; Haley, 1973a; Zeig, 1982). "I do the thing that stirs the patient into doing the right thing" (Erickson in Zeig, 1980, p. 143). It is a matter of leading the patient into experiential sampling of new ways of being and behaving.

These are the two functions of the therapist who, as the good form of the deeper potential, is this deeper potential in the extratherapy world, being and behaving in new and different ways, and thereby leading the patient into tasting and sampling the final experiential step in the session.

The Significance and Function of Being/ Behavior Change in Psychotherapy

On the one hand there is psychotherapy. On the other hand there is actual being/behavior change in one's actual world. The two domains are not all that interrelated nor friendly to one another. There are a number of considerations which apply to the significance and function of being/behavior change in psychotherapy.

Relations between psychotherapy and being/behavior change: Severely limited versus excitingly active. It is easy to speak glibly about psychotherapy and actual change, to say that psychotherapy is geared toward producing changes in ways of being and behaving. It is easy to presume that patients come to therapy to bring about changes in their problems or their general unhappy state or their specific bothersome behaviors. All of this is easy, but it is probably inaccurate. The relationship between psychotherapy and actual changes in ways of being and behaving is, I believe, a lot more complex. Here is a spokesman for a perspective which is different from the traditional one:

> People who enter therapy rarely wish to change themselves. They wish to be relieved of the suffering, anxiety, pain, failure, and uncertainty in their lives. People don't want to change their personalities. To the extent they identify with a neurosis, a facial tic, inadequate sexual performance, fears of dying, lack of meaning, phobias, etc., they do not see "change" as exchange, but rather as loss. People don't willingly give up, shed, or relinquish any part of their identity (Fadiman, 1980, p. 179).

Perhaps the commonest way of understanding reluctance or unwillingness to undergo actual change is the psychoanalytic axiom that the neurotic will resist and be threatened by the possibility of deep-seated personality change. Accordingly, the depressed patient, for example, will stoutly resist substantive changes arising out of intrapsychic processes: " . . . depression implies an unwillingness to consider alternatives to the threatened neurotic pattern. The patient proclaims, as it were, that his way is the only way, that he does want to play the game differently" (Angyal, 1965, p. 226).

It is understandable that patients may be reluctant to undertake behavioral changes which emanate from deep-rooted personality processes. It is understandable that many patients will hold back from changes which endanger large chunks of their personality. Even if we excuse and exclude such changes, it seems to be that psychotherapy has only the most tenuous of connections with changes in ways of being and behaving. There is a great deal of talk about change, a heavy presumption that changes should occur, a lot of implied wishes and wantings to change, but psychotherapy itself seems to need much more refinement and development before it actually qualifies as a medium of change. Indeed, there are several considerations which highlight the powerful limitations and blocks to the undertaking of new ways of being and behaving.

One has to do with the role-relationships which patients and therapists build with one another. If specific changes in ways of being and behaving fit in with and help play out the role-relationships, then they may occur. However, it is my conviction that most role-relationships sharply restrict the allowable being/behavior changes to those which contribute to the role-relationship, and effectively disallow any other (Mahrer, 1970b, 1978e, 1983a; Mahrer & Gervaize, 1983). The patient who is the helpless little child to the therapist as the good parent will tend to change in ways which play out the role of little child to the good parent. Changes which risk this role-relationship will tend to be disallowed. The role-relationships which therapists and patients conjointly construct define what changes are acceptable and stamp all other changes as either outside the bounds of this role-relationship or dangerous. Once you see the particular role-relationships that this therapist-patient dyad constructs, you can predict which changes are likely to occur, and you can predict that all other possibilities will not. This is a powerful restriction and limitation.

A second consideration is that the operating domain will do the same as the role-relationship. That is, the operating domain will allow only those behavior changes which serve the operating domain, and will do everything in its power to resist any other changes in ways of being and behaving. Whether it is called the operating domain, substantive personality, neurotic pattern, ego, or whatever, its investment is in maintaining itself. Changes are sharply restricted to mere unfolding, to whatever serves the operating domain. Whether through behavior therapy, psychoanalytic therapy, humanistic therapy, or any other kind of therapy, changes are easy if the changes fit in with and serve the continuing, conscious, functioning, operating, substantive personality. Changes that do not are unlikely to occur. The most powerful enemy of changes in ways of being and behaving is the patient himself—unless the changes serve the operating domain.

This means that some safe distal behaviors may be dropped, added, or replaced, and it means that the patient may impress others as different, but all of these changes are cordial to the person the patient is. The operating domain has not altered. It remains in place while its distal behaviors are refined. This also means that the range of allowable changes is truncated. The operating domain will only allow those changes which serve the operating domain, and other possibilities are not permitted. The net result is that psychotherapy is able to effect a tiny package of behaviors which are judged allowable by the reigning operating domain.

This is why the typical back and forth dialogue in many psychotherapies flows smoothly along until the therapist introduces the notion of actual changes in the patient's ways of being and behaving in the real world. There is no harm done if the therapist's statements can be incorporated into the flow of the back and forth dialogue, or if the therapist's statements can be encompassed by the role-relationship. But if the therapist has the audacity to interrupt the back and forth dialogue or the role-relationship by introducing the notion of actual changes in ways of being and behaving, the whole atmosphere changes. Things shut down. Resistances go up. Psychotherapy is hardly an enterprise geared toward effecting wholesale changes in ways of being and behaving.

There is a third consideration which sharply limits the possibility of changes. The patient may talk endlessly about changes. The dialogue may focus on how wonderful it would be to be a new and different person. The patient may even be quite a new and different person here in the interactive situation with the therapist. But once the situational context shifts from the therapy situation to the actual extratherapy world out there, it is a whole different matter. The reason is that the patient has worked long and hard to construct that world. Indeed, the patient is a master builder who has incredible proficiency in constructing the precise kind of world which fits the kind of person the patient is. Once the scene shifts to the actual world out there, the patient faces a world which has little or no room for actual changes in ways of being and behaving. While others may see all kinds of available space for the patient to effect serious changes, the patient's own external world closes ranks and stands in the most serious opposition to change. The patient's external world has a full investment in opposing changes.

These three considerations make actual changes unlikely, limited, and highly restrictive. One conclusion is that there are strong considerations which militate against all but a tiny package of actual changes in ways of being and behaving in the external world. The conclusion for experiential therapy is that the enterprise of actual changes in ways of being and behaving *can* be altogether open and free and excitingly active when potentials have been carried forward, when relationships between the operating and deeper domain become integrative, and when the patient has disengaged from the operating domain and entered into being the good form of the deeper domain. Then the possibility of changes in ways of being and behaving loses its limitations and restrictions; it is exciting, galvanizing, liberating, actualizing, spontaneous, rousing, energizing.

Following these experiential peaks, the exciting risk is that the patient at last has new and delightful alternatives and possibilities. It is as if the patient and his world transform into whole new possibilities. Indeed, it is common that this final step opens a cascading rush of whole new behavioral possibilities. Where the focus had been on a few new ways of being and behaving, the patient will often spontaneously open up new avenues of behavioral possibilities. Instead of being closed against actual changes, it is as if there is a dizzying new state of wholesale possibilities, a new world of actual new ways of being and behaving. The message in this final step is that there really is the wholesale possibility of being a new and different person, being and behaving in whole new ways, in a whole new and different world.

Instead of trying to modify a given behavior, instead of focusing on a given way of being and behaving which therapy is aimed at achieving or changing, the enterprise becomes one of the wholesale opening up of the incredible possibility of being a new and different person in a new and different world. Then the focus shifts to freedom and opportunity for whole new domains of ways of being and behaving. All in all, the relations between psychotherapy and being/behavior change can be a matter of facing powerful limitations and restrictions or, on the other hand, a matter of excitingly wide-ranging possibilities.

The struggle between the therapy world and the extratherapy world: Which one serves the other and the matter of termination. Once the patient reaches this final step in the session, it is the extratherapy world that is the major context. Patient and therapist attend to and exist in the extratherapy world, live and breathe in this encompassing world. In contrast, the therapy world is minimized. The context is not the world of interactions between patient and external therapist. In most approaches there is always a choice, a struggle, between the therapy world and the external world. In this final step, the extratherapy world is uppermost, and prospects for changes in ways of being and behaving are high. In many other therapies, the interactions and relationships of the therapy world are uppermost, and, we contend, prospects for tasting and sampling changes in ways of being and behaving are low.

In many approaches, the unspoken contract is that therapy is to be the jewel of the patient's life. Therapy is uppermost, the most important thing in the patient's world. The rest of the patient's world is secondary. It feeds and serves the therapy world. Patients and therapists talk about new ways of behaving, but the context is typically the relating therapist and patient talking to one another about behavioral changes in the extratherapy world. In the therapy context, such talk tends to feed the dominant role-relationship wherein the therapist is the good parent who is pleased by such talk, or the therapist is the authority who tells the patient how to be, or talking about new ways of being is the evidence that their relationship is paying off, or the patient bludgeons the therapist with threats of disastrous behavioral possibilities, or the therapist's steering the patient into particular behaviors is another means of showing that the therapist is a responsible manager. A large proportion of so-called changes are in the form of reportings by the patient, reportings which are fed into the world of the therapist-patient relationship. Instead of attending to and existing in the extratherapy world, the patient settles into the contextual world of the relating therapist and talks about or reports from the secondary extratherapy world.

If the patient should come face to face with a genuinely new way of being and behaving, many approaches rule that new ways of being are to be talked about and to occur exclusively in the context of therapy. The patient's newfound readiness to disclose more, to be close, to be warm and friendly, to be self-confident, angry, crying, laughing, assertive, wicked, risky—all of these changes are swept into the therapeutic relationship rather than occurring within real world contexts. When the therapy world is uppermost, it has first choice at incorporating whatever changes are ready to occur. Therapy becomes the place where behavioral changes occur, and the extratherapy world pales into secondary insignificance.

In experiential therapy, the final step in every session includes both therapist and patient testing and sampling new ways of being and behaving as the two of them are existing mainly in the extratherapy world. In contrast, many therapies dedicate months or years building the powerful dominance of the therapy world and forcing the extratherapy world to serve that enterprise. Then the inevitable time comes when, for whatever reasons, the therapist and patient are to disengage. This is labeled termination, and the problem is how to use the extratherapy world to serve, once again, the therapy world, now to entice the patient to leave; " . . . termination is a function of the patient's establishing those conditions outside the therapeutic situation which yield greater satisfaction than the therapeutic relationship itself. This is supplemented by the decreasing affective involvement of the therapist" (Whitaker, Warkentin, & Malone, 1959, p. 256). In termination, the predominant therapy world tries to use the extratherapy world to pry the patient loose from the therapy world.

After months or years of struggle to be preeminent over the extratherapy world, the therapist must resort to all sorts of techniques to terminate the patient's attachment to therapy. One technique is to give the patient a gift, a token of the therapy world which the patient is to carry with him in the extratherapy world. Accordingly, the patient is to carry an amulet of the therapist's voice or presence. "Patients frequently refer to the fact that after the interviews have ended, they carry the therapist around within them for some time as a dynamic part of their functioning in their social and real relationships" (Whitaker & Malone, 1953, p. 434). Termination is just another phase in the traditional struggle between the therapy world and the extratherapy world.

There are all sorts of "termination techniques" therapists use to dislodge the patient from the therapy world and out into the extratherapy world, after months or years of trying to make the therapy world utterly paramount. Therapists will stay away from deep topics, disclose a little of themselves, keep matters light and conversational, interpret the patient's ways of being and behaving as signifying readiness to leave, space appointments further and further apart. There are "experimental temporary interruptions" (Alexander, 1963) whereby the therapist invites the patient to stay away from therapy for a while to see what that is like, and therefore to ease reentry into the extratherapy world.

In experiential therapy, there is little basis for constructing a "termination problem" to be solved (Mahrer, 1978d). A large part of the reason is that each session ends with a wholesale turning to the extratherapy world and to harvesting the behavioral fruits of the session within the context of the extratherapy world.

All in all, most therapies favor the therapy world as paramount, and the extratherapy world is demeaned to providing some of the topics which patient and therapist talk about in the all-important therapy world. In these therapies, the lesser extratherapy world becomes useful toward the end of therapy when the therapist tries to "terminate" the patient by again talking about the extratherapy world. In experiential therapy, the therapy world is never supreme. In the final step in each session, the context is the extratherapy world simply because being/behavioral changes are most appropriately tasted and sampled within the context of the imminent, present, alive extratherapy world. The struggle between therapy world and extratherapy world is no contest, for the extratherapy world is the regular winner.

The therapist's personal investment in the patient's extratherapy world. How important is it to the therapist that the patient actually carry out changes in her extratherapy world? How invested is the therapist in particular kinds of changes in the patient's everyday world, or in having responsibility for what occurs in the patient's extratherapy world?

The experiential therapist trusts the experiential method and values the consequences of therapeutic work. In the course of this work it is important to experience the implications for being/behavioral changes in the context of the extratherapy world. The working therapist trusts and values this final step in the method. In contrast, some therapists have a deeply personal investment in the patient's extratherapy world. For example, it is very important for these therapists that patients report pleasant changes in their extratherapy world, that they feel better in that world, that they are changing in ways which are the fruits of the therapist's efforts. Such reports make the therapist feel good. Such reports enrich the therapist as the grand helper, the change artisan, the one who can make the patient's extratherapy world better. Such dialogue is a featured part of the role-relationships in which so many therapists are invested.

One common role includes that of manager or overseer of the patient's extratherapy world, the one who accepts professional responsibility for the patient's life outside therapy. This role was exemplified in, for example, Freud's rule to postpone important life decisions until psychoanalytic treatment was over:

> One best protects the patient from disasters brought about by carrying his impulses into action by making him promise to form no important decisions affecting his life during the course of the treatment, for instance, choice of a profession or of a permanent love object, but to postpone all such projects until after recovery (Freud, 1959, p. 373).

From here the role of responsible manager of the patient's extratherapy world had blossomed in many directions. The role has been ingrained in ethical, professional, and legal codes, investing the therapist with the right and responsibility for large chunks of the patient's external world. This includes the therapist's investment in dealings with the patient's family, social and health agencies, physician, clergyman, lawyer, parents, spouse, work, police, insurance company, friends. Virtually any involvement in the patient's extratherapy world lends itself to justification on professional, ethical, legal, moral, spiritual grounds — and therapists have proven adept at defining such justifications for the role of responsible manager of the patient's extratherapy world. For therapists and patients inclined toward such role-relationships, there are few if any problems here.

Does this mean that the experiential psychotherapist just turns her back on what others would refer to as concerned responsibility for the patient's welfare? Does the experiential psychotherapist really not care what happens in the patient's extratherapy world? There are at least a few answers to this question. One is that the experiential therapist is invested in the carrying out of the steps which comprise therapeutic work, but that does not include forcing the patient to have his wife also come to therapy or getting the patient to change jobs. The tasting and sampling of changes in ways of being and behaving are important to the experiential therapist. Pursuing an active investment in seeing to it that the therapist's "advised" extratherapy changes actually occur is beyond experiential psychotherapy.

Second, experiential psychotherapists accept the reality of the trouble they can avoid by carrying out the role of the responsible overseer, concerned professional, or managerial watchdog. Whitaker, Warkentin and Malone (1959) put it this way: "On rare occasions and for administrative purposes the environmental situation may be structured for suicidal protection or for the control of the patient's acting-out, so that the therapist will not be in trouble with his community" (p. 255). Ethical-professional-legal strictures are to be respected. But where the therapist's ethical-professional-legal responsibilities end, there remains a zone in which the therapist's personal investment in the patient's extratherapy world may be strong, moderate, or low. Quite outside of ethical, professional, or legal considerations, some therapists have a highly personal investment in their patients' lives outside therapy. On this score, the experiential method calls for little or no such personal investment.

The practice of experiential psychotherapy and its existential-humanistic theory and value system provide a third answer in which the patient is ceded a large measure of choice and responsibility. This applies not only to readiness and willingness to take the next step in the session, for example, but it applies also to the actual undertaking of being/behavioral changes in the extratherapy world. While the final step in each session includes the consideration of whether or not to undertake such changes (chapter 8), this is carried out within the context of the patient's choice and responsibility.

Fourth, before and after therapeutic work, the theory of experiential practice invites the therapist to be the person one is. Here is where many experiential therapists may well be quite honestly and genuinely concerned with the new car the patient just purchased, the patient's new hair style, whether or not the patient got the new job. The therapist is a person with her own ways of being, interests and concerns for the patient. But the specific content of this pre-therapy and post-therapy dialogue is outside the domain of actual therapeutic work where therapist and patient recline, put their feet up, close their eyes, and start the process of therapeutic change.

Finally, as will be discussed in chapter 8, the session closes with a checking of the bodily sensations of both patient and therapist. Only when these are pleasant and good-feelinged is the session brought to a close. If either or both of the participants are filled with bodily sensations which are bothersome, tight, dangerous, constricting, anxious, scary, menacing, the session is to continue. On rare occasions, the patient is geared toward leaving the office and going out into the extra-therapy world to carry out a behavior which fills the therapist with unpleasant bodily sensations. Not only does this mean that the steps of the work have not been carried out well, but it also dictates that the session is far from finished. How to negotiate this procedure and convert the therapist's (and/or the patient's) unpleasant and anxiety-ridden bodily sensations into effective therapeutic procedures is discussed in the next chapter.

In general, then, the experiential psychotherapist has little or no personal investment in the patient's external world, is not dependent upon the patient's reportings of changes in the external world, is not invested in being the responsible manager of the patient's extratherapy world. Instead, the experiential therapist is invested in insuring that the final step in the session deals effectively with the experiencing of new ways of being and behaving in the patient's extratherapy world.

Significance and functions: Practical, conceptual, and preventive. Tasting and sampling new ways of being and behaving can be seen as a rather practical enterprise. It is another practical way of bringing about experiencing. In fact, each of the five steps (Figure 1) is a soundly practical means of achieving experiencing. Of these five, this final means is the most effective. Once we set our task as the bringing about of therapeutic experiencing, and once we look around for practical means of bringing this about, this final step surfaces as the most useful and most practical of the methods available.

Next there is conceptual significance and function. Existential-humanistic theory invests human beings with the possibility of moving toward increasing integration and actualization, the pinnacles of human existence, the highest values of existential-humanistic theory. Patients who go through the step of experiencing new ways of being and behaving in their extratherapy worlds are taking giant strides in the direction of integration and actualization. From a conceptual perspective, the entire process of therapeutic experiencing has significance in terms of the state of integration and actualization (Arbuckle, 1975; Caruso, 1964; Hora, 1959; Mahrer, 1984c; Shaffer, 1978).

Then there is preventive significance and function. Tasting and sampling of new ways of being and behaving in the external world provide a measure of reassurance to therapist and patient alike. It is a reassurance of three worries to which both therapist and patient are entitled. For example, there may be disruptive eruptions into the patient's extratherapy world of what occurred earlier in the session, before we deal with the final step of being/behavioral change. The patient and the therapist may well go through a great deal of hell. They may plunge into the experiencing of going beserk, running amok, suicide, homicide, wild and crazy explosiveness. When awful and scary possibilities are stirred up in a session, it is so easy for the therapist—and the patient—to worry in the stretch between sessions. Is she going to kill herself? Is he going to end up walking mindlessly in the streets? Is she going to shoot her father? Is he going to slide into a state of complete withdrawal? These are the behavioral residuals of the experiencings which may be opened up in the first four steps. By undergoing the final step, such threatening behavioral possibilities are punctured. The reassuring preventive functions of this final step is to minimize the likelihood of disintegrative behavior implied or expressed in the course of the session.

Indeed, a preventive function of the final step is to take advantage of the good, integrative form of the behavioral possibilities generated in the course of the session. What started out as the experiencing of going beserk may become the experiencing of spontaneous looseness, opening up possible new ways of being and behaving on the basis of the newfound spontaneous looseness. The course of therapeutic work transforms disintegrative experiencings into their integrative good form, and the consideration of actual ways of being and behaving not only opens up these good behavioral possibilities but also serves to reduce the likelihood of threatening, bad-feelinged, disintegrative behaviors.

In the course of a session, there is often an activation of deeper experiencings which are risky, outlandish, wicked, bizarre, wild, impulsive, devilish. By subjecting these experiencings to the final behavioralizing step, there is a curiously reassuring effect. The behavioral possibilities are made forthrightly real and concrete. The deeper experiencings are converted into playfully integrative behavioral possibilities. There is a vividly real tasting and sampling of the behavioral implications of these deeper experiencings. The more these are played with, transformed, concretized, allowed to take specific form and shape, the more two consequences occur. One is that the changes in ways of being and behaving are transformed into their playful, positive, good-feel-inged, good form. The second is that there is a washing away of their frightening, awful, monstrous, disintegrative bad form. Without the final step of actual consideration of being/behavioral changes, the likelihood of such frightening changes is potentiated. When the final step is carried through, the likelihood of such frightening changes is washed away and replaced by more delightful behavioral possibilities.

There is another way in which this final step is preventive. In the course of the session, changes have occurred in that the patient carried forward experiencing, engaged in the integrative encounter, entered into being the deeper potential. If the session were to end there, many therapists know that patients will often tend to recoil against these forward movements. Between this and the next session, patients may be pulling in the other direction, balancing whatever therapeutic good steps were made. Angyal is representative of those who observe that a retrenchment " . . . is found after each decisive step forward in therapy. While the person is reaching toward health in a goal-conscious manner he may be assailed by temptations of the old ways, by acute anxieties, by accidents and somatic symptoms, or he may make 'slips' that have serious practical consequences and which may disarrange his life for a long time to come" (Angyal, 1965, p. 243).

By dealing with being/behavioral change, such retrenchments are reduced. Converting these experiential forward steps into being/behavioral possibilities tends to prevent the rest of the personality from rising up and countering experiential steps forward.

All in all, experiential tasting and sampling of behavioral possibilities have practical, conceptual, and preventive meanings. In experiential psychotherapy, the therapist has little or no personal investment in the patient's extratherapy world, nor does the therapist use the extratherapy world to serve to enhance role-relationships between therapist and patient. In our therapy, the experiential consideration of possible being/behavioral change is an excitingly active enterprise which caps the steps in each session.

THE DIRECTIONS OF POTENTIAL CHANGE: PROPADEUTIC CONSIDERATIONS

In order to undertake changes in the patient's ways of being and behaving, the therapist generally has some notions of the directions of potential change. How does the therapist arrive at notions of the directions of potential change for this patient? What data does the therapist use in framing out the directions of change for the given patient? What are the determinants of the directions of change for this patient? Changes in the patient's ways of being and behaving depend a great deal on the therapist's explicit and implicit notions of the directions of potential change in general and for this patient in particular.

Destiny of the Unchanging Personality: Degree and Specificity of Prediction

The therapist's picture of what this patient can become, the directions of potential change, depends on what the therapist believes about the ease of personality change and what determines personality change. Is personality relatively fixed and unchanging, or is it a fluid process? Either inside or outside of therapy, to what extent is personality seen as undergoing change, and to what extent is personality seen as relatively static and unchanging? While this issue falls outside the theory of practice, it has strong implications for practice (Mahrer, 1983a). If personality structure is held as relatively fixed and unchanging, it means that the therapist can assess directions of potential change against the backdrop of a relatively fixed and unchanging future. It means that the therapist can see something of the destiny of a personality structure which is relatively fixed and unchanging.

According to an existential-humanistic theory of human beings, it makes sense to speak of a destiny of the unchanging personality (Mahrer, 1978a; cf. Maddi, 1972; Mischel, 1969; Thomas, 1985). From the perspective of this theory, the personality structure of virtually every adult is relatively fixed and unchanging in its basic contours. Substantive changes in personality structure are preciously rare occurrences. That is what makes therapeutic change so very special. That is also what makes it quite possible to predict the destiny of the unchanging personality, once the therapist has a reasonable grasp of the patient's own personality structure.

The operating domain is relatively fixed and unchanging. The nature of relationships between the operating and deeper domains is relatively fixed and unchanging. To the extent that the therapist grasps all of this, it is quite possible to make some reasonable guesses of the likely destinies available for this particular patient. We may predict, for example, that this patient's likely destiny will include perpetual struggles against authority figures, struggles which will likely end in a series of valiant failures and disillusionments. We may predict that this other patient will spend his life inviting others to come close and then erecting barricades against their getting too close.

By presuming that the structure of the personality tends to remain pretty much unchanged, we can predict the nature of the experiencing for patients and get a hint or two of the means by which they may arrange for this experiencing. With one patient, the experiencing will be that of valiant failure and disillusionment, and the means of accomplishing this may consist of struggles against authority figures. For another patient, the destiny is the experiencing of safe distance, and the means may consist of various ways of inviting others to come close and then insuring that they do not. Predicting destinies is a matter of grasping the nature of the experiencings and having a few hints about how those experiencings may be enabled to occur.

It is easy to predict that the patient will continue to undergo this particular experiencing. On the other hand, it is quite difficult to predict the behavioral means the patient will use to provide for the experiencing. Binswanger (1958c) not only predicted the unchanging experiential destiny of Ellen West as including agonizing quiet, nothingness, and emptiness, but also went much further and predicted the specific behavioral means, viz. suicide: " . . . the existence in the case of Ellen West had become ripe for its death, in other words . . . the death, this death, was the necessary fulfillment of the life-meaning of this existence. . . . The suicide is a necessary-voluntary consequence of this existential state of things" (1958c, p. 295). I accept that the destiny is predictable in terms of the experiential state, but I part company with Binswanger in including the specific behavioral means in the predicted destiny.

In traditional theories of psychopathology, destinies are also predicted. However, where our theory holds for an unchanging personality structure, traditional theories of psychopathology speak of biologically grounded diseases (sicknesses, emotional illnesses) with built-in courses of development (Fenichel, 1945; Glover, 1925; Kendell, 1975; Klein & Davis, 1969; Millon, 1981; Noyes & Kolb, 1967). These theories speak of early stages, prodromal symptoms of what is to come, the development of the illness, middle and later stages of the illness. In contrast to the existential-humanistic theory, the destiny is predicted on the basis of the supposed course of the psychopathology rather than on the basis of an unchanging personality structure. Accordingly, our approach and the traditional psychopathological-psychodiagnostic approach would use different principles to predict different futures. If the therapist does not undertake some way of undergoing personality change, we foresee a destiny around an unchanging personality structure. In contrast, the traditional psychopathological-psychodiagnostic approach foresees a destiny around an unfolding series of stages of the illness. Where we lack principles to predict the precise behaviors the patient will use, the psychopathological-psychodiagnostic approach offers a more precise destiny filled with the symptoms of the development of the illness.

Determinants of the Directions of Change
for the Patient

How does a therapist arrive at some idea of the directions of change for a given patient? To what extent are the therapist's ideas about "directions of change" general for most patient versus distinctive for the given patient?

Psychotherapy researchers have repeatedly called for ways of studying change at the level of the individual patient. This is a serious matter, discussed by researchers of many stripes and colors, from clinician-researchers to research clinicians, from hard to soft psychotherapy researchers of several professions and many approaches to psychotherapy (Bergin & Lambert, 1978; Fiske et al., 1970; Frank, 1982; Gottman & Markman, 1978; Greenberg, 1983; Kiesler, 1971; Kiresuk & Sherman, 1968; Klonoff & Cox, 1975; Orlinsky & Howard, 1978; Waskow & Parloff, 1975; Weed, 1968). But this is more than merely a research matter, for the psychotherapist must have some ways of determining what this patient can become, the directions of potential change, and these directions are either general or specific, made up of large categories or tailored to the individual patient.

The perspective of experiential psychotherapy. After each session, the experiential therapist adds a note or two to a progressively cumulative picture of the patient's potentials for experiencing and their relationships. On the basis of this picture, and by invoking a set of change principles presented later in this chapter, the therapist can build an increasingly defined picture of the directions of change available to this given patient. In this way, the therapist does indeed have a set of ideas of the directions of potential change for this particular patient.

At the most general level, every patient is to change in the direction of increasing integration and actualization. Translated into therapeutic work, with a given patient, this means that the patient's potentials for experiencing will change to their good integrative form, and toward good, integrative relationships with other potentials. It also means that each of the patient's potentials changes in the direction of actualization, i.e., toward being realized, toward being a functional, working component of the patient's operating domain. Another way of putting this is that there are principles that guide the direction of change for every patient.

But "integration" and "actualization" are quite general and say little about the specific content and nature of the directions of change for the given patient. According to the existential-humanistic theory of human beings and the experiential theory of psychotherapeutic practice, each patient has her own distinctive package of potentials for experiencing, especially deeper potentials. These are the key to the given patient's distinctive directions of potential change. The predominant determinant of what this patient can be and become is the patient's own distinctive package of potentials, with heavy emphasis upon that person's deeper potentials.

The therapist does not determine the directions of potential change, nor does the patient. Because the determinants consist of the patient's own distinctive set of potentials, especially deeper potentials, there are at least two surprises. One is in discovering the actual nature of this person's potentials for experiencing. A second surprise is to see the good form of each of these potentials, the particular way in which this potential emerges into its own good form.

By accepting the determinant as the patient's own package of potentials for experiencing, especially deeper potentials, the direction of available change for each patient is a refreshingly individualized journey. This is one of the reasons why Erickson could assert that he had a different therapy for each patient (Erickson, 1980; Erickson & Rossi, 1981; Erickson, Rossi & Rossi, 1976), because he was explicit in seeking the directions of change from the given patient's own deeper personality processes, viewed in their more positive forms or possibilities.

Experiential psychotherapy determines the directions of available change by grasping the nature of the person's own distinctive package of potentials for experiencing, coupled with a set of principles for generating the directions of potential change. In contrast, many other perspectives have different ways of setting forth directions of change.

Some other perspectives. There are at least four contrasting perspectives for setting forth directions of change (Mahrer, 1985). One looks at patients in terms of psychopathology. Each patient is understood as falling along a dimension with one end variously described as psychopathological, sick, neurotic, abnormal, psychotic, having a psychodiagnostic condition of some kind, being maladjusted, maladapted. The other end of the dimension is described with words such as mature, healthy, adult, adjusted, normal, well, with reduced or little or no psychopathology. Patients are to change from the bad end to the good end of the dimension. It is as if the therapist faces the patient with the predetermined intent: "You are sick, I shall make you well. . . . You are immature, I shall make you mature. . . . You are abnormal, I shall make you normal. . . . You are maladjusted, I shall make you adjusted."

This perspective comes equipped with an explicit or implicit set of ideas about the meaning of mature, adult, healthy, adjusted, normal, well, and the direction of change is toward whatever comprises that therapist's meaning. It may consist merely of notions that normal people do not behave in ways which may be taken as untoward, out of the ordinary, abnormal, and that they generally function without making trouble or complaining too much. So the direction of change is away from indications, expressions, symptoms of the general meaning of psychopathology. Or, the direction of change is toward, for example, freeing oneself of self-defeating values and beliefs and replacing them with what the therapist considers to be rational, adjusted, non-defeating values and beliefs, more sensible basic premises (Adler, 1959; Dreikurs, 1956; Ellis, 1959a, 1959b, 1973). Some therapists identify particular areas of functioning which are regarded as normal, mature, well-adjusted, healthy, such as an enhanced self-image, pleasurable social network, age-appropriate intimacy (Lankton & Lankton, 1983). Many therapies have their own pictures of what the person is like who is normal, well, healthy, mature, adult, adjusted, and this picture constitutes the direction of change.

A second perspective starts with the idea of the patient's problems and frames the direction of change as the resolution of these problems. The problems may be defined by the patient in terms of presenting complaints, stresses, bothersome behaviors (Haley, 1976; Kanfer & Phillips, 1970; Krasner, 1975; Mischel, 1968). They may be defined by the referral source or third party complainant who cites the patient's drug abuse, relentlessness in school, alcoholism at work, irresponsibility in the family, or danger to the community; or problems may be defined by the therapist in terms of lack of impulse controls, excessive dependency, or unresolved Oedipal problems. The logic is to locate and identify the problem, and the direction of change is toward a resolution and reduction in whatever is identified as the problem.

A third perspective rests on favorite dimensions of personality with either a good end and a bad end or extremes and a midrange. Once the dimension is selected, the direction of change is toward the good end or the midrange. For example, Wyss (1973) describes the New Viennese School including V. E. Frankl, I. Caruso, P. R. Hofstätter, and W. Daim. According to this school, the paramount personality dimension runs from Godlessness to Godliness, and the direction of change is toward the acceptance of Godliness in one's innermost being. Other personality dimensions include internal — external control, self-centeredness — other centeredness, activity — passivity, social interest, dominance — submission, assertiveness, love — hate, flexibility — rigidity, detachment — involvement, dependence — independence. Equipped with such personality dimensions, there are built-in directions of change.

A fourth perspective is that patients are to become more like the therapist. The general idea is that the therapist is a model or exemplar of preeminent and healthy functioning, and the patient is gradually to identify with or become like the therapist. Some therapists explicitly serve as a model for how the patient is to be (e.g., Jourard, 1968, 1971a, 1971b). Most therapies are more circuitous in setting the goal of therapy as the attainment of maturity and healthy functioning and in identifying the therapist as an exemplar of maturity and healthy functioning.

The problem is that if patients were to be the way therapists are in therapy, the direction might be toward behaving in ways that seem removed, distant, calculating, manipulative, controlling, "paranoid", suspicious, distructful, bizarre, deranged (Laing, 1982). In some approaches, patients would tend to have private thoughts about others, be distant and removed, show very little of what they are thinking and feeling. They would presume that there is only one reality — their reality; if others do not share that reality then the others are out of contact, sick, unrealistic. The patient would categorize others in diagnostic entities and regard others as manifesting that diagnostic entity. The patient would use indirect and covert methods of controlling others, exerting pressure, influencing others to be different in specific ways that the patient privately maintains. The patient would listen by changing what others say into something else so that when others say one thing the patient really knows that the other person means something else. Whatever a person says is codified, symbolized, reduced, converted, interpreted as really meaning something else. In other approaches, if patients become more like their exemplar therapists, they might move in the direction of being kindly, caring, understanding, empathic, helping, positively regarding persons.

In contrast with these four perspectives, experiential therapy has no preset formulations for how the patient is to be or become. The picture is generated from the particular potentials of the given patient. Instead of preset formulations to which all patients are to conform, the direction of the change is distinctive to the given patient. The picture of the directions of change does not come from the therapist's theory of psychopathology, favorite dimensions of personality, or pictures of what is mature, normal, adult, adjusted, healthy. Each patient's directions for change emerge from a set of principles applied to the particular package of potentials, especially deeper potentials, characteristic of this particular person.

In-Therapy Data as Windows for Seeing the Directions of Potential Change

What data does the experiential therapist use to see the directions of potential change for this patient? On what basis does the experiential therapist actually generate the directions of potential change? The simple answer is that the therapist uses the peak experiencings in the session(s), applies principles of the directions of change, and thereby generates a picture of what this patient can become (Mahrer, 1985). The actual working data consist of the peak experiencings from each of the four steps in the session.

Peak experiencings in the session. Important and useful moments are when experiencing rises to its peaks, reaches its highest points. These may occur during the carrying forward of potentials. Whether at the operating or the deeper levels, there are moments when experienc ing is quite high as these potentials are carrying forward. How the patient is being in these moments, what the patient is doing, what is occurring in the patient, who and what the patient is in these moments— all of these are the important data for generating the directions of potential change. Included here are those precious moments when what is carried forward is a potential that occurred in early life, only to be left behind from then on. The current life does not include the early experiencing of joyful new discovery, or wonderful trust, or the sense of oneness, or delightfully open physical playfulness, or other experiencings whose appearance was limited to early life. These early positive experiencings offer a rich source of what can be rescued and used again in one's current world.

Similarly, peak experiencings may occur in the internal integrative encounter when the patient is engaged in the clashing of the encounter or in the new state of integration. These moments serve as a second package of in-therapy data for seeing the directions of potential change.

By far the most useful moments of strong experiencing are those which occur when the patient disengages from the operating domain and enters into being the deeper potential. The deeper potentials constitute the richest reservoir of data for new directions of potential change. This applies especially to those moments when the patient reaches the higher plateaus of experiencing the good form of the deeper potential. Even if this occurs for only a brief moment or so, it is akin to piercing the ceiling of a whole new plateau of possibilities for directions of change.

The steps of the therapeutic process are designed to foster moments of peak experiencing. When these actually occur, they constitute the priceless windows for seeing the directions of potential change for this patient in this session.

Applying the principles for seeing the directions of potential change. Once the therapist flags the peak experiencing(s) in the session, she has the data she needs. The therapist then applies the principles described later in this chapter and generates the directions of potential change for the patient.

Suppose, for example, that in step 2 (carrying forward the experiencing of potentials), the peak occurred when the patient erupted into gales of hilarious laughter as he was experiencing a sense of open sexuality, of exhibiting strong sexual feelings toward his lovely and highly attractive aunt. Here are the data of peak experiencing. One of the principles of generating the directions of potential change involves heightened experiencing of the good, integrated form of the operating potentials. On the basis of this principle, the therapist may see the directions of potential change for this patient as including free and wholesome expression of feelings of sexual attractiveness, easy and graceful acknowledgment of sexual feelings. All the experiential therapist does is to start with the data of the peak experiencings and to apply the various principles for generating directions of potential change for this particular patient.

Over the sessions, the therapist gradually accumulates an increasingly defined and accurate picture of the patient's own emerging and changing potentials for experiencing. On the basis of only a few instances, a potential may be described, for example, as the experiencing of defying, opposing authorities. However, after many more instances of this experiencing, it may disclose itself as the experiencing of standing up for oneself, being self-confident and intact, solid and firm. As more and more facets are revealed in subsequent peaks of experiencing, and perhaps as changes occur in the nature of the experiencing, the therapist gradually acquires a fuller and deeper picture of the present nature of the experiencing. Then, by applying the principles for generating directions of change, the therapist has a useful window for seeing what this patient can become, the directions of potential change for this individual person.

Directions of potential change and the patient's initial statement of problems and complaints, wishes and wants. To what extent are the directions of potential change generated from the patient's initial statement of problems and complaints? If the patient starts therapy by stating that he goes through cycles of gorging himself and then vomiting, or that he is unsure which career to follow, or that he lacks self-control, or that he is subject to bouts of gloominess and depression, do we build directions of potential change from these? Is the direction of change to be toward reduced cycles of gorging and vomiting, a clearer career choice, heightened self-control, minimized depression? From the experiential perspective the answer is no. Directions of potential change are constructed from the data contained in moments of peak experiencing in the session—not from the patient's initial statement of problems or complaints (cf. Wolpe, 1976).

Nor are the directions for potential change generated from the patient's initial statement of wishes and wants. "I want to be more assertive. . . . I want to be feeling and expressive. . . . My goal is to be respected, to respect myself, to feel self-respect. . . . I'd be happy if I had a sense of being needed and wanted, being useful and important to someone. . . . " Some refer to this as a description of the "ideal self" as contrasted with the "self," and psychotherapy is seen as a way of bringing about a "congruence" between the two. Clinicians then find it important " . . . to show that psychotherapy results in one kind of constructive personality change: increased congruence between the person's self and his ideal self" (Butler, 1968, p. 13). Experiential psychotherapy rejects this procedure. We do not generate directions of potential change from the referred-to wishes and wants in the patient's initial statements, nor from the initial statements of problems and complaints. There are several reasons for this.

One is simply that our data consist of the material in the moments of peak experiencing. Generally, initial statements of problems and complaints, wishes and wants, are not the moments of peak experiencing in the session. Accordingly, these initial statements fall outside the range of peak experiencings from which the directions of potential change are generated.

In experiential psychotherapy, what the patient says is received, processed, understood by means of experiential listening. This applies as much to initial statements as to any other statements by the patient. Accordingly, "listening" to these statements as initial problems, complaints, wishes, or wants is only one way of listening, and not ours. In the very beginning of the first session, the patient may say, "My problem is that I never have orgasms and my husband is getting frustrated. He yells at me and tells me that he's going to get another woman!" "I just don't have feelings. I am dead. Nothing affects me!" "Lately I'm starting to forget things and I drink more. I think the drinking is causing it, but I don't know. Things are just getting worse." To the experientially listening therapist, the data consist of the invoked images and experiencings rather than the denoted problems or complaints. Where one therapist may frame a problem as a marital conflict over orgasmic insufficiency, the experiential therapist may be sensing an anger-filled experiencing of pent-up uselessness directed at the husband. Where one therapist may identify a problem of lack of feelings, the experientially listening therapist may resonate to a resolute refusal and defiance against some external agency. Where one therapist may hear an initial complaint of forgetfulness and excessive drinking, the experientially listening therapist may be undergoing the terror of falling into a state of utter collapse, of complete chaos. We receive data of experiencing where other approaches may receive statements of initial complaints, problems, wishes and wants.

Initial statements by the patient are used as part of the first step in each session of experiential psychotherapy. These initial statements are used to enable the patient to begin therapeutic work by focusing attention upon some meaningful center so that bodily sensations are at least moderately strong. That opens the way for the subsequent steps in the session, and it is in those subsequent steps that the peak experiencings will occur.

Another reason is that the therapeutic process tends to yield fresh problems, complaints, wishes and wants as the session proceeds along, and as the patient moves from session to session. Even in the initial session or so, the beginning statements are taken as mere beginning points for the therapeutic process. As the therapeutic process moves along, the patient undergoes changes so that the person who had those initial problems and wants will move away from being that person with those same problems and wants. By the next session, or in subsequent sessions, the patient will likely be a new and changing person with a new set of initial problems, complaints, wishes and wants (cf. Angyal, 1965, p. 222).

Accordingly, the only likely condition under which initial statements of problems and wants would serve as data for generating the directions of potential change would be when the peak experiencing in the session lies in these initial statements. While that may happen occasionally in an initial session, it is not very likely, for the sequence of steps in the session is designed to yield better and better opportunities for peak experiencings. Furthermore, even if the peak experiencing occurs in the initial statements, the generating of directions of potential change is built on the nature of the experiencing which is present as the patient is stating the initial problems, complaints, wishes and wants. If the patient is experiencing a sense of loss of control and a frightening helplessness as he talks about the cycles of gorging and vomiting, the directions of potential change are constructed from the nature of the experiencing rather than the referred-to content of gorging and vomiting.

All in all, the directions of potential change have little to do with the patient's initial statement of problems and complaints, wishes and wants.

Criteria of Psychotherapeutic Depth, Breadth, and Profoundness of Change

I regard experiential psychotherapy as effecting the greatest depth, breadth, and profoundness of change. No other therapy can compare. If psychoanalytic therapists are ready for genuine depth, breadth, and profoundness of change, they should be seen in experiential psychotherapy. But experiential psychotherapy is not the only one singing this refrain. There are many therapies explaining why they are the deepest and most comprehensive therapy of all. For example, rational-emotive therapy stands above the others because it not only digs out the cognitive, but also the emotional and the behavioral (Ellis, 1976). But by far the most successful claimant to king of the therapeutic mountain is psychoanalysis. Proclaiming itself as the most complete therapy (Fine, 1973), it works hard to rise above other therapies as the deepest, most profound, most comprehensive approach. If you want real therapy, the supreme way of undergoing genuine depth change, psychoanalysis is the only way to go.

One problem is that we have few criteria upon which to assess psychoanaysis' claims. If we seek to evaluate therapies in terms of depth of work, profoundness of change, breadth of material covered, fullness and completeness at getting at the most basic of personality processes, what criteria do we use? Accordingly, the purpose of the present section is to answer the following questions: What are some criteria for assessing the degree of depth, breadth, and profoundness of change for experiential psychotherapy and for other therapies, including psychoanalysis? In terms of these criteria, to what extent may experiential psychotherapy and other therapies, including psychoanalysis, be regarded as deep, broad, and as effecting profound change?

Number of sessions, and for the rest of one's life. In order to get the greatest depth, breadth, and profoundness of change from experiential psychotherapy, three conditions should be met. One is to have up to two or three hundred sessions, distributed over perhaps two or three years. Following this, the patient should make experiential dream work a regular weekly enterprise for the rest of one's life (cf. Jones, 1953). In addition, the patient should return for therapeutic work every two years or so for about 10–15 sessions.

Experiential psychotherapy requires regular (e.g., weekly) therapeutic work throughout one's life. Even if the therapist has been in therapy for two to five years or so, genuine depth, breadth, and profoundness call for a continuation of effective therapeutic work the rest of one's life. Every week or so, the experiential psychotherapist is to engage in some kind of effective therapeutic work, whether it be individual experiential therapy or effective self-work, such as experiential dream work. In this, we are following the lead of practitioners of meditation and contemplation, who are encouraged to undertake this practice as a regular part of their entire lives. Therapies which end after a few years or many years, and which lack any systematic way of continuing therapeutic work for the rest of one's life, are regarded as less deep, less broad, and as effecting less profound change.

In this sense, the aim of experiential psychotherapy is to prepare the patient to carry on her own therapeutic work. At present, I see this as consisting of using experiential methods of working with one's own dreams, but it need not be limited to that. Experiential methods can be adapted to work with and by oneself, or with a partner who need not be an experiential therapist. In any case, truly deep therapy results in the patient's carrying out effective therapeutic work for the rest of her life.

In terms of number of sessions and their distribution, depth, breadth, and profoundness of change call for a minimum of around 300 sessions distributed over approximately three years of therapeutic work, followed by some kind of effective experiential work as a regular practice throughout one's life. As a provisional statement for psychotherapies in general, I suggest that psychotherapy that calls itself deep, broad, and profound should likewise aim at approximately 300 sessions over approximately three years, followed by some kind of change-facilitating practice as a regular part of one's continuing life. This provisional criterion applies to psychotherapies, to patients, and to psychotherapists who are enjoined to make their own therapeutic change a regular and continuing part of their lives (cf. Guntrip, 1969; p. 312).

Extinguishing of the operating domain; being the integrated and actualized deeper domain. Genuine depth of change means the wholesale extinguishing of the operating domain, and the patient's being the integrated, actualized deeper domain. This means that there is no more of the former operating domain, including its constructed external world, its experiencings, its behavioral means of constructing its external world, and its behavioral means of providing for its experiencings. In effect, the former personality is ended. In its place is a whole new person and personality comprised of the formerly deeper potentials, now in their integrated form and now actualized.

According to existential-humanistic theory, there are deeper potentials and there are basic potentials. A fully profound experiential therapy not only includes the extinguishing of the operating domain, but its replacement with integrated and actualized basic potentials. Such an achievement is rare, and is the goal of lifelong therapeutic work. However, whether replaced with deeper or basic potentials, deep change means the washing away of the substantive, continuing operating domain.

Consider all the problems which characterize the operating domain. The patient drinks too much, sinks into gloominess, has headaches, is always out of a job, on and on and on. Of all the ways of trying to do something about these problems and difficulties, one solution is deep, profound, and clean: The patient is no longer a person who has those problems. This is a wholesale, radical change. Once the whole operating domain extinguishes, all of its problems go away, for there no longer is any "person" who "has" these problems (Binswanger, 1958a, 1967; Boss, 1963; Ellenberger, 1958).

For example, consider the patient who is stuck between this and that, who is painfully this and painfully that, who hovers in the awful middle ground between this and that. Every therapy has words to describe this. Some refer to this as approach-avoidance, avoidance-avoidance, and approach-approach conflicts (e.g., Brown, 1942, 1948; Miller, 1944). Some speak of severe ambivalence. Every therapy has a few favorite versions of this and that. Patients move back and forth between being too manic and too depressed. Patients are caught between their top-dog and their under-dog, between their "child" and their "adult," between their introversive and extraversive tendencies. When patients have been in object-relations psychoanalytic therapy for many years, they are described as being, on the one hand, hesitant to throw themselves wholly into the psychoanalytic process and, on the other, hesitant to free themselves of the psychoanalytic career. How are these problems resolved in a manner which is regarded as deep, broad, and profound? Our answer is that the patient is no longer a person who has these problems. That is, the person with the problems extinguishes. As the person washes away, the problems are no more.

Because of differences in conceptualizations of personality and differences in vocabulary, it is difficult to compare experiential psychotherapy with others. If, however, the existential-humanistic "operating domain" may be roughly approximated with the psychoanalytic "ego," and if our "deeper domain" may be roughly approximated by the psychoanalytic "unconscious," then it seems that these two psychotherapies have rather different meanings of depth and breadth and profoundness of change. Throughout his writings, and notably in his introductory lectures (1976d) and his discussion of therapy as terminable or interminable (1976e), Freud asserted the aim of therapy as that of strengthening the ego, making it independent and autonomous against the inroads of the superego and the unconscious. In many psychodynamic and psychoanalytic therapies, depth of change includes the strengthening of the more or less conscious personality, the ego, the operating and functioning self (Allport, 1960; Fenichel, 1954b; Fromm-Reichmann, 1958; Hartmann, 1964; Rapaport, 1958). This conscious self is to be freed of the inroads and intrusions from deeper intrapsychic processes. If we can find a way of talking about personality structures, it seems that therapies would be regarded as deep and profound to the extent that there is a washing away or extinguishing of the conscious personality, the ego, the continuing self, the functioning personality, the operating domain. On this criterion, experiential therapy is deep and profound, of course, and many other therapies are not. On this criterion, psychodynamic-psychoanalytic therapies are expressly not deep or profound, for they work toward reinforcing and strengthening the operating, functioning, continuing ego or self or personality.

On our criterion, the operating domain is to be replaced with the integrated and actualized deeper domain. In broader terms, the goal is to replace the operating and functioning personality with the deeper personality processes (Adler, 1938; Angyal, 1965; White, 1959, 1960). Some other therapies accept this criterion and aim at bringing forth their own versions of deeper personality processes. If, for example, deeper personality processes are held as social interest, then deep and profound change means becoming a person with strong social interest. If deeper personality processes consist of Godliness or intimacy or competence or oneness with the world, then the becoming of these kinds of persons would evidence deep and profound personality change.

In many therapies, however, deeper personality processes are to be domesticated, gentled, understood, kept in place, resolved, not to be a source of conflict. In my opinion, most of the psychodynamic and psychoanalytic therapies do not aim at replacing the operating and functioning personality with some version of deeper personality processes. Accordingly, on this criterion, such therapies would not qualify as deep or profound.

Therapeutic involvement with basic personality processes. On this criterion I believe there can be more general agreement than on the one above. A therapy is deeper, broader, and achieves more profound change to the extent that the therapy deals with whatever is regarded as basic personality processes. Let us now turn our attention to three matters having to do with basic personality processes.

• Experiential psychotherapy includes a heavy emphasis on dream work. It holds that dreams express deeper and basic potentials for experiencing, and that dream work is necessary in order for experiential therapy to achieve changes which are deep, broad, and profound. In general, I would suggest that a psychotherapy which claims to be deep, broad, and profound should likewise work with dreams. Even if each therapy works with dreams in its own way, the therapy is dealing with material which contains basic personality processes.

• According to existential-humanistic theory, basic personality processes refer to material within the period from a few years prior to conception to several years following birth. Therefore, a deep, broad, and profound experiential psychotherapy will deal with material from that primitive period. It will go beyond the infant as the experiencing nexus, and into the experiencings of significant figures during this primitive period. Experiential psychotherapy will open up the mother's sense of defiance as she defies her parents' admonitions and keeps the baby even though she is not married and is living by herself. Basic potentials may consist of father's experiencing of desiccation and aging as he, in his late forties, finally has a baby and thereby disproves menacing fears of incapability, being over-the-hill. Experiential psychotherapy is deep, broad, and profound to the extent that it deals therapeutically with meaningful events in this primitive period.

Other therapies have their own concepts of what may be referred to as basic personality processes, the most fundamental stuff of personality and human functioning. For some therapies, the most fundamental material has to do with the birth events, or with early sexual and aggressive interactions, or with one's fundamental connectedness with human beings, or some other context in which the basic material derives. Some psychodynamic-psychoanalytic therapies regard as basic those processes involving separation and differentiation from the earliest mother figure, or Oedipal relations occurring early in one's life. Clearly, from the perspective of experiential therapy, those other therapies are rather superficial, for they are not designed to work with the genuinely basic personality processes.

Therapies which include a concept of basic and fundamental personality processes have their own ideas about the nature of such basic material. Each therapy is deep, broad, and profound to the extent that it deals with this material. Each therapy would tend to consider other therapies as less deep, broad, and profound to the extent that they fail to deal with the particular version of basic personality processes. While there may be a measure of agreement on the general criterion, there is little or no agreement on the results of trying to apply this criterion.

• Experiential psychotherapy has no preset list of the basic potentials. We surmise that we are at the basic level when we have penetrated down through the deeper potentials and arrive at fundamental potentials having their roots in the primitive period of personality development. But we hold that each patient will be characterized by a distinctive set of basic potentials. Truly deep experiential work deals with these basic potentials, whatever their explicit nature and content for this particular patient.

In contrast, many other therapies often have preset notions of the nature and content of basic personality processes. They can thereby identify their own therapeutic work as being genuinely basic when it involves given kinds of basic personality processes. They are also enabled, thereby, to reject other approaches as less basic because they do not deal with those given basic personality processes. Notable here are the psychoanalytic therapies which link depth, breadth, and profoundness with explicitly predetermined basic personality processes. The problem is that divergent schools of psychoanalytic thought are entitled to frame an unending list of increasingly fundamental floors to psychoanalytic work, and to decry others as being more superficial. For example, the object relations school holds that the traditional psychoanalytic basic processes, viz. Oedipal issues, are not really basic at all, and the truly basic issues involve the infantile ego's withdrawal, regression, and security in relationship with the earliest parental figures (Fairbairn, 1943, 1952; Guntrip, 1969; Hartmann, 1964; Klein, 1960; Winnicott, 1958, 1965):

> One can only keep a sharp lookout for whatever signs of "withdrawnness" the patient actually does present, and take care not to hold up the analysis by treating conflicts over sex and aggression as ultimates when the patient is ready to go behind them. We cannot afford to concentrate attention exclusively on any one thing, whether it be the oedipal problem, the depressive problem, or schizoid withdrawal and regression. We can only recognize that psychoanalytical investigation has discovered these problems in that order, as it has worked deeper (Guntrip, 1969, p. 286).

> The pathological Oedipus complex always masks poor relationships with parents in reality, and should be analyzed in such a way as to lead on to the discovery of the hopeless, shut-in, detached, infantile ego which has given up real object-relations as unobtainable and sought safety in regression into the deep unconscious (Guntrip, 1969, p. 305).

Psychoanalytic therapy is deep to the extent that it deals with whatever the regnant school of psychoanalytic thought names as universally basic personality processes. Similarly, every therapy which claims to be deep can argue that it is the deepest because it alone deals with its version of universally basic personality processes. Experiential psychotherapy has no preset list of basic personality processes, and therefore is not part of the competition on this particular matter.

With regard to basic personality processes, then, an experiential psychotherapy which is deep, broad, and profound will spend a good measure of time dealing with dreams and will involve itself with basic potentials whose roots lie in the primitive period from a few years before conception to a few years after birth. As a criterion for psychotherapies in general, it is proposed that psychotherapies which hold themselves out as deep, broad, and profound will involve themselves with their own versions of basic personality processes. However, it should be noted that because many therapies tend to have their own versions of the nature and content of what they regard as basic personality processes, comparisons are exceedingly difficult.

Bodily changes. Existential-humanistic theory includes the body as open to psychological understanding and description, just as is human behavior and the worlds in which human beings exist. Accordingly, an experiential psychotherapy which is deep, broad, and profound will include therapeutic changes in the body (Mahrer, 1978a). These will generally fall into two classes. One involves the washing away of bodily states, phenomena, events, and conditions which are bothersome and distressing. Included are bodily aches and pains, painful body sensations, bodily-felt feelings of tightness, tension, hurting, shakings and tremblings, palpitations in the heart region, faintness, shortness of breath, loss of muscular reflex, ear infections, miscarriages, glandular changes and changes in secretions, growth and tumors, warts, infections, skin eruptions. The second class includes changes in the direction of increasing bodily integration and actualization. There is a heightened bodily-felt sense of intactness and soundness, energy and vitality, togetherness and harmony, strength and firmness, fluidity and grace. In general, the body participates in and expresses the directions of change, including such dramatic changes as the washing away of what is termed cancer (Mahrer, 1980b) and the growth of what is termed physical bodily health. These kinds of changes occur in an experiential psychotherapy which is deep, broad, and profound.

As a criterion for psychotherapies in general, it is likewise proposed that psychotherapies which are deep, broad, and profound will be accompanied by the washing away of bodily states and conditions, and the promotion of good-feelinged bodily states and conditions of well-being and health.

Here, then, are four proposed criteria of the depth, breadth, and profoundness of change for psychotherapies in general and for experiential psychotherapy in particular. Experiential psychotherapy accepts these criteria for itself and defines its work as deep, broad, and profound when these four criteria are met. What about a comparison of experiential therapy with other therapies on these criteria? Two conclu-

sions seem to be in order. One is that few therapies, including psychoanalysis, seem to match experiential psychotherapy in terms of depth,
breadth, and profoundness of change on these four criteria. However,
a second conclusion is that reasonably rigorous comparisons are exceedingly difficult across different conceptions of personality, especially
with regard to deeper and basic personality processes.

PRINCIPLES OF THE DIRECTIONS OF POTENTIAL CHANGE

In order to have an idea of the patient's possible new ways of being
and behaving, the experiential therapist uses a set of principles which
start with the peak experiencing in the session and generate a picture
of the directions of change available to this patient. These principles
are invaluable. Given the peak experiencings in the session, the principles tell the therapist what this patient can be like, the kinds of
changes which can take place. These principles enable us to answer
the following question: On the basis of what you know about this patient, what are the directions of change available for this patient, and
what are the available or potential changes in ways of being and
behaving?

The balance of this chapter is given to a presentation of these principles. But first we must turn to the conceptual schema the experiential
therapist uses to understand the directions of potential change.

Schema of the directions of potential change. Just about every
psychotherapeutic approach has some conceptual map or schema of
personality, behavior, the external world, and the directions of potential change. This schema is that theory's more or less scientific conceptualization. On the other hand, the schema of what this patient can
become is an expression of the theory's value system, for every psychotherapy discloses its particular value system in its explicit or implicit picture of therapeutic goals, of what patients can be and become
(Ansell, 1979; Beutler, 1979; Mahrer, 1967a; Strupp, 1980). The
existential-humanistic schema of the patient's personality structure,
behavior, and external world is given at the left in Figure 6, and the
schema of the directions of potential change is given on the right. The
experiential psychotherapist fills in the schema on the left, and the picture of what the patient can become is given on the right.

In the course of the session, the therapist will be a part of strong experiencings which occur. They may occur when experiencing is carried forward, when the internal encounter is occurring, and when the patient is being the deeper potential. Whether these strong experiencings occur briefly or for many minutes, the therapist now grasps the nature of an operating (OP1-OP4, Figure 6) or a deeper potential (DP5-DP7), and the behaviors (B1-B4) used to construct and exist in that potential's external world. This may consist of an externalized deeper potential or an appropriate situational context (Figure 6).

When we come to the final step in the session, the therapist must have a picture of what this person can be and become, a picture of the directions of potential change. Based upon the strong experiencings in the session, the therapist must have a picture of what the patient is (given in the schema at the left in Figure 6), and, from that, a picture of the directions of potential change (given on the right in Figure 6). Indeed, the therapist must have these two schemas so ingrained that when therapist and patient are ready to taste and sample changes in ways of being and behaving, the therapist has a clear picture of what this patient can become, based upon the strong experiencings in the session.

Essentially, the schema at the right in Figure 6 gives the picture of movement toward integration and actualization. But this statement provides little help for the practicing therapist. In order for the practicing therapist to make practical use of what the patient can become, 12 principles show how the schema at the left in Figure 6 generates the schema at the right. These 12 principles are organized under several more specific meanings of integration and actualization. Principles 1–3 define changes in the direction of actualizing the good form of the operating domain, i.e., how the operating potentials on the left change toward their good form and move toward heightened actualization. Principles 4–8 define changes in the direction of integrative relationships between the operating domain and the deeper domain. Principles 9 and 10 refer to changes in the direction of actualizing the good form of the deeper potentials, and principles 11 and 12 define changes in the extinguishing of the old operating domain.

Using Figure 6 as a picture of what the patient is and what the patient can become, we now turn to the principles themselves as they show the specific directions of potential change and as they provide the conceptual basis for the therapist's undertaking the final step in each session.

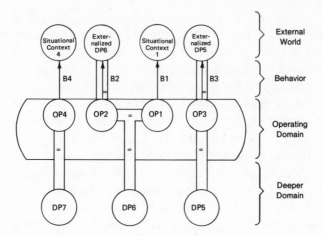

Figure 6. Schema of the Directions of Potential Change (left)

Actualization of the Good Form of the
Operating Domain

As given in Figure 6, the operating domain is comprised of the operating potentials (OP 1-4) which constitute what the patient experiences and how the patient behaves. Once the therapist has a picture of the operating potentials, the direction of change is toward transformation into their "good form" and increasing actualization of the good forms. Each operating potential shifts from a form in which the experiencing is painful, hurtful, disharmonious, torn apart, disjunctive, or anxiety-ridden toward a good form in which the experiencing is accompanied with tranquility, peacefulness, wholesomeness. The qualitative change is from the bad, disintegrative form to the good, integrative form; the quantitative change is toward heightened actualization of this good form. In all of this, the operating domain remains, but the essential nature undergoes a change both in form and in degree of actualization.

When the therapist grasps the nature of an operating potential, three principles define and specify the directions of change toward actualizing the good form of the operating domain.

1) There will be deeper and fuller experiencing of the good, integrated form of the operating potential. In the session, suppose that the peak experiencing consists of an operating potential involving the painful, disintegrative sense of separation, withdrawal, being at a distance

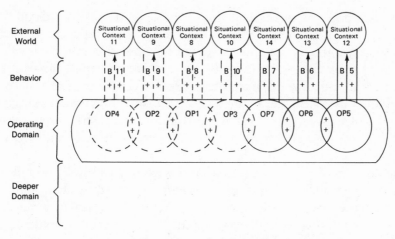

Figure 6. Schema of the Directions of Potential Change (right)

from people. What is a direction of potential change? If we use this first principle, it tells us that this patient is capable of becoming a person who (a) can experience the good, integrated form of that potential, and (b) can experience this good, integrative form in a fuller, more actualized way.

The therapist allows herself to resonate with, be filled with, "have" this experiencing. Because she can be on integrative good terms with it, the therapist can generate a picture of the patient as the deeper and fuller experiencing of the good, integrated form of this operating potential. The therapist quite literally can see a vivid picture of what this patient can become. By allowing this principle to generate a picture, the therapist may, for example, see a picture of this patient being a person who experiences a sense of intact independence, a sense of good-feelinged autonomy. Here is a distinct picture of what this patient can become, a direction of change generated by the first principle. The therapist sees a person being and experiencing this new way. When the therapist undergoes the operating potential, allows it to become its good, integrative form, and allows that to be experienced more deeply and fully, a distinct image will be generated. That image is the picture of what this patient can become.

In Figure 6, the change from bad, disintegrative form to good, integrative form is signified by the change from negative signs in the operating domain on the left (OP 1-4) to positive signs on the right. The change from truncated experiencing to deeper, fuller experiencing is signified by the increase in size of the operating potentials on the right (OP 1-4) as compared with the operating potentials on the left.

Whatever the nature and content of the operating potential which reached peak experiencing in the session, the therapist allows it to transform into its good, integrative form and into a picture of deeper and fuller experiencing. In the session, the operating potential occurs as a bad-feelinged sense of chaos, directionlessness, structurelessness, lack of any fixed anchor or certainty. By letting herself be filled with this experiencing, and by allowing a transformation into its good, integrative form, the therapist sees what this experiencing may become — for example, a new sense of impulsiveness, openness, freedom, spontaneity. In the session, peak experiencing discloses a frightening homosexual overture, taut and anxiety-ridden. What can this become in its good, integrated form? With one patient it transmutes into delightfully erotic sexuality with delicious lovers of one's own sex. With another patient it blossoms into an excitingly new closeness and intimacy with family, friends, acquaintances. By being inside the experiencing, by being on wholesomely integrative terms with the operating experiencing, and by allowing it to change in the direction of its integrative good form and also in the direction of deeper and fuller experiencing, the therapist sees the direction of potential change for this particular patient.

Some operating potentials already are in a more or less integrated form, accompanied with feelings of solidness, intactness, peacefulness, and harmony. He experiences caring, loving, kindly consideration. What is the direction of potential change here? It consists of deeper and fuller experiencing, toward still more intense, more amplified, more saturated, deeper and fuller experiencing of caring, loving, kindly consideration.

Patients often move back and forth between two operating potentials that are disintegratively related to one another. Consider the woman who operates on the basis of the experiencing of defiance and rebellion (OP1, Figure 6) and also the operating experiencing of sweetness and gentleness (OP2, Figure 6). These operating potentials are "yoked" together disintegratively so that the experiencing of one is (a) truncated and muted, and (b) made to feel painful, turmoiled, and hurtful by the other. That is, her life is trapped between these two operating potentials, experiencing each to a limited degree, and always in painful ways. On the basis of this first principle, what is the direction of potential change? As indicated on the right in Figure 6, it means the direction of change is toward the fuller, deeper experiencing of both potentials in their good, integrated form. She can become a person with a wonderfully good-feelinged, fuller and deeper experiencing of defiance, rebelliousness, a strong standing up for oneself and one's convictions, solid strength. In addition, she is able to enjoy fuller and deeper experiencing of genuinely good-feelinged sweetness, softness, and gentleness. Whether the referent is a single operating potential or a yoked set, the first principle yields a direction of change of deeper and fuller experiencing of the good, integrated form of the operating potentials.

2) There will be an increase in good-feelinged, bodily sensations of actualization. Whatever the nature of the operating potential, the direction of change is toward an increase in the good-feelinged, bodily sensations of aliveness, tingling, energy, excitement, lightness, buoyancy, vibrancy, vitality (Chang, 1959; Watts, 1961). The direction is toward a state of actualization, leaving behind a bodily state of being dead, frozen, numb, unfeelinged. Instead, the direction of change shows itself in at least four ways.

One is in terms of sheer intensity. There is a deepening and intensifying of bodily sensations of energy, excitement, aliveness. This increase is felt in the body. It is palpable and tangible. Second, these good-feelinged bodily sensations spread over more of the body. Instead of sensations of light tingling in the chest or the head, they occur over more or most of the body. For many patients, sensations of aliveness or vitality or other good sensations of actualization occur in some single favorite part of the body, such as the upper chest, face, head or genitals. The direction is toward these good bodily sensations occurring over the entire body, inside and out. Third, the sheer length of time stretches out. Most patients may have good-feelinged bodily sensations for perhaps a minute or so every day or two. The direction of change is toward a state in which good-feelinged bodily sensations are present nearly all the time. Finally, the good bodily sensations occur in relation to more and more operating potentials. Whereas some patients may have good-feelinged bodily sensations when they are undergoing one or two operating potentials, the direction of change is toward having these good bodily sensations in conjunction with all the operating potentials.

3) There will occur new behaviors for the experiencing of the good form of the operating potentials. Given the good form of the operating potentials, the direction of change is toward new behaviors which actualize this good form in two ways. One is to act upon the external world so as to build situational contexts well-suited for the good form of the operating potentials. The other is to be the direct avenue for experiencing the operating potentials. In Figure 6, the old behavior and situational context for OP4 are indicated as B4 and Situational Context 4, and the new ones as B11 and Situational Context 11, on the right.

Consider the woman whose disintegrative, bad form of the operating potential consisted of the experiencing of jagged aggressiveness, pushiness, icy superiority, and hurtful domination. While undergoing such experiencing, the feelings are turmoiled, tight, and the state is one of being torn apart in pieces. By applying the first two principles, the therapist knows that this selfsame experiencing has an integrative good form. It is the same experiencing, but it can occur in a form which is accompanied with integrated feelings. Now the therapist sees a picture of aggressive forthrightness, a tough firmness, a sense of strength, of leadership. But the third principle goes much further. It invites this good, integrated form of the operating potential to undertake new ways of being and behaving. The directions of change include an image of this person behaving in ways which construct marvelously appropriate situations for this good experiencing and directly enable the experiencing of aggressive forthrightness, tough firmness, strength, and leadership. The third principle dares to outfit the good form of the experiencing with actual behaviors. The picture is now more concrete, more vividly real, more behavioral.

The therapist allows herself to be filled with the jagged aggressiveness, the icy superiority, and the hurtful domination. Instead of being absorbed by feelings of disintegration, the therapist allows this experiencing to occur with the good feelings of integration. The experiencing feels whole, peaceful, organized, harmonious. There is a picture of actual new ways of being and behaving to provide for the experiencing of this potential in its good, integrative form. What does the therapist see? As the good, integrative form of the experiencing, the therapist sees a picture of the new person exchanging her current job for that of a departmental chair at another university. There it is! But there are further images. Here is one of the new person delegating authority to the right faculty members, and the experiential sense is that of good-feelinged toughness and leadership.

Once the behavioral pictures are opened up, new ones occur easily. Here is the person standing up to her full height, saying no in ways which feel wonderful. She calls up her gruff father and initiates a visit to him. This is new. There is a picture of her being with her father and being firm and tough in settling the family matter of his living with the patient's younger sister, now that mother has died. She raises her voice, overcomes his objections, and capably orders him to do what she says. Now there is a picture of her refusing to pay the bill for the shoddy paint job on her car, looking straight into the eyes of the fellow who worked on her car, grinning at him, swearing a little, and taking him out for a beer as they thrash through the matter.

Some of these new behaviors build the appropriate situations in her world, and other new behaviors directly open the way for the new-found experiencing in its good form. In a way, it is still the old jagged aggressiveness, icy superiority, and hurtful domination. But in another way it is a new, good form of it. Yet the added element is a whole series of actual new behaviors which provide for the new, good, integrative form of the operating potential.

Principles 1–3 involved directions of change coming from actualization of the good form of the operating domain. We now turn to the directions of change coming from integrative relationships with the deeper potentials.

Integrative Relationships
with Deeper Potentials

Relationships between the patient and deeper potentials are typically disintegrative, characterized by distance, separation, avoidance, opposition, resistance, pulling back from, denial, pushing away. Feelings are those of distrust, hatred, tension, anxiety, turmoil, disjunctiveness, disharmony, fragmentation, being in pieces. In Figure 6, these disintegrative relationships are indicated by the two negative signs in the channels of relationship between operating potentials 1–4 and deeper potentials 5–7, on the left.

The direction of change is toward integrative relationships between the patient and these deeper potentials, relationships indicated by the positive signs between the potentials (on the right, in Figure 6). There are five principles which specify the directions of change with regard to the increasingly integrative relationships between the patient and the deeper potentials for experiencing.

4) Disintegrative feelings will be replaced with integrative feelings. As integration occurs between the patient and the deeper potential, the direction of change is toward the washing away of disintegrative feelings and the new presence of integrative feelings. It does not matter what the nature is of the operating and deeper potentials. Regardless of their nature, the direction of potential change is toward a state of internal integration. Suppose that the operating potential is the experiencing of being unwanted, of intruding, being alien. And suppose the disintegratively related deeper potential is the experiencing of violent revenge, aggressive vindication. In the session, there is not only a sense of being unwanted but also a package of disintegrative feelings.

These disintegrative feelings are referred to by words such as being in pieces, being torn apart, a state of disjunctiveness, of disharmony, an inner jagged sense. These feelings are painful, hurtful. There is another way of describing these disintegrative feelings. It is as if there are painful and hurtful bodily sensations, signaling and expressing the disintegrative relationships between the operating and deeper potentials. There are headaches, low back pains, aches in the joints, butterflies in the stomach, a hot ball in the chest, searing pains in the neck, muscular crampings, shakings and tremblings in the arms and hands, weakness, hot or cold flashes.

As relationships with the deeper potentials become integrative, these painful feelings and bodily sensations go away. What is perhaps most dramatic is the newfound state of integrative bodily feelings and sensations. Not only is the person free of the painful feelings and bodily sensations, but there are now bodily feelings of oneness, inner harmony, wholeness, intactness, togetherness, peacefulness and tranquility. Not only is the body free of the pains and aches and hurts, but there is a newfound bodily clearness in the head, fluidity and grace, a being-one-with-the-body, a working-together, a firmness. There are bodily sensations of inner harmony and peacefulness, tranquility and oneness. These new bodily sensations and feelings are like a gift, a qualitatively new state of bodily integration.

The principle tells us that disintegrative feelings will be replaced with integrative feelings. The patient who spends her days in a state of bodily felt tightness, tension, and aches in the neck can become a person who is free of these and who enjoys the good, integrative, bodily felt sensations of inner wholeness, harmony, and peacefulness. While this direction of change is available for every patient whose operating and deeper potentials are related disintegratively, there is a special additional case.

There is a special circumstance where the disintegrative relationships occur between two "yoked" operating potentials (OP1 and OP2, Figure 6) and the patient is caught in the middle ground between the two.

Instead of experiencing either potential in any measure, the patient has the disintegrative feelings of being caught, stuck, trapped, bound, unable to move, hemmed in. If one potential is the experiencing of overwhelming sexuality and the other is the experiencing of icy superiority, the patient seldom gets off the disintegrative middle ground and into either of these operating potentials. Yet the direction of change continues to include a picture of a person free of these disintegrative feelings. With integration comes the possibility of newfound bodily feelings and sensations of oneness, inner wholeness and peacefulness, inner harmony, freedom of movement.

5) *Externalized and internalized forms of the deeper potential will extinguish.* According to existential-humanistic theory, if relationships between the patient and deeper potentials are sufficiently disintegrative, then it is likely that the deeper potential may occur in an externalized form in the external world or in an internalized form in the patient's body. Suppose that the deeper potential consists of the experiencing of nasty anger, aggressive jabbing and poking, always getting in the way and making trouble, incessantly striking out in anger (DP5, Figure 6). With sufficiently disintegrative relationships, his external world may include persons who exude nasty anger, who are aggressively cutting at the patient, who interfere with and make trouble for the patient, and who incessantly strike at the patient in anger. There is a wife or brother-in-law or older sister who serves the role of the externalized deeper potential (Externalized DP5, Figure 6). On the other hand, the deeper potential may take the form of some bodily phenomenon, a physical part of the body which shoots at him, jabs at him, strikes at him, always gets in his way and makes trouble for him, incessantly cuts at him. The patient may have what is termed an "ulcer." It is present and exceedingly tangible, just as the wife or brother-in-law or older sister are present and exceedingly tangible. What can this person become? As relationships with the deeper potentials move from disintegrative to integrative, these internalized bodily forms of the deeper potential will extinguish. There will be no ulcer. No longer will the body house internalized forms of the disintegrative deeper potential. Actual, tangible, real bodily phenomena will no longer occur. These internalized forms may include what is termed cancer, "lazy" eye muscles, warts, sloshy heart valves, fluid in the lungs, infections in the kidneys, crimpings in the colon, growths in the chest wall, glandular tumors, splotches on the skin, and dozens of other bodily phenomena

whose description and labeling have traditionally lent themselves to a medical vocabulary. When these are internalized forms of the disintegrative deeper potential, the direction of change is toward their evaporation.

With regard to externalized forms of the disintegrative deeper potential, the directions of change are a little more complicated, mainly because the external figure is likewise a person who builds and constructs external worlds. In general, the patient will move in the direction of no longer externalizing the deeper potential onto and into the external world (Perls, 1969a; Rose, 1976). The patient will no longer construct, select out, build, mould, fashion his older sister into someone who jabs at him, strikes at him, takes angry shots at him, always gets in the way and makes trouble for him, incessantly cuts at him. In effect, the direction of change is toward being a person who no longer externalizes the disintegrative deeper potential onto the external world. The older sister is no longer constrained (forced, constructed, architected) into being that way.

This means that the older sister is free to shine forth with new and different qualities. The patient and older sister are free to construct a new and different relationship. She may be disclosed as protective and loving, or petty and competitive, or whatever the older sister and patient now work out with one another. It may be better or it may be worse. They continue relating with one another, only now it is along different lines, for she no longer is forced into being the externalization of the disintegrative deeper potential.

Another possible consequence is that there are no further relationships with her. It may be that she had died 12 years ago and he maintained her in his world where no one else could see her. His wife and friends considered him crazy because he talked to his older sister and saw her on the streets where no one else could see her. Or it may be that, having withdrawn his own externalization, it turns out that she has her own basis for jabbing at people, striking out, taking aggressive shots. The difference is that it now comes from her own nature rather than from his own externalization of that role upon her. Accordingly, he may well have few if any further relationships with his older sister.

All in all, the direction of change is one in which the internalized and externalized forms of the deeper potentials are no longer present. They extinguish. The body itself is now free of internalized bodily forms of the disintegrative deeper potential, and the world in which he exists no longer includes externalized agencies of the disintegrative deeper potential. This fifth principle promises massive internal and external changes.

6) Disintegrative relationships with the external world will extinguish, and integrative relationships will occur. As relationships between the patient and the deeper potential move from disintegrative toward integrative, the direction of change is toward the washing away of disintegrative relationships between the patient and the external world, and their replacement with integrative relationships. Given the disintegrative relationships with the deeper potential, these relationships are constructed with the externalized deeper potential. These are indicated by the two negative signs in the channel of relationships between OP3 and externalized DP5, on the left in Figure 6. Between the patient and the externalized deeper potential are disintegrative feelings of tension, misunderstanding, disharmony, distrust, hatefulness.

Consider the woman whose operating potential is the experiencing of friendliness and concern, and whose deeper potential is the experiencing of closed-in withdrawal. One way in which disintegrative relationships occur is when she constructs figures as externalizations of the deeper potential and then suffers from disintegrative relationships with those externalized figures. The brother-in-law sees through her veneer of friendliness. It is cheap and shallow. He hates her as a phony who does not really care for others. He scorns her overtures of concern as manipulative and untrue. She is tight and constrained with him, and relationships are disintegrative. Another way in which disintegrative relationships occur is when she externalizes the deeper potential upon others and bears disintegrative relationships toward them for being closed-in and withdrawn. She hates her daughter for being so cold, for having private thoughts, for being not part of the family, for never sharing what she is thinking. Something must be wrong with the daughter. Relationships with daughter and with the brother-in-law are characterized by separation, distance, charged dislike, hatred, disharmony, conflicts, problems. Once disintegrative relationships are present with the deeper potential, there is generally an externalized figure or figures toward whom the patient bears the same disintegrative relationships, and who bear the same disintegrative relationships toward the patient.

Occasionally these disintegrative relationships spread out to include the whole external world. The deeper potentials are externalized onto the entire external world, and it is the whole external world which bears disintegrative relationships toward the patient or with which the patient bears disintegrative relationships.

In any case, the change toward integrative relationships means that the direction of change can include the wholesale washing away of the disintegrative relationships and their replacement with integrative ones. Whether relationships are with the brother-in-law, the daughter, or the whole external world, they are no longer charged, hostile, menacing, pushing away, distancing, avoidant, hateful. Instead, they inevitably move in the direction of closeness, warmth, cordiality, playfulness, intimacy, ease, grace, harmony, togetherness, oneness, mutual letting-be, welcoming, acceptance, trust, unity and fusion (Binswanger, 1958c; Fromm, 1956; Jourard, 1971b; Maslow, 1970; May, 1953; Seguin, 1965). These changes are indicated by the two positive signs in the channel of relationships between operating potential 3 and the external world on the right in Figure 6.

The therapist can envision what this person can become by using this principle to see the direction of potential change in the patient whose disintegrative relationships with deeper potentials mean that disintegrative relationships also occur with the external world.

7) Disintegrative ways of being and behaving will extinguish. As integrative relationships occur between the patient and the deeper potential, there are changes in the patient's feelings (principle 4), in the patient's body (principle 5), in the patient's external world (principle 5), and in the relationship with the external world (principle 6). There will also be changes in the patient's behavior.

The logic is that as relations between the patient and the deeper potential move from disintegrative to integrative, then the patient no longer needs to use (disintegrative, painful) behaviors which (a) construct and maintain externalized forms of the deeper potential, and (b) construct and maintain disintegrative relations between the patient and those parts of the external world. Accordingly, these disintegrative behaviors decrease, they wash away. In Figure 6, disintegrative behaviors are indicated as behaviors 2 and 3. As integrative relationships occur between operating and deeper potentials, these disintegrative behaviors extinguish and so they are omitted from the right in Figure 6.

Sam is the owner of a small neighborhood restaurant. He is in his early fifties, staid, conservative, hardworking, and with seriously disintegrative relationships with a deeper potential whose bad form consists of the experiencing of sexual wantonness, wildness, and lasciviousness. What disintegrative behaviors does he use to construct and maintain an externalized form of this deeper potential? He may select such a person ready-made by, for example, picking just the right kind of waitress. Screening a number of applicants, Sam always ends up with a waitress who is exceedingly seductive, exudes sexual attractiveness, gets the men all worked up. Or Sam fashions and moulds some figure into being that kind of person. For years he architected and shaped his daughter into being a shapely, suggestive, seductive, wanton young woman. He commented on her body, always accused her of being oversexed, kept her away from boys because "you never know what can happen," carefully avoided touching her in sexual body parts, even when she was a young child, patrolled her room for pornographic material, stayed up at night to make sure that he could interrogate her about what she was really doing with boys, feasted his eyes on her developing breasts and legs, and generally shaped her into being the lascivious person she became. Another behavioral means consisted of mutual cooperation between the patient and another person whereby the two work together conjointly. Sam always seemed to cultivate a customer into the kind of relationship in which she was attracted to this older, hardworking man. He would be interested in her troubles, comment on the fine person she was, give her special treats in her meals. If she responded, he always seemed to be over at her apartment, fixing the plumbing or putting in the air conditioner or caulking a window. With the right companion, he engaged in a back-and-forth sexual dance which always seemed to culminate in her allowing and inviting him to be sexually intimate with her.

By means of effective little behaviors, Sam managed to construct and maintain particular women in his world, externalizations of his own deeper potential for sexual wantonness, lasciviousness, and wildness. Yet relationships were always uniformly disintegrative, filled with distance and separation, hurt and pain, tension and anxiety, rage and hatred. Disintegrative behaviors not only constructed and maintained the externalized form of the deeper potential, but also constructed and maintained disintegrative relationships between the patient and the other figures.

Whenever his sexy waitress was a few minutes late in the morning, Sam angrily alluded to her sleeping with some guy. He frequently touched her on the shoulder and back in sexually suggestive ways. In front of others, he stared at her body in ways which invited customers to share in aggressively denigrating snickers. When she was clearly bothered by his behaviors, he surrounded himself in an envelope of superior coldness, and hinted about firing her if she openly protested. He never looked her straight in the eyes. Most of his words were suggestive innuendoes. As she withdrew more and more from him, Sam became more openly tight, short-tempered, and critical, accusing her of stealing money, being lazy, being stupid. Sam behaved in ways which effectively constructed and maintained highly disintegrative relationships with the waitress, his daughter, and his "friend" so that they hated him, he hated them, they withdrew from him and he from them, they maintained charged distance from him and he from them. Relationships on both sides were hurtfully pained.

The direction of change is toward the washing away of all these behaviors. The whole slab of disintegrative behaviors merely extinguishes. Whether delicately subtle or gross, these disintegrative behaviors go away. The picture of what patients can become always includes the washing away of these disintegrative behaviors, and because these disintegrative behaviors typically constitute a large proportion of behaviors, the direction of change is generally dramatically different. The whole class of disintegrative behaviors is missing, gone. This is the picture generated by the seventh principle of the directions of potential change.

8) New integrative ways of being and behaving will occur. As relationships between the patient and deeper potentials become integrative, at least six classes of new integrative behaviors will occur.

• One class includes integrative behavioral skills of using bodily sensations to monitor behavior. As internal relationships become increasingly integrative, the patient comes into closer and closer touch with a whole spectrum of immediately ongoing bodily sensations (Gendlin, 1964; Lankton & Lankton, 1983). Some of these are pleasant; some are unpleasant. They are the bodily sensations that occur when what the patient is doing feels fitting, fulfilling, happy, pleasant, or dangerous, menacing, constricting, and unpleasant. The new integrative way of being and behaving consists of listening to these bodily signals and acting on the basis of them (Mailloux, 1953; Maslow, 1963).

The patient becomes able to recognize his own particular bodily sensations that signal that something is wrong and then to act effectively. How do you know when your body is signaling danger, threat, imminent menace? How do you know when bodily sensations signal that you are twisting yourself out of shape or that the situation is too much for you? Each patient must learn his own danger signals. They may consist of a drawing up of the muscles around the chest wall, or becoming warm all over, or a constricted throat, or a pressure ache at the back of the head, or butterflies in the stomach, or the skin gets prickly and itchy.

Once the bodily danger signs are noticed, the patient learns to act effectively on the basis of these signs. Instead of staying at the party, asking innocuous questions of the stranger, the patient is to stop what she is doing and withdraw from the situation. Having asked the silly conversational question, she feels the muscles drawing together across the chest wall. Closing her eyes for a few seconds, she attends to the bodily sensations, puts her hand on the stranger's shoulder, says, "I have to stop, sorry about the silly question," and exits from the situation.

You may be inviting someone to come over to your house, chatting with your mother on the phone, asking a friend to go shopping with you, defending yourself in the argument, walking alone in the street with your husband, sitting and reading a book, petting a cat, getting a second helping of roast beef. It does not matter if the situation is mundane or extraordinary, unimportant or important. It does not matter if you are aware of what is causing the trouble or even what the problem is. None of that matters. What does matter is that the patient is learning to be aware of her own particular bodily sensations which signal danger, that the patient stop what she is doing, and that the patient withdraw from the situation. Here is one skill in using bodily sensations to monitor behavior.

A second skill is to use bodily sensations to assist in making a decision or choice, to consider doing this or that. Should I return to the party or go home? Should I go to elementary school and talk to my son's teacher or not? Should I buy this sweater or not? Should I order a steak or a small salad? Should I start divorce proceedings or not? Whether the choices and decisions are momentous or innocuous, the patient learns how to use bodily sensations to monitor the choice. She envisions the possibility, listens to the bodily sensations, and decides accordingly. She envisions sitting in the classroom, talking with her son's elementary school teacher. As this scene becomes clear, she is aware of the clutching up in her stomach, a hurtful clenching. Something is wrong; she will not do this. Or her body issues sensations of a light, buoyant tingling in the chest. It feels great; she will talk to the teacher. Each patient has a distinctive set of bodily sensations which either feel good or bad, pleasant or unpleasant, and these are used to monitor behavioral choices and decisions.

The therapist envisions what this patient can become, the directions of potential change, by framing a picture around this new class of integrative behaviors. The therapist sees a picture which includes being aware of the patient's own particular set of pleasant and unpleasant bodily sensations as monitoring signals and using these signals to monitor behavior.

• A second class of new behaviors consists of having integrative reactions and responses to one's own immediate way of being and behaving (May, 1953). The patient is able to stand a little to the side, see how delightfully or disgustingly he is just being and behaving, and have integrative self-reactions. It requires that the patient be able to stand off and be aware of the way he is being right now.

While some patients are plagued with being too aware of how they are being, plagued with a split in which they are always standing off and having reactions, always observing and commenting on their behavior, most patients are pristinely unaware. They behave, know they are behaving, feel and sense what they are doing, but are unable to stand aside and have a different perspective on the way they are being right now. These are the patients who behave in hurtful, damaging, cutting, nasty, distancing, aggressive ways, but who sail through these behavings in frozen unawareness. There may be a brief sense of numbness or tightness, but nothing more. If their victims protest, the patients nevertheless protect themselves from seeing or knowing how they behaved.

The direction of change is toward being able to step aside and have a different perspective, and then to express that reaction integratively. It is as if the patient, being operating potential 3 and behaving on the basis of behavior 10 (on the right, Figure 6), is picking at his colleague, issuing little invitations to fight. Then the patient moves into operating potential 7, and the integrative behavior (B7, Figure 6) consists of saying, "What a tight little sonuvabitch I am! If I keep that up, I'll probly get a sock in the jaw!"

The integrative behavior may involve being pleased or displeased with the way one just was. Regardless, the self-reactive behavior is integrative in that it is welcoming, friendly, accepting, playful, cordial, harmonious. After singing a few bars, "That's a pretty good voice!" After saying something which got his friends into knee-slapping hilarious laughter, "I'm funny! I can crack people up!" After looking at oneself in the mirror, "Not bad for an old broad." After delivering a fine short speech at the committee meeting, "Well! That was short and to the point, pretty good!"

On the other hand, integrative relationships between potentials mean that the patient can criticize himself, apologize, see how silly he was, highlight the mistake, have reactions to his being a pompous tyrant. After using an impressive big word, "What a big word! That sure impresses people—if it's right:" After bawling out the secretary, "Jesus! What got me in such a bad temper today?" After being sickeningly sweet, "I hate acting so sickeningly sweet." After making a motion to the committee, one which was so poorly thought-out and worded that no one could follow it, "That's the dumbest motion I ever heard!" Quite often the patient is merely expressing what others are also thinking. The difference is that it can come from the patient, and the tone and sense of the expression are integrative.

• A third class of integrative ways of being and behaving is that of letting-be, giving other persons the gift of freedom and space to be however they are (Laing, 1982; Overstreet, 1949; Prescott, 1957). No longer must the patient crowd the aunt into being coldly superior. Instead of forcing or expecting or perceiving or moulding the aunt into being that way, the patient gives her plenty of freedom and space to be however she is, even if this includes being coldly superior.

There are two faces to this class of integrative behaviors. One face is freedom from the patient's own forcings. In so many ways, the patient fashioned her aunt into being coldly superior. The patient's postures, glances, pauses, facial expressions were designed to mould the aunt into being the coldly superior one. What the patient said, how the patient responded, every verbal dance the patient carried out with the aunt was toward constructing and maintaining the aunt as the coldly superior one. No longer does any of this occur. The patient gives the aunt freedom and space to be however the aunt may be. It is a letting-be which is free of shaping the aunt into being that particular way.

The other face is a willingness to receive the aunt as being something other than the patient's cold superiority. The aunt is free to be nasty and petulant, or sexy or grasping or funny or however the aunt is, and the patient welcomes that. The patient provides the aunt with space to be however she is. It is as if the integrative space gives the aunt plenty of room to do and be whatever is here at the moment. It means the patient has the widest possible range of receiving what may come from the aunt. Nothing is out of bounds. It is as if the integrative letting-be were to express the following: "At this moment, whatever comes from you is your choice, your freedom." All of this is shown in the patient's looks, direct and indirect behaviors, body postures, tone of voice, presence.

• A fourth class of integrative behaviors expresses a readiness and willingness to be close and intimate. The patient is welcoming and receptive to whatever measure of closeness and intimacy is present, and welcoming and receptive to its ripening (Binswanger, 1958c; Lovlie, 1983; Rowen, 1983; Suzuki, 1949). There is no force or pressure of having to be close or intimate. Instead, the integrative behaviors are more gracefully receptive to the presence and growth of such a relationship.

The therapist pictures the patient being intimate and close and behaving in ways that are intimate and close. There is a moving closer, being more with, a being together with. The patient is friendly, welcoming, gracious and inviting a closeness and intimacy with the other one.

• A fifth class of integrative ways of being and behaving consists of sharing what is occurring in the other one. At the far reaches of empathy, and beyond, the patient senses or feels what the other one is sensing and feeling (Havens, 1973; Rogers, 1975). It is a matter of fusing or assimilating or aligning, a matter of resonating. When it is occurring in you, it is also occurring in me.

When my older brother is having a sense of loyalty and pride in the family, I likewise share in his sense of loyalty and pride. When the other one is being resistant and defiant, I share in that. I resonate to her sense of resistance and defiance. I share her awful experience of being brutally insulted, violated, and intruded upon by the adolescent kid who tried to rape her. I go beyond the usual meaning of empathy. I feel it. I have it. I let it occur in me. Being and behaving so that I share the ongoing experiencing in the other individual constitutes this fifth class of integrative ways of being and behaving.

• The final class of integrative ways of being and behaving consists of engaging in integrative encounters with others. It is a matter of allowing a playful, friendly staying at the place where the patient and the other meet, and going just a bit beyond (Schutz, 1973; Searles, 1963). Instead of preserving a safe distance, that ordinary moat of separation from others, the patient is willing to risk going an integrative step further. By means of an encountering next step, an interactive offering, the patient goes just a bit into the periphery of the other, a brief incursion into the private zone. The patient risks the encounter. Yet it is an integrative encounter, meaning that it is friendly, respectful, gracious, cordial. It is not an aggressive confrontation or an intrusive forcing of oneself, not a tense having-it-out-with or a forceful challenge.

It stops when the other one declines. It stops the instant it loses its friendly, playful, welcoming tone.

Actualization of the Good Form of the Deeper Domain

The direction of change starts with deeper potentials. Whatever their nature, they can transform into their integrative good form and become a part of the operating domain. Actualization is the shift from deeper to operating potential. In Figure 6, deeper potentials 5–7 on the left become operating potentials 5–7 on the right.

9) There will be new potentials for experiencing in the operating domain. The direction of change is toward becoming a new person with new potentials for experiencing. The therapist starts with what the deeper potential is like, its nature and content. Almost always this is in its disintegrative form. Then the therapist envisages what this person can become if (a) this disintegrative deeper potential were to convert into its good, integrative form, and (b) the good form were to rise into the operating domain and be a part of the way the person actually experiences.

There are at least three ways for the therapist to get a picture of the actualized good form of this deeper potential. One is to merely note what has occurred in the session, in either the internal encounter or the fourth step of being the deeper potential. When patient and therapist go beyond a peak clashing encounter, a plateau is reached where patient and therapist stand on top of the (deeper) potential and experience what it is like to be the good form of this potential. Also, when the patient disengages from the operating domain, enters into being the deeper potential, and carries forward the experiencing, there typically is a moment when the patient is now being the good form of this deeper potential. So the therapeutic work of the session will present the live appearance of the good integrative form of the deeper potential.

A second method is for the therapist-as-deeper-potential to do the work of seeing what the deeper potential can be in its good, integrative form. This is one of the advantages of the therapist over the patient. While the patient recoils from the monstrous disintegrative form of the deeper potential, the therapist can enter into it, wallow in it, allow it to take its good, integrative form, and frame a picture of the new person as this new potential.

A third method is somewhat less trustworthy, for it relies to some degree on the therapist's thinking. When the therapist has accumulated decades of therapeutic work, there are commonalities built up as similar deeper potentials transform into their good forms. On this basis, the therapist may come to expect that a particular deeper potential will likely move from this disintegrative form to that likely integrative form. In effect, the therapist gradually accumulates a wealth of expectations about likely conversions from bad form to good form.

By means of these methods, the therapist sees a picture of what this patient can become as a deeper potential converts into its good, integrative form, and as it moves (actualizes) into being a part of the operating domain. The deeper experiencing of being hurt, made to feel bad, sensitive to the slights of others, may lead to the picture of a new patient who can experience genuine closeness and intimacy with others. The disintegrative deeper potential for control, manipulation, icy superiority, may translate into a new person who experiences leadership, genuine responsibility, strength of purpose. What has existed as a deeper potential for experiencing impotence, fecklessness, wimpishness, may develop into a new person who experiences passivity, trust, secure dependency. A deeper potential for experiencing depression and heaviness generates a picture of a person with the new experiencing of making life changes, getting away from entrapping situations, having the capacity for withdrawing and letting go. The disintegrative deeper experiencing of being a hated troublemaker, being bad and causing problems, may transform into an image of a new person who experiences a pleasant wickedness, devilishness, mischieviousness, spontaneous spunkiness.

What had occurred as a deeper fear-laden homosexuality generates a picture of the experiencing of closeness and genuine intimacy with one's own sex. The deeper experiencing of being abandoned and rejected becomes a new experiencing of letting the other go, allowing space and freedom. The deeper terror of death, dying, ending, may convert into an experiencing of peacefulness, all-over harmony, calmness. The awful deeper sense of being a pawn, owned and defined by others, plastic to their wishes, may yield a new experiencing of secure trust, fitting into, the strength of ego-lessness.

All in all, the therapist envisages a new person whose operating potentials include the good, integrative form of the deeper potentials. It is a seeing of what this person can become — in terms of new potentials for experiencing as the deeper disintegrative potentials give rise to integrative operating potentials.

10) There will be new ways of being and behaving for the experiencing of the new operating potentials. When deeper potentials become a part of the operating domain, there are incredible opportunities for new ways of being and behaving which build new situations and provide for the new experiencing. Some of these new ways of being and behaving build new situations which provide a context for the new experiencing. Others provide for the actual experiencing of these new potentials. In Figure 6, deeper potentials 5–7 on the left become operating potentials 5–7 on the right and are linked with new behaviors and new situational contexts.

Consider the woman who now has the new operating potential for experiencing freedom and spontaneity, open expressiveness and space. Given this new potential for experiencing, what new ways of being and behaving could provide for new situational contexts and for new ways of direct experiencing? The possibilities are enormous, and stretch all the way from slight refinements in her current life situations and behaviors to magnificently new ones. She may walk to work instead of driving, and her walking stance is free and open, receptive to sights and smells, sounds and movements. Instead of always having things to be done with her four-year-old daughter, she now allows her daughter time and space to lead, to explore, to play, to carry out all sorts of new behaviors. The woman may take up the cello, watch the clouds move, write poetry, take time to be aware of herself. Her life unlocks its constrictions and becomes less demanding, more enabling of freedom and space. She has unfilled time, moments for drifting. She laughs and cries more easily and spontaneously. She can seek out new persons with whom there is greater freedom and space. She is more attuned to the panoply of her own bodily sensations and reactions. She follows the flow of bodily sensations, and behaves effortlessly and spontaneously on their invitations. She sleeps when she is tired, and makes love when she is aroused. She allows her feelings and emotions to be present and to have easy and graceful expression. In a thousand new ways she can be and behave so as to open new situational vistas and open up direct experiencing of freedom and spontaneity, open expression and space.

There is a wonderful new experiencing of childlike wonder and bewilderment, curiosity and open-eyed involvement. This fellow had been branded as "obsessive-compulsive" by a psychiatrist and a psychologist he had seen previously, and he was moved out of his job as a personnel officer because he would get bogged down in the details of the procedures. In its disintegrative form, the deeper potential consisted of being caught by the forces, swept in, losing his integrity, having his very identity sucked away. What would be the new ways of being and behaving to accommodate the newfound childlike wonder and bewilderment if it were to become part of the operating domain? When a person in the apartment house said something he really did not quite understand ("I live in 1204, on the other wing"), he becomes a person who asks ("There are other wings? I didn't know that"), and he is really interested in what people say, entranced in the stories people tell, truly interested in the content of what others tell him. People will start kidding him, "Watch out for Marvin; he listens to what you say!" He gets down on his stomach and looks intently into the eyes of the old brown dog, lying there grinning at him. He stares at the moving clouds, watching their evolving new formations. He becomes a photographer of inner-city scenes, and his photographs are on display in galleries. He loves talking with people who have interests, and he often spends a few hours intently talking, and mostly listening, to the fellow who repairs watches, the bricklayer, the woman who owns the small restaurant, as each of them describes more and more of what they are fascinated with in the watch repairing, the bricklaying, and the small restaurant business. He behaves in quite specific ways which construct situations and make for delightful, wholesome experiencing of the newfound childlike wonder, candid bewilderment, curiosity, and open-eyed involvement.

Actualization of the deeper potential into the operating domain means that the patient now has freer and wider choice. Instead of reacting to inner and outer pushes and pulls, he has a dilated sense of choice. This new way of behaving is extolled in existential thought, a main feature of the ways persons can become. It is likewise valued in the derivative psychotherapies:

> Wellness is perceived as fundamentally the increasing capacity to choose. Shorn of all its frills, sickness is perceived as any hindrance to free choice. Choice is seen as more than a conscious intellectual exercize. The well person chooses correctly without thinking. This is the essence of what the Buddhist refers to as the hallmark of the mature person in their Mushin (without thought) . . . (Whitaker & Malone, 1953, p. 417).

Principles 9 and 10 apply to the directions of potential change as the deeper disintegrative potentials become integrative parts of the operating domain. Just knowing the nature and content of the deeper potentials allows the therapist to see a picture of what this person can become. The final two principles have to do with the risked fate of the former operating potentials.

Extinguishing of the Old Operating Domain

The picture of what the patient can become includes the risk of extinguishing the old operating domain. This means that the patient may become a person who no longer experiences what she had experienced, no longer behaves in the ways she had, and no longer builds and exists in the same external world. In effect, the old operating domain extinguishes, together with its ways of being and behaving and its own external world. As indicated in Figure 6, operating potentials 1–4 are now signified with dotted lines to indicate that these former operating potentials either transform radically or they extinguish altogether. Behaviors 1–4, on the left, are omitted from the right. Situational contexts 1 and 4 are missing on the right, and so too are externalized deeper potentials 5 and 6.

The basis for this radical extinguishing are contained in the previous ten principles. The first three principles flow out of the idea that the former operating potentials actualize into their good (integrative) form. These are substantive changes which risk the wholesale extinguishing of the former experiencings, the former ways of being and behaving, and the former external world.

Principles 4–8 involve therapeutic changes toward integrative relationships between the operating and deeper domains. As these relationships become integrative, operating potentials lose their reason for existing. No longer having to block and avoid what is deeper, no longer having to deny and mask the deeper potentials, no longer having to establish disintegrative relationships, the operating potentials tend to fade away.

Principles 9 and 10 express the movement of the deeper potentials into the operating domain, the actualizing of the deeper potentials. For many operating potentials, this signals the end of their function, for they existed to serve the deeper potentials, to be their instrumental means for providing a whiff of experiential air.

All in all, these changes converge on the extinguishing of the operating domain. The nature and content of the experiencing change dramatically or wash away, old behaviors are gone, and the constructed external worlds are no more. The final two principles concretize the directions of change ensuing from the extinguishing of the old operating domain.

11) The operating domain's external world will extinguish. The patient exists in an external world constructed by and fitted to the operating domain. She has a job, a lover, several friends who admire her a great deal. Her brothers clutch at her and give her a feeling of being suffocated. One of her supervisors is quite rigidly authoritative. She has a six-year-old child from a former marriage. The ex-husband visits the daughter, and there are monthly flare-ups, jaggingly aggressive. If we keep our eye on her operating potential for experiencing being a victim, being assaulted, intruded into, then the risk is that those parts of the external world linked to this experiencing will extinguish. What will that mean?

If the job feeds the experiencing of being a victim, if that is the predominant function it serves, then the likelihood is that she may leave the job. The same holds true for her lover, ex-husband, brothers and daughter. If the main function they all serve is to enable the experiencing of being a victim, being assaulted and intruded into, then the very real likelihood is that she may simply leave them go, walk away, and they will extinguish as component parts of her external world.

Similarly with specific situations: Her world may be filled with very real situations in which she is beaten up by her lover, in which her brothers refuse to pay back the money they borrowed, in which her daughter never gives her a moment's respite, in which her ex-husband takes her to court to sue for custody. The direction of change is toward the extinction of these situations. They no longer occur in her life.

It may also mean that some or all of these parts of her external world in one sense remain, yet in another sense lose their experiential meaning and fade out of her life. She may remain with her daughter, but now everything around the daughter is different. Her brothers may continue to borrow money from her, but the whole enterprise no longer leaves her experiencing the sense of being intruded into and assaulted. She stays at the job, but the whole meaning of the job shifts.

These changes in the external world appear justifiable when the operating domain is twisted and painful. But the external world is slated for extinction even for operating potentials which feel good. He may derive a wonderful sense of power and strength within an external world consisting of large bank accounts, being a major executive of the newspaper, being chairman of a community board, being catered to and respected by gardeners, tailors, mechanics, people who work at the newspaper, from the large house and the prestigious neighborhood, from the translations of his wishes into program changes, personnel changes, policy changes at the newspaper.

Alas, the processes of therapeutic change signal the end of this world too. Carrying forward of this operating potential for power and stength, its shift into the good, integrative form, change from disintegrative to integrative relationships between this operating potential and deeper potentials, and actualization of the good form of deeper potentials — all of these changes mean risked extinguishing of the operating experiencing of power and strength. This fellow's external world risks the distinct possibility of no longer having large bank accounts, being the major executive of the firm, the large house. Situations which service the sense of power and strength may extinguish so that, for example, people who work at the newspaper no longer cater to him in ways which instill the sense of power and strength. It may also mean that parts of his external world remain but their whole former meaning extinguishes. He may still have gardeners and cars and a job at the newspaper, but the whole meaning changes so that they no longer feed a sense of power and strength. What can be safely predicted is that those parts of the external world that support the operating potentials will indeed extinguish in one or more of these ways.

As a special case, externalized forms of the deeper potential will extinguish. I am referring to those persons whose operating domain swings around some centrally compelling external agency, some external figure or force that is the axis around which the patient's life revolves. This external agency is powerful, and the operating domain builds it, sustains it, lives and exists in relationship to it. Here is the patient whose whole world revolves around some extra-powerful agency such as a parent, evil people out there, key figures who plot against and torment the patient, the all-powerful "other." The patient spends his life trying to overcome father, protecting himself against father, struggling against him, trying to win him over, trying to please him. The patient twists and turns to free himself of father, resists against and defies him, tries to be a human being in spite of him, tries to get out of being defined and ruled by him. This is the organized external world in which such persons exist.

Here is a woman whose life revolves around the feared and hated, all-powerful "man." She struggles to be dutiful to him, please him, defer to his wishes. She must be equal to him, on a par with him, be acknowledged by him. She hates her father, her grandfather, the male boss, bad men out there, men in positions of authority, male friends, lovers, husbands, male enemies, men in general, evil and menacing men who are the central axis of her world. She must destroy him, yet he always reappears. She rails against his superior demands, his control and domination. She struggles to be free of the man, to be a person on her own right. The "man" is the linchpin for her whole world.

The direction of change is likewise toward the receding away of the centrally compelling external agency around which the person's world revolves, the extinguishing of the "primal participation mystique" (Jung, 1962). This key component of the external world extinguishes. There are no further evil figures who plot against him. The agency that terrorized the patient washes away. There are no further relationships with the all-powerful parent or spouse or enemy whose powerfulness likewise extinguishes. The whole centrality of these figures and agencies extinguishes.

On the right in Figure 6, there are no externalized deeper potentials. Nor are there the situational contexts which had been there on the left. Principle 11 forecasts the extinguishing of the external worlds of the former operating domain.

12) The operating domain's behaviors will extinguish. The behaviors which serve the operating domain will fade away as the steps of the therapeutic process do their work. Conversion of the operating potentials to their integrative good form signals the end of the old behaviors. Sheer carrying forward of both operating and deeper potentials means the former behaviors will wash away. The occurrence of integrative relationships with the deeper potentials removes the very basis for the old behaviors. As the good, integrative form of the deeper potential enters into and comprises the operating domain, there is less room for the old ways of being and behaving. All in all, the actual behaviors which helped to construct the external world extinguish, and so too do all the behaviors which provided for the experiencing of the former operating potentials. The overall direction calls for the extinguishing of these behaviors. In Figure 6, B1–B4 do not appear on the right.

This includes wicked and bad behaviors that get the patient in trouble and make him feel rotten, as well as behaviors that are pleasant and fun-loving, that make the patient feel good. They include those special behaviors which make the patient what he is, a distinctive individual, one of a kind. They include behaviors that psychologists like to use to spell out what is normal, adjusted, mature. Indeed, the terrible risk is that all of these behaviors will extinguish. All your bad behaviors, like picking your nose and stealing items from stores, loafing instead of working, and being drunk so much—all of these extinguish. All your good and charming behaviors, like smiling so sweetly and remembering birthdays and telling funny jokes at parties and being punctual — all of these extinguish. If everyone went through this process of change, psychologists would have to revise the list of behaviors they hold up as the standards of being normal and ordinary. As the operating potentials sink into the sunrise, so too do their behaviors.

What behaviors served to provide her with the experiencing of being a victim, being assaulted and intruded into? Knowing that she was to be at work at 9:00, she typically inched her way into the vicinity of her supervisor around 9:15. She would gaze directly at her supervisor with a look of terror, her body almost poised to flinch, as if her supervisor were raising her arm to strike her. Having worked to create the right situation, when her supervisor would tell her to make sure she was at work on time, the patient would rapidly tap her nails on the desk, half turn to the side with eyes vacantly staring away from the supervisor. When the supervisor's voice would then have a tough edge to it, the patient would finally look straight at her and, lip trembling, accuse the supervisor of picking on her. The patient was a deftly skilled professional in behaving precisely to experience the sense of being a victim.

The physician gained a sense of assiduous dedication and devotion by being instantly available to his patients. Virtually every call was returned within an hour. He lived within walking distance of both his office and the hospital. He spent extra time with interns and residents. He read as much as he could in the field of his specialty. There were many patients whose illnesses were serious and, even after they were fine again, he would call to see how they were. He lived in the aura of an experiencing of dedication and devotion. He felt uplifted, and to many persons around he was a very special physician indeed. However, in the course of therapy the deeper potential for being the God-like special one, the one who was worshipped and sanctified by one and all, converted into its more integrative form and emerged as a new-found sense of understanding, a gentle kind of transcendence, a fuller humanness, a broad wisdom. No longer was there a basis for having to be and behave in ways which had provided for the former operating potential of dedication and devotion. No longer was this operating potential in place to serve the deeper experiencing of the God-like special one. As a consequence, the old operating behaviors faded away.

There is one special class of behaviors which deserves mentioning. Many bodily states, conditions, and phenomena serve the operating domain faithfully. They work right alongside the usual meaning of behaviors to build appropriate situations and to provide directly for the experiencing of operating potentials. What happens to these bodily behaviors, these bodily states, conditions, and phenomena? They fade away.

What bodily behaviors can contribute to the experiencing of being engulfed, taken over, invaded, deprived of mandate and intactness? The body offered its contribution by means of dizziness and passing out, complete with physical bodily phenomena which go with dizziness and passing out. As the old operating domain extinguished, so too did the occasional bouts of dizziness and passing out, together with the accompanying bodily phenomena.

Aggressively tinged avoidance of sexual intercourse may be experienced in several ways which call upon bodily states, conditions, and phenomena—sudden headaches, shooting low back pains, overwhelming fatigue, together with bodily conditions and phenomena which go with and explain the headaches, low back pains, and fatigue. As the operating potential extinguishes, as the basis for the experiencing is no longer, the headaches go away, the low back pains extinguish, and the fatigue washes away.

The body is effective in contributing to the experiencing of avoiding punishment, of providing a sense of "It's not my fault . . . I'm not responsible for that." Promising candidates include, for example, so-called epileptoid fits and seizures, fugue states, and all manner of powerfully incapacitating "physical illnesses." When the operating potential extinguishes, so too will the bodily states, their bodily conditions, and the supporting cast of bodily phenomena.

Here are 12 principles for generating a picture of the directions of potential change. All the therapist starts with is the experiencing in the session. Then the appropriate principles take over and generate a picture of what this patient can become. What is essential is the automatic, ingrained use of the appropriate principles. Given the experiencing in the session, all the therapist does is allow space for the picture of the directions of potential change. These 12 principles then do their work, and a vivid picture is present. To accomplish this, the therapist must be trained, practiced, studied, and experienced so that the proper application of these 12 principles is an automatic, ingrained skill. Then, with a vivid picture of what this patient can be and become, the therapist can use methods to provide an experiential sample of what it can be like for the new and different person to be and behave in new and different ways. This is the subject of the next chapter.

CHAPTER 8

Being/Behavioral Change: Methods

THE PURPOSE OF THIS CHAPTER is to answer the following questions: What methods may the therapist use to enable the patient to experience being/behavioral change? Once the patient has gone through the preceding steps of the session, what methods may be used to enable the patient to sample new ways of being and behaving which facilitate heightened integration and actualization within the extratherapy world? The last part of this chapter deals with refining the patient's own sense of choice in carrying out or in declining to carry out the experienced new ways of being and behaving, as well as with the ending of the session and the consideration of the next session.

The essentials: Experiencings in the session and the picture of the directions of potential change. In order to use these methods, it is essential that peak experiencings occur in the session and that the therapist have a picture of the directions of potential change. The high point of experiencing may have occurred when the potentials were carrying forward, or when the patient was engaging in an integrative encounter with the deeper potential, or when the patient disengaged from the operating domain and entered into being the deeper potential.

When the patient shifts into being the deeper potential, something almost magical happens. The patient is experiencing as a new and different person, being and behaving in a whole new way, and existing in a qualitatively new and different world. Even if this occurs for a brief moment, it has occurred. This experiencing is priceless for being/behavioral change.

But that alone is not enough. The therapist must also have a picture of the kind of person this patient can become. Given the high experiencings in the session, the therapist uses the principles described in chapter 7 to generate a picture of the directions of potential change for this person with this strong experiencing. Given this experiencing, and given this generated picture of what the patient can become, the methods now make sense. They start with the strong experiencings, and they give the patient an experiential taste of what it is like to move in the direction of that picture.

Throughout each of the methods, the reader will see these two essentials. Every method requires both.

Remember that the therapist is already within the zone of the integrated and actualized deeper potential. That is, the therapist is exceedingly ready and willing and able to be and behave in ways which are quite in line with that picture. Whether the therapist talks to the patient who is being the deeper potential, like two peas in a pod, or whether the therapist talks to the patient who has had a taste of being the deeper potential, the therapist is drenched in the integrated and actualized deeper potential, and is quite inclined to be and behave in these new ways.

Determinants of which method(s) to use. There are at least three determinants. One is that the patient will already be selecting a method if he spontaneously turns to the external world. The patient who is being the deeper potential and then turns to the extratherapy world is thereby determining the use of particular methods. A second determinant is the nature and content of what the patient is doing when the experiencings reach a peak in the session. If, for example, the patient is laughing hard as he is thoroughly enjoying telling someone that he is an asshole, then the patient is inviting a particular method to be followed, namely the method of starting with that kind of behavioral achievement and seeing where it fits in the patient's extratherapy world. The third determinant is the skill and competence of the therapist in each of the methods. Some therapists are more effective with some methods than with others.

The criterion of effectiveness: Experiential effect. There are two ways of describing the effective use of these methods. One is that the patient would seem to have actually gone through the actual carrying out of the behavior in a defined scene. It is as if the patient did it, actually tasted and sampled the behavior in the scene. The effect is experiencing the carrying out of this new way of being/behaving within the context of the extratherapy world—and all of this occurs in the session. The question may be put in these words: In the session, did the patient experience the new way of being and behaving within the context of the possible extratherapy world? If the answer is yes, then we have achieved the experiential effect.

Another way to describe the experiential effect is in terms of special kinds of bodily sensations. New ways of being and behaving are accompanied with bodily sensations, some corresponding to actualization and others to integration. Bodily sensations of actualization include: energy, excitement, tingling, headiness, a surge of aliveness, vitality, an increase in pressure, a sense of risk, a lightness and buoyancy. There are also sensations of integration: a bodily centeredness, intactness, "rightness," internal harmony, sense of oneness, togetherness. These occur as palpable, tangible bodily sensations that also constitute the experiential effect. When the right behavior is here, the body has appropriate sensations.

These bodily sensations are the effects of experiencing, and it is reasonable that they should occur. If the patient is coming closer to what she can become, she is truly entering the state of new experiencing. In other words, the patient is undergoing new experiencing, new integration, and new actualization. It is understandable that the new state of integrated and actualized experiencing will be accompanied with bodily sensations. Accordingly, the net result is a palpable experiential effect, the criterion that the method is successful.

THE WORKING METHODS

My purpose here is to describe and illustrate seven working methods for experiencing new ways of being and behaving in the external world.

1) Invite the New Potential to Be and Behave in Its Own Way and in Its Own World

For a few seconds or minutes or so, the patient was a new and different person. It may have occurred after experiencing carried forward just enough to let the operating or the deeper potential experience more or after the internal encounter brought that new state of integration. It typically occurs when the patient disengages from his ordinary operating domain, enters into the deeper potential, and experiences as this deeper potential. For our purposes, the patient is, even momentarily, a new and different potential, a little more integrated and actualized.

For example, the patient was experiencing the wonderfully integrated and actualized deeper potential, the sense of physically doing it, of exhilarated accomplishment, of effecting it. He was being a seven-year-old boy, learning to play hockey, and he managed to slide the puck right past the nine-year-old goalie and into the net. Everyone cheered and he felt fantastic. Or, the patient is being the deeper potential and is in the midst of rollicking hilarity as she is saying, "No, I don't want to," and experiencing a delightful sense of defiance, of having an impact, of expressing herself. Or, as the deeper potential, she is experiencing an incredible new sense of creation, fruitfulness, bringing forth, as she is touching the sculpture which she brought to life, fascinated with its beauty and freshness, its gracious form and shape. In any case, the patient is being this good-feelinged potential, usually the deeper potential. Here is a new and different person, alive and present.

The therapist separates this new personality from the ordinary patient, addresses the new potential and distinguishes this from the former, old, continuing operating domain. In so doing, the therapist enables the new potential to be a genuinely new and different person, separate and distinct from the former operating domain. Here are two examples of the therapist bringing forth the patient-as-new-potential and setting aside the patient-as-old-operating-domain:

T: OK, so you are tough, and you fight. I believe you. Listen, can we leave old Jane alone? I mean she's so busy attending to the pains in her chest, doing her dance with cancer, and heading toward death. Let's let her be. She'll do OK by herself.

T: You are really something! You are gentle and touching and considerate. Can I talk to you? You're just not like Henry, all wrapped up in struggles with Kathy the warden, the one who keeps him in line. He spends his time getting her to put limits on him while he whines about how mean she is. But you—you got a different life. You see the tenderness in the world. You know what it's like to be really gentle with another one. What a person you are!

Then the therapist invites this new potential to be and to behave in its own way, to live and be in its own world. The therapist regards this new person as having its own distinctive ways of being and behaving, and as living and existing in its own distinctive world. Thereby new ways of being and behaving are brought forward.

What is so singular is that the person-as-operating domain will live and be in one reality, and the person-as-deeper-potential will live and be in a qualitatively different reality. It is the new perspective which makes all the difference. In the same session, the patient will shift from one reality to another. Here is the patient as operating domain:

Pt: I don't even have free time at lunch. Three times a week I have to go to the classification office to check on things. And I bring my lunch, a cold sandwich. I work at night, at least once a week. You know what that leaves me? Wednesdays and Friday nights! I'm coming unglued, and there isn't any way out. I wish I'd get sick, except I know what's behind it. Even death . . . anything.

And that is the way it is for the operating domain. A little over an hour later in the session, the new potential is alive and enjoying itself in its own extratherapy world. By using this first method, the new potential of trusting, of being with, of sharing can be and behave in its own world. The new potential is with Diane, a woman he knows from another province, someone he writes to and calls and sees three or four times a year:

Pt: She is a social worker at the community agency in Edmonton, and I'm going to be with her. Yes, dammit! She's just too wonderful to let all these months go by. I'm free. What the hell! I can get a transfer out there, for three years. Easy! I'll be in the Edmonton office! Yeah! And we'll be together and live together, finally! Why not? It seems so easy! It's like I put myself in handcuffs for years. They're mine! Nobody did it to me! Hell, I can be out there by November! And we can walk through the park and touch and play house and have evenings. What a waste! I can taste it! Making suppers together. She's almost as good a cook as I am. Better! Hours and hours of being together. We'll have at least three years! What a feeling!

The patient-as-operating-domain lives in one real world, and the new patient-as-deeper-potential lives in a different world. To each, the world is available and real. Shift the perspective and the world changes.

Once the world changes, so do ways of being and behaving. The patient-as-deeper-potential no longer lives in a world of being pressed-in and suffocated, no longer experiences hopelessness and frustration. For the new patient-as-deeper-potential, the experiencing of trusting, being with, of sharing is so very natural and graceful. Appropriate new ways of being and behaving flow easily from this new potential. He exudes "being with," and all manner of new behaviors are now naturally forthcoming. The whole world becomes accommodating to ways of trusting, being with, sharing. He talks differently to close friends. smiles more openly, discloses more, touches a little more, fills his conversation with trusting. New behaviors just appear and flow from this new potential. It is as if an incredible resource for new ways of being and behaving is the person who is the integrated form of the deeper potential, situating itself in the external world.

The therapist begins by talking to the new potential:

T: What a guy you are! Gentle and loving and kind. You're really something! Now leave old Conrad go. You remember, old Conrad who has the arthritis all over his body, and forgets meetings and fights with his wife, and has all those temper tantrums, and, well, you know the poor old sucker.

Pt: He's a mess, yeah.

T: Yeah, just let him go. He's a real mess, and nothing much is going to happen to him. But you! You're something! What kind of a life have you got? Who are you? What do you do with yourself? When you feel all caring and gentle and kind and like that?

Pt: (Here is the beginning of the experiencing of new ways of being and behaving.) This is weird. I see white flowers, white, and I think I'm growing them. They're mine. And I feel like I'm in a greenhouse. The strangest thing! I see white roses. There such a thing? White roses? Aren't they red or pink or something?

T: Hey! Roses! Are you really white? You're white roses. If anyone asks you, tell 'em you're white roses, 'cause I said so!

Pt: (These are new ways of being and behaving for this patient.) I'm touching them. White, and they smell nice. A whole bed of them. In a greenhouse. I have a greenhouse. It's got water, a faucet, and a hose and earth, and flowers, lots of really pretty flowers. . . . And now I am . . . Christ, I'm touching a woman's neck, and we're sitting in lawn chairs, real close, and I'm in love with her. A woman, a slender neck, and she's slender. I see her neck and feel what it's like touching her neck and really loving her. A soft slender neck. I love you! I say, "I love you." I like loving you. It feels so nice being with you and loving you.

T: I'm getting a little embarrassed. I should leave you two be alone.

Pt: It's like having a house and a big yard and a greenhouse, and being with a slender woman I love, and I touch. I have hands that like to touch, gently, really gently. A flower and a shoulder. I feel things and I like it. Raise flowers and take care of them. And being with a woman where we love each other. I'd recognize her, slender and tall, and dressed in white slacks and running shoes, long hair, a real friend, someone I love. Loving her and touching her, raising flowers together. It's nice, it's really nice, really damned nice. What a delicious life.

Here is the new Conrad, experiencing what it is like to be and to behave in ways which were not part of the old Conrad. This new potential is living in its own world and is behaving in its own ways.

In being the deeper potential, Lucille reached a point where she was filled with gales of rollicking laughter as she was living in a scene in which she is startling a fellow by whispering wickedly lewd and lascivious inclinations. Lucille was in her late forties, divorced for nearly 16 years, and she is not the sort of woman who ever acted that way.

T: You know, I know good old Lucille pretty well, and she is real nice, but she just isn't very sexy. I mean, she doesn't have sex with anyone, not even with herself. But *you*! You're dirty! I mean, you're a bad woman! And at your age! You ought to be ashamed of yourself!

Pt: I'm not ashamed. (Laughs)

T: (Talking to this new and sexy woman) No, you really aren't. What do sexy old ladies like you do with your lives? Screw around with dirty old men? How do you spend your time? I know what Lucille does, and there's no sex. But you? Your life must be different. What do you do at night?

Pt: I screw! (Laughs hard) I love men!

T: Men? More than one?

Pt: Hell yes! I like big men, big, like me. I'm big, and I like men that can handle me. I like to yell and make noises when we screw. And I have to have a big heavy bed.

T: You use beds?

Pt: I use anything I can get. I have friends and we go to their place or my place, and I use the floor or the bed. Anything I can get. Every night! Till I'm all tuckered out.

T: All what? "Tuckered"? What's that?

Pt: (Laughs) Tuckered. We screw like hell and I get tuckered. I hold him on my breast and I love sucking. Oh dear! I love a good sucking. Mmmmm. Delicious. And then it's my turn to get sucked, and I twist and turn and moan and groan and scream. I love this! I have my own place and I live alone and I bring men home and I go to the hospital. I'm a nurse too, like Lucille. I work in emergency. Better there, and you meet all kinds of people. I like the ER. It's exciting, and I feel exciting, and I am exciting. I like the night shift. Keeps things exciting. That's when the action is.

T: How do you find men?

Pt: They're everywhere! I just am open, and honest! And I love sex. I have coffee in the cafeteria and tell someone that I'm turned on and I want a screw. Some say fine and some get all scared and polite. It feels fantastic. I get horny in my thighs. They start shaking and tingly, and that's how I know that I'm all sexed up, and then I tell whoever I'm with, "I'm all sexed up, you wanta screw?" I love it!

Here is a tasting and sampling of new ways of being and behaving. The newfound deeper potential has a chance to come to life, to build its own world, and to engage in its own ways of behaving.

The therapist may invite the new potential to have a chance to do what it wants with the situations which the old operating domain maintains as problems. Here are the externalized deeper potentials, the persons whom the old operating domain makes into compellingly axial centers of her world, and with whom the old operating domain has disintegrative relationships. The therapist guides the new potential into framing out its one way of being and behaving in these situations.

The operating domain lives in a world of two grownup sons who live with her, hang on her. There are neighbors who withdraw from her and regard her as someone to be pushed around. There is a series of men who try her out and abandon her. As the new potential, she dances with this world in a new way, from a new perspective. She exists and behaves in that world in a new and different way, from within this new and different potential.

T: OK, so there are the boys, in their twenties, living at home, there when you leave for work, there when you come home, usually with two or three of their friends, drinking beer, waiting for you to make dinner.

Pt: She's waiting for Tom to come back.

T: Huh?

Pt: Tom, her husband, ex-husband, of seven years an ex. I'd sell the house, inform the young men, get myself a nice apartment, and live a life— instead of pretending that nothing's changed.

T: Oh.

Pt: They're not bad kids. They can be all right. On their own that is. The whole scene is sad. Sad. And silly. I'd start leading my own life. Sure I would. So long kids! You're free! And me too!

Whether in its own world or bumping up against problematic situations and parts of the old patient's world, the new potential is invited to be and behave in its own way and in its own world. By means of this first method, the new potential gains an experiential taste of its own new ways of being and behaving within a new world of its own construction and existence.

2) Invite the New Potential to Communicate with the Old Operating Domain About How to Be and Behave in the External World

As with the above method, the therapist starts with the patient as the new potential. While this may be the new potential who has carried forward the heightened experiencing, or the new potential in an integrative encounter, the most fitting starting point is the patient who is being the deeper potential.

The therapist likewise addresses this new potential and differentiates this new person from the former personality, the old operating domain. There is the same sharp separation between this new personality and the former one who has the difficulties and problems. The distinctiveness of the second method consists of the invitation for the new potential to respond and react to the former old personality. Tell that former person how you want her to be, what you think of her, how she could be and should be, how you feel about the way she is, how she could and should be different, and the kind of life she could and should have. It is an invitation for the patient to be a qualitatively new potential who behaves in qualitatively new ways within the context of the imminent extratherapy world. In its interaction with the old personality, the new potential is being and behaving in new ways as it pushes and pulls the old personality into new ways of being and behaving.

In the session, Donald had made the radical shift into being a deeper potential who is open, straightforward, and honest, in contrast with the usual operating Donald who is tight, defensive, clamped up, avoiding, hiding, deceiving, indirect, living in a world of ever present threat. The therapist addresses the new person:

T: I see! I see! You're bubbling! OK, but tell me something. You're like the better twin of clamped-up old Donald.

Pt: Yeah, like a clone. I look like him.

T: Nyaa, you look better.

Pt: (Starting to compare and contrast the two) He's a little overweight. I feel harder, less fat. (The implied changes are now starting.)

T: Sure! Better. You're different, in lots of ways. Say, what do you think about the old slug, your clone there, screwed-up old Donald, the slug? How do you feel about him? What do you think? You know, about the way he is, about his life? You satisfied?

Pt: Hell no! To begin with, the hiding and deception got to end. No more! His whole life is not telling, not talking about it, hiding this from his wife and hiding that from his parents. He lies and hides and deceives. He never tells the truth. The poor bastard is never straight! He never even tells what he really means. He hints, or he alludes without ever really coming out and saying. He should say, "Wait, that's not true. That's a lie!" That's what he should say.

T: That'd be a change!

Pt: (Continuing) And he should lose weight. He has about 30 pounds, all in the belly and it just sits there. It's disgusting! It's like a sort of big thing, and it's crazy! He hides behind it.

T: You and your jargon. What do you call that? Insight? (The new vantage point of the patient allows him to see more of what the former person is, and could and should be.)

Pt: He ought to lose weight, and he hates being a lawyer. The only time he gets excited is when he works on political committees. He ought to go into politics much more. He's a lousy lawyer!

T: (Here are all sorts of new ways of being.) What are you going to do, change his whole damn life?

Pt: (Warming up to the changes) He'd be better off in politics. He's diplomatic. That means he lies! (Laughs) If he's going to hide, he at least should get something from it. He'd be better off. He would! He should run for alderman, and step up in the committees. Ottawa is a great place for that. He knows lots of people. Drop the law, or keep it on the side, a sideline. Yeah.

T: You done with the poor old sucker? What about all his problems? (The therapist guides potential changes into this particular situational context.)

Pt: In the firm? He bitches all day long about the partners, and he asks for problems. His headaches? His sweating all the time? He never is straight with anyone in the firm. He's even scared of the secretaries for God's sakes!

T: So? What do you think? (What are the possibilities for actual change in these problem situations?)

Pt: Be honest! Stop the damned hiding! You get annoyed. Let them know. You ought to start complaining. I'd sure as hell complain. I'm going to have my office painted and get some damned good furniture! I'm not the lackey in this place. Even the secretaries have nicer desks. Bitch bitch bitch! John has his own secretary! That's crazy! Be honest! Drop the tight stuff, it's ridiculous! Stop hiding and lying. Start growling about the inequities and all the damned injustices in the damned offices! You've got to own up! Yeah! Bitch a little! Yeah!

Here are bunches of new ways of being and behaving offered by the patient from the perspective of the new deeper potential.

Patients typically are in early situational contexts when they undergo the step of disengaging from the operating domain and enter into being the deeper potential. The therapist starts with the patient-as-deeper-potential, within the early situational context, and invites this new person to communicate with the person-as-operating-domain within the context of the current world. In the next excerpt, the good form of the deeper potential emerged as a forthright toughness, a firm decisiveness. She then recollected a special incident which first showed this quality before it disappeared. Iris had been kept after school by her first grade teacher who praised her drawings. Exhilarated, Iris took her sketchpad and drew the low brick fence and gnarled old tree of a lovely stone home near the elementary school. Arriving home late, her mother was furious and in no mood to hear Iris' happy explanation. Maddened by her mother's reception, Iris marched over to her girlfriend's house, right into the family dinner, and announced that she wanted to live with them from now on, brightly recounting the reasons for this serious decision, and facing them squarely with the proposition. Here was a deeper potential which emerged in its good form through therapeutic work, topped off by the memory of having momentarily experienced as that person. Now the therapist turns to being/ behavioral change by using the second method.

T: Fantastic! What a tough kid you are! You really act! I mean when the situation is bad and not fair, you do something! And you tell them right out that you want to live with them. Fantastic! (The therapist is talking to the patient-as-deeper-potential.)

Pt: Ha! I remember the look on Mr. Bronstein's face. He was half laughing and half surprised by this tough little kid. I was serious!

T: If you had known what Iris would grow up into! Well! What do you think of her? I like you! You're tough, and you take things in hand. But Iris. Do you know what happened to her? Huh? She grew up to be 35 years old, and she got married and she had two bratty kids, and she's sullen and depressed, and her husband is disgusted with her and she has no backbone, and she has bad colds and she's tired all the time, and she practically never has sex, and that's just for openers. What the hell do you think of her? Take a look at her! You're like her sister or something. You're a different person, thank God for that, but you get inside her body every so often. So what do you think? Proud of the lady Iris turned out to be? (Will the patient-as-deeper-potential turn her attention to the ordinary Iris?)

Pt: Maybe she can do other things, it's not too late. She's not getting any younger. Actually I'd like to kick her in the ass, or throw her in the garbage can, or something.

T: Yeah?

Pt: She has to have everyone approve of her. That's silly. She goes around asking if everything's OK. She's missing everything. She could have sex, real sex, with lots of men. And she loved to draw and sketch. She could take classes and evening classes, and help the art teacher, and just paint. Golly, she doesn't even paint. Dear! That's so missing things! She could take vacations and . . . she has never been to Mexico or Japan or New

York or South America. She could have picnics in the mountains and
go skiing and have real friends and take her husband to Europe and play
with the kids. She's missing so much! For nothing! I'd do all these things.
T: Nine-year-old kids can't get credit cards! Talk to her. Hey, Iris . . .
Pt: I'd kick her in the pants, and get her to do all sorts of things. Have an
affair! Try a new man! See what it's like with women! Wake up and
have some courage! I'd do all sorts of things!
T: I believe you! (But the patient tosses more new ways of being and behaving at the old Iris.)
Pt: No reason to live four blocks from your mother. You've never gotten away
except for school. Three years, what's that? You have your mother
babysit. No reason! No reason to call up mother every other day, and
have the family over, and they all pitch in and help with the fence, and
then they swarm all over her house like flies! Move away! That's not
so hard. Jim wants to go to Toronto. He turned down a move there.
I'd tell him to take it. I'd be a better wife than she is! I know I would!
T: I believe you!

Here again is a flurry of behavioral possibilities coming from the
new potential giving its version of how the old personality could and
should be different. It is important to note the changes which the new
potential offers to resolve the problem situations. The new potential
sees how the old Iris invites all sorts of problems by behaving in specific
ways with her mother and her family. Dropping such behaviors is a
major shift in Iris' way of being, and it is the new personality who identifies these behaviors and simply tells Iris to drop them. The new personality is in a delightful position to see how the patient behaves so
as to construct problems, and it is the new personality who is in a position to invite the old personality to give up those behaviors.

As the new potential, relationships with the former operating domain can be delightfully integrative. New ways of being and behaving spring to life as the new potential communicates with the former
operating domain along an integrative relationship, and within the context of the current world. As the new potential, Stephan can now relate
integratively with the old operating domain, including its thorough-
going self-centeredness. In this integrative communication with the former Stephan, he is being and behaving in new ways as he chides the
operating domain to try out new ways of being and behaving.

Pt: You could learn to flutter your eyes. You used to do that when you were
very little, and everyone thought it was so sweet. Try it out. Who
knows, maybe there's an old lady somewhere who'll get sucked in. Probably not. You'll be fluttering for nothing.

T: Listen! Don't you think Stephan should have a series of shots of his ordinary day? He's got a camera. Take pictures of Stephan. Big ones, of
Stephan brushing his hair, and Stephan thinking about Stephan. It'd be
great.

Pt: Right! And they should be blown up to be maybe real life size. And he
can have a room containing nothing but these shots, all over the walls
and ceiling.

This second method starts with the patient being the new and different, sounder and happier potential. The therapist then invites this
new personality to react and respond to the old operating personality; in so doing, the new potential is expressing new ways of being and
behaving within the context of a new and changing extratherapy world.

3) Invite the Old Operating Domain
to See the Picture of the Directions
of Potential Change

When the patient is still in the vicinity of being the new potential,
the previous two methods enabled the patient to (a) live and be and
behave in the potential's own way and in its own world, or (b) communicate with the old operating domain about how to be and to behave
in the external world. But often the center of the patient has drifted
out of the new potential, typically the good form of the deeper potential, and is now back inside the old operating domain. The patient is
once again the old patient—with a very important exception. The patient has carried forward the experiencing, has engaged in an internal
encounter, has lived and existed as the deeper potential.

The key to this third method lies in the patient's seeing the picture
of the directions of potential change. Back inside the operating domain,
safely removed from any pressure to be and behave differently, this
method merely invites the patient to see the picture of a personality
which can be, a person who could exist and be and behave. The image must be clear, defined, vivid. It is akin to an optimal person, a happy person, free of the patient's ways of being and behaving, an ideal
or fulfilled image, a picture of the directions of potential change.

The picture may be that of a twin, someone who looks like the patient but who is happy and secure, joyful and good-feelinged. It may
be a clone who is everything the patient could be but isn't. It may be
the dream version of the patient, a person who lives in a happy and
delightful dream world and behaves in his own distinctive ways. It may
be in the form of an actor or actress, living the role of the optimal ver-

sion of the patient. It may start with a nucleus of some deeper potential in the patient, one which grew into a wholesomely integrated and actualized new person of its own. It may be a potential which had a breath of life when the patient was a child and then was buried, only to reemerge now as a grownup optimal whole person, integrated and actualized. The therapist frames in this other personality, this person who can be, this image of the direction of potential change. While safely ensconced within the operating domain, the patient is invited to see this new and possible personality.

Bandler and Grinder (1982) organize this method into two steps. The first consists of the patient visualizing herself being and behaving in optimal ways, accompanied with good feelings. For example, they describe a woman with little or no feelings in her pelvic region, and they invite her to visualize herself, as clearly as possible, in the throes of enjoying sexual intercourse. The second step is to join into that image, to float into being that image of herself. In our version, the method begins with the therapist framing the picture of what the patient can become, starting with the experiencing in the session. Here is where the 12 principles of chapter 7 come into play. Beginning with the experiencing in the session, it is a matter of using one or two of the principles in generating a picture of what this person can become.

It is curious and interesting that some patients will indeed be able to visualize this new, happy optimal person who behaves in new ways — and other patients will not and cannot. Some will see the picture clearly, and some will either see it in a cloudy, hazy way or not at all. Some can put the picture on hold and see it for a while, and others will allow only a cursory sidelong glance for a fraction of a second. Some will be able to visualize a new world without the precious booze or job or hash or spouse or kids or gun collection, and some cannot imagine a world without its present components.

Seeing the new image carries with it some powerful challenges. One is to allow significant other figures to be different. If father is moulded into being the cold and critical one, is the patient able to visualize herself as an equal, as a genuine friend who can josh and kid with father? This means allowing father to no longer be in the crucial role of the cold and critical one:

Pt: Yes! Yes! She's really a pal, and she likes the old codger! She grins at him and touches him on the shoulder. Wow! This is really something! They're buddies! He's grinning, and he looks . . . sheepish. They are buddies!

On the other hand, some patients are not prepared to leave go of the old relationship, and must preserve father as the distantly critical one:

Pt: (Tight and hard) When he does it, when he says those things to her, yeah, then she can tell him, she can stand up to him. She doesn't have to take it anymore. He's mean, and she should stand up to him!

A second challenge is to leave go of the world components which are precious to the operating domain. In being the deeper potential, the very heart of the patient let go of the operating domain. Can the patient visualize living without the operating domain's precious world? Is it possible to see a world without his wife? Can she visualize a life where she no longer lives with her mother? Can he imagine a world without his being the head of the firm, the main executive officer, the important committee member? Is it possible to see a happy self who is no longer seductive and sexually appealing? Can the patient see the new person building a wonderful life free of everything which is so exceedingly precious to the ordinary continuing patient? This is the second great challenge.

Patients who can visualize the optimal person living and behaving in an optimal world are capable of allowing behavioral changes to occur. Those who cannot visualize this change are not yet ready to allow behavioral changes to occur.

The patient is a sociologist with a raging ulcer. He is quiet, tense, tight, and in the session there was a moment when he was a different person, free of the ulcer, and verging on being a fellow who was inviolate—no one could ever corner him; he was very defiant, antagonistic, rebellious. It felt great—for less than a minute.

T: Can you picture a guy, also named Dr. Firmo Pugnazzi, same name as you, hell he even looks like you, but he is not you. He's like a twin brother. Only he is happy. You're miserable. He's a guy who enjoys his life. He doesn't even know you. He is a fellow who is delightfully antagonistic, joyfully rebellious. See him? He is tough, and enjoys his life, really happy. He is a defiant sonuvabitch, and he is great at being like that. What the hell would he do? What would his life be like? Can you see this other, happier Dr. Firmo Pugnazzi?

Pt: That's easy. He'd be in politics. He'd put his politics where his mouth is. He'd tell the truth about the kinds of programs the government should have, and he'd do it on the basis of sociology, not the damned lawyers and self-seekers. He'd write a column in the paper. That's what he'd do.

T: What sort of a column?

Pt: Honest, straightforward, and tough. He knows sociology. He knows the history of programs the government is fooling around with. He's a sociologist with smarts and he can show how the changing times mean changes in what we conveniently call welfare programs or job creating programs. He'd give the background of the programs, the wider and deeper scope, and he'd suggest real alternatives, real ones, with stature and toughness to them. That bastard would have fun!

T: He's got a column!

Pt: He's got a life! He has friends that he talks to. He has a place, that's a home, a real home. Damn! I've never even unpacked. I see his home. Wait! He doesn't have an ulcer! He doesn't even stand like a little mouse or a praying mantis, skinny and tight and tense. He stands up and looks people in the eyes, and he smiles. He's got a face that smiles. He is happy! That guy is happy! Hey! (New features emerge as the patient sees the image more clearly.)

T: What about the fights in the department? They fuel your ulcer and you suffer. How is he? What is he like in the department, especially when there is fighting and arguments?

Pt: He'd say it's mostly a bunch of shit! He could say it's childish! He'd say that changing the spring break from two days to three days is horseshit, and he didn't give a damn, except that 14 grown people are spending two hours arguing like babies about it. I admire that guy! I salute a guy like that! I'd applaud him, that's what I'd do. He'd enjoy ridiculing them, and I'd be in the audience wishing I could do it. I like that guy. Give 'em hell, brother!

Ann is in her late forties, lives with her 20-year-old daughter, hasn't had sex in six years, and, as the good form of the deeper potential, was recounting stories of how she and a girl friend used to leave school in the fourth grade, go into the back of an old store with "older boys" of 12 and 13, take off all their clothes and "do things." Ann was excitedly shrieking and raucously laughing as she told these stories. It is common that therapy will illuminate a potential which had a brief career in childhood. What if it grew up into its own integrated and actualized personhood?

T: That Ann was a sexual devil! No one knew?

Pt: (Laughing) I think everyone knew. Except my parents. They never found out. I think. But everyone else did. (Laughs)

T: Now suppose, just suppose, that that wicked, nasty little 11-year-old sexpot grew up, there she goes, and all she knows is being with boys, having girl friends, teasing the guys, having guys that she could kid with, really kid with, and exhibiting herself, and being sexual. That's it! That's her personality. Then she grows up, zoom, 16, 26, here comes middle age, 35, 40, and now the old lady is 47 big ones.

Pt: Oh, what happened to her? Sad.

T: She's Lisa.

Pt: That's my middle name.

T: Sure! There's Ann. Step forward Ann. And there's Lisa. Here she is, ladies and gentlemen. Lisa is a fantastic woman. She is happy. Oh she doesn't have your fine qualities, but she is the happiest Lisa possible. See her? See her?

Pt: She's slender! She's slender. Look at her face! No big bags under her eyes, no fat hanging on her arms. No belly! She doesn't have a belly.

T: Jealous old lady!

Pt: She looks good. Her age, but very attractive. Mainly she weighs around 118, and I weigh a very round 150! That's the difference. It's funny. I'm looking at her and she's looking at herself in the mirror.

T: Where's the mirror? In a store, in a home? Is she still stripping for 13-year-old boys?

Pt: She doesn't have a daughter. Her daughter is not living there. She's got her own place. She looks a helluva lot better than I do. She enjoys her body and she's healthy and attractive. I just got dumpy and sexless and depressed. She has sexual feelings. She has them, in her thighs. And even the way she walks. Look at her. She walks like a sexual woman. I admire that. I walk like a dumpy old woman. She walks briskly. Look at her! You know, this is embarrassing. I can feel it coming. She can have sex, and it is natural and nice. I don't want to watch her have sex. That would be too much for me. She probably knows some men her age and they love sex with her and she enjoys sex. I don't want to see her in bed with a man. That's too much. She'd take off his clothes and he'd take off her clothes and they'd do things. I don't want to see her having sex. She'd be happy with men, and that's all fine enough, but I don't want to watch.

In framing the image of the direction of potential change, the therapist is free to define scenes in which this optimal person is being and behaving. One of these is the situation which is problematical for the patient, the one in which the patient feels rotten in her own way. How would this other, optimal personality be and behave in that situation? The therapist frames in the problem situation, and then describes the way the optimal person is, the qualities and characteristics, the kind of person who is the optimal individual this patient can become. Putting the patient safely on the sidelines, the therapist fills in the picture of the directions of potential change:

T: You are sitting in the living room with Bill. Lucy, your kind-of friend
   comes over, and in her usual way, she says, "No one in the neighborhood likes the awnings you just put up." Your insides seize up, you
   freeze, and you feel the knife inside. Right?

Pt: Uh huh. Never again!

T: Tell you what. I'm going to hire an actress. She looks just like you. You
   can sit hidden in the dining room. Be under the table. Here's what's going to happen. This actress is the spitting image of you. You can't imagine. First she calls Lucy and asks her to come over for coffee. With
   you hiding under the dining room table. Bill's sitting in the living room,
   smoking as usual, like he was. The actress, sounds remarkably like you,
   says, "Lucy, I'm going to recreate the scene from a couple of days ago,
   when you were here, but this time, I'm going to do a few new tricks,
   a couple of new lines. Will you just listen? You don't have to do a thing,
   just listen for three minutes. Yes? No?"

Pt: She'd say yes.

T: Great, now you just stay quiet in the dining room. OK. Then the actress,
   looks just like you, she says, "Remember you said something like, 'No
   one in the neighborhood likes the awnings you just had installed?' Ah!
   Lucy! You promised to just listen. When I'm done you can talk. OK.
   Well, here!" And the actress shoves a big juicy lemon pie right in Lucy's
   kisser!

Pt: (Shrieks)

T: Be quiet! There's more! And then the actress says, "You little bitch! What
   a childish, nasty, awful thing to say. I'm damned tired of you smiling
   and telling me how someone else hates my guts! Do it again and bammo,
   another pie!" And then the actress says, "OK, darling. That's all the time
   I wanted to take. Now it's your turn, Lucy. And be careful, don't mess
   with me." And all this time you are sitting quietly in the dining room.

Pt: She's hired! I need her!

   The more the patient sees the new picture, the closer the patient
comes to welcoming the new ways of being and behaving. Throughout
the session, the older man became less and less terrified of the awful
carnality. Then it began to occur in its good form, a sensuous mutuali-
ty, oneness with another, a harmonious blending of bodies, sweet and
graceful and joyous. Now the question: How can the patient bring this
into his life? How can he "see" a picture of this newfound wonderful
sexuality?

T: I can see that fellow, Jonathan, looks like you, same little cigar that the
   two of you like, same long legs. He has a lovely work of art on the small
   marble table near the entryway. A man and a woman, metal, lovely,

entwined around one another, sexual, each figure about 20 inches high, smooth curves. It is sensuous. I like it. (The patient brings these behavioral images into the vicinity of his own life.)

Pt: Our house is so sterile. That's a change. Never had anything like that. Going to the ballet. He would watch them move gracefully together, touching, he would go, and he'd watch. He'd go. He would go.

T: And pictures, lovely pictures of women and men, holding and touching.

Pt: I saw a Japanese drawing, on a white ceramic base, a lamp. Big lamp. Beautiful. Lovely. A man and a woman, sort of intertwined, like sex, but pretty. Few lines. Sensual and he'd have something like that. (Now he brings the new way of being and behaving into his life.) I could have it. I could have Japanese drawings and sketches. Pictures. I could have paintings. Sensual, sexual paintings. Japanese and all sorts, old masters. Big paintings, lovely frames. There could be some in our house. We have nothing. Women and men. It could be, sure. Yes indeed.

Safely situated in the old operating domain, the patient witnesses the clear image of the directions of potential change. From this vantage point, the patient gains an experiential shot at new ways of being and behaving, new possibilities in situations comprising the currently available external world, and the consequence is an experiential taste of these new ways of being and behaving.

4) Walk the Patient Through the Carefully Detailed, Concretely Specific New Way of Being and Behaving

The patient experiences the new ways of being and behaving by actually going through them very slowly, very explicitly, in vividly etched, concrete detail, inch by inch. In so doing, the therapist and patient almost seem to be in the actual situation, undertaking the actual behavior in a hypnogogic, as if, manner.

How does the therapist identify these new ways of being and behaving? The therapist may witness these new behaviors in the session itself. They occur as the patient goes through the strong experiencing of each previous step in the session. Or the therapist starts with the raw experiencing in the session, uses the principles given in chapter 7, and generates a picture of the directions of potential change, including new ways of being and behaving.

How does the therapist identify the situational contexts in which these new ways of being and behaving are to occur? The therapist has several choices. The new ways of being and behaving may be inserted into problem situations in which the patient has feelings of tension, pain and anguish. It may be current versions of recent or remote situations from the patient's life. Or it may be a situation invented by the therapist to accommodate the picture of the directions of potential change.

The key to this method is careful, detailed description of the concrete specifics of both the "inside" and "outside" behavior. That is, the therapist describes the details of carrying out the actual behavior, but the therapist also describes what is occurring inside—what it feels like inside, the immediately ongoing bodily sensations, the inner thoughts and ideas.

Something quite special occurs as the therapist walks the patient through the detailed minutiae of the new ways of being and behaving in the concretely specific situational context. There is a gliding into the new experiencing and owning of this new way of being and behaving. Generally the patient quietly listens and then starts to feel it, to nod and say "yes," to sigh or grunt acknowledgment, to laugh or groan. Next the patient makes the new way of being her own by actively remembering similar experiencings, similar ways of behaving in the past, locating her own life situations where it is fitting to be and behave in these ways. The quite special consequence consists in this taking into herself these new ways of being and behaving.

The high point of experiencing, for this patient, consisted of the integrative relationship with his own craziness, his own out-of-control bizarreness, his chaotic lunacy. Building a picture of what this patient can become, the prominent feature was a person who could be friendly and integratively welcoming of this tendency. Instead of cloaking and defensively distancing himself, he can become a person who can step aside from and play with this very real quality in him.

T: You are walking downtown with Claire, and you see the fellow who is walking toward you. He is slight, wearing a dark brown old overcoat, and you see the gun. It is a gun! He holds it in his right hand, sort of half hidden behind the fold of the coat, and your whole body freezes. You are riveted on the gun, and your thoughts stop. Now he is about eight feet away, and your body is panicked. Breath is hard and short, legs are jerky and weak and—and it is an umbrella! An umbrella!

Pt: I'd die!

T: And you notice, he's past, it all took about four seconds. And you say out loud, Claire hears, "I'm a looney! I see things! A few more of these and I'm going to turn myself in." Claire turns and looks at you a little quizzically.

Pt: She should! (It is as if the patient shared in this new way of being and behaving.)

T: And you say, "Claire, I though that guy—Jesus. I hope you saw the guy, the slight little assassin in the old dark brown overcoat. I saw him carrying a gun, a nasty, ugly gun. Then, just as he passed, the damn thing turned into an umbrella. Isn't that a sign? I'm crazy! I know I'm a damned nut!"

Pt: Boy, I wish! I wish! If I could do that. I couldn't.

T: And those voices in your head? "Don't get trapped. Watch out, don't get trapped. Be careful." (The patient is terrified of the harsh inner voice.)

Pt: Oh no!

T: It's Christmas, and you're at home, with the old family.

Pt: I'm going in two weeks.

T: Your cousin Don is there. That one. The loser, the family bum, the wheeler-dealer who always cons everyone in the family. Keep it in the family. He's asking you if you read about the new watchman, the portable tiny little TV that's going to sweep the country, bigger than Walkman. Here's the voice. Whispering as usual. "Don't get trapped." Oh, oh, the nuttiness is showing. The voice is here. Shit! You lean toward Don. Forget about his cigar. Put your head next to him. "Can you hear the voice, Don? I got a voice inside my head. It's whispering nasty little things to me. It's my own private little voice. It's 'cause I'm deranged. Are you deranged?" And you look him straight in the eye, right directly in the eye.

Pt: (Laughing) He'd swallow his cigar!

T: That's a helluva way to avoid a straight answer.

Pt: I could start another group, crazies anonymous. Wait a second, Crazies. The crazy guys. No! BONKERS! (laughs) That's it, the bonkers. There were three of us in elementary school, and we used to be nuts. They called us the bonkers. A teacher called us that 'cause we did crazy things. Bonkers, nuts. And we used to explain everything, we'd be late, or forget to bring some homework, you know? And we'd say, "We're bonkers." It was great. Jesus Christ, we admitted being weird. I don't know what happened. I used to do it, I used to. I felt good then. I'm bonkers. I'm bonkers. I think I got a lot of the signs. I'm one of the looney kids. Damn!

Susan agonized over situations such as the executive board meetings. In the middle of the session, there was a carrying forward of a potential for experiencing frustration, a screaming out of frustration. Later, she was able to be that potential and to live and experience from within it. This was a sharp contrast to her ordinary tendency to appease and understand, and then to be withdrawn and terribly fatigued. The therapist framed in the problem situation.

T: Sue, Susan, Doctor Susan . . . It's starting again. Here are the seven on
the executive committee, and they are discussing the person who rep-
resents the association in the government council, that very plum position. Hampton's four years are up, and they are going to replace him
with one of the people on the executive committee. One of us!

Pt: I hate this kind of stuff!

T: Sure! It's unfair. Let's put ourselves in the best slots. That's a plum. Put
one of us there. Martin wants it. The board wants Martin. Here it
comes. "I move that we nominate Martin to the government council."
Wham! The pressure in your head starts. It freezes you up, in the head,
and your throat tightens. All the signs. Then you pound the table. Pound
it hard. Bam! No! No! No! I hate this! Louder! NO NO NO!!! I HATE
THIS DAMNED PUSHING OURSELVES! NO!

Pt: I'd turn the corner if I could do that!

T: Be my guest. Go ahead, doctor!

Pt: If I could say no, and really mean it, oh wow! NOOOOOOO! (She screams.)

T: They all look at you as if you lost your mind!

Pt: Noooooo! You're all a bunch of moralistic self-centered pricks! I could
do it! Damn right I could do it! Why not! Oh why the hell not!

T: ARE YOU ALL LISTENING TO ME!

Pt: You know what? I always wanted to tell my husband how damned cruel
he is to our son. I was a good wife for years. (It is common that going
through one situation leads the patient to open up another. The therapist
knows the new situation well.)

T: Here's what you do. You tell Sam that you want to talk to him and he
has to listen for ten minutes. He's got to keep his mouth shut for ten
minutes. OK Sam? Right. Then you take him into the office. It's quiet
there, can't hear much, right? And you say, "I tolerated it for years, for
years! But Sam, you are going to stop being so damned cruel to Philip
or I'm going to ram my fist down your throat! You are mean! You treat
him like he's your slave, and a stupid one at that! No more!"

Pt: (Moving into place) You crowd him and you lord over him and you never
let him do anything on his own, and you are just a SHIT! You impose
penalties as if you're still a major in the damned army! Leave him
alone!!! My God I'm yelling! I never yell! I like yelling! I have a lot of
yelling to do! I could spend half of my time yelling NO! Don't step all
over me! No! Leave me alone! Get the hell out of here! Stop pushing
at me! Get off of me! NOOO!. . . . My body's been trying to say no
for me, poor old body of mine. Nice body. You're my friend. It seems
so simple. No, Lester. No, Adrian. No, Evan. No, Sam. No, Pearson.
No, no, no. It's easy. No. Ha!

In the course of earlier steps in the session, the patient may uncover
delightful experiencings which were marvelously present in childhood
and conspicuously absent today. The technical problem is how to

reconstruct the childhood situations in the current life, modify the childhood behaviors as needed and thereby regain the delightful experiencings. For example, Rob recollected precious moments when he was five years old, built a snow fort, and, when it was done, sat inside. The sense was a wonderful sense of safety, protection, being enclosed, womblike, cozy. Did he have that today? Never. The therapist fabricated current replications of the snow fort and, using this fourth method, walked the patient slowly through appropriate ways of being and behaving to open up the precious experiencing. As is common, the patient then suggested his own new behavioral possibilities.

T: You have a four poster bed, with big strong posts. There is a roof to the bed, made of heavy material, and on all three sides are the same heavy material, enclosed, inside, and there are four big pillows. The drapes around the bed are very thick and very heavy, and they surround the whole bed. You are enclosed inside, no one can see in. The material is light brown, thick, heavy, hanging. And there is a feeling of peaceful security, a wonderful feeling of being protected, all enclosed here. It's about midnight, and you are a little tired, and you are in the bed, and no one is going to bother you, and your body is cozy, and you feel so very protected.

Pt: I am thinking about camping. I've never gone camping. I always thought about being inside a tent. Yee Gods, I would love to go camping with Liz. She said she used to when she was a kid. I've never done it. Camping, going camping. Being inside the tent, in the evening. Wonderful! Seems so just you and me. I want to do it, the weather's perfect. I would love to. And the bed, I'm a gadget nut. I'd want to have a room like that. A bed room. I've always, the little tiny room. We remodeled the house and made three bedrooms instead of four, and we got a tiny little room, about the size of a big bed. Paint the walls dark. I would make the whole room a water bed, and just that, the whole room, dark walls and dark ceiling, and the whole floor is the water bed, and it's on the floor, and we'd have a panel too, a console, for making coffee and a tiny refrigerator for drinks, and music and TV, all operated from where we are in the bed, I've always had something like that in the back of my mind. Liz would love that. I'd go bananas! Yeah!

The key is careful, detailed description of the new way of being and behaving. From the picture of the directions of potential change, the therapist has images of new ways of behaving in appropriate situational contexts. In this defined situation, the therapist walks the patient through the carefully detailed, concretely specific new way of being and behaving. The patient then experiences what it is like to be and behave in new ways which bring the patient closer to the picture of what this particular person can become.

5) Be the Integrated, Actualized Potential Who Carries Out the New Way of Being and Behaving

The patient has carried forward the experiencing, has moved along an integrative encounter with the deeper potential, and has moved into being the deeper potential. In all of this, the therapist is the voice of the integrated and actualized potential, is its identity and its agency. Being and behavioral change occurs when the therapist turns this identity to the extratherapy world. The key is that it is the therapist who enacts the new way of being and behaving, who does it, expresses it, shows it, undertakes it.

In being this agency, the therapist truly is the "I." The therapist is the voice of this new patient, speaks as "I," refers to herself as "I," refers to the patient as "you," and regards that patient as a separate and distinct entity. I am the identity who is ready and willing to carry out new ways of being and behaving. As this "I," I do not need you at all. You can do whatever you must do, if you wish. You can lead your life and I will lead my integrated and actualized life. I can go my way and you can go yours. I can also invite you to come on along with me, perhaps. I can even order and command you to do what I want to do. I can say, "I'm going to move to Vancouver and accept that job and see what it's like to have a real executive position." Or I can say, "I command you to call the fellow tonight and tell him that you accept the position." I am the I. I am the integrated and actualized potential who is ready and willing to be and behave in new ways.

Another way of putting this method is that the therapist-as-deeper-potential does it for and as the patient. The therapist is the model, the exemplar. The difference is that the therapist is truly being the good form of the potential, actually living as the "I" who is quite ready and willing to be and behave as the potential.

The important point is that the therapist is the one to carry out the new behavior. If the new behavior is taking a trip and enjoying it, the therapist simply does it or tells the patient to do it. There is no need to embellish the new behavior in lights or to feature it as some new behavior. The doing is the key feature. For example, in the following, Erickson merely tells the patient to do it, without drawing the patient's attention to the new behavior:

. . . I told her, "Enjoy your trip to Dallas. Enjoy your trip back, and tell me how much you enjoyed it." She didn't know that she was keeping her promise, but she was. I knew what I intended by that promise. She didn't know. And it was said so gently, "Enjoy the trip there and back." And she had promised to do whatever I asked of her. She didn't notice that I asked that of her (Erickson in Zeig, 1980, p. 158).

As the new integrated and actualized potential, the therapist explodes into dozens of new ways of behaving. Set within the context of the real world, each potential erupts like a popcorn machine into bunches of new behaviors. What had been a feared childishness, a "regressed" immaturity, converts into a sense of naive, childlike delight, a freshness in new-seeing, a wonder at shapes and forms and touches and colors. This explodes into bunches of behaviors: inspecting the big toe, bending over and seeing the world from between one's legs upside down, the sense of inhaling and exhaling slowly, discovering teeth and nipples and armpits, the joy of being able to tie shoes, the fun of reciting the alphabet, the delight of urinating, the wonderful headiness of looking way up to the top of the tall building.

The new potential is also able to give up and to step away from all the unfortunate life situations the patient constructs in order to feel rotten. The patient builds and clings to life situations which enable her to feel bad in a hundred different ways. While the patient must have these in her life, the therapist-as-deeper-potential does not. So the therapist can enter a life free of these, leaving the patient unhappily dangling in those awful life situations:

T: I can work and fight and live for the next 20 years. But you, you poor baby, the cancer's going to get you, maybe in the next eight months. You're going to die, sucker. Not me. You go ahead.

T: I have an apartment and a new man, and we're going to get married 'cause we love each other. You want to come to the wedding? You and your big house, and your three grownup kids hanging on you. You got one helluva a life. Come visit me every so often. Eat your heart out. You want to complain how your kids don't work and expect you to be the breadwinner and their servant? Go ahead. I can listen, and even understand. 'Cause I am living with Ed, and we're happy.

The therapist is infused with the integrated and actualized experiencing, and is quite free to be the behaving identity. If the therapist is now on integrative terms with the little ways of behaving that provoke others, that refuse to cooperate with what others want, that successfully drive others wild, the therapist can be these in interaction with significant others:

T: A-ha! You had your heart set on pancakes! I went to the store and lookee lookee! No pancakes. Ha! Pretty good, eh! Does that get your blood pressure up? How am I doing?

T: Oh, I don't know. You're handing me a great opportunity. Pick you up at the airport at 10:15? I think I'll just forget about it and then have my innocent look when you come in around midnight. I'll practice: "Golly gee, it must have slipped my mind, ha ha ha ha." Sure you want me to pick you up?

The patient was describing his two little girls. As he was returning them to his ex-wife, after his weekly visitation, Linda turned to him and blew him a kiss. In the session he caught himself. Almost starting to cry, he managed to catch himself. His reaction to almost crying is disintegrative. He must change the subject quickly and make sure that he is on top of "things," meaning the possibility of crying. The therapist can have an integrative reaction to being on the verge of crying:

T: I am going to be on the verge of sudden crying again. It may happen tonight or tomorrow or next week. The damned tears leap out on my face. With Linda and every so often with real people, big ones. The next time it happens, that instant when I got to stop them, I say, "There are tears starting! No way! I will not cry! Never! Only babies cry! I will not! I am a man! You hear? A man!"
Pt: Well, that's what I think!
T: Step aside, son. You do the thinking; I'll say it out loud.
Pt: I couldn't.
T: Damned right you couldn't, you sniveling little two-faced, false macho, little baby, toothless little liar!
Pt: Now wait a minute!
T: Easy, I got tears starting in my eyes. I have to stop them from pouring out 'cause I'm the real man around here.
Pt: I could do it (meekly).

Being the good form of the deeper potential, and being on integrated terms with the operating domain, the therapist can play with the exaggerated version of these behaviors. Claire behaves in ways which invite others to overlook her, to hurt something precious within her. It is as if she presents something of herself and others then malign it. The therapist can start with the mild ways Claire actually uses to accomplish this and raise the stakes:

T: Do you want to come to my party? It will be October 15, and I am going to have everyone sit around while I open up some of the things I have in specially marked boxes.

Pt: What do you mean?

T: Well, I'll show everyone the dress I wore when I went to church when I was seven years old. It's so lovely. Everyone will oow and aaaah, 'cause it really is so pretty. And I'll read a poem I wrote last year when I saw a leaf turn red, the first one in my little tree in the backyard.

Pt: That's ridiculous.

T: (Snapping)) You're not very nice to me! I don't think I'm going to invite you. You'll miss all the good things.

Pt: What?

T: I have a whole bunch of hair that I saved from brushing my hair. And old pictures of me when I was in elementary school. And I'm going to tell people about some of my thoughts about other thoughts. And then everyone will take turns telling how wonderful I am. (The patient is laughing now.) Wait, that's not the highlight. I got more.

Pt: (Laughing) That's enough.

Victoria is in her late forties. What emerged in the session was a deep-seated rivalry and competitiveness with her daughter who has a new baby, is youthful and vital, has a new home, and who is entering a fine professional career. All of these feed the mother's intense competitiveness.

T: Well? It's time for some changes. I am going to have my hair done in a new style, youthful, long, long and beautiful hair. And I'm going to look even better than Elaine 'cause I'm going to start exercise classes and I'll be great, youthful and lithe and slender again. No problem.

Pt: Sure.

T: A baby. Shit! I'm in the prime of life. I'm mature enough now to be a good mother. I'm going to get pregnant. I'll have a baby. And I'll wear shorts. I got great legs, a flat stomach, and a nice body. I'll give up the old apartment and have a real home. And I'm going to go to school and become a social worker. I'd be wonderful.

Pt: I'm too old!

T: You sure are. But not me! I can do it.

Pt: Well, I could exercise a little.

T: See, that's a start. We'll both exercise, and I'll start school.

Pt: It is a little ridiculous. (Laughing)

T: Stop fighting me! (Victoria laughs quite hard.)

Pt: I'm 49! I don't want to have a baby! Let Elaine have the kids. Say, I guess
I have a lot to talk to her about, huh! I'll be the momma. She'll do the
rest. I have a lot to say to her. Sure do.

In the session, the deeper potential surfaced. Unlike the operating
domain, the deeper potential need not have the operating experiencing of dashed hopes, bitterly unhappy vindictiveness. This 64-year-old
man had lost his laundry business, and his wife divorced him. He is
in debt and spreading his venomous gloom around the house of his
daughter and son-in-law. It was the perfect setup for the painful operating potential. The deeper potential surfaced as a momentary intimacy with men, a chum relationship, a genuine friendship. The
therapist allowed this deeper potential to fashion a life, and the therapist was its agency:

T: Joe Goody has a place. My old buddy. His wife died three years ago, and
he hinted at my living with him. Shit, he's older than I am! I got just
enough to share expenses with him and I'm going to live with him. We
both love cigars! And we can cook, both of us. We argue about everything, politics, that bastard, and religion, that old Jew! We've known
each other for years! Yep, I'm going to live with old man Goody! Damn!
What a great idea!

Pt: I could ask him.

T: Me first! Take your turn. Besides, I don't think I want to live with a bitter old kid like you. No, I'm going to do omelets. I'm good with omelets.
And we'll argue over who cleans the kitchen. He's got a great place. I'll
buy in. Half for him. We'll split the expenses. Half and half. I got the
money. Barely.

Pt: Sounds good.

T: Thank you. Come visit, once!

In being the good form of the deeper potential, the therapist inhaled
what it is like to step out of the operating domain, the long-suffering
matriarch of the large family, the one with the responsibilities and the
self-imposed burdens, the problems and the never-ending complaints.
I am free, liberated, breathing easy. I am free to do what I want to
do. It's wonderful!

T: I'm 36, have four kids, and a reasonable husband, Bill, and that's where
I'm going to be. No more big momma in the whole family. Alice gets
a breast removed? She can figure out where to stay. She's got a husband

and a teenaged kid. I don't have to chair a big family conference. Uncle George has glaucoma and Aunt Harriet is all upset? Not my problem! I'm resigning! Everybody listening? No more big momma! I'm resigning! No more Christmas dinners at my house! It's someone else's turn! Over with! Done!

Pt: (Laughter) I couldn't!

T: No one asked you to.

Pt: I couldn't do that.

T: *I'm* going to do it. You can do whatever the hell you want to do.

Pt: Well, I wish I could.

T: (Continuing) I hate these damned long Ottawa winters, cold and gray for months. Everyone I know goes south for a week. I'm going to go to Florida for a week in February, cold gray, no-sun February.

Pt: Bill would kill me. He has to work.

T: You stay with Bill, I don't give a damn. But I'm going to go, and I'm going with my sister, she always wanted to go. And this time I'm going! Warmth, sunshine, just lying on the beach. Ah! You keep your miserable life. Take care of the family. Nurse your bursitis. Take naps 'cause you're dead tired. Enjoy yourself. I'm going to Florida, and I'm buying myself a bicycle.

Pt: What?

T: (A little miffed at the question) I'm buying myself a bicycle. I want to take rides in the evening, along the parkway, like everyone else. I used to do it when I was a kid, and I'm going to do it again now. Next spring. A shiny one, red, 10-speed, mine. With a lock and a carrier for egg salad sandwiches.

Pt: (Quietly) Can I come along?

T: Maybe.

The range of this method is quite broad. As the voice of the good form of the potential, the therapist carries out the experiencing in all sorts of situational contexts. In the following, the therapist is the voice of a deeper potential which, in its good form, occurs as a kind of delightful sense of befuddlement, a whimsical confusion, incapability, fecklessness. The therapist finds himself in a mundane problem situation, confronting the uncooperative refrigerator.

T: I'm in the kitchen here, and Liz is gone. She's at school for the evening class. I open the freezer, it's got the light on, the light works, but oh damn, look at the food! It is no longer frozen! It is melted! I see the water in the cellophane bags of the food which used to be frozen. Something is wrong with the freezer. Oh yes, something is wrong with the freezer section. The refrigerator part is working. See, I open it up and it is still working. But the freezer is screwed-up. That's a technical term because I don't know what the hell to do now and I think I'm going to panic.

Pt: Oh yeah! That's a bad moment for sure!

T: And I have no idea what to do, and I can't fix it, 'cause I think I got a bad problem here. It's called not knowing what the hell to do. I know nothing about this. I know about labor relations. I think I'm going to call a plumber, or Fred—he knows about plumbing, and I'll tell him that I know nothing about this. Help!

Pt: I can't repair anything.

T: Me neither! It's a damned mystery, all that damned mechanical shit in the refrigerator. I sink to my knees in front of the freezer, put my hands together in prayer. Please! Freezer, fix yourself! Heal! I don't know anything about fixing you. Please get better.

Pt: It's even when I take my car in. I don't know what the hell the mechanic is talking about. I try to bluff my way. I'm tall, I get confused. I don't know what the hell you're talking about. It's hard to say that. I don't know what you're talking about. I'm confused.

T: So am I. Let's go together, a couple of dummies.

As the voice of the deeper potential, the therapist may confidently order the patient to carry out the new behavior. Here is a woman who gets a sense of nausea and who vomits nearly every time her parents and husband push her to get pregnant. For a few moments, she was a deeper potential with a newfound sense of being tough and firm and standing up for herself. During these moments the nausea stopped. How nice! The therapist says the following:

T: I do not want a baby! Not now, maybe later.

Pt: (Giggles)

T: The answer is no, for the present, and if anyone tells me to have a baby, screw 'em. It's my decision, not theirs. Beatrice Johnson! I hereby order you to go home and tell Edgar the following. "I am not ready to get pregnant. We can discuss this matter each month, and when we both, underscore that, Edgar, *both* . . . decide we want a baby, then we shall try and get pregnant. Do you understand what I am saying, dummy?"

Pt: (Laughing) You want me to tell him that?

T: No, you keep your nausea and you throw up every day. I'll tell him. And when do you want me to tell Mom and Dad?

Pt: I will! I will! I'll do it!

T: Toss you for it.

Pt: It's my belly. I'll do it.

T: No more nausea.

In the following, the new experiencing consisted of forthright complaining, open yelling. It was wonderful. Applying this to the problem situation meant undergoing this experiencing in situations where his wife has to have evening appointments with two or three people from the office. It happens about once a week, and he typically pulls into an enveloping pouty mope:

T: Tonight you will go home and tell Christine the following: "No more announcing at dinner that you have an evening appointment. That is over. We are going to coordinate, 'cause it drives me wild to be told that. I hate it." Then you tell her that you are going to join the tennis club and play tennis in the evenings, and you'll need three or four hours to reserve a court. So no more last minute announcements from her.

Pt: Well, I don't know.

T: Good! The little fart head doesn't know. Great! Then don't! You sit in the corner and pout, get tight! I'll tell her! We'll both go home and I'll tell her! I want to play tennis anyhow!

Pt: I couldn't tell her that.

T: As a matter of fact, there's Joanne and Betty and Gabrielle. We could play doubles. They are good, and wonderful women.

Pt: I'll do it! I'll do it.

T: No! I'll do it.

Pt: Well, I'm the one who's mad!

T: The hell you are! I want to yell at Christine!

Pt: Me too!

T: OK! Deal! You bawl her out and I'll play tennis!

In this fifth method, the therapist is the voice and the identity of the new behaving part, separate and distinct from the ordinary, continuing patient. As the voice of the new behaving part, the therapist can thoroughly enjoy all sorts of new behaviors in all sorts of situational contexts. The ordinary patient-as-operating-domain sits on the sidelines, watching the integrated and actualized self go about its business of carrying out the new ways of being and behaving.

6) Be the Old Operating Domain Who Integratively Objects to the New Potential

After going through the four therapeutic steps, the patient may slide into being the new potential who is ready and willing to be and behave in new ways within the extratherapy world. "Something feels different!

I feel happy! I don't even feel like drinking anymore. I think I'll give up the booze! Yeah!" The patient has the audacity to be different, to behave in new ways. Sometimes, in the final step of the session one of the methods works and the patient may also dare to be different, to taste and sample new ways of being and behaving. So here the patient is, being the new potential, being and behaving in new ways.

In this sixth method, the therapist takes on the identity of the old operating domain and carries out an integrative objecting (chiding, ridiculing, disapproving, opposing, dissenting) relationship. In fact, the old operating domain is the enemy of any prospective change, for any genuinely deeper change will threaten its very life. Little changes that consolidate the operating domain are permitted. But the kind of changes that come from the deeper potentials are of a different order. The old operating domain knows that its very life and world are threatened, and therefore the old operating domain is quite entitled to object to any such changes.

The key to this method is that the therapist can do all this in an integrative relationship with the patient. The therapist can object playfully, can resist wholesomely, can bring up a hundred considerations in an almost whimsical, enjoyably open and harmless way. Thereby the patient is playfully pushed into the new ways of being and behaving. The therapist catastrophizes, yelps and yowls, fabricates horrible possibilities, scolds and finger points, sees the monstrous consequences, and generally backs the patient into experiencing the new ways of being and behaving.

If the patient is the new way, inclined to be and behave in new ways, the therapist speaks with the voice of the balance of the operating domain, with its lower lip out. If the separated husband really starts living with the new woman, the therapist is the balance of the personality, scolding the patient for even daring to consider such a rash action:

T: Now just a minute here! If you go live with her, that other woman, how can I still do things with Elaine, my almost ex-wife? Huh? You want an example? (As the old operating domain, the therapist speaks as "I.")

Pt: Uh huh.

T: Well, Elaine and I have to see the marriage counselor at 5:00. And we see her till about 6:00, and have supper together and we talk. Fine. How the hell can I do that if you are living with some new woman? Suppose you and she want to make dinner together and I want to go to the marriage counselor with Elaine? We can't do both! What about that?

Pt: Uh huh. Something's got to change.

T: Right, but what? Let's negotiate. You can go visit your new woman but don't live together.

Pt: That's not fair.

T: Negotiation's not fair. Remember, I have a whole game worked out with Elaine. So, OK? I go to the marriage counselor with Elaine?

Pt: How about we both get divorced and leave Elaine alone. (New behavioral possibilities are bubbling up.)

T: No way!

While the patient has the audacity of entering new experiential territory and telling her 28-year-old son to move out, the therapist objects vociferously. The patient moved out of the operating potential of control, hanging on, being a burden. She allowed her son to recover from a simple divorce by living with her in her small home. She wound her web around him, with his helpful posturings, and now she was being the new potential, a sense of letting go, a freeing.

Pt: (To her son) You may as well admit it, I'm a burden. I should be on my own and so should you. I run your life, yes I know. And I know you ask for it and you resent me. Hell, I'm an old woman, and I force you to take care of me. I tie you up in knots and we're bad for each other. I'm going to live here alone and you're going to leave.

T: What a thing to say! You can't do that! You're an old woman and he ought to take care of you. What are you saying?

Pt: (Laughing suddenly, but still addressing her son) I don't know. Maybe I'll get married! I'd rather have a husband than you. I have something to offer a man! Why not! I can cook and take care of things, and spend years taking care. I can meet men my age! That's a helluva better life! Yeah! Right!

As the new potential, the patient was able to visualize succulent little girls without having an erection. He tested himself with images of the most sexually exciting little children, tightly packed and seductive. Nothing. He was delighted. What was hanging in the air was the balance of his personality, the part which had sustained that way of being for so many tantalizing years. While the patient is being the newly integrative and actualized potential, the therapist speaks from the identity of the grumpy old operating domain.

T: I'm not all that sure I like this. What's going to happen to me? I get turned on by the right little girls. I roam the playgrounds and the neighborhoods and every so often, whammo! I find a juicy little morsel!

Pt: Grow up.

T: Grow up, grow up! Shit! That's easy for you to say. I want to fool around with little girls! You don't have any right to do this to me! You know what you're becoming? You know? You're going to be . . . NORMAL! What a fate! You're going to miss all the good old days. Come on, Ronald, fight this. Don't let them do this to us!

Pt: Shut up!

T: Ha Ha! I got you worried!

Pt: Yes! I used to spend maybe a week clean, and then it'd come over me again.

T: Good! I got a chance. Glory be!

Pt: You're impossible!

The channel of communication should be open and free and integratively friendly to grease the way to actual behavior change.

Seymour was furious in the session. He got really mad and screamed, an ear-piercing, shattering scream of rage. He later was telling himself that there are lots of times when he at least *feels* like screaming, maybe he could growl a little. The therapist exchanged places with the patient and spoke with the voice of the balance of the operating domain:

T: (Burlesqued gloominess) Well, frankly I think whenever anyone mistreats you, you should be depressed. Let your face hang down, like a Bassett hound. Look down, be real sad.

Pt: I do that!

T: Just promise me you'll always do that. You got me worried. And make sure you get people to yell at you. How about Genevieve. Is she going to keep yelling at you? She always used to. I like that.

Pt: She'll keep yelling.

T: Thank you. That reassures me a little. Is it OK if I say something?

Pt: What?

T: I think if you scream like that it sounds like a crazy person. Nobody screams like that.

Pt: How about a punch in the mouth?

T: You going to hit me, Seymour? Huh?

Pt: (Laughing) No, I mean if . . . oh never mind. I'll go home and practice looking fierce and growling.

T: Didn't I see you on Hill Street Blues?

Pt: Just a little screaming? One teenie weenie scream when someone drives me crazy?

T: One. Don't make a habit of it.

From the perspective of the operating domain, new experiencings in the session are dangerous. The therapist sees the awful behavioral possibilities, and describes exactly how that experiencing can be translated into real life current behaviors which would wreak havoc with the patient's life. "See what awful experiencings you have in you? See how they can occur as actual behaviors in your life? See how behaving in that way would wreck your life?" That is the work of the therapist speaking as the voice of the operating domain. It is interesting that one consequence is a sort of freeing relief. It is as if the defining of the actual, concrete, disastrous possibility is reassuring and liberating. Another consequence is that the patient typically is spurred into added behavioral possibilities.

During the session this competent woman, cold and capable, unflappably controlling, entered into an epoch of momentary chaotic confusion. She shook; her tongue was numb; she couldn't think straight; she could barely utter a sound. In the final phase of the session, the therapist says:

T: Now look! Remember when you were terrified, mixed up, frozen, couldn't talk?
Pt: I was a little girl and they caught me, yes.
T: Well, for God's sakes, keep that shit in here, in therapy. You'd better not ever be that way in your real life. If they saw you that way! If you were backing your proposal at the trustees meeting and, just for a second or so, you were scared and confused, really! Dead! You'd be dead! They'd see all the chinks in your armor! They'd look at each other and smile! You'd be finished!
Pt: (Calm and in good humor) That really got me. I don't know. Maybe it's not so bad. Not with the others at meetings. I'm not ready. But with Paul (her husband). He gets rattled, and confused, and he manages. I wondered why I'm like stone. It really wasn't all that bad. What the hell. I'm human. Even in board meetings. It's really not all that awful. Actually.

The high point of experiencing in the session was when he momentarily was being a small child, incontinent. It was the experiencing of urinating in his diapers, that instant of just letting go. The therapist is the operating domain who vividly witnesses the possibility of being this way in the patient's current life, and who playfully lets it occur:

T: You'll be at the tavern where you love to go with the guys after work. Then, as they're laughing and shooting the shit, you know what might happen? It will come over you and what happened to good old Steve? Why he's sliding onto the floor. He's lying on the floor, on his back,

arms flung every which way, gurgling like a baby and you'll, you'll
. . . you're peeing. He's peeing in his pants! Look at him!

Pt: Never!

T: At the restaurant, your wife's talking to you and then you go blank, the
food dribbles all over your mouth, and you babble like an infant! She'll
have to wipe the food off your jacket.

Pt: She'd divorce me!

T: That's OK, you'd never know. You'll be in a crib, playing with your toes.
Someone'll have to tell you when you get older, if you get older. Maybe
you'll just be a complete baby.

Pt: That might not be so bad.

T: Who said it's bad?

The therapist starts with the new experiencing in the session, and
celebrates it, has a festival of playing with the monstrous possibility
of actually behaving on that basis in the current life. What if that experiencing were translated into actual behaviors in the immediate
world? See what would happen! If the patient tastes what it is like to
give in, allow herself to be caught, is controlled and manipulated, then
what would it mean if she allowed this to take the form of actual behavior in her life?

T: Just give Sam and Jerry the controlling interest in the firm. Don't fight
them. They are tough and they have a lot of moxie. Hand it over to
them. Don't make a profit, just do what they want. Give them the controlling interest.

Pt: In my next life maybe. Maybe in a hundred years.

T: You're 46 years old! Retire! Be nice! Give in gracefully! You got a 26-year-
old daughter, and she is pregnant. You'll be a great gramma. Give in!
You can still go to the meetings. Just smile and keep your mouth shut.

Pt: You know, I think of that! I have thoughts of doing just that! I thought
I was losing my mind. So maybe not. I never mentioned that to anyone.
I thought of that. I'd never do it, but I thought of getting out of the
business. I did!

One procedure is for the old operating domain to cling to itself for
the rest of its life. See the image of oneself as an old woman, relentlessly
unchanged. When the patient is veering toward a new way of being,
the therapist speaks for the operating domain who wishes to continue
and continue and continue. Florence is in her middle thirties, and she
spends most of her life with her parents, hovering between being
dangerously close to them and taking backward steps away from them.
She always hovers in the middle ground, never going too far one way

or the other. In the session she exists as the deeper potential, free of both sides of this, being a significantly different person who no longer is caught between being too close and too removed. It felt wonderful, and she was seriously considering remaining this qualitatively new person, behaving in this qualitatively new way. The therapist spoke with the voice of the ordinary, continuing Florence who is determined to remain this way forever:

T: I don't like the way you are. It interferes with my plans for the future. You're wrecking my plans.
Pt: What plans? What?
T: When I'm 83 years old, and my mom and dad are dead and buried, I look forward to driving my old Plymouth to the cemetery. And as I get closer and closer, my rickety old body'll start to shake a little more and more, and my old car will slow down, and when I get right near the cemetery, I'll put the car in reverse and very slowly back up 'cause I don't want to touch their gravestones. Yech! And everyday I'll start out and spend my afternoons going toward them and away from them . . . and those are my plans, and you're wrecking my plans! I won't be able to do it anymore.
Pt: (Laughing) Oh, you poor old dear. I'll visit their graves every so often, and I'll get someone to be with you so you won't back into someone on the road.

In speaking as the old operating domain, the therapist fabricates awful situations and awful behaviors as the grotesque form of the prospective changes. In its bad form, the potential had started as fears of being enclosed, and transformed into a new potential including good feelings of being reached, gotten to, affected, naked, free of defenses. While the patient enjoys this new experiencing, the therapist concocts ways in which the patient can bring about horrible forms of the experiencing in grotesque situations:

T: I know what you should do. Hire a bunch of dwarfs, tell them to put on scary masks, pay them $50 each, about a dozen of them, and tell them that to earn the money they have to swarm all over you till you suffocate. They aren't supposed to stop till you are completely helpless and almost dead. How about that?
Pt: Yikes! I used to scream bloody murder when I'd walk through a field and grasshoppers would get on me. I couldn't get them off, and I remember my brother used to push me into the closet and shut the door. I'd go crazy!
T: Is he still around? I know the closet, and I could get about a thousand big hungry grasshoppers and . . .

Pt: I'm sorry I mentioned that!

T: I can see it now! Can I watch?

Pt: No! You'd enjoy it too much. I'll get Terri to sit on me. She's big, and she can swarm all over me. And I'll let people touch me. A handshake, and touching. My hands are itchy to touch. Terri to cuddle and be all over me. Sounds wonderful.

T: No fair, you're going to like that!

Pt: Sure am!

T: Curses!

The therapist may be the voice of the operating domain which is scared that things can get out of hand, the new ways of being will go too far. The patient will become wild or frenzied or out of control. Awful consequences will occur. Here is the operating domain which imagines extreme possibilities, gross exaggerations, catastrophic consequences. What starts out as little behavioral changes, the therapist energizes into gross and dangerous possibilities. Radical new behavioral possibilities are bent and redirected into their monstrous form. John had opened up a sense of real rage, and briefly expressed how great it would be to hurl a cup across the room and smash it. He enjoyed what it felt like to throw the cup against the wall and considered the possibility of having a few old cups handy in the kitchen when he got really worked up.

T: You know what's going to happen? Next thing you're going to get a machine gun and kill people. You're out of control, you aggressive monster! You ought to be locked up. You can't go around shooting people!

Pt: Shooting people? Shit! I just want to throw a dinky cup against the wall.

T: See! It's starting! Next it will be little furry animals, and then . . . you know what comes next! Mailmen who deliver bills! Visitors to the house who don't act the way you want! You'll throw innocent little children against the wall and smash their little brains apart. You MONSTER! WHY DID YOU KILL MY BABY?

Pt: CALM DOWN, WILL YOU?

T: No! You're a homicidal maniac!

Pt: You're crazier than I am!

T: See! You admit it! You're crazy! Lock him up! Lock him up!

Pt: All this from a silly cup? How about if I tell my wife that I "feel" like smashing a cup. I won't even do it.

T: Well, OK, if you say it gently. Don't scream.

Pt: A little annoyance maybe?

T: Just a little, OK.

The balance of the personality is entitled to be quite threatened by the prospective new ways of being and behaving. Not only may the balance of personality bring up all sorts of frightening and worrisome possibilities, it may use its big guns:

T: If you really start being that way, I'm going to have a relapse, see! I'm going to have an asthma attack. I haven't had one in years, but I'll do it! You'll see!

T: Go ahead. Go on! You do that and I'll, I'll . . . I'll be depressed and suicidal again! That's what! I'll kill myself! And it'll be your fault. Just think about that, Dorothy! I was suicidal before and I can be that way again!

T: Remember when you started therapy? Your life was falling apart and you were showing signs of crumbling into lunacy? Well, it's starting again! I feel unsure of myself. Mixed up, shaky. The world's starting to be scary again. It's all coming back. How am I doing? Scaring you? Ha ha ha . . . just watch out!

The therapist promotes behavioral change by speaking from the perspective of the integrated operating domain. The therapist responds and reacts to the patient who is leaning toward changes, who is considering possible behavioral changes. The difference that makes a difference is that the therapist-as-operating-domain is on good terms with the new patient who is veering toward possible behavioral change. The therapist can be welcoming and accepting, honestly worried and concerned, receptive and genuinely empathic toward the part of the patient that is considering new ways of being and behaving. In this way, the therapist can visualize the pessimistic destiny or fate, the therapist can invent all sorts of far-out and catastrophic situations, the therapist can define the awful consequences, the dangerous possibilities. And thereby the therapist opens the way to the promotion of possible new behavioral ways of being.

7) Use the New Way of Behaving in the External World

The steps of the session serve to invite the patient into new ways of behaving. As the patient carries forward experiencing, engages in the internal encounter, and enters into being the deeper potential, the chances are very high that the patient will behave in some new way.

But these new behaviors occur in the session and not in the extratherapy world. If we look carefully at the session, there is almost always some specific new behavior. It may last only a few seconds. It may be natural and appropriate in the session. But here it is. The task of the therapist is to seize that new behavior and put it to use in the extratherapy world (Lankton & Lankton, 1983; Wolstein, 1965). The seventh method shows how to carry out that task. It is divided into three sub-methods.

(a) Fabricate situations in which to use the behavioral achievement from the session. This method starts with what may be termed a "behavioral achievement" in the session. That is, the patient actually behaved in some new way, and, what is more, the accompanying feelings were good ones. These are indeed behavioral achievements, for the patient genuinely accomplished something here in the session. It may have occurred in carrying forward the potential, in the integrative encounter, or especially in being the deeper potential, but here it is—a behavioral achievement.

For example, in the session the patient was able to tell his mother that he loved her, and really feel it. Only in the session was she able to let tears come as she shared the joy of her sister's wonderful forthcoming marriage. Only in the session did he break out of his meat and potatoes meals and freely sample all sorts of exotic foods. In the session she could plead for help and be a frightened and confused little kid. In the session he could say, with good feelings, "That's enough! Now shut up!" or excitingly, "I did it! I finally did it! I'm great!" or firmly, "No! I will not! No! No! No!" Only in the context of an encounter with the therapist did he really get mad and explode in anger. Only as the deeper potential did she openly berate and criticize the other person. It is as if the new way of being and behaving is a precious gift; the challenge is to let this new way of being and behaving come to life in the patient's actual external world.

How does the therapist identify life situations in which the new behavior is to occur? Suppose that the behavioral achievement consisted of saying, "No! I will not! No! No! No!" Here is a delightful new behavior of which the patient is the proud owner. Where is it to be used in the external world? Working down from the picture of the directions of potential change, there are several situational contexts in which the new behavioral achievement may be used:

• Use the new behavior in the patient's favorite "problem" situations, when she feels miserable and rotten in her own way. Some of these consist of appropriate situational contexts, like when the ex-husband decides to drop in, intrusively, ostensibly to "talk." In these situations she feels tight, scared, angry, boxed in, thoroughly miserable and rotten. The possibility is of facing the bastard squarely upon arrival, and determinedly belting him with, "No way! Never! Get the hell out! No talking! No! NO NO NO NO!!!" There are also externalized deeper potentials, figures whom she invests with the deeper properties, and with whom relationships are rotten. Her externalized deeper potential occurs in the form of her imperious aunt, the matriarch of the family, whose every slight wish is an order. What would it be like to confront the old auntie and to attack her with "No, I will not! No, no, no!" These are situations where the new behavior might be used.

• Use the behavioral achievement in situations when the patient's ordinary ways of being and behaving try to say no, but always in hurtful and painful ways. When her supervisor loads her with extra work and expects her to do special favors for him, she gets very tired, her stomach muscles tighten up, she feels physically ill. Instead of starting down that path, the possibility is facing him immediately and saying, "What? More extra work? No way! No! I will not! Impossible!"

• Use the behavioral achievement in situations where the patient ordinarily sidesteps and avoids with accompanying bad feelings. How does the patient indicate no without directly expressing no? When her ex-husband brings up the possibility of having Jon and Ann over the weekend, she typically indicates that she would like to but cannot because she really should shop for the new bunkbeds for the kids. This is a saying no in an indirect, muted way. Instead, the therapist fabricates the situation in which the patient openly and directly says, "No! I will not! No! No! I hate spending weekends alone, fretting, getting little sleep! No way! No!"

• Use the behavioral achievement in situations which figured prominently earlier in the session. The opening portion of the session revolved around situations at work where she was annoyed with people who signed up for committees but who didn't bother coming or who arrived just before the committee broke up. "No! You can't do this! No way! If you're going to be on the committee, attend meetings! No! Not allowed! No way! No!"

• Use the behavioral achievement in current versions of earlier situations in which the patient blew the behavioral opportunity. When Sherry was 14, the situation involved her mother's volunteering her in a manipulative manner. Mother tells the neighbor, in front of Sherry, "Of course Sherry would love to babysit for you." Sherry did nothing. In the session, the new behavioral achievement exploded: "No! I will not! No!" But in the actual earlier moment, she only froze. In her life today there are many situations where others manipulatively volunteer her services, and in these situations the new behavioral achievement is marvelously appropriate. Sherry's adolescent daughter reassures her girlfriend on the phone that her mother will take them to the party. Sherry's brother offhandedly mentions that Sherry wouldn't mind making coffee and "a little something to eat" for the poker group he has tomorrow. Sherry's mother informs her that she wouldn't mind taking care of their cat while Mom and Dad go to Florida for a week. "No! I will not! Never! No way! Hell no!"

• Use the behavioral achievement in current versions of earlier situations in which the patient behaved that way magnificently. One of her preciously delightful memories was when she was around seven years old and she recollects her mother, her aunt, and her six-year-old cousin visiting. The aunt was going to take her daughter to a play, and Sherry's mother was holding Sherry's favorite dress. "Tell your cousin that she can have the dress, Sherry." At that moment, Sherry grabbed the dress, was enraged, screamed "NO!", planted her feet firmly, and dared anyone to take it away from her. It felt simply wonderful. Starting from there, the therapist fabricated current situations characterized by others' appropriating her things, taking over her possessions, intruding into her territory. In each of these current situations, the therapist inserted the new way of behaving: "No! No way! I will not allow this! No!"

• Use the behavioral achievement in fresh new situations where the patient actively arranges conditions conducive for the new behavior. Here is where the therapist is to be creative and inventive, with a healthy dash of whimsical unreality. Yet the serious theme is that the patient can construct situations, can take an active hand in moulding situations to enable the behavioral achievement to occur. There are always protest meetings, dissidents being dissenting. Ask around to see what group is getting together to protest, and mix in with them during the protest. Be the cheerleader: "No! We protest! We will not!

We will never give in! No way!" Keep speeding and going through red lights until some policeman follows you, tells you to pull over, and asks for your driver's license. Then you look outraged at him and say, "No! I will not! No! No way!"

In inserting the behavioral achievement into the external world, the therapist may take the role of the part of the patient which is ready and willing to be this way. "I'm going to tell my mom that I love her. I am! I'm going to do it tonight or tomorrow." The therapist speaks as the "I." Or the therapist may carry the patient through the new way of being, describing in concrete detail the actual situation, the detailed minutiae of confessing her love to her mother. It does not matter which role the therapist takes as long as the therapist starts with the behavioral achievement in the session and then fabricates situations where it can be used in the extratherapy world.

T: You cried! You had real tears rolling down your cheeks. I was here, I saw them. You cried, and what's more, you felt great when you were crying and even after. I know. You cried, you can cry.

Pt: I know.

T: Here, you cry here. I know you almost come close in your life, and you don't, you stop. "No crying. Not allowed here." You verge, you start, and there are almost tears.

Pt: I can't even remember. I can't. I don't even know when I cried. Here, I know I cry here. Come close? You know when? I saw the pope on television, and he, he (laughs) was humming along with the little kids singing camp songs. No! He was tapping his foot. Right! They showed him, his robes, he was tapping, shaking his leg with the music. I got tears in my eyes. I was sitting there with Edna and I got tears in my eyes! Right!

T: So where the hell can this guy let himself cry? He can cry, and once in a while he almost, he can cry, where? There must be somewhere. I know! When he watches a movie? Something on television. . . . Damn, there must be someplace.

Pt: When I get mad at one of the kids—Jenny's five and Donald is just seven. I spank 'em or scream at them. And I get up sometimes in the morning and go into their bedroom and see them sleeping.

T: Oh here it comes. He's going to kneel down by their beds, and there will be tears, like when he talks about it in therapy, and he's going to have drops of water on his face, cheeks, and he'll run his fingers over their face and he'll put his head against Donald's face, and he cuddles him, and there are tears, and if he's ready, he says, "I love you," and there are light little tears on his face.

Pt: Yeah, yeah. I am. I feel that way. I am. I love them so much. And with
Edna. I have a real bad day? We get the kids to bed and we sit and have
a beer, maybe two or three, before bed. And I get quiet, and I wish I
could be like a kid, put my head in her lap and tell her I think I'm in
over my head in this contracting shit, too much for me, and I want to
just cry sometimes. I feel like a kid and I feel like crying. I could. I could
do it, and even . . . I don't go out to the cemetery where my mom and
dad are. I stay away. I get to feeling real blue sometimes and I wish they
were here. I think about going to the cemetery. But I don't. I feel like
going out there and being alone with them and spilling my troubles to
them, and (he is crying) talking to my mom and dad (more tears). I still
have them in a way . . .

Whether or not therapeutic work began with problem situations,
behavioral achievements may be inserted into the problem situation.
The therapist describes the precise problem situation, and then the opportunity is to use the behavioral achievement on that precise situational context. For example, being the good form of the deeper potential carried through to her screaming out in sheer anger. She had been
talking about a friend's son who ran through her flower bed. In ac-
tuality she said nothing as she saw him do that, and was nasty and
critical of the friend who mildly chided the son. But in the session the
patient was mad. "You little bastard! Get the hell out of there! Damn
you!" Of course she never talked that way, but in the session it felt
great. How wonderful it would be to get mad. Problem situations for
her consisted of weekly visits to her parents who exerted head-pounding
pressures on her as they pushed her on everything from her lazy husband to her working, from the way she dressed to her not having children. The behavioral achievement was introduced into the problem
situation.

T: You little bastard! Get the hell out of there! What a fantastic feeling that is!
Pt: I wish I could say that!
T: Your wish is granted. There! Poof! DO IT!
Pt: I'm still furious at the little bastard!
T: Yeah! Too bad there's no place for you to say that and really mean it!
Pt: Well, if he ever tramples on my bed again, I'll nail him.
T: I got it! How's this? Ask sweet darling little Brad if he will do you a favor.
    Take him outside and tell him to tromp through the garden. Just to do
    you a favor. Then, when he does it . . .
Pt: (Laughing) Damn you! Get the hell out of there! (Laughs more) A game!
    Yeah, a game! I can do it! But what if he wants to play some other game,
    like, I don't know.

T: Risky, eh!

Pt: Brad's not the problem. My Dad's the problem.

T: I know, let me have a whack at it. Sure as hell Dad's going to start in on you this weekend. He'll start putting the old pressure on. You ought to have children. What is this working stuff? You aren't getting any younger. Pretty soon you're going to be too old. Then you say . . .

Pt: Damn you! Get the hell out of my life!

T: Get the hell out of my bed, Daddy!

Pt: (Laughing) Yeah! Stay in your own bed. Leave me alone! Just leave me the hell alone! Don't trample on my life — or I'll start walking all over your life, you bastard!

T: Fantastic! I like this!

Pt: Shit! Half the world walks all over my flower bed. Damn you, you bastard, get the hell out of here! I love it! I could say it three times a day and it would probably fit! At work. At home. At work! Oh yeah, at work! Damn you, get the hell out of here! It feels right! Damn you, get the hell out of here! Mother, if you're going to come to my house, call first! Don't just intrude! You pushy bitch! Get the hell out of here. (Laughs.)

Sometimes the situation is fabricated from a combination of a person, who is the central theme of the session, and the new deeper potential. Throughout the session, the central figure was her explosive, animal-like, low-class, rude father. The new deeper potential consisted of the experiencing of her own grossly explosive, unmannered, rude, earthy animalness. Combining the two led to the following fabricated situation into which the new way of behaving was inserted:

T: I am with my Dad. I went over to his apartment, called first. I arranged for the visit, and I'm bringing him a fifth of whisky. Really good, aged whisky. Here you are, you old fart! I never gave you a gift. Well, here.

Pt: Daddy. (Spoken quietly, almost murmured)

T: I never asked you. Since Mom died. Are you getting any ass?

Pt: I can just picture him falling over!

T: Get up! Get up! What's the matter? Are you shy? How's your sex life?

Pt: How about inviting me over for supper sometime? I want to see what the hell you're like. Hmmm. I never had supper with him. Ever! Never! Mom's dead, and we never had a meal together, the two of us. That's weird! I think I'm going to invite him to come over for a meal. Strange. That's really strange. I never had a meal with him! I'm going to invite him over. That'd be something! I don't even know what he's like. What the hell's he like? I want to know. I never had a meal with him, just the two of us. That's really weird. Never? Never. I'm going to invite him over. Sure I am.

Fabricating a situation may begin with little more than a delightful interpersonal behavior uncovered in childhood. Therapeutic work led to an experiencing of warmly spontaneous companionship as a 10-year-old. The behavior consisted of a pleasantly sexualized bear-hugging, clapping one another on the back. Since then, everything disappeared, and we are left with a pleasant childhood behavior and the challenge of fabricating new situations where this leftover behavior may be used.

T: You have a great feeling, solidness with a guy, you and me, together, the two of us, closeness. And you even have a way of letting that happen. You grab another guy and you touch. You bearhug each other or physically hold one another. You know the problem? Where the hell could you feel something like this and do something like this today? Anywhere? Look around.

Pt: (Snickers) Hold some other guy? I don't know. My wife maybe, and Jessica and I don't do that, and I don't feel that way with her. But yeah, it was great doing it with Henry. But I was maybe 10 years old. And we were buddies. I have no buddy today. I don't. I'm married and have kids. Little kids. (Pause)

T: What a shame!

Pt: It just wouldn't happen.

T: I know. What a damned pity. Here you got all this in you and it is just possible to bearhug another guy, but nowhere in your life, nowhere.

Pt: Even if I tried, wanted to a lot, no place. It wouldn't fit.

So true. Here is where the therapist shakes up his life a bit. The net result is to open up the possibility of making some changes in the kind of life he has built around himself.

T: You know, if they told you that you have one week. One week. Or they put you away forever, down in the deepest hole. You must feel solidness and doing it together, you and the other one, the two of you, and that happens when you bearhug one another. You know what? I think you couldn't do it. With no one, nowhere.

Pt: Well I don't know anyone.

T: You're finished.

Pt: My kids are too young. I have no neighbors like that. I don't do anything with guys alone. I don't bowl or go fishing or . . . and my sister's in Vancouver. I . . . no. No one at work. Nurses, the doctors. My office. Jesus, I don't have any idea.

T: There are probably fellows right now in town, feeling a fantastic good feeling of buddy, me and you, closeness, the two of us, and the two of you will stagger around, never meeting. But your life won't let it happen? It won't!

Pt: No.

T: (Fabricating playful situations) Learn how to play tennis, doubles. You and your partner work your way through a tournament, win it, look at each other as buddies, really achieved together, and bearhug.

Pt: Sure, by next week.

T: Oh yeah! Hire a buddy! That's it. Get either an actor or hire a fellow who is an expensive paid sexual companion, a male whore. Be a little kinky. Tell him that the two of you will be building a fence together and then when you're done, feel real buddy buddy and hug each other.

Pt: I don't even work like that at the hospital. If I hugged a nurse or another doctor they'd think I went bolo or something.

T: Advertize! Let's see. One guy, ready and eager to be close and feel buddy buddy with another, wants a partner, someone to be close with, and must bearhug.

Pt: You know what I'd get. Crazies answering a gay kinky ad.

T: That's it! Be gay! And find a real buddy who can be your friend.

Pt: My life, I have no one like that. Like a brother.

T: You could end up doing anything, the two of you, you and any other person. When you do something together, feel close and warm and hug.

Pt: (Laughs) After every operation! We could all hug! (Laughs) That'd be something! They'd throw us out of the hospital!

He is beginning to entertain the possibility of letting it happen in risky ways.

T: (Laughing) And after every committee meeting. We accomplished it, together. Oh let's clasp one another!

Pt: They'd run me out of the neighborhood. Watch out, here he comes. He'll feel close and hug you. Aren't there groups like that? Encounter groups!

T: Sure! That's it! Why didn't I think of it! Wait, I think I have a list somewhere. There's groups for sex and groups for yelling at each other, and for touching-feeling and yeah, here it is, there's a group for you. "Closeness and buddy buddy. Closeness and being together and group hugs!" That's it.

Pt: I'd rather start with Jessica and the kids. Why not? We get loose and silly. (We have opened up the possibility of inserting the behavioral achievement into the external world.)

We began with the cancer and the fighting against it. Then we moved into the deeper experiencing, a sense of peaceful, trusting giving in. He curled up, cried softly, allowed himself to be enfolded in peaceful death. The therapist fabricated this way of being within today's context:

T: How nice this is. So peaceful. So lovely. Listen, Laura, old wife, just let me sleep here in your lap. Put your arms around me, yes. Pat my head just a little. There. My body is starting to feel so heavy, and restful, and peaceful. Quiet, all quiet. Ah yes, yes, I can smell you, feel your heart beating. Mommy! Hmmm. So nice.

Pt: (With light tears in his voice) We have separate beds. Me, I was the one. I did a bad thing. Years ago. Twelve years, married, and I never curled up, held, never held.

T: Just all curled up. Thanks, Laura. You feel so good. Tomorrow I'll do whatever you want. So sleepy. I want to die for about ten hours. Sleep. In your lap. Little baby.

Pt: I want a big bed, the two of us. Ours. I look at her sometimes and I don't want to have supper in the dining room. I want to put my head in your lap and just tell you about what happened to me. I want to talk to you. (He is now crying more.) I am crying. Crying. I feel so good. I feel so very good. Like a happy little baby. We have years yet. Me and my cancer, just being here, lying down, and you're holding me. I love you. I really love you.

The therapist starts with the new behavioral achievement of the patient in the session, one which felt good. Then the therapist uses it in some fabricated situation in the patient's world, utilizing any of the procedures for defining specific situations for this patient right now. The therapist may give the new behavior life and form by serving as the model or exemplar. Or the therapist may carry the patient through by careful and detailed description. In any case, the new behavior is thereby transferred or generalized from the behavioral achievement in the session to the external world.

(b) Recycle old effective behaviors as substitutes for the current problematic behaviors in the situation. Rather than some behavioral achievement in the session, this method begins with an effective behavior from the past. Given the same or similar situations, then and now, we uncover old effective behaviors, recycle them, and substitute them for the current problematic behavior in the situation.

This method combines one proposition from Ericksonian hypnotherapy and one from Wolpean desensitization. My impression is that one of the propositions used by Erickson was to recycle childhood behaviors that were effective and to arrange circumstances so that they are used in the patient's current life (Erickson, 1980; Erickson & Rossi, 1981; Lankton & Lankton, 1983; Zeig, 1982). Wolpe's desensitization therapy is based at least in part on the proposition that prospective effective behaviors reciprocally inhibit the current problematic behavior (Wolpe, 1958, 1973). Our method combines the two propositions.

For example, when he got into trouble as a child—when he broke a window or spilled milk on the table—he would face the offended party straight on and give her a favorite marble or a picture that he drew, saying forthrightly, "I am sorry. I did a bad thing." In his current life, when he gets into trouble, he gets drunk, wallows in gloomy self-recrimination, and feels rotten. The method calls for the patient's handling the current situation by recycling the old effective behavior, i.e., forthrightly confessing, saying he is so sorry, and giving a meaningful personal gift.

T: It's going to cost you $32. That's the cost. On York Street, only about four blocks from your apartment, is a florist. It has a white front, and it is open until 5:30 tonight. When you leave here, you drive there and ask the lady for $28 worth of roses. She has lovely roses now. There is a card which goes with the roses. You write on the card, "I am sorry," and sign your first name, "Joel." The lady wraps flowers in very attractive packages. Then you pay for them and you give her a $4 tip. That's $32. You drive to your apartment house. Go to the apartment next door, ring the bell. Mrs. Anderson will answer. She's very old, and she seldom goes out. You hand her the flowers and you say, "Mrs. Anderson, I am sorry that I kept you up most of the night with the loud music and the noise." By then it will be around 5 or 5:15. If you feel that you then want to get drunk, go ahead, but only after you do what I told you to do.

Jerry drove a truck for a construction company. His awful headaches started when he made a terrible mistake on the job. He had just deposited a load of bricks at 1217 Donnell Street. An hour later, looking through the billings, he saw that they were to have been delivered at 1217 O'Connell Street. Bam, the awful headache started, there at the back of his head. His headaches were driving him crazy. They started in such situations and lasted for at least a few days, almost incapacitating him. In the session, Jerry lived in very old scenes when he was around six years old. When Jerry got in trouble, when he did something wrong—like stealing money from Mommy's purse or pushing down a neighborhood kid and making him cry—so that he knew he was going to get yelled at by his parents, Jerry would do a strange thing. With sheer glee, thoroughly reveling in every nuance, he would go down to the basement and urinate on the floor. Why he would do that in the basement and not upstairs, he never knew. Why he would do it at all, he was never really sure—though counselors and friends and the family had all sorts of good explanations. In fact, one of the reasons this behavior was so strange was that Jerry was a model child. He never did anything wrong, ever. Well, practically never. Living through these childhood scenes was the experiential highlight of the session. Then Jerry slid into glumness about his headaches and the job, and his half-hearted inclination to stay away from work because of the headache.

T: Jerry, you have a basement at home, and you're proud of the recreation room you built there.
Pt: (He suddenly broke into laughter.) Oh no!
T: (The laughter was infectious, and the therapist was laughing as she said . . .) You got it. As soon as you do something wrong on the job, that instant, wherever the hell you are or whatever you're doing, go home, right home, down to the basement, whip it out, and splash, right on the floor. And leave it there! Piss on it!
Pt: (Jerry's laughing was so hard that he was blubbering, and he nearly rolled out of the chair. He said sporadic words, but they were unintelligible. It seemed to be something about rushing home to beat the headache, driving like a maniac, and then the laughing was almost uncontrollable when he mentioned that he could drive over to his parents' place instead of his. He toned down somewhat when he mentioned that the headache was now gone, and maybe just thinking about peeing in the basement would work.)

You know that wonderful sense of one-on-one competition when you were a child and you played pingpong with your friend? You were pretty good. Remember when you would free-fall into the hay? What a joyous sense of adventure when a few of you ride your bikes out to the country, with everyone having a packed lunch, and riding just to explore. Therapeutic work uncovers all sorts of old effective behaviors which can be recycled in the current world. Some may have occurred a few years ago, in adolescence, in later childhood, or when you were just an infant. Some may have occurred in your primitive world from a few years before conception to a few years after birth, when the effective behaviors were carried out by a parent rather than by you yourself. There is a rich reservoir of old effective behaviors, all of which may be recycled and substituted for current problem behaviors in current problem situations.

(c) Fabricate situations in which to use the acquired "therapy process skills." There is a rather extensive literature based on the idea that there are explicit skills which constitute the role of psychotherapeutic patient, that these skills are teachable and learnable, and that therapy moves along better when patients are competent in the use of these skills (Imber, Pande, Frank, Hoehn-Saric, Stone, & Wargo, 1970; Jacobs, Charles, Jacobs, Weinstein, & Mann, 1972; Lennard & Bernstein, 1960; Orne & Wender, 1968; Pierce, Schauble, & Farkas, 1970; Sloane, Cristol, Pepernik, & Staples, 1970; Truax & Wargo, 1968; Truax, Wargo, & Volksdorf, 1970; Warren & Rice, 1972; Yalom, Harts, Newell, & Rand, 1967). If we look closely at virtually any therapy, there are quite explicit skills that their patients acquire, skills in being a good patient who fits into the sheer process of therapy. I refer to these as "therapy process skills."

Gestalt patients typically acquire the skill of taking the role of significant other persons, objects, or body parts. Psychoanalytic-psychodynamic patients acquire the skill of talking without censoring thoughts, as well as the skill of recognizing and labeling blocks, stops, and obstructions. Psychotherapies are replete with all sorts of skills that patients learn, from hitting a mat when they are angry to gazing straightforwardly into the other person's eyes, from having regular hours where they talk to someone about themselves, to self-relaxation skills, from trying out the feared act little by little, to talking about feelings (Singer, 1980).

Experiential therapy joins with other therapies in providing its own array of "therapy process skills." In the process of experiential psychotherapy, patients learn such skills as stepping aside and having playfully integrative reactions to oneself, being aware of and describing immediate bodily sensations and spontaneous images, allowing bodily sensations and states to become fuller and deeper, concentrating attention on a meaningful focal center, using bodily sensations to monitor ongoing behavior, working therapeutically with one's own dreams, sharing the experiencings occurring in another person, penetrating through threat to the critical moments, entering into deeper potentials (alternative states of experiencing), engaging in integrative encounters, entering into stronger and more intense levels of experiencing, saying it openly and directly, reversing what others do to the patient.

This is a kind of incidental learning that patients gain as they go through experiential psychotherapy. The key is that many of these skills are effectively useful as new ways of being and behaving in the external world. It is a form of simple behavioral skill training in the explicit skills which constitute part of the very process of experiential psychotherapy. When patients are using these skills in the moments of strong experiencing, especially in being the deeper potential, then the stage is set for the patient to taste the possibility of using these skills in the external world.

For example, experiential patients learn a number of skills which enable the patient to give in to experiential states and bodily sensations which are immediately present. If there is a bodily sense of dizziness, patients learn how to let that deepen and intensify. If there is an inner pull to feel concerned and genuinely interested, patients learn to give in and let that occur. If there is a sense of sexuality, patients learn to be passive to it and to let it grow. All of the therapy process skills have generous implications for actual new ways of being and behaving in the patient's world.

But where? In what situations? The answer is that the therapist fabricates the same seven kinds of situations as were described in regard to the use of behavioral achievements in the session. If experiencing is strong as the patient is using a given "process skill," then the picture of the directions of potential change accommodates all sorts of appropriate situations. Here is an illustration:

T: Finally you can talk about old Richard, and play with him, comment on what a self-centered spoiled brat he can be. I know it. You know it, you might as well admit it.

Pt: I never did anything like that at home, or with anyone.

T: And it's about time. There you are at home, and you expect your wife to get up and get the ketchup just 'cause the spoiled brat wants it. (Here is one fabricated situation.)

Pt: "Thank you, Maude. Thanks for catering to the spoiled brat." I could never say that.

T: You just did!

Pt: I'm a spoiled brat. I *am* a brat! I am self-centered.

T: Maude, would you get me the ketchup? Jesus that sounds self-centered.

Pt: Maude, please get me the ketchup? 'Cause I'm a self-centered little brat. Yeah! I am! I really am! I'm a self-centered brat. Do this for me. Hell, it's OK to admit that I'm a self-centered brat? I sound like a baby. I really sound like a little kid. Maude, I act like a little baby. Maude, half the time with you I act like a baby. You know, there are lots of times when Maude's thinking that, she gives me a look, and my kids think that, and it's in the air, and I can say it out loud. Well, I'm a little brat. That sounds like a spoiled kid. Yeah! I can comment on the way I am and it's OK. I never did that! I never did! I felt it, but I never said it! Ain't I a spoiled brat? Yes, I am a baby! It's not so hard!

T: Hey, Maude! You agree with me? Don't I sound like a spoiled brat? I expect you to do things for me. Aren't you married to a little baby?

Pt: She'd agree! I know she would! What the hell!

Patients acquire the skill of openly acknowledging thoughts, ideas, fantasies, and impulses that are bizarre, risky, loose, crazy, a little wacky, far out. They learn to express them, to share them, to have fun with them, to admit and confess them. It is a learned "therapy process skill" which could be used in their extratherapy world—especially if the patient, in the session, felt happy and playfully comfortable in doing so.

T: You were laughing! I heard you! You were actually happy about noticing the way Sally (the patient) is weird, I mean she does some pretty weird things!

Pt: I have delusions! I see things!

T: OK, but don't tell anyone! Keep it to yourself, you idiot! You want to get thrown into the monkey ward?

Pt: I saw blood, I really saw blood there, on the white drapes, and I thought something had bled on the drapes! They're 20 feet long, in a huge restaurant! I really thought!

T: OK, now admit it, this isn't the first time in your life that you were bonkers. I know that. You're probably going to have one or two moments in the next couple of weeks, moments when you . . . you know, don't say. You have a weird thought, or you walk down the wrong street, or you think your name is Susan or Kelly instead of Sally, or you hear voices and no one does. A-ha! That proves you are out of your mind! It's going to happen!

Pt: Sure! I go to a restaurant, and I sometimes forget what I am. I don't remember what I order. I forget! When they bring it, I have no idea that's what I ordered.

T: (Whispering) So you lean over to . . .

Pt: Harvey, no! With Celia and Catherine. I say, "I have no idea what I ordered. I have no memory of ordering anything."

T: (Carrying on as the patient) . . . does that mean I'm deranged or is that the second sign of a fried brain?

Pt: I hear voices! I do! When I listen to Harvey reading the book at night. We read together. Sometimes I drift off and I really hear a voice inside my head. It's like a real person, and it says, "He's a fat slob" or "His voice is grating." All right, if I tell him, Harvey, I hear voices, and I really do! He'll try to understand. Oh my Lord, he'll really try hard. The trou-

ble is that he's a nice guy, but he's . . . Harvey is well-meaning. He's
DUMB! "Harvey, I hear voices when you read! I just heard a voice in
my head—and DON'T TRY TO UNDERSTAND, YOU DUMMY."
(She starts laughing.)

T: Don't laugh, that'll give it all away. You *are* nuts, you nut!

Pt: Yes! I think I'll tell Celia that I saw blood on the drapes. Maybe she did
too! Oh, maybe she didn't! I got hallucinations. Celia, you got hallucinations! I do!

Another "therapy process skill" is learning to recognize bodily danger
signals, bodily sensations that indicate threat, danger, something wrong.
Each patient has a unique set of such bodily warning signals. More
specifically, these bodily sensations may indicate that right now someone is menacingly aggressive, or I am starting to sink, or I am starting
to go a little mad, or what I just did was stupid or wrong, or the immediate situation is closing in on me. The bodily sensations may consist of a tight throat, an airiness in the voice, clearing the throat, a
headache at the base of the head in back, heart racing, tightness across
the chest, a sense of listening to one's own voice and observing one's
behavior a little "to the side," a leatheriness of the skin of the face,
sweating, a sense of being frozen, a hot ball of threat in the chest, butterflies in the stomach. The first step is being aware of one's own particular set of bodily threat sensations.

The second step is stopping what you are doing. Instead of letting
the situation proceed on, instead of your continuing to behave this way,
just stop. This may consist of a deliberate closing of one's eyes and
letting attention go to one's own body, attending wholly to these bodily
sensations. It may consist merely of halting whatever you are doing,
even in mid-sentence.

The third step is exiting, leaving, withdrawing from the momentary situation of threat. This may consist of a literal leaving of the room.
It may consist of going into a sort of threat-free sanctuary for a few
minutes or so.

T: OK, so you know! You get this false smile and your belly is clutched up.
Is this going to happen?

Pt: Hell yes! Tonight we're going to an open house and I hate most of the
people there. I know damn well I'll smile and I'll pick a fight with Fred
on the way home, and I'll be up all night with a stomachache. I don't
even want to go but I got to.

T: Here's what you do. Ready? Now listen carefully. You have to be aware
of the exact moment when you have that false smile, and you have to
be aware of the clutched up belly.

Pt: That's easy. I always wonder what the hell I must look like with this phony smile on my face.

T: Good, that's the first step. You got it down. Next. Right then and there, you say, "Wait! I got to stop! See, phony smile? My gut is killing me. I can't stay here anymore. Sorry. I have to get the hell out!" And you can even say all this with the phony smile on your face.

Pt: Wow! That'd be novel!

T: Then leave! Just get the hell out of there!

Pt: That's so easy! Shit! Can I do it?

T: Probably not!

Pt: It would save our marriage! (Laughs) And my social life! And my belly! (Laughs)

These are the working methods for providing the patient with an experiential taste of new ways of being and behaving. Starting with peaks of strong experiencing in the session, the therapist then generates a picture of the directions of potential change. With this precious picture of what the patient can be, the therapist uses these working methods so that the patient actually senses, tastes, samples, and experiences what it is like to be and behave in new integrative and actualizing ways, closer to the directions of potential change. These working methods constitute the final step in therapeutic experiencing, the process of change. However, there are a few unfinished issues before the session is ended.

THE END GAME

There are three matters which are to be taken up before the session is over. One has to do with the issue of whether or not the patient actually undertakes to carry out the new way of being and behaving. How does a patient decide to do it or not? The second has to do with the issue of bringing the session to a close. Finally, there is the issue of arranging for a next session.

Determining Whether or Not to Go Ahead
With the New Behaviors

Sometimes a patient will come face to face with the issue of actually carrying out the new behavior. Experiential tastes and samples are one thing, but now the patient seriously considers actually doing it. The patient says, "I'm going to do it! I'm going to! I'm going to do it tonight. . . . " "I'm going to call her and ask her. Why wait? I'm ready to do it now!" Sometimes the patient's serious intent to carry out the new behavior is not explicitly stated, but it is strongly implied, hanging there in the air. When this issue presents itself, what does the therapist do?

Most of the work is already done: The degree of integration. New behaviors are always tied to some potential for experiencing. Whether or not the patient determines, in the session, to carry out the new behavior is already decided by the degree of integration between the new potential and the rest of the operating domain. If there is a high degree of integration, then the patient will tend to be quite cordial toward actually carrying out the new behavior. With or without the therapist, the patient will be quite ready to undertake the new behavior, and the patient's consideration of this issue will lean heavily in the direction of actually going ahead and carrying it out.

Therapeutic work in the session contains a series of checks and balances. The step of working the relationship between patient and deeper potential, i.e., the internal integrative encounter, paves the way for this determination. If relationships become sufficiently integrative, then the patient is ready to determine to go ahead with the behavior. The other steps in the session also depend upon the degree of integration both within the patient and within the therapist. Carrying forward of the potentials, being the deeper potential, and experiencing new ways of being/behaving will be therapeutically successful to the degree that integrative relationships within both patient and therapist allow these to occur. Accordingly, if the patient considers the issue of actually carrying out the new behavior, most of the work is already done in terms of the degree to which the new potential sits integratively in relation to the other operating potentials.

Using bodily sensations as the final monitor. The patient experiences what it is like to carry out the new way of being/behaving within the context of the actual, real, current life situation. This is the major work of the final step of the session. The issue of whether or not to undertake this behavior is determined by the bodily sensations in the patient and in the therapist. As we consider actually undertaking the new way of being and behaving, what are the bodily sensations like? If they are good and fine, integrated and actualized, then the body is giving its OK. If either patient or therapist has negative, scary, unpleasant, bothersome bodily sensations, then the answer is no; do not go ahead. The therapist applies this test and acts upon its results.

If we are inclined toward a serious consideration of actually doing it, we rehearse the behavior. Let us try it out and then check our bodies. If the bodily sensations are all right, then maybe the green light is on. If we try it out and either one of us has has bodily danger signals, then the answer is no. Do not actually carry out the proposed behavior. It is in this open way that we rehearse the possible new behavior. We go ahead and try it out with the explicit purpose of seeing how our bodies react.

Pt: I've been hiding that from Selma for two years. I think I really am ready to tell her that I steal things from women. Lipstick, cigarettes, perfume, crazy things, and I hide them in the garage. It felt great telling her. I felt free. I'm going to do it. I think I'll tell her tonight.

T: Oh! I don't know. I get tense about that. Let's try it out. For real. Rehearse it. Look right at her, do it all the way, like you were really doing it. Got me? And when you're done, you check your body and I'll check mine. Just to see. Really, like you were going to do it tonight, or tomorrow maybe.

Pt: (Immediately in the scene with Selma, and with a voice full of energy) I think you've known, or suspected. I hide things in the garage, in the old big black suitcase. Women's things! Selma! I steal them! I steal them! I snitch a lipstick or a cigarette lighter, or anything! Personal little things! I'm sick! But what's worse! I get off on it! Selma, I'm a nut . . . (sighs).

T: (Touching his chest) Well, I got something!

Pt: My head is light and I feel charged up. I feel full of energy. My hands are charged. I feel good.

T: Yeah! Me too! Mainly my head is all light and dizzy, but light, nice dizzy. Shit, let's do it!

Pt: I think I'm really going to tell her.

T: For real? Really?

Pt: I think so! It feels great!

Because of the checks and balances built into the steps of the session, it is exceedingly rare that there is a serious consideration of undertaking behaviors which strike the patient or the therapist as dangerous, frightening, or threatening. These are behaviors such as beheading a cat, stuffing a child down a toilet, defecating on police cars, shooting oneself in the head, throwing an aunt out a window, gouging the eyes of the priest, raping the librarian. On the other hand, many prospective behaviors may be accompanied with good bodily sensations in the "as if" final step, but are accompanied with negative bodily sensations when patient and therapist confront the distinct possibility of actually undertaking the new behavior. Then the patient is enjoined to decline undertaking the prospective new behavior. Indeed, the therapist absolutely forbids carrying it out.

T: So you're really serious?
Pt: Why not? I used to pee in the basement. What the hell. Why not? I screw
    up, I go home. I pee on the basement floor. Why not?
T: OK. Let's try it out. You're really serious. Let's go through it. Start with
    the basement door. Right here. And you are headed down the basement.
Pt: I open the door. I go down the basement. I'm in the basement. It's around,
    let's see, yeah, it's afternoon, around the middle of the afternoon. In
    the basement. I unzip my pants. Unzip it. Take it out. I'm near the fur-
    nace. I pee. Starts to pee. I pee on the floor. There's a whole pool of
    piss on the floor. (Pause) Hmmm.
T: My chest is tight. I got butterflies in my stomach. Not good.
Pt: Well, I don't have a headache.
T: Me neither. But my whole chest and stomach are tight, tense.
Pt: (Pause)
T: And I don't want to do it.
Pt: I feel all right.
T: Well, I don't, and that's it! No! The answer is no!
Pt: Just a little whiz?
T: No way.
Pt: Chicken.
T: Right. You may be ready. I'm not.
Pt: (Coyly) You want to talk about this?
T: Never mind! Just don't do it!
Pt: OK. OK!

Patient and therapist try it out, rehearse the prospective new behavior and use the bodily sensations as the final monitor to help determine whether or not to go ahead with the new way of being and behaving. While the truly final decision lies with the patient (Arbuckle, 1975; Holt, 1968), the therapist stands by the nature of the bodily sensations occurring in her body as she rehearses the new behavior. "No, by golly, it makes my chest tight and my throat all constricted. I'll figure out 20 airtight reasons for saying 'no way.' Don't quit your job." "Well, it leaves that awful heaviness in your head and you're going to have to decide no, but I got to tell you, I feel all excited and light and tingly. But I'll respect your body. So the answer is no. So that's it."

If the bodily sensations in the therapist are tight, full of anxiety and threat, constricting, negative, then the therapist stands by her decision to discourage, prevent, stop, resist the actual carrying out of the behavior. While this situation is exceedingly rare, when it happens the therapist is firm. With this quite rare exception, however, the therapist and patient go through as thorough and specific a behavioral rehearsal as is needed, and this constitutes the final monitoring test, for both patient and therapist, of whether or not to actually go ahead with the new behavior.

Bringing the Session to a Close

The session winds to a close after finishing this last step, the experiencing of being/behavioral change. But there are some indicators that the session is over, and there is one final check.

The indicators. There is a package of indicators that the session is over. One is that therapist and patient have indeed finished the work on the final step. Another is that the "therapeutic edge" is gone, i.e., the readiness for continued therapeutic work is over. Instead, the body tells both patient and therapist that it has had enough: No more tension or bodily felt tingling, buttocks have had enough reclining in the chair; the body knows. Thoughts of ending the session come wafting through, accompanied with easy bodily sensations. Attention turns casually to topics such as the next session, getting the car started on the cold wintry evening, being a little hungry.

Sometimes the patient provides the cues that therapeutic work is done. There is a long pause. The patient seems ready to wind up, and his attention turns to non-therapy matters: "I think I'm ready to finish. . . . My ass hurts; I'm done tonight, I think. . . . I can never tell how long the sessions are. This one seemed to be longer than usual. . . . I'm getting hungry. Hope Jack has a good meal ready. . . . I'm done. I think I'm finished today. . . . "

Sometimes it is the therapist who initiates bringing the session to a close. Things seem to be done. Work feels over. The therapist's thoughts shift to finishing. Bodily sensations shut down and experiencing lowers. The therapist is ready to stop: "I'm ready to stop. . . . Well, I think I'm done. . . . My ass is starting to hurt. That usually means we're done. . . . My mind is going to food and that must mean I'm heading toward the end. . . . I'm done; you done?"

The session comes to a close, and this is sensed by patient, therapist, or both. Either patient or therapist may acknowledge the indicators, put them into words. Yet, in any case, it is the patient who has the final say. If the patient is ready to go on, to do more work, then the session is not really over. In experiential therapy, the session is over when both patient and therapist have finished the work, and when both therapist and patient indicate their readiness to end the session. In many other therapies, sessions are defined by the therapist as ending when the 50 minutes are up, and this invites last-minute skirmishes over how the patient accedes to these therapist demands. For example, patient overtures to complete the session may be regarded as problems with dependency:

> . . . (Some) patients feel that they must routinely be the ones to ter-minate the interviews. Either these patients feel threatened by the im-pending dependence on a person to whom they would grant the power of deciding when to dismiss them for the day; or they conclude the hour in an attempt to ward off their longings for dependence, which seems fraught with danger for some biographically determined reason; or they conclude the interview because of a need to live up to what appears to them the valid proof of independence, upon which they rely for their alleged security and integrity . . . (Fromm-Reichmann, 1958, p. 186).

If a committee of patients were to draft a contract for terminating sessions, the final document might well use the above words, with "therapists" substituted for "patients." In experiential therapy's open-ended sessions, with patient and therapist free to note indicators that work is over for this session, the session completes itself without these invited or forced skirmishes.

The final check. Ending the session means that therapist and pa-tient open their eyes and thereby close the work. Work is indeed over when patient and therapist undergo a final check on their bodies to note the body sensations. It works like this:

T: OK, as you open your eyes, and as I open mine, check your body. Take your time. Do it gradually. Take five or ten seconds or so. If the sensa-tions in your body are all right, feel good, if everything is OK in yours and mine, we're done. So take your time.
Pt: (Pause) I got a little tiny tension, like a thin pencil, just a little tension, in my stomach. But it's all right. Mild.
T: My fingers are tingling a little. All right, I'm opening my eyes too. There.

This is the ordinary dialogue. On rare occasions, either patient or therapist or both will have strong bodily sensations of a negative sort. It is quite rare, but it does occur.

Pt: My heart is really going, a mile a minute. My head hurts, I got a headache. Just started a minute or so. My heart's really going!

T: Yeah! Well, I got the same thing, but no headache. My heart too. OK, we have more work to do. We aren't ready to finish . . .

The therapist essentially starts the session from the beginning and gives the opening instructions for the patient to let attention go to whatever is there. We go on with therapeutic work.

Once in a while, the patient may indicate that she is ready to open her eyes, but the therapist is the one who is not ready. Under these conditions, which are even rarer, the therapist continues:

T: Well, everything is OK with you, but my whole insides are tight as hell! My stomach is in a knot, and my chest is so tight I can barely take in a breath! Something's really wrong!

Pt: What should we do?

T: Let's go on a bit. Wow! My chest is tight as hell!

We continue therapeutic work until both patient and therapist have bodily sensations which indicate that they are both ready to finish work. It must be mentioned that it is exceedingly uncommon for the therapist to be the only one not prepared to complete the session, and it is almost as rare that therapist and patient as a pair are not ready to finish the work for that session.

Negotiating the Subsequent Appointment

The most common arrangement is for the patient and therapist to settle into a routine. The patient settles into a routine of three or two or one session a week, and negotiations for the next session are easy and brief:

T: Next session, next session. What's your pleasure?

Pt: Monday, 2:30, same.

T: Right. OK.

Or it is the therapist who lapses into the routine:

T: Today's Tuesday. Next Thursday, 6:00, right?

Pt: Right.

T: All right.

The next appointment is a matter of negotiation. It may be cursory, as above, or it may be a little back-and-forth. But it is important to note that the larger hand is held by the patient. It is the patient who has the final choice for the next appointment, and when to have it. The patient has the choice (Enright, 1970), even though there is a back-and-forth negotiation between therapist and patient. Often the therapist opens with her preference:

T: Now if it were up to me, I'd have another session on Thursday, but that's my preference. You're the boss, what do you think?
Pt: Thursday's fine. Right.
T: Time?
Pt: Same? 5:00?
T: Good. Right.

Sometimes the therapist reacts to the patient's selection:

T: Next session? Gimme a day.
Pt: Tomorrow.
T: Five times this week? You really want another session tomorrow? . . . I think he really wants another session tomorrow.
Pt: Something wrong?
T: Oh no. Everything's fine. Five times a week, for maybe 30 years, he'll get to be such a good patient. . . . Why am I complaining?
Pt: I don't know.
T: (Sighs) OK, tomorrow. How about 1:30?
Pt: That's the usual time.
T: Oh, right. OK, 1:30.

Or the patient wants a session later on and the therapist wants one earlier:

T: Wait a minute! We got to decide on the next session.
Pt: It's been once a week. Let's have one in two weeks, I'm going to be in Toronto for Monday and Tuesday.
T: Two weeks! Two weeks! Too long. No. Too long.
Pt: I'll be back Tuesday evening. Wednesday evening?
T: Sounds good. Name a time.
Pt: Nine?
T: Nine? So late? How about 7:30. That sounds nice to me.
Pt: 7:30. Right.

The therapist is the person he or she is. That means negotiations for the next session may proceed slightly differently each time. But the continuing guideline is that the patient has the major and final choice, even if the patient and therapist settle into a brief and mechanical routine.

This completes the work of the session. My aim has been to walk with the reader through the theory and the methods of experiential psychotherapy, to provide rationale and practices whereby patients and therapists can undergo a sequence of therapeutic experiencings. I hope that this book allows practitioners to have a sense of understanding of the experiential theory of practice, and to follow the experiential method. My invitation is to carry forward the methods of experiential psychotherapy, to venture into new territory which these methods open up and symmetrically to discover new methods which can go even further.

REFERENCES

Abraham, K. *Selected papers of Karl Abraham*. London: Institute of Psychoanalysis and Hogarth Press, 1927.

Adams, H. E. & Frye, R. L. Psychotherapeutic techniques as conditioned reinforcers in a structured interview. *Psychological Reports*, 1964, 4, 163–166.

Adler, A. Compulsion neurosis. *International Journal of Individual Psychology*, 1931, 9, 1–16.

Adler, A. *Social interest: A challenge to mankind*. London: Faber and Faber, 1938.

Adler, A. *The practice and theory of individual psychology*. Patterson, NJ: Littlefield, Adams, 1959.

Adler, A. *The science of living*. New York: Anchor Doubleday, 1969.

Alexander, F. *Psychosomatic medicine*. New York: Norton, 1950.

Alexander, F. The dynamics of psychotherapy in the light of learning theory. *The American Journal of Psychiatry*, 1963, 120, 440–448.

Alexander, F. & French, T. M. *Psychoanalytic therapy*. New York: Ronald, 1946.

Alexander, F. & French, T. M. *Studies in psychosomatic medicine*. New York: Ronald, 1948.

Allport, G. W. *Personality: A psychological interpretation*. New York: Holt, 1937.

Allport, G. W. *Personality and social encounter*. Boston: Beacon Press, 1960.

Allport, G. W. *Pattern and growth in personality*. New York: Holt, Rinehart and Winston, 1961.

Anderson, W. *Open secrets: A western guide to Tibetan Buddhism*. New York: Penguin Books, 1980.

Angyal, A. *Neurosis and treatment: A holistic theory*. New York: John Wiley, 1965.

Ansbacher, H. L. The structure of Individual Psychology. In B. Wolman (Ed.) *Scientific Psychology*, New York: Basic Books, 1965. Pp. 340–364.

Ansell, C. Counter-transference: A story. *Psychotherapy: Theory, Research and Practice*, 1979, 16, 261–268.

Ansell, C., Mindess, H., Stern, M., & Stern, V. Pies in the face and similar matters. *Voices: Journal of the American Academy of Psychotherapists*, 1981, 16, 10–23.

Arbuckle, D. S. *Counseling and psychotherapy: An existential-humanistic view*. Boston: Allyn and Bacon, 1975.

Arieti, S. The psychotherapeutic approach to depression. *American Journal of Psychotherapy*, 1962, 16, 392–406.

Auerswald, M. C. Differential reinforcing power of restatement and interpretation on client production of affect. *Journal of Counseling Psychology*, 1974, 21, 9–14.

Ayllon, T., & Azrin, N. *The token economy: A motivational system for therapy and rehabilitation*. New York: Appleton-Century-Crofts, 1968.

Azrin, N., & Holz, W. Punishment. In W. Honig (Ed.). *Operant behavior: Areas of research and application*. New York: Appleton-Century-Crofts, 1966.

Bach, G. R., & Goldberg, H. *Creative aggression*. Garden City, NY: Doubleday, 1974.

Bachrach, H. Adaptive regression, empathy, and psychotherapy: Theory and research study. *Psychotherapy: Theory, Research and Practice*, 1968, 5, 203–209.

Banaka, W. H. *Training in depth interviewing*. New York: Harper and Row, 1971.

Bandler, R. & Grinder, J. *Reframing: Neuro-linguistic programming and the transformation of meaning*. Moab, UT: Real People Press, 1982.

Bandura, A. Psychotherapy as a learning process. *Psychological Bulletin*, 1961, *58*, 143–159.

Bandura, A. *Principles of behavior modification*, New York: Holt, Rinehart and Winston, 1969.

Barnabei, F., Cormier, W. H., & Nye, S. L. Determining the effects of three counselor verbal responses on client verbal behavior. *Journal of Counseling Psychology*, 1974, *21*, 355–359.

Bateson, G. The biosocial integration of behavior in the schizophrenic family. In N. W. Ackerman, F. L. Beatman, and S. H. Sherman (Eds.) *Exploring the base for family therapy*. New York: Family Service Association of America, 1961. Pp. 116–122.

Bateson, G., Jackson, D., Haley, J., & Weakland, J. Toward a theory of schizophrenia. *Behavioral Science*, 1956, *1*, 251–264.

Beck, A. T. *Depression: Clinical, experimental and theoretical aspects*. New York: Harper and Row, 1967.

Beier, E. G. *The silent language of psychotherapy*. Chicago: Aldine, 1966.

Berg, L. & Steinberg, H. *In search of a response*. New York: Tiresias Press, 1973.

Bergin, A. E. Some implications of psychotherapy research for therapeutic practice. *Journal of Abnormal Psychology*, 1966, *71*, 235–246.

Bergin, A. E., & Lambert, M. J. The evaluation of therapeutic outcomes. In S. L. Garfield & A. E. Bergin (Eds.). *Handbook of psychotherapy and behavior change*, 2nd ed. New York: John Wiley, 1978, Pp. 139–189.

Bergman, D. V. Counseling method and client response. *Journal of Counseling Psychology*, 1951, *15*, 216–224.

Bergman, P. The germinal cell of Freud's psychoanalytic psychology and therapy. *Psychiatry*, 1949, *12*, 265–278.

Berne, E. *Principles of group treatment*. New York: Oxford University Press, 1966.

Berne, E. *What do you say after you say hello?* New York: Grove Press, 1972.

Beutler, L. E. Values, beliefs, religion and the persuasive influence of psychotherapy. *Psychotherapy: Theory, Research and Practice*, 1979, *16*, 261–268.

Bibring, E. Psychoanalysis and the dynamic psychotherapies. *Journal of the American Psychoanalytic Association*, 1954, *2*, 745–770.

Binswanger, L. The existential analysis school of thought. In R. May, E. Angel & H. F. Ellenberger (Eds.). *Existence: A new dimension in psychiatry and psychology*. New York: Basic Books, 1958a. Pp. 191–213.

Binswanger, L. Insanity as life-historical phenomenon and as mental disease. In R. May, E. Angel, and H. F. Ellenberger (Eds.). *Existence: A new dimension in psychiatry and psychology*. New York: Basic Books, 1958b. Pp. 214–236.

Binswanger, L. The case of Ellen West: An anthropological-clinical study. In R. May, E. Angel, & H. F. Ellenberger (Eds.). *Existence: A new dimension in psychiatry and psychology*. New York: Basic Books, 1958c. Pp. 237–364.

Binswanger, L. *Being-in-the-world: Selected papers of Ludwig Binswanger*. J. Needleman (Ed.). New York and London: Harper Torchbooks, 1967.

Bordin, E. S. Inside the therapeutic hour. In E. A. Rubenstein & M. B. Parloff (Eds.). *Research in psychotherapy*. Washington, DC: American Psychological Association, 1959.

Boss, M. *Psychoanalysis and Daseinsanalysis*. New York: Basic Books, 1963.

Boverman, M. Some notes on the psychotherapy of delusional patients. *Psychiatry*, 1953, *16*, 141–157.

Bowen, M. F. *Family therapy in clinical practice*. New York: Jason Aronson, 1978.

Bowlby, J. *Attachment and loss, volume 1: Attachment*. New York: Basic Books, 1969.

Bowlby, J. *Attachment and loss, volume 2: Separation: Anxiety and anger*. New York: Basic Books, 1973.

Breuer, J. & Freud, S. *Studies in hysteria*. New York: Nervous and Mental Diseases Publications, 1936.

Brown, J. S. The generalization of approach responses as a function of stimulus intensity and strength of motivation. *Journal of Comparative Psychology*, 1942, *33*, 209–226.

Brown, J. S. Gradients of approach and avoidance responses and their relation to level of motivation. *Journal of Comparative and Physiological Psychology*, 1948, *41*, 450–465.

Brown, M. The new body psychotherapies. *Psychotherapy: Theory, Research and Practice*, 1973, *10*, 98–116.

Buber, M. *Between man and man*. Boston: Beacon, 1955.

Buber, M. Guilt and guilt feelings. *Psychiatry*, 1957, *20*, 114–129.

Buber, M. *I-thou*. (2nd ed.). New York: Scribners, 1958.

Bucklew, J. *Paradigms for psychopathology: A contribution to case history analysis*. Chicago: Lippincott, 1960.

Bucklew, J. The use of symptoms to assess case history information. *Multivariate Behavioral Research*, 1968, Special Issue, 157–168.

Budge, S. A critical look at the psychotherapeutic outcome research paradigm. *Psychotherapy: Theory, Research, and Practice*, 1983, *20*, 294–306.

Bugental, J. F. T. The person who is the psychotherapist. *Journal of Consulting Psychology*, 1964, *28*, 272–277.

Bugental, J. F. T. *The search for authenticity*. New York: Holt, Rinehart and Winston, 1965.

Bugental, J. F. T. Commitment and the psychotherapist. *Existential Psychiatry*, 1967, Fall, 285–292.

Bugental, J. F. T. *The search for existential identity*. San Francisco: Jossey-Bass, 1976.

Bugental, J. F. T. *Psychotherapy and process: The fundamentals of an existential-humanistic approach*. Reading, Massachusetts: Addison-Wesley, 1978.

Buhler, C. Human life goals in the humanistic perspective. *Journal of Humanistic Psychology*, 1967, *7*, 36–52.

Bullard, D. M. (Ed.) *Psychoanalysis and psychiatry: Selected papers of Frieda Fromm-Reichmann*, Chicago: University of Chicago Press, 1959.

Bullard, D. M. Psychotherapy of paranoid patients. *Archives of General Psychiatry*, 1960, *2*, 137–141.

Butler, J. M. Self-ideal congruence in psychotherapy. *Psychotherapy: Theory, Research and Practice*, 1968, *5*, 13–17.

Buytendijk, F. J. The phenomenological approach to the problem of feelings and emotions. In M. L. Reymert (Ed.) *Feelings and emotions*. New York: McGraw-Hill, 1950. Pp. 127–141.

Byles, M. B. *Journey into Burmese silence*. London: George Allen and Unwin, 1962.

Camus, A. *Resistance, rebellion, and death*. New York: Alfred A. Knopf, 1961.

Carkhuff, R. R. & Berenson, B. G. *Beyond counseling and therapy*. New York: Holt, Rinehart and Winston, 1967.

Caruso, I. A. *Existential psychology*. New York: Herder and Herder, 1964.

Cashdan, S. *Interactional psychotherapy: Stages and strategies in behavioral changes*. New York: Grune and Stratton, 1973.

Casriel, D. *A scream away from happiness*. New York: Grosset and Dunlop, 1972.

Caudill, W. *The psychiatric hospital as a small society*. Cambridge, MA: Harvard University Press, 1958.

Cautela, J. R. The application of learning theory "as a last resort" in the treatment of a case of anxiety neurosis. *Journal of Clinical Psychology*, 1965, *21*, 448–452.

Cautela, J. R. Treatment of compulsive behavior of covert sensitization. *Psychological Record*, 1966, *16*, 33–41.

Cautela, J. R. Covert sensitization. *Psychological Reports*, 1967, *20*, 459–468.

Chang, Chen-Chi. *The practice of Zen*. New York: Harper and Row, 1959.

Chrzanowski, G. Interpersonal treatment method with the difficult patient. In B. B. Wolman (Ed.) *International encyclopedia of neurology, psychiatry, psychoanalysis, and psychology*. New York: Aesculapius, 1977.

Chrzanowski, G. Malevolent transformations and the negative therapeutic reaction. *Contemporary Psychoanalysis*, 1978, *14*, 405–413.

Chrzanowski, G. Problem patients or troublemakers? Dynamic and therapeutic considerations. *American Journal of Psychotherapy*, 1980, *34*, 26–38.

Claiborn, C. D. Interpretation and change in counseling. *Journal of Counseling Psychology*, 1982, *29*, 439–454.

Cole, M. *Violent sheep: The tyranny of the meek*. New York: Times Books, 1980.

Condrau, G. & Boss, M. Existential analysis. In J. G. Howells (Ed.). *Modern perspectives in world psychiatry*. New York: Brunner/Mazel, 1971. Pp. 488–518.

Cormier, W. H. & Cormier, L. S. *Interviewing strategies for helpers*. Monterey, CA: Brooks-Cole, 1977.

Craighead, E. W., Kazdin, A. E., & Mahoney, M. J. *Behavior modification*. Boston: Houghton Mifflin, 1976.

Dalal, A. S. & Barber, T. X. Yoga and hypnotism. In T. X. Barber (Ed.). *LSD, marihuana, yoga, and hypnosis*. Chicago: Aldine, 1970. Pp. 117–132.

Davis, J. D. *The interview as arena*. Stanford: Stanford University Press, 1971.

Denes-Radomisli, M. Existential-Gestalt therapy. In P. Olsen (Ed.) *Emotional flooding*. New York: Penguin Books, 1977. Pp. 25–39.

Dreikurs, R. The four goals of children's misbehavior. *Nervous Child*, 1947, *6*, 3–11.

Dreikurs. T. *The challenge of parenthood*. New York: Duell, Sloan, and Pearce, 1948.

Dreikurs, R. Adlerian psychotherapy. In F. Fromm-Reichmann and J. L. Moreno (Eds.). *Progress in psychotherapy*. New York: Grune and Stratton, 1956. Pp. 111–118.

Dreikurs, R. Goals of therapy. In A. R. Mahrer (Ed.). *The goals of psychotherapy*. New York: Appleton-Century-Crofts, 1967. Pp. 221–237.

Dunlap, K. *Habits: Their making and unmaking*. New York: Liveright, 1932.

Dupont, H. Social learning theory and the treatment of transvestite behavior in an eight year old boy. *Psychotherapy: Theory, Research and Practice*, 1968, *5*, 44–45.

Dusay, J. Script rehearsal. *Transactional Analysis Bulletin*, 1970, *9*, 117–121.

D'Zurilla, T., & Goldfried, M. Problem solving and behavior modification. *Journal of Abnormal Psychology*, 1971, *78*, 107–126.

Edelwich, J., & Brodsky, A. *Burn-out: Stages of disillusionment in the helping professions*. New York: Human Sciences Press, 1980.

Edie, J. *Speaking and meaning: The phenomenology of language*. Bloomington: Indiana University Press, 1976.

Eigen, M. The recoil in having another person. *Review of Existential Psychology and Psychiatry*, 1973, *12*, 52–55.

Ellenberger, H. F. A clinical introduction to psychiatric phenomenology and existential analysis. In R. May, E. Angel, and H. F. Ellenberger (Eds.). *Existence: A new dimension in psychiatry and psychology*. New York: Basic Books, 1958. Pp. 92–124.

Ellenberger, H. F. *The discovery of the unconscious*. New York: Basic Books, 1970.

Ellis, A. A homosexual treated with rational psychotherapy. *Journal of Clinical Psychology*, 1959a, *15*, 338–343.

Ellis, A. Requisite conditions for basic personality change. *Journal of Consulting Psychology*, 1959b, *23*, 538–540.

Ellis, A. *Reason and emotion in psychotherapy*. New York: Lyle Stuart, 1962.

Ellis, A. Goals of psychotherapy. In A. R. Mahrer (Ed.) *The goals of psychotherapy.* New York: Appleton-Century-Crofts, 1967. Pp. 206–220.

Ellis, A. *Growth through reason.* Palo Alto: Science and Behavior Books, 1971.

Ellis, A. *Humanistic psychotherapy: The rational-emotive approach.* New York: Julian Press, 1973.

Ellis, A. Rational-Emotive Therapy. In V. Binder, A. Binder & B. Rimland (Eds.). *Modern Therapies.* Englewood Cliffs, NJ: Prentice-Hall, 1976.

Enright, J. An introduction to Gestalt techniques. In J. Fagan & I. L. Shepherd (Eds.). *Gestalt therapy now.* New York: Harper and Row, 1970. Pp. 107–124.

Erickson, M. H. *The collected papers of Milton H. Erickson on hypnosis.* 4 volumes. Edited by E. L. Rossi. New York: Irvington, 1980.

Erickson, M. H. & Rossi, E. *Experiencing hypnosis.* New York: Irvington, 1981.

Erickson, M. H., Rossi, E. L., & Rossi, S. *Hypnotic realities.* New York: Irvington, 1976.

Erikson, E. H. *Childhood and society.* New York: W.W. Norton, 1950.

Esterson, A. On breakdown in psychiatry. In J. L. Fosshage and P. Olsen (Eds.). *Healing: Implications for psychotherapy.* New York: Human Sciences Press, 1978. Pp. 350–368.

Fadiman, J. The transpersonal stance. In R. N. Walsh and F. Vaughan (Eds.). *Beyond ego: Transpersonal dimensions in psychology.* Los Angeles: J. P. Tarcher, 1980. Pp. 175–181.

Fagan, J. Three sessions with Iris. *Counseling Psychologist,* 1974, 4, 42–60.

Fairbairn, W. R. D. The repression and the return of bad objects. *British Journal of Medical Psychology,* 1943, 19, 342–369.

Fairbairn, W. R. D. *An object-relations theory of the personality.* New York: Basic Books, 1952.

Farber, M. *The aims of phenomenology: The motives, methods, and impact of Husserl's thought.* New York: Harper and Row, 1966.

Farrelly, F. & Brandsma, J. *Provocative therapy.* Fort Collins, CO: Shields, 1974.

Federn, P. *Ego psychology and the psychoses.* New York: Basic Books, 1952.

Feifel, H. (Ed.). *The meaning of death.* New York: McGraw-Hill, 1959.

Feldenkrais, M. *Body and mature behavior.* New York: International Universities Press, 1949.

Feldenkrais, M. *Awareness through movement.* New York: Harper and Row, 1972.

Fenichel, O. *The psychoanalytic theory of neuroses.* New York: Norton, 1945.

Fenichel, O. From the terminal phase of an analysis. In H. Fenichel & D. Rapaport (Eds.). *The collected papers of Otto Fenichel: First Series.* New York: Norton, 1953a. Pp. 27–31.

Fenichel, O. Psychoanalytic method. In H. Fenichel and D. Rapaport (Eds.). *The collected papers of Otto Fenichel: First Series.* New York: Norton, 1953b. Pp. 318–330.

Fenichel, O. The symbolic equasion: Girl = phallus. In H. Fenichel & D. Rapaport (Eds.). *The collected papers of Otto Fenichel: Second series.* New York: Norton, 1954a. Pp. 3–18.

Fenichel, O. Symposium on the theory of the therapeutic results of psychoanalysis. In H. Fenichel and D. Rapaport (Eds.). *The collected papers of Otto Fenichel: Second series.* New York: Norton, 1954b. Pp. 19–24.

Fenichel, O. Early stages of ego development. In H. Fenichel and D. Rapaport (Eds.). *The collected papers of Otto Fenichel: Second series.* New York: Norton, 1954c. Pp. 25–48.

Fenichel, O. On masturbation. In H. Fenichel & D. Rapaport (Eds.). *The collected papers of Otto Fenichel: Second series.* New York: Norton, 1954d. Pp. 81–88.

Fierman, L. B. (Ed.). *Effective psychotherapy: The contributions of Hellmuth Kaiser.* New York: Free Press, 1965.

Fine, R. *The healing of the mind*. New York: McKay, 1971.

Fine, R. Psychoanalysis. In R. Corsini (Ed.). *Current psychotherapies*. Itasca, Illinois: F. E. Peacock, 1973.

Fingarette, H. Real guilt and neurotic guilt. *Journal of Existential Psychiatry*, 1962, 3, 145–158.

Finney, B. C. Say it again: An active therapy technique. In C. Hatcher & P. Himelstein (Eds.). *The handbook of Gestalt therapy*. New York: Jason Aronson, 1976.

Fiske, D. W., Hunt, H. H., Luborsky, L., Orne, M. T., Parloff, M. B., Rieser, M. F., & Tuma, A. H. Planning of research on effectiveness of psychotherapy. *Archives of General Psychiatry*, 1970, 22, 22–32.

Fleischl, M. F. A note on the meaning of ideas of reference. *American Journal of Psychotherapy*, 1958, 12, 24–29.

Flugel, J. C. *Man, morals, and society: A psycho-analytical study*. New York: International Universities Press, 1945.

Framo, J. Symptoms from a family transactional viewpoint. In C. J. Sager & H. S. Kaplan (Eds.). *Progress in group and family therapy*. New York: Brunner/Mazel, 1972.

Frank, G. H. & Sweetland, A. A study of the process of psychotherapy. *Journal of Consulting Psychology*, 1962, 26, 135–138.

Frank, J. D. The dynamics of the psychotherapeutic relationship: Determinants and effects of the therapist's influence. *Psychiatry*, 1959, 22, 17–39.

Frank, J. D. *Persuasion and healing: A comparative study of psychotherapy*. Baltimore, Maryland: Johns Hopkins Press, 1961a.

Frank, J. D. The role of influence in psychotherapy. In M. I. Stern (Ed.). *Contemporary psychotherapies*. New York: Free Press of Glencoe, 1961b. Pp. 17–41.

Frank, J. D. The present status of outcome research. In M. R. Goldfried (Ed.) *Converging themes in psychotherapy*. New York: Springer, 1982. Pp. 281–290.

Frankl, V. E. *The unconscious God*. New York: Simon and Schuster, 1949 (2nd ed., 1975).

Frankl, V. E. *Man's search for meaning: An introduction to Logotherapy*. Boston: Beacon Press, 1963.

Frankl, V. E. *The doctor and the soul*. New York: Alfred A. Knopf, 1965.

Franks, C. Can behavioral therapy find peace and fulfillment in a school of professional psychology? *The Clinical Psychologist*, 1974, 28, 11–15.

Freud, A. *The ego and the mechanisms of defense*. New York: International Universities Press, 1946.

Freud, S. On the history of the psychoanalytic movement. In *Collected Papers of Sigmund Freud*. Vol. XIV:3. New York: Norton, 1976a.

Freud, S. The dynamics of the transference. In *Collected papers of Sigmund Freud*. Vol. XII:99. New York: Norton, 1976b.

Freud, S. Fragment of an analysis of a case of hysteria: Prefatory remarks. In *Collected Papers of Sigmund Freud*. Vol. VII:249. New York: Norton, 1976c.

Freud, S. *New introductory lectures on psycho-analysis*. Vol. XV & XVI. New York: Norton, 1976d.

Freud, S. Analysis terminable and interminable. *Standard edition of the complete psychological works of Sigmund Freud*. Vol. XXII:209. New York: Norton, 1976e.

Freud, S. *The interpretation of dreams*. Vol. IV & V. New York: Norton, 1976f.

Freud, S. Mourning and melancholia. In *Collected papers of Sigmund Freud*, Volume XIV:239. New York: Norton, 1976g.

Freud, S. Analysis of a case of hysteria: The clinical picture. In E. Jones (Ed.) *Collected papers of Sigmund Freud*. New York: Basic Books, 1959.

Freudenberger, H. J. The staff burn-out syndrome in alternative institutions. *Psychotherapy: Theory, Research and Practice*, 1975, 12, 73–82.

Freudenberger, H. J., & Robbins, A. The hazards of being a psychoanalyst. *Psychoanalytic Review*, 1979, 66, 224–236.

Fromm, E. *Escape from freedom*. New York: Farrar, Straus, and Giroux, 1941.

Fromm, E. *Man for himself*. New York: Holt, Rinehart and Winston, 1947.

Fromm, E. *The art of loving*. New York: Harper and Row, 1956.

Fromm, E. Value, psychology, and human existence. In A. H. Maslow (Ed.). *New knowledge in human values*. New York: Harper and Row, 1959.

Fromm, E., Suzuki, D. T., & de Martino, R. *Zen Buddhism and Psychoanalysis*. New York: Harper and Row, 1960.

Fromm, M. G. Impasse and transitional relatedness. In T. Seretsky (Ed.). *Resolving treatment impasses: The difficult patient*. New York: Human Sciences Press, 1981. Pp. 5–29.

Fromm-Reichmann, F. *Principles of intensive psychotherapy*. Chicago: University of Chicago Press, 1958.

Gendlin, E. T. Experiencing: A variable in the process of therapeutic change. *American Journal of Psychotherapy*, 1961, 15, 233–245.

Gendlin, E. T. A theory of personality change. In P. Worchel & D. Byrne (Eds.). *Personality change*. New York: Wiley, 1964. Pp. 100–148.

Gendlin, E. T. Existentialism and experiential psychotherapy. In C. Moustakas (Ed.). *Existential child therapy*. New York: Basic Books, 1966. Pp. 206–246.

Gendlin, E. T. Client-centered: The experiential response. In E. F. Hammer (Ed.). *Use of interpretation in treatment*. New York: Grune and Stratton, 1968. Pp. 208–227.

Gendlin, E. T. Focusing. *Psychotherapy: Theory, Research and Practice*, 1969, 6, 4–15.

Gendlin, E. T. Therapeutic procedures with schizophrenic patients. In M. Hammer (Ed.) *The theory and practice of psychotherapy with specific disorders*. Springfield, Ill.: Charles C Thomas, 1972. Pp. 333–375.

Gendlin, E. T. *Focusing*. New York: Everest House, 1978.

Gervaize, P. A., Mahrer, A. R., & Markow, R. Therapeutic laughter: What therapists do to promote strong laughter in patients. *Psychotherapy in Private Practice*, 1985, 3, 65–74.

Glasser, W. *Reality therapy*, New York: Harper and Row, 1965.

Glasser, W. & Zunin, L. M. Reality therapy. In R. Corsini (Ed.). *Current psychotherapies*. Itasca, Illinois: F. E. Peacock, 1973.

Glover, E. Notes on oral character formation. *International Journal of Psychoanalysis*, 1925, 6, 131–154.

Goldfried, M. & Davison, G. *Clinical behavior therapy*. New York: Holt, Rinehart & Winston, 1976.

Goldstein, A. P., Heller, K., & Sechrest, L. B. *Psychotherapy and the psychology of behavior change*. New York: Wiley, 1966.

Goldstein, A. J. & Wolpe, J. Behavior therapy in groups. In H. I. Kaplan & B. J. Sadock (Eds.). *Comprehensive group psychotherapy*. Baltimore: Williams & Wilkins, 1971.

Gottman, J. M., & Leiblum, S. R. *How to do psychotherapy and how to evaluate it*. New York: Holt, Rinehart and Winston, 1974.

Gottman, J. M., & Markman, J. H. Experimental designs in psychotherapy research. In S. L. Garfield & A. E. Bergin (Eds.). *Handbook of psychotherapy and behavior change*. New York: Wiley, 1978.

Greben, S. E. On being therapeutic. *Canadian Psychiatric Association Journal*, 1977, 22, 371–380.

Greenberg, L. S. Psychotherapy process research. In E. Walker (Ed.). *Handbook of clinical psychology*, New York: Dorsey, 1983.

Greenberg, L. S. Resolving splits: Use of the two-chair technique. *Psychotherapy: Theory, Research and Practice,* 1979, *16,* 310–318.

Greenson, R. Empathy and its vicissitudes. *International Journal of Psychoanalysis,* 1960, *41,* 418–424.

Greenson, R. R. *The technique and practice of psychoanalysis.* New York: International Universities Press, 1967.

Greenwald, H. *Direct decision therapy.* San Diego: Edits, 1974.

Grinker, R. R., & Gottschalk, L. Headaches and muscular pains. *Psychosomatic Medicine,* 1949, *11,* 45–52.

Grotjahn, M. *Beyond laughter: Humor and the subconscious.* New York: McGraw-Hill, 1966.

Guntrip, H. *Schizoid phenomena, object-relations, and the self.* New York: International Universities Press, 1969.

Gurwitsch, A. *Phenomenology and the theory of science.* L. Embree (Ed.). Evanston, Ill.: Northwestern University Press, 1974.

Hackney, H., Ivey, A., & Oetting, E. Attending, island, and hiatus behavior: Process conception of counselor and client interaction. *Journal of Counseling Psychology,* 1970, *17,* 342–346.

Haley, J. The art of psychoanalysis. In S. I. Hayakawa (Ed.). *Our language and our world.* New York: Harper, 1959.

Haley, J. *Strategies of psychotherapy.* New York: Grune and Stratton, 1963.

Haley, J. (Ed.). *Advanced techniques of hypnosis and therapy: Selected papers of Milton H. Erickson, M.D..* New York: Grune and Stratton, 1967.

Haley, J. *Uncommon therapy: The psychiatric techniques of Milton H. Erickson, M.D..* New York: Norton, 1973a.

Haley, J. Control in psychotherapy with schizophrenics. In D. Jackson (Ed.). *Therapy, communication and change.* Palo Alto, CA: Science and Behavior Books, 1973b.

Haley, J. *Problem-solving therapy: New strategies for effective family therapy.* San Francisco: Jossey-Bass, 1976.

Halpern, H. An essential ingredient in successful psychotherapy. *Psychotherapy: Theory, Research and Practice,* 1965, *2,* 177–180.

Hartmann, H. *Ego psychology and the problem of adaptation.* New York: International Universities Press, 1958.

Hartmann, H. *Essays on ego psychology.* New York: International Universities Press, 1964.

Hartmann, H., Kris, E., & Loewenstein, R. M. Comments on the formation of psychic structure. In A. Freud (Ed.). *The psychoanalytic study of the child.* New York: International Universities Press, 1947.

Havens, L. L. *Approaches to the mind: Movement of the psychiatric schools from sects toward science.* Boston: Little, Brown, 1973.

Havens, L. *Participant observation.* New York: Jason Aronson, 1976.

Heidegger, M. *Existence and being.* London: Vision Press, 1949.

Heidegger, M. *Being and time.* New York: Harper and Row, 1963.

Hekmat, H. Reinforcing values of interpretations and reflections. *Journal of Abnormal Psychology,* 1971, *77,* 25–31.

Herrigel, E. *Zen in the art of archery.* New York: Pantheon, 1956.

Highlen, P. S. & Baccus, G. K. Effects of reflection of feeling and probe on client self-referenced affect. *Journal of Counseling Psychology,* 1977, *24,* 440–443.

Hill, C. E. & Gormally, J. Effects of reflection, restatement, probe, & nonverbal behaviors on client affect. *Journal of Counseling Psychology,* 1977, *24,* 92–97.

Hobbs, N. Sources of gain in psychotherapy. *American Psychologist,* 1962, *17,* 741–747.

Hoffnung, R. J. Conditioning and transfer of affective self-references in a role-playing counseling interview. *Journal of Consulting and Clinical Psychology*, 1969, *33*, 527–531.

Hogan, R. A. & Kirchner, H. Preliminary report on the extinction of learned fears via short-term implosive psychotherapy. *Journal of Abnormal Psychology*, 1967, *72*, 106–109.

Holt, H. The problem of interpretation from the point of view of existential psychoanalysis. In E. F. Hammer (Ed.). *Use of interpretation in treatment*. New York: Grune and Stratton, 1968. Pp. 240–252.

Hora, T. Tao, Zen, and existential psychotherapy. *Psychologia*, 1959, *2*, 236–242.

Hora, T. Psychotherapy, existence, and religion. In H. M. Ruitenbeek (Ed.).*Psychoanalysis and existential philosophy*, New York: Dutton, 1962. Pp. 70–81.

Horner, A. *Object relations and the developing ego in therapy*. New York: Jason Aronson, 1979.

Imber, S. D., Pande, S. K., Frank, J. D., Hoehn-Saric, R., Stone, A. R., & Wargo, D. G. Time-focused role induction. *Journal of Nervous and Mental Disease*, 1970, *150*, 27–30.

Jackins, H. *The human side of human beings: The theory of re-evaluation counseling*. Seattle: Rational Island Publishers, 1965.

Jackson, D. The eternal triangle. In J. Haley & L. Hoffman (Eds.). *Techniques of family therapy*. New York: Basic Books, 1967.

Jacobs, D., Charles, E., Jacobs, T., Weinstein, H., & Mann, D. Preparation for treatment of the disadvantaged patient: Effects on disposition and outcome. *American Journal of Orthopsychiatry*, 1972, *42*, 444–474.

Jacobson, E. *Progressive relaxation*. Chicago: University of Chicago Press, 1938.

James, M. & Jongeward, D. *Born to win*. Reading, Mass.: Addison-Wesley, 1971.

Janov, A. *The primal scream*. New York: Dell, 1970.

Janov, A. *The anatomy of mental illness: The scientific basis of primal therapy*. New York: Putnam, 1971.

Janov, A. *The primal revolution*. New York: Simon and Schuster, 1972.

Janov, A. & Holden, E. (Eds.). *The primal man*. New York: Crowell, 1975.

Jaspers, K. *Reason and existence*. New York: Noonday Press, 1955.

Jaspers, K. *Man in the modern age*. Garden City: Doubleday, 1957.

Johnson, R. E. *Existential man: The challenge of psychotherapy*. New York: Pergamon, 1971.

Jones, E. *The life and work of Sigmund Freud*. New York: Basic Books, 1953.

Jourard, S. M. *Personal adjustment: An approach through the study of the healthy personality*. New York: Macmillan, 1963.

Jourard, S. M. *Disclosing man to himself*. Princeton, New Jersey: Van Nostrand, 1968.

Jourard, S. M. *Self-disclosure: An experimental analysis of the transparent self*. New York: Wiley, 1971a.

Jourard, S. M. *The transparent self*. Princeton, New Jersey: Van Nostrand, 1971b.

Jourard, S. M. Existential quest. In A. Wandersman, P. Poppen, & D. Ricks (Eds.). *Humanism and behaviorism: Dialogue and growth*. New York: Pergamon, 1976.

Jung, C. G. The aims of psychotherapy. *Collected works*, volume 16. London: Routledge and Kegan Paul, 1929.

Jung, C. G. *Modern man in search of a soul*. New York: Harcourt, Brace, 1933.

Jung, C. G. The relation between the ego and the unconscious. *Collected works*. Volume 7. London: Routledge and Kegan Paul, 1934.

Jung, C. G. The detachment of consciousness from the object. In R. Wilhelm, *The secret of the golden flower: A Chinese book of life*. London: Routledge and Kegan Paul, 1962. Pp. 122–127.

Kanfer, F., & Phillips, J. *Learning foundations of behavior therapy.* New York: John Wiley and Sons, 1970.

Karpman, S. Script drama analysis. *Transactional Analysis Bulletin*, 1968, 7, 39–43.

Keleman, S. We do have bodies and we are our bodies. *Psychology Today*, 1973, 7, 64 –70.

Kelly, G. A. *The psychology of personal constructs. Volumes I, II.* New York: Norton, 1955.

Kelly, G. A. A psychology of the optimal man. In A. R. Mahrer (Ed.). *The goals of psychotherapy.* New York: Appleton-Century-Crofts, 1967. Pp. 238–258.

Kelman, H. Kairos: The auspicious moment. *American Journal of Psychoanalysis*, 1969, 29, 59–83.

Kempler, W. Experiential psychotherapy with families. *Family Process*, 1968,7,88–99.

Kempler, W. *Principles of Gestalt Family Therapy.* Costa Mesa, California: The Kempler Institute, 1974.

Kempler, W. *Experiential psychotherapy within families.* New York: Brunner/Mazel, 1981.

Kendell, R. E. *The role of diagnosis in psychiatry.* Oxford: Blackwell, 1975.

Kernberg, O. *Borderline conditions and pathological narcissism.* New York: Jason Aronson, 1975.

Kernberg, O. *Object-relations theory and clinical psychoanalysis.* New York: Jason Aronson, 1976.

Kierkegaard, S. *The concept of dread.* Princeton, NJ: Princeton University Press, 1944.

Kiesler, D. J. Experimental designs in psychotherapy research. In A. E. Bergin and S. L. Garfield (Eds.). *Handbook of psychotherapy and behavior change: An empirical analysis.* New York: John Wiley, 1971. Pp. 36–74.

Kiresuk, T. J., & Sherman, R. E. Goal attainment scaling: A general method for evaluating comprehensive mental health programs. *Community Mental Health Journal*, 1968, 4, 443–453.

Klein, D. F., & Davis, J. *Diagnosis and drug treatment of psychiatric disorders.* Baltimore: Williams and Wilkins, 1969.

Klein, M. *The psycho-analysis of children.* London: Hogarth, 1960.

Klonoff, H., & Cox, B. A. Problem-oriented approach to analysis of treatment outcome. *American Journal of Psychiatry*, 1975, 132, 836–841.

Knight, R. P. Evaluation of the results of psychoanalytic therapy. *American Journal of Psychiatry*, 1941, 98, 434–446.

Knight, R. P. An evaluation of psychotherapeutic techniques. *Bulletin of the Menninger Clinic*, 1952, 16, 113–124.

Koestenbaum, P. *The new image of the person.* Westport, CT: Greenwood Press, 1978.

Kohut, H. *The analysis of the self.* New York: International Universities Press, 1971.

Kohut, H. *The restoration of the self.* New York: International Universities Press, 1977.

Kondo, A. Intuition in Zen Buddhism. *American Journal of Psychoanalysis*, 1952, 12, 10–14.

Kondo, A. Zen in psychotherapy: The virtue of sitting. *Chicago Review*, 1958, 57–64.

Kopp, S. *The hanged man: Psychotherapy and the forces of darkness.* Palo Alto: Science and Behavior Books, 1974.

Kovacs, A. L. The intimate relationship: A therapeutic paradox. *Psychotherapy: Theory, Research and Practice*, 1965, 2, 97–104.

Krasner, L. Techniques of assessment in behavior therapy. In I. E. Waskow & M. B. Parloff (Eds.). *Psychotherapy change measures.* Rockville, MD: National Institute of Mental Health, 1975. Pp. 65–74.

Kubie, L. S. The nature of psychotherapy. *Bulletin of the New York Academy of Medicine*, 1943, 19, 183–194.

Kurz, R. R. & Grummon, D. L. Different approaches to the measurement of therapist empathy and their relationship to therapy outcomes. *Journal of Consulting and Clinical Psychology*, 1972, *39*, 106–115.

Labov, W. *Sociolinguistic patterns*. Philadelphia: University of Pennsylvania Press, 1972.

Labov, W. & Fanshel, D. *Therapeutic discourse: Psychotherapy as conversation*. New York: Academic Press, 1977.

Lacan, J. *Ecrits*. New York: Norton, 1951 (1977).

Lacan, J. Some reflections on the ego. *International Journal of Psychoanalysis*, 1953, *34*, 11–17.

Laing, R. D. *The self and others*. Chicago: Quadrangle Books, 1962.

Laing, R. D. *The divided self*. London: Tavistock Publications, 1975.

Laing, R. D. *The voice of experience*. New York: Pantheon Books, 1982.

Laing, R. D. & Esterson, A. *Sanity, madness and the family*. Harmondsworth, Middlesex: Penguin Books, 1970.

Lambert, M. J., & Bergin, A. E. Psychotherapeutic outcome and issues related to behavioral and humanistic approaches. In A. Wandersman, P. Poppen, & D. Ricks (Eds.). *Humanism and behaviorism: Dialogue and growth*. Oxford: Pergamon Press, 1976. Pp. 173–188.

Langs, R. *Technique in transition*. New York: Jason Aronson, 1978.

Langs, R. *Psychotherapy: A basic text*. New York: Jason Aronson, 1982.

Lankton, S. R., & Lankton, C. H. *The answer within: A clinical framework of Ericksonian hypnotherapy*. New York: Brunner/Mazel, 1983.

Lankton, S., Lankton, C. & Brown, M. Psychological level communication in transactional analysis. *Transactional Analysis Journal*, 1981, *4*, 287–299.

Lawton, G. Neurotic interaction between counselor and counselee. *Journal of Counseling Psychology*, 1958, *5*, 28–33.

Lazarus, A. *Behavior therapy and beyond*. New York: McGraw-Hill, 1971.

Lennard, H. L., & Bernstein, A. *The anatomy of psychotherapy: Systems of communication and expectation*. New York: Columbia University Press, 1960.

Levine, J. Humor as a form of therapy: Introduction to a symposium. In A. J. Chapman & H. C. Foot (Eds.). *Humor and laughter: Theory, research and applications*. London: John Wiley and Sons, 1976.

Levitsky, A. & Perls, F. The rules and games of Gestalt therapy. In J. Fagan & I. L. Shepherd (Eds.) *Gestalt therapy now*. New York: Harper and Row, 1970. Pp. 140–149.

Levy-Bruhl, L. *Primitive mentality*. London: MacMillan, 1923.

Lewis, C. S. *The four loves*. New York: Harcourt Brace, 1960.

Lewis, H. & Streitfeld, H. *Growth games*. New York: Bantam, 1972.

Liberman, R. *A guide to behavioral analysis and therapy*. Elmsford, New York: Pergamon Press, 1972.

Locke, E. A. Is "Behavior Therapy" behavioristic? (An analysis of Wolpe's psychotherapeutic methods). *Psychological Bulletin*, 1971, *76*, 318–327.

Loevinger, J. Three principles for psychoanalytic psychology. *Journal of Abnormal Psychology*, 1966, *5*, 432–443.

Loevinger, J. *Ego development*. San Francisco: Jossey-Bass, 1976.

London, P. The end of ideology in behavior modification. *American Psychologist*, 1972, *27*, 913–920.

Lovlie, A. L. *The self of the psychotherapist*. New York: Columbia University Press, 1983.

Lowen, A. *Physical dynamics of character structure*. New York: Grune and Stratton, 1958.

Lowen, A. *Love and orgasm.* New York: Macmillan, 1965.

Lowen, A. *The betrayal of the body.* New York: Collier, 1967.

Lowen, A. Bioenergetic analysis: A development of Reichian therapy. In G. Goldman and D. Milman (Eds.). *Innovations in psychotherapy.* Springfield, IL: Charles C Thomas, 1972.

Maddi, S. *Personality theories: A comparative analysis.* Homewood, IL: Dorsey Press, 1972.

Mahler, M. S. *On human symbiosis and the vicissitudes of individuation.* New York: International Universities Press, 1968.

Mahrer, A. R. (Ed.). *The goals of psychotherapy.* New York: Appleton-Century-Crofts, 1967a.

Mahrer, A. R. The goals and families of psychotherapy: Implications. In A. R. Mahrer (Ed.). *The goals of psychotherapy.* New York: Appleton-Century-Crofts, 1967b. Pp. 288–301.

Mahrer, A. R. Interpretation of patient behavior through goals, feelings and context. *Journal of Individual Psychology,* 1970a, *26,* 186–195.

Mahrer, A. R. Motivational theory: A system of personality classification. In A. R. Mahrer (Ed.). *New approaches to personality classification.* New York: Columbia University Press, 1970b, Pp. 277–308.

Mahrer, A. R. Metamorphosis through suicide: The changing of one's self by oneself. *Journal of Pastoral Counseling,* 1975a, *10,* 10–26.

Mahrer, A. R. Therapeutic outcome as a function of goodness-of-fit on an internal-external dimension of interaction. *Psychotherapy: Theory, Research and Practice,* 1975b, *12,* 22–27.

Mahrer, A. R. Infant psychotherapy: Theory, research and practice. *Psychotherapy: Theory, Research and Practice,* 1976a, *13,* 131–140.

Mahrer, A. R. Some known effects of psychotherapy and a reinterpretation. In A. G. Banet, Jr. (Ed.). *Creative psychotherapies: A source book.* La Jolla: University Associates, 1976b. Pp. 334–344.

Mahrer, A. R. Theory and treatment of anxiety: The perspective of motivational psychology, *Journal of Pastoral Counseling,* 1977, *7,* 4–16.

Mahrer, A. R. *Experiencing: A humanistic theory of psychology and psychiatry.* New York: Brunner/Mazel, 1978a.

Mahrer, A. R. Sequence and consequence in experiential psychotherapies. In C. L. Cooper and C. P. Alderfer (Eds.). *Advances in experiential social processes.* Volume 1. New York: John Wiley, 1978b.

Mahrer, A. R. Experiential psychotherapists: A "prognostic test" and some speculations about their personalities. *Psychotherapy: Theory, Research and Practice,* 1978c, *13,* 24–31.

Mahrer, A. R. Turning the tables on termination. *Voices: Journal of the American Academy of Psychotherapists,* 1978d, *13,* 24–31.

Mahrer, A. R. The therapist-patient relationship: Conceptual analysis and a proposal for a paradigm-shift. *Psychotherapy: Theory, Research and Practice,* 1978e, *15,* 201–215.

Mahrer, A. R. An invitation to theoreticians and researchers from an applied experiential practitioner. *Psychotherapy: Theory, Research and Practice,* 1979, *16,* 409–418.

Mahrer, A. R. Value decisions in therapeutically induced psychotic states. *Psychotherapy: Theory, Research and Practice,* 1980a, *17,* 454–458.

Mahrer, A. R. The treatment of cancer through experiential psychotherapy. *Psychotherapy: Theory, Research and Practice,* 1980b, *17,* 335–342.

Mahrer, A. R. Research on theoretical concepts of psychotherapy. In W. De Moor and H. R. Wijngaarden (Eds.). *Psychotherapy: Research and training.* Amsterdam:

Elsevier/North Holland Biomedical Press, 1980c. Pp. 33–46.

Mahrer, A. R. Humanistic approaches to intimacy. In M. Fisher and G. Stricker (Eds.). *Intimacy*. New York: Plenum, 1982. Pp. 141–158.

Mahrer, A. R. *Experiential psychotherapy: Basic practices*. New York: Brunner/ Mazel, 1983a.

Mahrer, A. R. An existential-experiential view and operational perspective on passive-aggressiveness. In R. D. Parsons and R. J. Wicks (Eds.). *Passive-aggressiveness: Theory and practice*. New York: Brunner/Mazel, 1983b. Pp. 98–133.

Mahrer, A. R. Fully experiencing the therapist's ailments. *Voices: Journal of the American Academy of Psychotherapists*, 1983c, *19*, 33–35.

Mahrer, A. R. The care and feeding of abrasiveness. *The Psychotherapy Patient*, 1984a, *1*, 69–78.

Mahrer, A. R. Humanistic theory of development. In T. Husen & T. N. Postlethwaite (Eds.). *International Encyclopedia of Education: Research and studies*, New York: Pergamon Press, 1984b.

Mahrer, A. R. Existential psychology and psychotherapy. In R. J. Hunter (Ed.). *Dictionary of Pastoral Care and Counseling*. Nashville, TN: Abingdon, 1984c.

Mahrer, A. R. *Psychotherapeutic change: An alternative approach to meaning and measurement*. New York: Norton, 1985.

Mahrer, A. R. A challenge to communication therapy: The therapist does not communicate with the client. *Journal of Communication Therapy*, in press.

Mahrer, A. R. & Bornstein, R. Depression: Characteristic syndromes and a prefatory conceptualization. *Journal of General Psychology*, 1969, *81*, 217–229.

Mahrer, A. R., Brown, S. D., Gervaize, P. A., & Fellers, G. Reflection, self-exploration, and client-therapist communication: Some unexpected in-therapy consequences. *Journal of Communication Therapy*, 1983, *2*, 1–13.

Mahrer, A. R., Clark, E. L., Comeau, L., & Brunette, A. Therapist Statements as prescriptions-for-change: A method for assessing psychotherapeutic change. *Journal of Communication Therapy*, in press.

Mahrer, A. R., Durak, G. M., Lawson, K. C., & Nifakis, D. J. Interpretation as a means of enhancing the role of the therapist. *Journal of Communication Therapy*, in press.

Mahrer, A. R., Edwards, H. P., Durak, G. M. & Sterner, I. The psychotherapy patient and the initial session: A study of patient effects and alternative strategies. *The Psychotherapy Patient*, 1985, *1*.

Mahrer, A. R., Fellers, G. L., Brown, S. D., Gervaize, P. A., & Durak, G. M. When does the counsellor self-disclose and what are the in-therapy consequences? *Canadian Counsellor*, 1981, *15*, 175–179.

Mahrer, A. R. & Gervaize, P. A. Impossible roles therapists must play. *Canadian Psychology*, 1983, *24*, 81–87.

Mahrer, A. R. & Gervaize, P. A. An integrative review of strong laughter in psychotherapy. *Psychotherapy*, 1984, *21*, 510–516.

Mahrer, A. R. & Kangas, P. Suicidal attempts and threats as goal-directed communication in psychotic males. *Psychological Reports*, 1970, *27*, 795–801.

Mahrer, A. R., Levinson, J. R., & Fine, S. Infant psychotherapy: Theory, research and practice. *Psychotherapy: Theory, Research and Practice* 1976, *13*, 131–140.

Mahrer, A. R., Nifakis, D. J., Abhukara, L., & Sterner, I. Microstrategies in psychotherapy: The patterning of sequential therapist statements. *Psychotherapy*, 1984, *21*, 465–472.

Mahrer, A. R. & Pearson, L. The working processes of psychotherapy: Creative developments. In A. R. Mahrer & L. Pearson (Eds.). *Creative developments in psychotherapy*. Cleveland: Press of Case Western Reserve University, 1971. Pp. 309–329.

Mailloux, N. Psychic determinism, freedom, and personal development. *Canadian Journal of Psychology*, 1953, 7, 1–11.

Maslow, A. H. *Toward a psychology of being*. New York: Van Nostrand, 1962.

Maslow, A. H. Fusion of facts and values. *American Journal of Psychoanalysis*, 1963, 23, 117–131.

Maslow, A. H. *Motivation and personality*. New York: Harper and Row, 1970.

Masson, J. *The assault on truth: Freud's suppression of the seduction theory*. New York: Farrar, Straus, and Giroux, 1983.

Malleson, N. Panic and phobia. *Lancet*, 1959, 1, 225–227.

Maupin, E. W. Zen Buddhism: A psychological review. *Journal of Consulting Psychology*, 1965, 29, 139–145.

May, R. *Man's search for himself*. New York: W.W. Norton, 1953.

May, R. Contributions of existential psychotherapy. In R. May, E. Angel & H. F. Ellenberger (Eds.). *Existence: A new dimension in psychiatry and psychology*, New York: Basic Books, 1958. Pp. 37–91.

May, R. *Psychology and the human dilemma*. Princeton: D. Van Nostrand, 1967.

May, R. The daemonic: Love and death. *Psychology Today*, 1968, 1, 16–25.

May, R., Angel, E., & Ellenberger, H. F. (Eds.). *Existence: A new dimension in psychiatry and psychology*. New York: Basic Books, 1958.

McGill, V. J. *The idea of happiness*. New York: Praeger, 1967.

Mead, G. H. *Mind, self, and society*. Chicago: University of Chicago Press, 1934.

Meichenbaum, D. *Cognitive-behavior modification*, New York: Plenum, 1977.

Meichenbaum, D. & Goodman, J. Training impulsive children to talk to themselves: A means of developing self-control. *Journal of Abnormal Psychology*, 1971, 77, 115–126.

Michels, R. Treatment of the difficult patient in psychotherapy. *Canadian Psychiatric Association Journal*, 1977, 22, 117–121.

Miller, N. E. Experimental studies of conflict. In J. Mc. V. Hunt (Ed.). *Personality and the behavior disorders*. New York: Ronald, 1944. Pp. 431–465.

Millon, T. *Disorders of personality: DSM-III, Axis II*. New York: John Wiley, 1981.

Milner, M. *The hands of the living God*. New York: International Universities Press, 1969.

Mindess, H. *Laughter and liberation*. Los Angeles: Nash, 1971.

Minuchin, S. *Families and family therapy*. Cambridge, MA: Harvard University Press, 1974.

Minuchin, S., Montalvo, B., Guerney, B., Rosman, B. & Schumer, F. *Families of the slums*. New York: Basic Books, 1967.

Mischel, W. *Personality and assessment*. New York: John Wiley, 1968.

Mischel, W. Continuity and change in personality. *American Psychologist*, 1969, 24, 1012–1018.

Moreno, J. L. *Psychodrama: Foundations of psychotherapy*, vol. 2. New York: Beacon House, 1959.

Mosak, H. & Dreikurs, R. Adlerian psychotherapy. In R. Corsini (Ed.). *Current psychotherapies*, Itasca, Ill.: F. E. Peacock, 1973.

Moustakas, C. E. Honesty, idiocy and manipulation. *Journal of Humanistic Psychology*, 1962, 2, 1–15.

Moustakas, C. (Ed.). *Existential child therapy*. New York: Basic Books, 1966.

Mullan, H. & Sangiuliano, I. *The therapist's contribution to the treatment process*. Springfield, Illinois: Charles C. Thomas, 1964.

Naranjo, C. *The unfolding of man*. Menlo Park, California: Stanford Research Institute, 1969.

Needleman, J. The concept of the existential a priori. In J. Needleman (Ed.). *Being-in-the-world: Selected papers of Ludwig Binswanger*, New York: Harper Torchbooks,

1967. Pp. 9–31.

Nichols, M. & Zax, M. *Catharsis in psychotherapy*. New York: Gardner Press, 1977.

Noyes, A. P., & Kolb, L. C. *Modern clinical psychiatry*, 6th edition. Philadelphia: W.B. Saunders, 1967.

Ofman, W. V. *Affirmation and reality: Fundamentals of humanistic-existential therapy and counseling*. Palo Alto: Western Psychological Services, 1976.

Olsen, P. *Emotional Flooding*. New York: Human Sciences Press, 1976.

Orlinsky, D. E., & Howard, K. I. The relation of process to outcome in psychotherapy. In S. L. Garfield and A. E. Bergin (Eds.). *Handbook of psychotherapy and behavior change*. New York: Wiley, 1978. Pp. 283–329.

Orne, M. T., & Wender, P. H. Anticipatory socialization for psychotherapy: Method and rationale. *American Journal of Psychiatry*, 1968, *124*, 1202–1212.

Osborn, A. *Applied imagination*. New York: Scribners, 1963.

Osipow, S. H., & Walsh, W. B. *Strategies in counseling for behavioral change*. New York: Appleton-Century-Crofts, 1970.

Ostow, M. The psychic function of depression: A study in energetics. *Psychoanalytic Quarterly*, 1960, *29*, 355–394.

Ouspensky, P. D. *In search of the miraculous*. New York: Harcourt, Brace, Jovanovich, 1949.

Ouspensky, P. D. *The fourth way*. London: Routledge and Kegan Paul, 1957.

Overstreet, H. *The mature mind*. New York: Norton, 1949.

Park, J. *An existential understanding of death: A phenomenology of ontological anxiety*. Minneapolis: Existential Books, 1975.

Pasternak, S. A. The explosive, antisocial, and passive-aggressive personalities. In J. R. Lion (Ed.). *Personality disorders: Diagnosis and management*. Baltimore: Williams and Wilkins, 1974. Pp. 45–69.

Patterson, C. H. Relationship therapy and/or behavior therapy? *Psychotherapy: Theory, Research and Practice*, 1968, *5*, 226–233.

Patterson, C. H. *Relationship counseling and psychotherapy*. New York: Harper and Row, 1974.

Paul, I. H. *The form and technique of psychotherapy*. Chicago: University of Chicago Press, 1978.

Pelletier, K. R., & Garfield, C. *Consciousness: East and West*. New York: Harper and Row, 1976.

Perls, F. S. *Gestalt therapy verbatim*. Moab, Utah: Real People's Press, 1969a.

Perls, F. S. *Ego, hunger and aggression*. New York: Random House, 1969b.

Perls, F. S. Dream seminars. In J. Fagan & I. L. Shepherd (Eds.). *Gestalt therapy now*. New York: Harper and Row, 1970. Pp. 204–233.

Perls, F. *The Gestalt approach and eyewitness to therapy*. New York: Bantam, 1976.

Pierce, R. A., Nichols, M. P., & DuBrin, J. R. *Emotional expression in psychotherapy*. New York: Gardner Press, 1983.

Pierce, R. M., Schauble, P. G., & Farkas, A. Teaching internalization behavior to clients. *Psychotherapy: Theory, Research and Practice*, 1970, *7*, 217–220.

Poland, W. S. The place of humor in psychotherapy. *American Journal of Psychiatry*, 1971, *128*, 127–129.

Polster, E. & Polster, M. *Gestalt therapy integrated*. New York: Brunner/Mazel, 1974.

Prescott, D. A. *The child in the educative process*. New York: McGraw-Hill, 1957.

Prince, M. *The dissociation of a personality*. London: Longmans, Green, 1905.

Prochaska, J. & DiClemente, C. *The transtheoretical approach: Crossing the traditional boundaries of therapy*. Homewood, Illinois: Dow Jones-Irwin, 1984.

Rado, S. The problem of melancholia. *International Journal of Psychoanalysis*, 1928, *9*, 420–438.

Rado, S. *Psychoanalysis of behavior: Collected papers. Volume I*. New York: Grune and Stratton, 1956.

Rado, S. *Psychoanalysis of behavior: Collected papers. Volume II*. New York: Grune and Stratton, 1962.

Rank, O. *The trauma of birth*. New York: Harcourt Brace, 1929.

Rank, O. *Will therapy and truth and reality*. New York: Knopf, 1945.

Rapaport, D. The theory of ego autonomy: A generalization. *Bulletin of the Menninger Clinic*, 1958, 22, 13–35.

Reich, W. *Character analysis*. New York: Orgone Institute, 1945.

Reik, T. *Listening with the third ear*. New York: Farrer, Strauss and Young, 1948.

Rimm, D. & Masters, J. *Behavior therapy*. New York: Academic Press, 1974.

Ritvo, S. Psychoanalysis as science and profession: Prospects and challenges. *Journal of the American Psychoanalytic Association*, 1971, 19, 3–21.

Roche, M. *Phenomenology, language, and the social sciences*. London: Routledge and Kegan Paul, 1973.

Rogers, C. R. The characteristics of a helping relationship. *Personnel and Guidance Journal*, 1958, 37, 6–16.

Rogers, C. R. A theory of therapy, personality, and interpersonal relationships as developed in the client-centered framework. In S. Koch (Ed.). *Psychology: A study of a science*. Volume 3. New York: McGraw-Hill, 1959.

Rogers, C. R. The concept of the fully functioning person. *Psychotherapy: Theory, Research, and Practice*, 1963, 1, 17–26.

Rogers, C. R. *Client-centered therapy*. Boston: Houghton Mifflin, 1965.

Rogers, C. R. The process of the basic encounter group. In J. F. T. Bugental (Ed.). *Challenges of humanistic psychology*. New York: McGraw-Hill, 1967. Pp. 261–276.

Rogers, C. R. *On becoming a person*. Boston: Houghton-Mifflin, 1970a.

Rogers, C. R. Being in relationship. *Voices: Journal of the American Academy of Psychotherapists*, 1970b, 6, 11–19.

Rogers, C. R. Empathic: An unappreciated way of being. *Counseling Psychologist*, 1975, 5, 2–10.

Roheim, G. *The origin and function of culture*. Garden City, New York: Doubleday Anchor, 1971.

Rose, G. J. King Lear and the use of humor in treatment. *Journal of the American Psychoanalytic Association*, 1969, 17, 927–940.

Rose, S. Intense feeling therapy. In P. Olsen (Ed.). *Emotional Flooding*. New York: Human Sciences Press, 1976. Pp. 80–95.

Rosen, J. *Direct analysis*. New York: Grune and Stratton, 1953.

Rosen, V. The reconstruction of a traumatic childhood event in a case of derealization. *Journal of the American Psychoanalytic Association*, 1955, 3, 211–221.

Rosenfeld, H. Considerations concerning the psychoanalytic approach to acute and chronic schizophrenia. *International Journal of Psychoanalysis*, 1954, 35, 135–140.

Rosenheim, E. Humor in psychotherapy: An interactive experience. *American Journal of Psychotherapy*, 1974, 28, 584–591.

Rowen, J. *The reality game: A guide to humanistic counselling and therapy*. London: Routledge and Kegan Paul, 1983.

Sagarin, E. (Ed.). *Humanistic psychotherapy*. New York: McGraw-Hill, 1973.

Salter, A. *Conditioned reflex therapy*. New York: Farrar, Straus, & Giroux, 1949.

Saretsky, T. *Resolving treatment impasses: The difficult patient*. New York: Human Sciences Press, 1981.

Saul, L. J. *Technique and practice of psychoanalysis*. Philadelphia: Lippincott, 1958.

Schachtel, E. G. *Metamorphosis*. New York: Basic Books, 1959.

Schaffer, R. Regression in the service of the ego. In G. Lindzey (Ed.). *Assessment of human motives*. New York: Rinehart, 1958.

Schofield, W. *Psychotherapy: The purchase of friendship*. Englewood Cliffs, NJ: Prentice-Hall, 1964.

Schur, M. *The id and the regulatory principles of mental functioning*. New York: International Universities Press, 1966.

Schutz, W. C. *Here comes everybody*. New York: Harper and Row, 1971.

Schutz, W. C. Encounter. In R. Corsin: (Ed.). *Current Psychotherapies*. Itasca, IL: Peacock, 1973.

Schwartz, O. *The psychology of sex*. New York: Penguin, 1951.

Searle, J. R. A classification of illocutionary acts. *Language in Society*, 1976, *5*, 1–23.

Searles, H. F. The place of natural therapist responses in psychotherapy with the schizophrenic patient. *International Journal of Psychoanalysis*, 1963, *44*, 42–56.

Searles, H. F. *Collected papers on schizophrenia and related subjects*. New York: International Universities Press, 1965.

Seguin, C. A. *Love and psychotherapy: The psychotherapeutic eros*. New York: Libra, 1965.

Serban, G. The existential therapeutic approach to homosexuality. *American Journal of Psychotherapy*, 1968, *22*, 491–501.

Shaffer, J. B. P. *Humanistic psychology*. Englewood Cliffs, NJ: Prentice-Hall, 1978.

Shepherd, I. L. Intimacy in psychotherapy. *Voices: Journal of the American Academy of Psychotherapists*, 1979, *15*, 9–14.

Sherman, A. *Behavior modification: Theory and practice*. Monterey, CA: Brooks/Cole, 1973.

Shorr, J. E. *Psycho-imagination therapy*. New York: Intercontinental Medical Book Corporation, 1972.

Shorr, J. E. *Psychotherapy through imager*. New York: Intercontinental Medical Book Corporation, 1974.

Simkin, J. S. *Gestalt therapy mini-lectures*. Millbrae, CA: Celestial Arts, 1977.

Singer, J. The scientific basis of psychotherapeutic practice: A question of values and ethics. *Psychotherapy: Theory, Research and Practice*, 1980, *17*, 372–383.

Sloane, R. B., Cristol, A. H., Pepernik, M. C., & Staples, F. R. Role preparation and expectation of improvement in psychotherapy. *Journal of Nervous and Mental Disease*, 1970, *150*, 18–26.

Stampfl, T. G. Implosive therapy. In P. Olsen (Ed.). *Emotional flooding*. New York: Penguin, 1977. Pp. 62–79.

Stampfl, T. & Lewis, D. *Implosive therapy: Theory and technique*. Morristown, NJ: General Learning Press, 1973.

Steiner, C. *Scripts people live by*. New York: Grove Press, 1974.

Stieper, D. R. & Wiener, D. N. *Dimensions of psychotherapy: An experimental and clinical approach*. Chicago: Aldine, 1965.

Strupp, H. H. Humanism and psychotherapy: A personal statement of the therapist's essential values. *Psychotherapy: Theory, Research and Practice*, 1980, *17*, 396–400.

Sullivan, H. S. *Conceptions of modern psychiatry*. New York: Norton, 1953a.

Sullivan, H. S. *The interpersonal theory of psychiatry*. New York: Norton, 1953b.

Suttie, I. *The origins of love and hate*. New York: Julian Press, 1935.

Suzuki, D. T. *Living by Zen*. Tokyo: Sanseido Press, 1949.

Suzuki, D. T. *Zen Buddhism*, Garden City: Doubleday, 1956.

Taylor, W. S. & Martin, M. F. Multiple personality. *Journal of Abnormal and Social Psychology*, 1944, *34*, 281–300.

Teilhard de Chardin, P. *The phenomenon of man*. New York: Harper and Row, 1965.

Thomas, R. M. (Ed.). *Comparing theories of child development*. Belmont, California: Wadsworth, 1985 (2nd ed.).

Thorne, F. Eclectic psychotherapy. In R. Corsini (Ed.). *Current psychotherapies*. Itasca, IL: Peacock, 1973.

Tillich, P. *The courage to be*. New Haven, CT: Yale University Press, 1952.

Towbin, A. P. The confiding relationship: A new paradigm. *Psychotherapy: Theory, Research and Practice*, 1978, *15*, 333–343.

Truax, C. B., & Wargo, D. G. Effects of vicarious therapy pre-training on group psychotherapy. *International Journal of Group Psychotherapy*, 1968, *18*, 186–198.

Truax, C. B., Wargo, D. G., & Volksdorf, N. R. Antecedents to outcome in group counseling with institutionalized juvenile delinquents: Effects of therapeutic conditions, patient self-exploration, alternate sessions, and vicarious therapy pre-training. *Journal of Abnormal Psychology*, 1970, *76*, 235–242.

Ullmann, L. & Krasner, L. (Eds.). *Case studies in behavior modification*. New York: Holt, Rinehart & Winston, 1965.

Van Dusen, W. The theory and practice of existential analysis. *American Journal of Psychotherapy*, 1957, *11*, 310–322.

Van Dusen, W. Wu Wei, no-mind; and the fertile void in psychotherapy. In J. Welwood (Ed.). *The meeting of the ways: Explorations in East/West psychology*. New York: Schocken Books, 1979.

Van Kaam, A. *Existential foundations of psychology*. Pittsburgh, PA: Duquesne University Press, 1966.

Wachtel, P. What should we say to our patients?: On the wording of therapists' comments. *Psychotherapy: Theory, Research and Practice*. 1980, *17*, 183–188.

Wallerstein, R. S. The psychotherapy research project of the Menninger Foundation: A semifinal view. In J. M. Shlien (Ed.). *Research in psychotherapy*. Volume 3, Washington, D.C.: American Psychological Association, 1968. Pp. 584–605.

Walsh, R. N. & Vaughan, F. (Eds.). *Beyond ego: Transpersonal dimensions in psychology*. Los Angeles: J. P. Tarcher, 1980.

Warkentin, J. & Whitaker, C. A. Time-limited therapy for an agency case. In A. Burton (Ed.). *Modern psychotherapeutic practice*. Palo Alto: Science and Behavior Books, 1965. Pp. 249–304.

Warren, N. C., & Rice, L. N. Structuring and stabilizing of psychotherapy for low prognosis clients. *Journal of Consulting and Clinical Psychology*, 1972, *39*, 173–181.

Waskow, I. E. & Parloff, N. B. (Eds.). *Psychotherapy change measures*. Rockville, MD: National Institute of Mental Health, 1975.

Watts, A. W. *This is it and other essays on Zen*. New York: Random House and John Murray, 1960.

Watts, A. W. *Psychotherapy East and West*. New York: Pantheon, 1961.

Watzlawick, P., Beavin, J., & Jackson, D. *Pragmatics of human communication*. New York: Norton, 1967.

Weed, L. I. Medical records that guide and teach. *New England Journal of Medicine*, 1968, *278*, 593–657.

Weiss, S. Therapeutic strategy to obviate suicide. *Psychotherapy: Theory, Research and Practice*, 1969, *6*, 39–43.

Welwood, J. (Ed.). *The meeting of the ways: Explorations in East/West psychology*. New York: Schocken Books, 1979.

West, W., Jr. Combined approaches in the treatment of the orally regressed masochistic character disorder. *Journal of Contemporary Psychotherapy*, 1978, *9*, 155–161.

Wheelis, A. W. *The quest for identity*. New York: Norton, 1958.

Wheelis, A. W. How people change. *Commentary*, 1969, 56–66.

Wheelright, J. Jung's psychological concepts. In F. Fromm-Reichmann & J. L. Moreno (Eds.). *Progress in psychotherapy*. New York: Grune and Stratton, 1956. Pp. 127–135.

Whitaker, C. A., Felder, R., Malone, T. P., & Warkentin, J. First stage techniques in the experiential psychotherapy of chronic schizophrenics. In J. Masserman (Ed.). *Current psychiatric therapies*, Vol. 2, New York: Grune and Stratton, 1962. Pp. 147–158.

Whitaker, C. A. & Malone, T. P. *The roots of psychotherapy*. New York: Blakiston, 1953.

Whitaker, C. A., Warkentin, J. & Malone, T. P. The involvement of the professional therapist. In A. Burton (Ed.). *Case studies in counseling and psychotherapy*. Englewood Cliffs, NJ: Prentice-Hall, 1959. Pp. 218–257.

White, R. W. Motivation reconsidered: The concept of competence. *Psychological Review*, 1959, 66, 297–333.

White, R. W. Competence and the psychosexual stages of development. In M. R. Jones (Ed.). *Nebraska symposium on motivation*. Lincoln: University of Nebraska Press, 1960.

Whitehorn, J. C. The goals of psychotherapy. In E. A. Rubinstein and M. B. Parloff (Eds.). *Research in psychotherapy*. Washington, DC: American Psychological Association, 1959. Pp. 1–9.

Whitmont, E. C. & Kaufmann, Y. Analytical Psychotherapy. In R. Corsini (Ed.). *Current psychotherapies*. Itasca, IL: Peacock, 1973. Pp. 85–117.

Wilber, K. *No boundary: Eastern and Western approaches to personal growth*. Boulder, CO: Shambhala, 1979.

Wilber, K. *The Atman Project: A transpersonal view of human development*. Wheaton: Theosophical Publishing House, 1980.

Wilber, K. *Up from Eden: A transpersonal view of human evolution*. Garden City, NY: Anchor Doubleday, 1981.

Wilhelm, R. *The secret of the golden flower: A Chinese book of life*. London: Routledge and Kegan Paul, 1962.

Winnicott, D. W. *Collected papers*. New York: Basic Books, 1958.

Winnicott, D. W. *The family and individual development*. London: Tavistock, 1965.

Wolberg, L. R. *The technique of psychotherapy*. New York: Grune and Stratton, 1954.

Wolpe, J. *Psychotherapy by reciprocal inhibition*. Stanford, CA: Stanford University Press, 1958.

Wolpe, J. Isolation of a conditioning procedure as the crucial psychotherapeutic factor: A case study, *Journal of Nervous and Mental Diseases*, 1964, 134, 316–329. (Also in L. Diamant (Ed.). *Case studies in psychopathology*. Columbus: Charles E. Merrill, 1971. Pp. 143–158).

Wolpe, J. *The practice of behavior therapy*. Elmsford, NY: Pergamon, 1973 (2nd ed.).

Wolpe, J. Behavior therapy—A humanitarian enterprise. In A. Wandersman, P. Poppen, & D Ricks (Eds.). *Humanism and behaviorism: Dialogue and growth*. Oxford, England: Pergamon, 1976. Pp. 55–82.

Wolpe, J. & Lazarus, A. A. *Behavior therapy techniques*. Oxford: Pergamon, 1966.

Wolpe, J., Salter, A., & Reyna, L. J. (Eds.). *The conditioning therapies*. New York: Holt, Rinehart, & Winston, 1964.

Wolstein, B. *Freedom to experience: A study of psychological change from a psychoanalytic point of view*. New York: Grune and Stratton, 1965.

Wyss, D. *Psychoanalytic schools from the beginning to the present*. New York: Jason Aronson, 1973.

Yalom, I. D. *Existential psychotherapy*. New York: Basic Books, 1980.

Yalom, I. D., Harts, P. S., Newell, G., & Rand, K. H. Preparation of patients for group therapy, *Archives of General Psychiatry*, 1967, 17, 416–427.

Yates, A. J. Symptoms and symptom substitution. *Psychological Review*, 1958, 65, 371–374.

Yates, A. J. *Theory and practice in behavior therapy.* New York: John Wiley, 1975.

Zeig, J. K. (Ed.). *A teaching seminar with Milton H. Erickson,* New York: Bruner/Mazel, 1980.

Zeig, J. (Ed.). *Ericksonian approaches to hypnosis and psychotherapy.* New York: Brunner/Mazel, 1982.

Zilboorg, G. Rediscovery of the patient. In F. Fromm-Reichmann and J. L. Moreno (Eds.). *Progress in psychotherapy.* New York: Grune and Stratton, 1956. Pp. 108–110.

Zinker, J. *Creative process in Gestalt therapy.* New York: Brunner/Mazel, 1977.

NAME INDEX

SUBJECT INDEX

abreaction, carrying forward of experiencing vs., 25
actualization:
  approximation of, 191–92
  bodily sensations of, 295, 321
  of good form of deeper potentials, in direction of change, 309–13, 321–26
  of good form of operating domain, 292–97
  integration of potentials and, 7, 112, 191–92, 225, 246, 269–70, 274–75, 284–86, 295, 328–30
  see also internal integrative encounter
altered state, as actual being in real situation, 65–69
anthropomorphizing potentials, in discovering early scenes, 77–80
anxiety:
  counter-conditioning of, 254
  deeper potentials and, 109, 143
  existential, 185, 186–87
  in experiential vs. external therapies, 18, 22–23
approach-avoidance conflicts, 285
assimilation terror, 237
attentional center:
  at beginning of session, 3, 51
  bodily experiencing and, diagrammed, *xvi*
  compelling, 61–63
  deflection of, 44–45
  phenomenological description and, 27–29, 44, 54
  shared by therapist and patient, 17
  special listener as, 56–59
  therapist's, 98
  see also centers of gravity; focal center, in situational context; peak experiencings
autistic conceptual systems, 138–39
avoidance:
  compelling bodily events as, 163
  crazy ploys as, 163
  in experiencing relationship with deeper potential, 117–19

externalizing therapist as, 163
  other situational contexts as, 162
  of stronger experiencing, 162–66
  withdrawal as, 163
  see also distancing; resistance
awareness, in Gestalt theory, 195–96

"behavioralizing," 90
behavioral therapies, 206
  catastrophic situation and, 197–98
  "earlier the better" rejected by, 47–48
  emphasis on new behaviors in extra-therapy world in, 254–55
  external contingencies altered via, 8, 21, 45
  intrapsychic change deemphasized in, 256
  methods of, as new vocabulary only, 254
  see also specific therapies
birth:
  basic personality processes and, 286–87
  experience of, 82
  memories from before, 82
  primitive field and, 80–84, 226, 237
blocking:
  carrying forward of experience vs., 21–24
  see also avoidance; resistance
bodily sensations, 27, 29, 289
  actualization and, 295, 321
  at beginning of session, 3, 51
  direction of change and, 99, 102, 289, 295, 298
  disintegratively related deeper potentials and, 298, 299
  empathy and, 30
  at end of each session, 269, 374–77, 378–79
  in experiencing relationship with deeper potentials, 108–9, 111, 212–13, 223
  experiential effect and, 321
  as final check in decision to terminate session, 377–79

DATE DUE